THE
FORGOTTEN
TERRORIST

Other Books by Mel Ayton

The JFK Assassination: Dispelling the Myths

Questions of Controversy: The Kennedy Brothers

A Racial Crime: James Earl Ray and the Assassination of Dr. Martin Luther King, Jr.

THE FORGOTTEN TERRORIST

SIRHAN SIRHAN AND THE ASSASSINATION OF ROBERT F. KENNEDY

MEL AYTON

POTOMAC BOOKS, INC.
WASHINGTON, D.C.

Library of Congress Cataloging-in-Publication Data
Ayton, Mel.
  The forgotten terrorist : Sirhan Sirhan and the assassination of Robert F. Kennedy / Mel Ayton. — 1st ed.
    p. cm.
  Includes bibliographical references and index.
  ISBN 978-1-59797-079-2 (alk. paper)
  1. Kennedy, Robert F., 1925–1968—Assassination. 2. Sirhan, Sirhan Bishara, 1944– 3. Assassins—Biography. 4. Terrorists—Biography. I. Title.
  E840.8.K4A98 2007
  364.152'4092—dc22
                                    2006100845
ISBN 978-1-59797-080-8 (Paperback)

Printed in the United States of America on acid-free paper that meets the American National Standards Institute Z39-48 Standard.

Potomac Books, Inc.
22841 Quicksilver Drive
Dulles, Virginia 20166

First Edition

10 9 8 7 6 5 4 3 2 1

CONTENTS

ACKNOWLEDGMENTS

It is not possible to thank everyone who gave so graciously of their time, but I owe a special debt of thanks to a number of people. Anyone who writes about the Robert Kennedy assassination must acknowledge a large debt to Dan Moldea. His book about the murder is indispensable to researchers. Dan has given generously of his time in reading my manuscript and clarifying issues raised. I also owe a debt of gratitude to Robert Blair Kaiser, whose book *RFK Must Die* is also indispensable to anyone who wishes to gain insight into Sirhan Sirhan's state of mind and motives for the assassination.

This book would not have been possible without the assistance of experts, academics, and scientists who have decisively cleared up many anomalies arising from the evidence in the case. I am therefore grateful for the work done by Steve Barber, Larry Sturdivan, Philip Harrison, Dr. Chad R. Zimmerman, and Michael O'Dell. Their contributions to my research have been outstanding.

I also wish to thank others whose contributions have been invaluable, including Anthony Summers, Archivist Nancy Zimmelman of the California State Archives, Larry Sneed, Dr. Graham Wagstaff, Dr. Etzel Cardena, James W. Kenney, Don Bohning, Manny Chavez, Grayston Lynch, and Lonnie Athens. I also wish to acknowledge the work of my literary agent Barbara

Casey and my editors at Potomac Books, Don Jacobs and Julie Kimmel, who have given excellent advice in the editing of my manuscript.

Finally, I would not have been able to undertake this work had it not been for the love and support of my wife, Sheila, my daughter Laura, and my son Tim.

TIME LINE

March–April 1948	Twenty-two-year-old Robert F. Kennedy covers the Arab-Israeli conflict for the *Boston Post*.
May 1948	The new State of Israel is declared.
June 1948	The first of RFK's four articles about the conflict in Palestine appears in the *Boston Post*.
December 1956	The Sirhan family secures sponsorship from two families belonging to the First Nazarene Church in Pasadena. The family arrives in the United States the following year, and Sirhan enrolls in public school.
1958	Bishara Sirhan, Sirhan's father, abandons his family and returns to Jerusalem.
November 1960	John F. Kennedy is elected president of the United States. During the election campaign he states that friendship with Israel is not "a partisan matter. It is a national commitment."
March 1963	Sirhan becomes a part-time student at Pasadena City College.
November 1963	JFK is assassinated.
March 1964	Sirhan secures employment at John Davies's service station.
May 1964	Sirhan is dismissed from Pasadena City College for poor attendance.

August 22, 1964	After resigning his position as attorney general in the Johnson administration, RFK announces his candidacy for the Democratic senatorial nomination in New York. In a campaign speech RFK declares, "we will stand by Israel and come to her assistance" in the event of an attack.
November 1964	RFK is elected senator for New York. As senator, he stands by his brother's commitment to Israel.
October 1965	Sirhan secures employment at Santa Anita Racetrack.
March 31, 1966	Sirhan quits his job at the Santa Anita Racetrack.
June 2, 1966	Sirhan secures employment at the Granja Vista del Rio Horse Farm.
September 25, 1966	Sirhan suffers head injuries in a fall from a horse.
November 13, 1966	Sirhan is fired from his job at the horse ranch. He then secures employment at the Del Mar Racetrack but is fired after a few weeks.
May 24–June 23, 1967	RFK gives five pro-Israeli speeches and describes Israel as a "gallant democracy" equipped with "arms and courage."
September 24, 1967	Sirhan secures employment at John Weidner's health food store.
March 7, 1968	After an altercation with his boss, Sirhan is fired from his job at John Weidner's health food store.
March 16, 1968	RFK declares his candidacy for president of the United States.
April 10, 1968	Sirhan tells Alvin Clark he is going to kill Robert Kennedy.
May 15, 1968	John Frankenheimer's CBS television documentary *The Story of Robert Kennedy* is broadcast. A few days later Sirhan Sirhan learns from a radio broadcast on KFWB that RFK has committed himself to supplying Israel with fifty Phantom jets. (Note: Sirhan said he believed he watched the CBS television documentary on May 18 or 20, 1968)
May 18, 1968	Sirhan writes in his notebooks, "Robert Kennedy must be assassinated. . . . My determination to eliminate RFK is becoming more the more [*sic*] of an unshakable obsession."
May 20, 1968	RFK, wearing a yarmulke, gives a speech at the Temple

	Isaiah in West Los Angeles in which he declares that the United States "must fully assist Israel—with arms if necessary."
May 24, 1968	Sirhan attends a Kennedy rally at the Los Angeles Sports Arena.
May 27, 1968	At Temple Shalom in Portland, Oregon, RFK, wearing a yarmulke, declares that the United States must defend Israel against aggression "from whatever source."
June 1, 1968	
12:50–3:00 p.m.	Sirhan visits the Corona Police Department pistol range. On his way home from the range, he purchases two boxes of .22-caliber hollow-point bullets from the Lock, Stock 'N Barrel Gun Shop in San Gabriel, California.
June 2, 1968	RFK takes his family to Disneyland and returns to the Ambassador Hotel at 7:00 p.m. Sirhan attends a Kennedy rally at the Ambassador Hotel and observes the senator standing on an outdoor terrace.
June 3, 1968	
8:00 p.m.	RFK flies to San Diego after a ride through the African-American Los Angeles suburb of Watts and a rally in Venice.
8:45 p.m.	RFK arrives at the El Cortez Hotel in San Diego. Evidence suggests that Sirhan may have stalked RFK at the El Cortez Hotel.
12:00 midnight	RFK returns to Los Angeles.
June 4, 1968	
afternoon	Sirhan fires his gun at the San Gabriel Valley Gun Club and then meets friends at the Pasadena City College campus before going to the Ambassador Hotel.
7:15 p.m.	RFK travels to the Ambassador Hotel for his victory rally after having spent the day with his family at the Malibu home of film director John Frankenheimer.
9:00–9:30 p.m.	Sirhan voices disdain for RFK at the Ambassador Hotel campaign victory party.
10:30 p.m.	Sirhan is observed in the Ambassador Hotel pantry area. He asks a hotel busboy if RFK will be coming through the pantry.
11:00 p.m.	Sirhan is asked to leave the anteroom behind the Embassy Ballroom stage.

June 5, 1968

12:15 a.m.   RFK concludes his victory speech and is led behind the
                        stage to the kitchen pantry. Sirhan meets the Kennedy
                        party in the pantry, where he fires eight shots. Kennedy
                        and five others are wounded.

1:44 a.m.   Kennedy is pronounced dead at age forty-two. All other
                        victims of the shooting survive their wounds.

June 8, 1968   Robert Kennedy is buried at Arlington National Cem-
                        etery, Arlington, Virginia.

INTRODUCTION

> *"What I think the [RFK] assassination did was to sour the whole*
> *public, and particularly the Democratic Party, on the election and*
> *on the political process. We'd had the Tet offensive—which was a*
> *political disaster in this country—and then you get McCarthy*
> *on the road, you get Bobby in the primaries, and you get Martin*
> *Luther King's assassination, and the party is now torn in many*
> *ways, in disarray. . . . I think this was just too much. It was like a*
> *mental breakdown for the American political community."*
>
> —HUBERT HUMPHREY

The year 1968 was marked by death and heroes, war and peace, revolution, and uprisings in Czechoslovakia and France. The sequence of events had a disturbing effect on the American psyche—the intensity of emotions, whether in response to class or racial, ideological, or spiritual injustice, forever changed the way a generation thought about the direction of politics. Americans listened to protest music, protest speeches, and a never-ending debate about the old ways and the new. Over the previous eight years the country had endured continual tragedies—President John F. Kennedy's assassination, the Cuban Missile Crisis, the murder of three civil rights workers in Mississippi, the murder of Malcolm X, and the riots in Watts, Harlem, Detroit, and various major cities across the land.

In 1968, however, the tragedies arrived one after another, month after month. It seemed as if the United States was coming apart at the seams. Never before had American television screens played out such a drama of change, producing an indelible collage of photographs, television footage, and images of people responding to death, violence, and protest. The drama began with the North Koreans' capture of the U.S. spy ship *Pueblo*. The *Pueblo*'s capture was quickly followed by the Tet offensive, which shocked Americans into an awareness that victory in Vietnam was an illusion. In April President Lyndon B. Johnson's announcement that he would not seek another term as president was quickly followed by the news that an assassin's bullet had killed Martin Luther King. America was in turmoil as buildings across the land, torched by African Americans who rioted in the streets, erupted in flames. Throughout the year police officers confronted rebellious youth who protested against the injustices in American society and American involvement in a foreign conflict that was, essentially, a civil war with no end in sight.

But it was the tragic death of presidential candidate Robert F. Kennedy that finally persuaded many Americans that the grave problems their country confronted were insoluble. From the start of that terrible year, Americans had been looking for a political savior to disengage them from the racial, economic, and foreign predicaments; someone who could engender real change without bringing chaos to the system. They wanted someone like Franklin Delano Roosevelt, a president who rescued Americans from the Great Depression while keeping the fundamental capitalist and democratic system in place.

Following a prolonged period of indecisiveness, Senator Robert F. Kennedy put himself forward as the answer to America's problems. In his brief campaign for the presidency he elevated the spirits of many who saw him as the only candidate who could unite the country. He was the most original politician of his time: he told his audiences uncomfortable truths and changed forever the way they judged their leaders. Although a fundamentally shy and genuinely self-deprecating man, Robert Kennedy believed he and he alone could provide solutions to the bitter battles fought through the 1960s—battles to end poverty, ensure equal rights, provide an enlightened foreign policy, and end civil disorder.

Kennedy's supporters were euphoric when he secured victory in the final and most important primary state—California—at the end of his 1968 presidential primary campaign. The victory propelled him in front of his main rivals, Vice President Hubert H. Humphrey and Senator Eugene J. McCarthy, in the nation's popularity polls. But the Democratic Party's presidential nomination was another matter, and it would be a long uphill struggle to secure a majority of the Democratic National Convention delegates.

After Kennedy finished his victory speech on the night of the California primary election by thanking everyone who assisted in the campaign, he stepped down from the podium and walked through a kitchen pantry on his way to the Ambassador Hotel's Colonial Room, where the nation's press were waiting.

For most Americans over forty-five years old the images are still vivid—Robert Kennedy shaking hands with kitchen staff; Kennedy lying in a pool of his own blood, rosary beads pushed into his hands by a hotel worker; Kennedy's unofficial bodyguards and friends grabbing the young Palestinian,

Sirhan Sirhan, as he rapidly fired off his pistol shots before he could be subdued; the prostrate bodies of the other victims wounded by Sirhan's indis-
criminate shooting spree; the nation once again mourning the loss of an
American hero dead before his time.

Kennedy's followers believe he would have not only ended the war
in Vietnam but also pursued a political agenda to decisively change American society, closing the gap between rich and poor, black and white. What
Robert Kennedy might have done as president is one of history's great unanswered questions.

Although the grief over Robert Kennedy's death has subsided over
the years, the suspicions about the circumstances of the assassination have
grown. Opinion polls during the past thirty-five years have shown that a
majority of Americans believe Kennedy's assassination was part of a larger
conspiracy. The list of possible culprits has grown as the years have passed
to include organized crime, that wanted Kennedy dead because as U.S. attorney general he had cracked down on the Mafia; the military-industrial complex, that feared Kennedy would put an end to the Vietnam War; rogue elements of the CIA bent on revenge for the Kennedy brothers' abandonment
of the Bay of Pigs exiles during their 1961 invasion of Cuba; western ranch-
ers upset with Robert Kennedy's support for migrant farm workers; and the
Ku Klux Klan (KKK) and the American Nazi Party, upset with Kennedy's
support for civil rights.

The RFK assassination conspiracy theories are rooted in witness
testimony that a girl in a polka-dot dress, who had been standing near Sirhan,
proclaimed after Kennedy had been hit, "We shot him!" In 1970 Robert Blair
Kaiser published *RFK Must Die*, an account of Sirhan's arrest and trial, which
endorsed suspicions that the assassin had been part of a plot. Kaiser's important contribution to the case was his study of Sirhan. He had an exclusive writer's contract with Sirhan and saw the accused assassin two or three
times a week while he was awaiting trial. In return for this privilege Kaiser
gave about $32,000, about half what he received from magazines before the
case ended, to Sirhan's lawyers and served them as an investigator.

Kaiser believed there was more to Sirhan's act than the American
public knew. He was critical of the lawyers who failed to move the jury in
1969, the psychiatrists for their conflicting conclusions, and the Los Angeles police for not pursuing possible links between Sirhan and organized crime,
the right wing, the left wing, and the terrorist organization, Al Fatah. Kaiser
believed Sirhan had conspired with someone and had not acted alone. He
advanced two possibilities: The first, initially proposed by novelist Truman
Capote, posited that Sirhan had been an unwitting conspirator, hypnotized

by others, as in Richard Condon's *The Manchurian Candidate*. There was no hard evidence to support this theory. The second was that Sirhan, who studied the occult, managed to hypnotize himself, to program himself to kill Kennedy. This theory was the creation of Dr. Bernard Diamond, a respected and ingenious defense psychiatrist. He testified that Sirhan used mirrors to hypnotize himself and that the light and the mirrors at the Ambassador Hotel made him commit murder.

Several legislative and judicial panels from the early 1970s to the mid-1980s found serious problems with the original investigation, which had been carried out predominantly by the Los Angeles Police Department's team of detectives headed by Robert Houghton. The LAPD team, managed day-to-day by Houghton appointee Captain Hugh Brown, was named Special Unit Senator (SUS) and was aided by a team of FBI investigators. Houghton wrote, "I was resolved to make certain that the investigation into the assassination would leave no questions unasked, no answers untested, no evidence unchecked, no possible conspiratorial doors unopened. Perhaps it was an unattainable goal, but it was THE goal."[1] While this statement is not proof that the SUS pulled out all stops to follow all of the leads that suggested conspiracy, it does show that the unit at least acted in good faith, despite the protestations of conspiracy writers who suspected the LAPD was part of a cover-up. As it happens, not all leads were followed, not all avenues pursued. The investigation was flawed. Critics presented witnesses who had allegedly observed a second gunman and pointed to anomalies in the ballistics evidence. They sufficiently established doubt about Sirhan's guilt and a growing legion of supporters, including RFK aides, joined in the chorus of disapproval at the way the case had been investigated. The Los Angeles Police Department and District Attorney's Office attempted to frustrate these challenges to the official version of the shooting with secrecy restrictions, bureaucratic maneuvers, silence, and counterattack. The way the LAPD acted did nothing except fuel a sense of injustice, which in turn eroded public trust.

The testimony and evidence presented during the trial was wrought with definite and disconcerting inconsistencies. A panel judicially appointed in 1975 found bullet markings from tests that were different from the markings on Sirhan's gun. Dr. Thomas Noguchi, the Los Angeles coroner who autopsied Robert Kennedy's body, concluded with certainty that Kennedy's mortal wound in the head was made by a shot that came from behind the senator at a point only a few inches away, point-blank range. Yet witnesses said that Sirhan had been in front of Kennedy and not closer to him than a few feet. These glaring discrepancies led many to believe a second gunman had been positioned behind Kennedy.

The principal incongruity in the investigation turned on the number of shots fired. Sirhan's .22-caliber revolver held eight bullets, and all were thought to have been discharged in a few moments of pandemonium. Three hit Kennedy and one passed through his jacket; the shot to the head was fatal. The remainder struck other members of Kennedy's entourage, and a couple of shots hit the ceiling, one of which was lost in the ceiling interspace. But the photographs of the crime scene and the recollections of some of the police officers involved in the investigation immediately afterward identified two additional bullet holes or bullets lodged in the wooden frame of the pantry's swinging doors, meaning ten shots could possibly have been fired and thus another gun—and another killer—must have been involved. There were also allegations that the assailant, Sirhan, had been hypnotized when he carried out the murder, and critics questioned why the LAPD destroyed the doorframes and other physical evidence following Sirhan's trial.

The campaign for a comprehensive and thorough reinvestigation grew as writers continued to point out flaws in the original investigation. Although the SUS provided a mountain of evidence that pointed to the assassin's guilt, respected investigators and journalists, like Theodore Charach, Vincent Bugliosi, Paul Schrade (a victim of the shooting who worked with conspiracy advocates to reopen the case), and Allard Lowenstein, were not satisfied and began to question whether Sirhan did indeed kill Kennedy. According to Bugliosi, "I think there [were] enough substantial unanswered questions in this case that the House Select Committee on Assassinations should have reinvestigated this case in 1977 and 1978 along with the assassinations of John F. Kennedy and Martin Luther King." Other writers attempted to prove that Sirhan had been part of a widespread conspiracy involving the LAPD, the government, and/or organized crime. The real assassins, they alleged, wanted to eliminate a dangerous and radical politician who had been willing and eager to challenge the powerful and sinister political forces that held control over the U.S. government.

In 1995 investigative reporter Dan Moldea, a former conspiracy advocate, published the results of his investigation into Kennedy's murder in *The Killing of Robert F. Kennedy: An Investigation of Motive, Means, and Opportunity*. Moldea pored over the mountain of evidence in the case. He studied the forensic and ballistic reports and interviewed scores of witnesses, including many of the police officers involved who had not been interviewed previously. What he found suggested a botched investigation involving the mishandling of physical evidence, the failure to correctly interview some witnesses, the premature destruction of key pieces of physical evidence, and the lack of proper procedures in securing and investigating the crime scene.

Earlier efforts to clear up the mystery suggested an accomplice, Thane Eugene Cesar, a part-time security guard who carried the only other pistol in the pantry that night. But Cesar was never a serious suspect. Moldea tracked him down and eventually persuaded him to take a polygraph test, which he passed. Moldea also questioned Sirhan in California's Corcoran Prison and concluded that the assassin had been lying when he said he could not remember shooting Kennedy. Moldea's research was truly a tour de force, and ultimately cleared up the many inconsistencies in the evidence and provided sufficient answers to establish what is likely the best understanding of what happened on the night of June 5, 1968.

The Killing of Robert Kennedy became the definitive book on the subject, as the national media proclaimed Moldea had finally provided answers to the many questions and mysteries that had plagued government investigations and private researchers for the past three decades. According to Christopher Lehmann-Haupt of the *New York Times*, Moldea's book was "carefully reasoned . . . dramatic. . . . The author has brought order out of a chaotic tale and turned an appalling tatter of history into an emblem of our misshapen times."[2] Steve Waldman of *Newsweek* said, "If there had been a conspiracy to assassinate Robert F. Kennedy . . . Dan Moldea would have found it. . . . Moldea concluded he was wrong the first time—and that the sole killer of Robert Kennedy on June 5th, 1968, was a deranged Sirhan Sirhan. . . . Moldea shows that simple (and sometimes hilarious) human error explain these suspicious coincidences."[3]

Moldea's book did not satisfy the conspiracy theorists, however, and Internet sites flowered as writers and researchers criticized his work, pointing out supposed flaws in his research. RFK researcher and author Philip Melanson rightly criticized Moldea for not competently inquiring into the allegations that Sirhan had been hypnotically manipulated. Sirhan Sirhan's attorney, Larry Teeter, and Sirhan family friend Lynn Mangan also met Moldea's conclusions with ridicule. Their research into the case provided critics with enough ammunition to infer that doubt still resided in Sirhan's guilty conviction. In the late 1990s, Teeter and Mangan joined forces with Sirhan and Sirhan's brother, Adel, in calling for an independent investigation and a new trial for the assassin.

In addition, Sirhan retracted his many statements admitting guilt and said that he did not kill Kennedy and that conspirators had "hypno-programmed" him. According to Teeter, the RFK assassination was a "sequel" to the JFK murder, and "There were good reasons for [the CIA/FBI/Pentagon] to have wanted Robert Kennedy eliminated. He wanted to end the war in Vietnam. He wanted to get to the bottom of his brother's assassination. He wanted to break the power of the Teamsters Union. He wanted to end the wild adventurism of the CIA." The "adventurism" Teeter spoke of included the notorious MK-ULTRA program, which was designed by the CIA to see if it was feasible to use drugs and hypnosis to create a "programmed assassin." William Klaber in his 1993 documentary, *The RFK Tapes*, proposed that a California sex therapist and alleged CIA hypnosis expert, Dr. William Bryan Jr., programmed Sirhan. Bryan, a self-proclaimed eccentric character, once boasted to two of his favorite prostitutes that he, in fact, had hypnotized Sirhan and had worked on "top secret" CIA projects. Bryan's most famous hypnotic subject was the notorious Boston Strangler, Albert DeSalvo, whose name appeared in Sirhan's notebooks.

Teeter's claims that Sirhan had been hypnotized were supported by Dr. Herbert Spiegel, a New York psychiatrist who taught at Columbia University and was regarded as one of America's leading experts on hypnosis. Spiegel said, "Sirhan, being an outstanding hypnotic subject, was probably programmed through hypnosis to shoot Senator Kennedy and to experience a genuine amnesia of the shooting."[4]

The publication of three books criticizing Moldea's work and the republication of Robert Blair Kaiser's *RFK Must Die* in 1999 decisively placed the RFK assassination back on the agenda of unsolved crimes. In 1997 William Klaber and Philip Melanson published *Shadow Play: The Murder of Robert F. Kennedy, the Trial of Sirhan Sirhan, and the Failure of American Justice*, in which the authors insisted that the case had sufficient anomalies to infer that Sirhan was the unwitting patsy in a conspiracy and that his guilty verdict should be considered unsafe. The authors also believed Moldea did not provide a credible motive for Sirhan's act. These conclusions were mirrored in James DiEugenio and Lisa Pease's *The Assassinations:* Probe Magazine *on JFK, MLK, RFK, and Malcolm X* (2003) and ex-FBI agent William Turner's *Rearview Mirror: Looking Back at the FBI, the CIA and Other Tails* (2001).

As will be made clear in this book, the conspiracy advocates' claims to overturn Dan Moldea's conclusions about Sirhan's guilt remain speculative at best.

Although Moldea successfully addressed the issue of Sirhan's guilt and the unlikelihood of a conspiracy, the issue of motive and the suspicions that Sirhan had been hypnotized remained problematic. Moldea believed Sirhan's claim to have acted in response to America's policy on the Middle East was merely an excuse. He wrote, "The problem here is that Sirhan— who claimed to be angry at Kennedy over his advocacy of sending the jets to Israel—had written about his 'determination to eliminate RFK on May 18— two days before the television broadcast [implying RFK's support for Israel] and eight days before the speech at Temple Nevah Shalom [advocating the sale of fifty Phantom jets to Israel]."[5] Moldea concluded that Sirhan had acted for personal reasons: "Did Sirhan kill Robert Kennedy because of the Senator's support for Israel? I don't believe that for a second, and Sirhan certainly never mentioned anything about Kennedy's position on the Middle East in his notebooks. . . . I believe that Sirhan's motive had less to do with politics and more to do with his own personal problems. . . . He had become a desperate young man, somehow losing all hope. . . . I believe that Sirhan's unilateral motive consisted of nothing more than his desire to prove to himself and those who knew him that he still had his nerve. He wanted everyone to know his name and be forced to recognize him. . . . To Sirhan, Kennedy had become a symbol of everything he wanted and didn't think he would ever have a chance to get."[6] Moldea also believed that Sirhan's self-confessed motive—that he was a champion of Palestinian rights—had been constructed following his arrest and had been planted in his mind by supporters of the Palestinian cause.

Moldea and others, especially those writers who claim that a "motiveless" Sirhan was used a "patsy" in the crime, have argued that since Sirhan had written down his resolve to kill RFK two days before the senator spoke of supplying bombers to Israel, the political motive was an "invention." The chapters that follow, however, will show that there is no discrepancy here. Sirhan's anti-Semitism was a part of his makeup. He had expressed extreme disdain for U.S. politicians who gave their support to Israel, especially following the 1967 Arab-Israeli war, and had thoughts about killing an American politician (President Johnson was among his potential victims) for a considerable period following the 1967 conflict. He began to focus his anger on RFK some months before the assassination (for reasons explained in later chapters) and expressed his desire to kill the senator shortly after Martin Luther King's murder. Sirhan had some ambivalence toward RFK and at times saw him as a "savior for the poor and disadvantaged," that is, people like himself. At the trial, however, he said that after watching a television documentary about RFK, broadcast on May 15, and discovering that the senator had been pro-Israel since 1948, he could have killed him "right then and there." Kennedy's promise to send bombers to Israel, if he were elected, only reinforced Sirhan's prior determination and gave it new meaning.

Conspiracy authors concluded Sirhan's motive was a moot point; he, unaware he had fired a pistol, which might have been loaded with blanks, had been a mere "patsy," hypnotically programmed to either kill Kennedy or act as a diversion for the real killer. Philip Melanson told researcher Paul Nellen,

My theory about Sirhan's involvement is that he was definitely firing a gun and therefore should have been convicted of some kind of attempted murder if in fact they couldn't prove diminished responsibility. But I see Sirhan basically as a pawn in a conspiracy. My view is that while he was there shooting he didn't mastermind a plot to kill RFK. He was not a conscious participant with others where he was recruited into a plot. I see him as someone who is/was manipulated through his mind largely, through hypnosis, to shoot, firing a gun, to be a distraction for others who assassinated RFK. Unfortunately, Sirhan doesn't know enough about that to be able to provide leads or show leads on it for us and it is something that people other than Sirhan will have to try to figure out.[7]

And, according to both Melanson and Klaber, "equally baffling was that, although [Sirhan] had been cooperating in his interrogations . . . during his seven months in custody the defendant had been hard pressed to come up with a coherent explanation as to why he would commit such a crime."[8]

I believe that both Moldea and the conspiracy writers have been wrong about Sirhan's true motives. As far as the subject of mind control is concerned I have provided evidence that the idea that Sirhan had been programmed is spurious. And, while I do not disagree with the accounts of the assassination that give Sirhan's motive a personal dimension, I have concluded that political factors played a larger role than has previously been stated. When Sirhan was arrested the media referred to him as a Jordanian citizen, and the source of his rage, bitterness, and anger at "Jews" was not explained in most news stories. In those days most Americans had no idea what a "Palestinian" was and even fewer understood their grievances. The 1967 Six Days' War was barely a year old, and the Palestine Liberation Organization (PLO) had not yet begun its terrorist campaign of bombings and hijackings that eventually brought Yasser Arafat to the attention of the world. Commenting at the time of the murder, *New York Times* editorial columnist James Reston described Sirhan's motive as "a wholly irrational act" devoid of political inspiration. The *Boston Globe* stated, "So now it develops that Sirhan Sirhan was a 'mad man.'"[9]

Sirhan tried to explain his motives at the time of his arrest when he cried out, "I can explain" and "I did it for my country." But America either didn't listen or failed to understand. As Yitzhak Rabin, Israel's ambassador to the United States at the time said, "The American people were so dazed by what they perceived as the senseless act of a madman that they could not begin to fathom its political significance."[10] Had the assassination been carried out in a European country it would have no doubt been classified as a terrorist political act. The State Department was afraid that relations between the United States and Arab nations would deteriorate if the political aspects of the crime were highlighted. Taking their cue from the State Department, politicians in Congress avoided fanning the flames and downplayed the Arab/Israeli connection to the crime. The press followed suit. Without any lead from the American government, American commentators speculated that the questions surrounding the murder could be answered with psychoanalysis—or they tried to link RFK's death with the suspicions surrounding the JFK assassination. Furthermore, the FBI was at a loss to explain why Sirhan shot Kennedy. According to William C. Sullivan, No. 3 man in the Bureau in 1968, "We did finally decide that Sirhan acted alone, but we never found out why. Although he was a fanatic for the Arab cause, we could never link Sirhan with any organization or to any other country. He never received a dime from anyone for what he did. We sometimes wondered whether someone representing the Soviets had suggested to Sirhan that Kennedy would take action against the Arab countries if he became president. But that was only a guess. . . . Investigating Sirhan was a frustrating job, for in the end we were never sure."[11]

In fact for the next three decades RFK biographers espoused the idea that Sirhan's act held no real political underpinning. Some referred to Sirhan as "a disturbed Jordanian immigrant,"[12] "a mentally unstable, unemployed drifter,"[13] and "a twenty-four-year-old Jordanian."[14] Others, like Arthur Schlesinger Jr., William Vanden Heuval, and Milton Gwirtzman, similarly failed to address Sirhan's politics.

Sirhan might have been mentally unstable and angry at a society that had relegated him to the bottom of the heap, as Dan Moldea concludes, but there is sufficient evidence, originating years before the shooting, that Sirhan clearly saw himself, like today's suicide bombers, as an Arab hero. The PLO and most Palestinians certainly judged him this way. In February 1973 the Palestinian terrorist organization, Black September, killed three American diplomats on Yasser Arafat's orders. The terrorists had demanded Sirhan's release but President Nixon refused to submit to their request. It seems clear that Sirhan's fellow Palestinians became convinced, following RFK's assassination, that high-profile violent acts would advance their cause. One month after the assassination, the Popular Front for the Liberation of Palestine hijacked an Israeli passenger jet. A year later the organization hijacked an American plane.

A wealth of evidence illustrates that Sirhan's political explanations for the killing were not constructed, as some writers allege, to justify his act—this will be made clear in the pages that follow. Perhaps now, following the tragic events of September 11, 2001, we can arrive at a greater awareness of the nature of Sirhan's act, an act that overlooked evidence in the case points to as a "terrorist" assault against a leading American target. The assassination might be the first act of the tragedy that culminated in 9/11.

1
THE AMBASSADOR HOTEL

"We think the Ambassador is of national significance as the as-
sassination site of Robert Kennedy and as one of the most noted
sites in Hollywood history. It's one of the buildings that people
across the country associate with Los Angeles."
—LOS ANGELES CONSERVATORY EXECUTIVE DIRECTOR LINDA DISHMAN

The sprawling Ambassador Hotel on Wilshire Boulevard, with its red
tiled roofs, graceful gardens, and 23.5 acres of velvet lawns, was one of
the world's most famous hotels. It was the meeting place for the rich and
famous—movie stars, princes, eccentric millionaires, athletes, and politicians. For decades everybody who was anybody stopped at the Ambassador
if they were visiting Los Angeles.

The Ambassador Hotel was built on land owned by dairy farmer
Reuben Schmidt. Schmidt had sold the twenty-three-acre section of his land
to Ella Crowell, who then sold it to the Los Angeles Pacific Railway Company for the purpose of constructing an interurban railway. The railway
plans did not develop, and in 1919 both Crowell and the railway company
sold their halves to a hotel company. The hotel was originally called "The
California," but its name was changed after millionaire, S. W. Straus, stepped
in with much needed funding. The hotel then became a part of the Ambassador Hotels chain, which included properties in Atlantic City and New
York. The hotel was distinguished by its "H"-shape plan, which allowed the
sun to shine into every room, and also by its views of the Santa Monica
Mountains. The panorama included mountains on two sides, the sea on the
west, and the distant reaches of the sea and valley to the south and over the
Palos Verdes Hills and the Channel Islands in the distance.

The Ambassador opened its doors to the public on New Year's Day
1921, and its "grand opening" came on January 18, 1921. Three thousand

local society leaders as well as politicians and visitors who traveled in for the party attended the opening. The hotel soon became the center of social life for the rich and famous. Up until the 1970s the stretch of Wilshire between McArthur Park and Western Avenue was as close as Los Angeles ever came to having its own 5th Avenue. The area included world-famous nightclubs and restaurants like the Brown Derby, Perino's, the Windsor, and I Magnin.

The Ambassador Hotel had more than 500 rooms and bungalows and over 200 staff members. On April 21, 1921, the Ambassador's Cocoanut Grove nightclub opened and quickly became the most renowned nightspot on the West Coast. The grove's interior had palm trees adorned with stuffed monkeys and a blue ceiling painted with twinkling stars. From its opening until the 1960s the Ambassador was the place to be seen. The first Oscars were awarded in the Cocoanut in 1930—it was the third Academy Awards ceremony but the first featuring the golden statues. The hotel was used throughout the 1920s and '30s for the Academy Awards, and in 1944 it hosted the first Golden Globe Awards.

Bing Crosby started his career at the Ambassador's Cocoanut Grove. Mack Sennet discovered Crosby singing with a group called the Rhythm Boys. Famous columnist Walter Winchell, who announced on November 22, 1963, that President John F. Kennedy had been shot, lived in one of the Ambassador's bungalows until his death in 1972. Hollywood star John Barrymore stayed at the hotel with his pet monkey Clementine. Gloria Swanson and newspaper tycoon William Randolph Hearst were also residents. Hearst lived there with his mistress, actress Marion Davies, taking up the entire east wing of the second floor. Movie producer and future billionaire Howard Hughes used to sit at a table in the back of the Cocoanut Grove and eat ice cream. Amelia Earhart's flying club, which included aviators Jimmy Doolittle and Roscoe Turner, met at the hotel. Charles Lindbergh visited following his famous transatlantic flight of 1927.

At the Ambassador Richard Nixon wrote his famous "Checkers Speech," and then, ten years later, he delivered an angry concession speech, directed mainly toward the press, for the California governorship there. Throughout its history the hotel's patrons included not only Hollywood stars but also every president from Hoover to Nixon, explorer Rear Adm. Richard Byrd, and members of the British royal family. Soviet Premier Nikita Khrushchev and his wife stayed at the hotel during their 1959 visit to the United States.

During the 1970s and 1980s the hotel slowly but surely fell out of favor because it could not compete with newer hotels in the Beverly Hills area and also because the managers failed in its upkeep. Gradually it had become rundown; floor after floor was closed until it finally shut its doors to the public on January 3, 1989. Nearly sixty-eight years to the day from its opening, the Ambassador closed along with its timeless memories of Hollywood's golden age. Its contents were auctioned off in the 1990s, and most of the hotel was demolished in 2006 in a controversial move by the Los Angeles Unified School District.

The Ambassador Hotel continued to play a part in American film culture even as it declined and even after its doors had been closed to the public. Before its closing it had frequently been used by moviemakers for interior and exterior film scenes. Directors were impressed with the Ambassador's veneer walls, high ceilings, and general 1930s decor. *The Graduate*, starring Dustin Hoffman and Anne Bancroft, was filmed there. The Ambassador's lobby, reception desk, and Palm Bar were all shown extensively as the young graduate conducted his love affair with Mrs. Robinson. Numerous directors and stars continued to film movies there after it closed. Among the films that used the Ambassador as a set in the 1990s are *Hoffa*, *Forrest Gump*, *Pretty Woman*, *Apollo 13*, and *True Lies*.[1]

The Ambassador Hotel, however, will always be associated with one of America's darkest moments: the shooting of Senator Robert F. "Bobby" Kennedy, brother of assassinated president John F. Kennedy, on June 5, 1968. Kennedy's murder was a significant turning point in the hotel's history: it initiated the once-grand hotel's decline. To many, a brighter American future was also destroyed when Kennedy died. Following the removal of Senator Kennedy from the presidential sweepstakes that year, the nation endured Nixon, Watergate, and another five years of war. Some might wonder how many names on the Vietnam War Memorial could be removed had the gunman who shot Bobby Kennedy failed in his efforts.

To disillusioned Democrats that spring of 1968, Robert F. Kennedy was a potential savior, a politician independent of the party bureaucracy who could articulate their anger and idealism. Although Kennedy was an "insider," he understood the depth and urgency of the nation's problems. Like Martin Luther King, who was murdered two months before him, Kennedy linked the tragedy in Vietnam with the struggles in the inner cities and the plight of the poor and disenfranchised and the generational struggles within American society.

RFK, as he was known to the American public, was a complicated man. He wore the tragedies of his brother's death, his own dark internal struggles, and the empathy he felt for people who suffered on his sleeve. Although RFK's personae very much fit in with the liberal and radical image popular during the mid-1960s, he was essentially a conservative. He believed in the rule of law, the work ethic, and family values, and he had worked on the staff of infamous Communist hunter Senator Joseph McCarthy in the early 1950s. Some of the policies RFK espoused, such as federalism, welfare reform, and individual liberty rather than state control, later became cornerstones of the conservative platform. However, RFK's fundamental strength was his ability to understand how politics affected the human condition, and he appealed to minority groups, America's youth, and middle-class and blue-collar workers alike.

Following his election to the Senate in November 1964, Robert Kennedy continued to fight for minority groups that he had championed as attorney general in his brother's administration. During the last four years of his life, his passion to help became more intense. The celebrated Kennedy charisma added force to his every activity. He began to differentiate himself from his brother by advocating more radical programs to help the poor and the less powerful in American society and around the world. During his first two years in the Senate, he initiated a number of projects in New York of which even veteran legislators were proud. They included assistance to underprivileged and emotionally disturbed children, the establishment of a corporation to bring industry to Brooklyn slums, and the setting up of regional development councils for upstate New York. Nationally RFK spoke out for jobs, housing, and education. Whereas JFK's call for action was disinterested and remote, according to Kennedy biographers Arthur Schlesinger and Ted Sorensen, RFK became personally involved in his work. He visited American Indian reservations and experienced firsthand the plight of the natives. On trips to places like the Mississippi Delta, inner-city ghettoes, and the homes and workplaces of California migrant workers, where poverty was endemic, he became enraged.

The possibility of violence and danger were ever-present during RFK's 1968 presidential campaign. A number of Kennedy's friends and relatives, still haunted by the loss of JFK, believed a run for the presidency was simply an invitation for danger. Not a week went by without one news story or another making reference to the tragic events in Dallas in 1963. Bomb threats and crank calls plagued the Kennedy campaign organization. In Salt Lake City, at the end of March, the police chief appeared in front of a campaign rally to announce that the police had received an anonymous call saying a bomb was about to go off at the rally. The police chief said everyone who stayed, stayed at their own risk. No one left the venue. Later RFK joked about the incident: "That's what I call opening my campaign with a bang. I hope we are all able to see each other at the end of my speech. In case we don't I just want you to know that I couldn't have wanted to go with a greater group of fellows."[2] During campaign visits to cities and towns across America police officers were alerted to Kennedy's presence. Newspaper and television reporters joked about being on a "death watch," ready at any moment for a waiting gunman poised to claim the life of another charismatic leader.

Outside Gary, Indiana, in May, the open car in which Kennedy and his wife, Ethel, were riding suddenly pulled off the road in a scene eerily reminiscent of the November 1963 assassination. As it turned out, the car had stopped to allow RFK's wife to put on a topcoat. In San Francisco's Chinatown, on the last day of the California primary campaign, the sound of exploding firecrackers frightened Kennedy aides and reporters and paralyzed Ethel with fear. Many onlookers had mistaken the explosions for gunshots. The sound of balloons bursting caused similar moments of fright. Friends and campaign workers repeatedly expressed fears for RFK's safety as the senator plunged into adoring crowds or stood up in cars surrounded and mobbed by excited supporters. During one incident, in Los Angeles on May 16, after a visit to Valley State College, RFK was hit by a stone hurled from a bridge. The stone left a mark on the senator's cheek and landed in the car. Soon after, a mistaken newspaper report flashed around the world suggesting that RFK had been the target of an assassin.[3]

Kennedy's fatalism was an eerie presence during the campaign and unnerved many of his aides and supporters. *Time* reporter Hays Gorey believed it hastened the senator's "undoing." Gorey talked to Kennedy about how exposed he was—the open car, people grasping for him. Gorey said RFK was "aware. But he knew no other way to campaign. He had to go to the people." "If someone out there wants to get me badly enough he will," Gorey quoted Kennedy as saying.[4] Friends recalled that when RFK was asked about the dangers of plunging into crowds he shrugged them off saying, "It doesn't bother me, the physical part of getting hurt. What happens beyond that . . ."[5] Kennedy did not like talking about the danger he had learned to live with. His personal bodyguard, Bill Barry, was concerned about the senator's safety at many campaign rallies and intended discussing the issue with him on their return to New York. Barry was particularly concerned about Kennedy's desire to allow as many supporters as possible to be close to him.[6]

During the 1968 presidential primary campaign, Kennedy, looking not so much like a politician but a pop culture idol followed by excited fans, attracted friendly crowds everywhere he went. America had not seen such an outpouring of adulation for a politician since the John Kennedy days. Some believed that the American people gave their love to the martyred president's brother in an effort at reaching catharsis. Others believed RFK was opportunistically exploiting his brother's memory.

On May 29 RFK led a motorcade into downtown Los Angeles. Police were assigned to observe the motorcade's course to ensure the even flow of traffic. At one point in the motorcade, at Ninth and Santee Streets, the vehicles came to a halt as the crowd enveloped the Kennedy car and pulled the candidate from the vehicle. A traffic enforcement officer tried to assist RFK back to his vehicle, but Kennedy aides berated the officer for interfering. Later, Kennedy aide Fred Dutton "shouted obscenities" at several officers who were trying to manage the crowd of enthusiastic supporters. The police considered arresting Dutton but decided it would simply inflame an already difficult situation.[7]

At 3:00 p.m., Sunday, June 2, RFK, his wife, and four of their children arrived at Orange County Airport to begin the final two days of the California campaign. RFK and his entourage went to Bolsa Grande High School for a campaign rally, then visited Disneyland with their children around 6:00 p.m., returning to the Ambassador Hotel at 7:00. On Monday, June 3, Kennedy left Los Angeles International Airport and flew to San Francisco to give a brief speech at Fisherman's Wharf and returned to Long Beach at 4:00 p.m. RFK gave a twenty-minute speech in Lincoln Park to a crowd that included a few hecklers, before his motorcade journeyed to the Watts area, where Kennedy stopped numerous times to give short campaign speeches from his car. Except for a drunken man who jumped on the hood of the senator's car, the people Kennedy spoke to were enthusiastic and friendly. Hays Gorey quoted one observer as saying, "This is madness. Some nut with a gun could climb one of these trees and it would be all over."[8]

At 5:30 p.m. the motorcade left Watts for the Venice area, where Kennedy again gave speeches from his car, exciting the crowds who poured out to see him. That evening Kennedy toured some of the poorest areas of Los Angeles. People surged against the convertible in waves. His official bodyguard, ex-FBI agent Bill Barry, became exhausted protecting the candidate. His unofficial bodyguards, Los Angeles Rams star Roosevelt "Rosey" Grier and Olympic decathlete Rafer Johnson, held Kennedy as he jumped on the trunk of his car. Kennedy suffered blisters from shaking so many hands. His bodyguards were buffeted by hordes of admirers. By the evening RFK was tired and emotionally drained, his face burned and his hair bleached by the sun of an open car. In public he personified youth and vigor. In private his friends saw he had been pushing himself to the limits while also risking death.

Kennedy knew that his efforts on the campaign trail were the only way he could persuade the American people to turn to him instead of his opponents. He had entered the race late and did not have the advantage of consolidating his support among those delegates who were appointed outside the primary election system. He needed the delegates in the primary contests if he was to secure the Democratic nomination at the convention to be held in Chicago that August. Following his electioneering, Kennedy, his wife, and six of his ten children went to the Malibu Beach home of their friend, movie director John Frankenheimer, who had spent 102 days working with Kennedy on his television ads during the campaign. Frankenheimer had directed the 1962 movie *The Manchurian Candidate*, which starred Frank Sinatra and Laurence Harvey. The movie's plot centered on a captured American soldier who was brainwashed by the North Koreans and their Chinese allies to assassinate a presidential candidate.

The movie director and his wife gave up their bedroom for Bobby and Ethel to give them some escape from the frantic campaign. Later that evening Frankenheimer intended to have a dinner party and had invited Hollywood celebrities, including Roman and Sharon Polanski, to share the meal with RFK and Ethel. However, the candidate did not return until the wee hours of Tuesday morning and the dinner was cancelled.

At 8:00 p.m. on June 3, Kennedy and his entourage flew to San Diego for a campaign rally at the El Cortez Hotel. Because the candidate was exhausted and hoarse, he decided he couldn't continue with his prepared speech, and the rally was cancelled. Kennedy—feeling sickly and nauseous, according to his driver Don Weston—returned to Los Angeles International Airport at 12:30 a.m. on June 4 and proceeded to John Frankenheimer's house in Malibu.[9]

RFK slept late on Tuesday, June 4. Shortly after noon he went with his children to swim and play on the beach. He talked with them about the beauty of the Pacific coastline and about how pollution had scarred many parts of it; the beach reminded him of Cape Cod and of how he loved the place the Kennedys thought of as their home. The sun did not break through the clouds that morning and a chilly mist hung over the sea. Nonetheless, RFK plunged into the surf with his children. A large wave came in and crashed over two of them. RFK dived under and came up with David, whom he had pulled from an undertow and who now bore a bruise on his forehead. At Frankenheimer's house, RFK told author and Kennedy family friend Romain Gary that he expected an attempt on his life "sooner or later" but not for any political belief, rather because of "contagion."[10]

RFK and his children returned to the Frankenheimer swimming pool, but three-year-old Max wanted to bury coins in the sand, so he set off with his father. Returning to the pool the family continued their play. At approximately 3:00 p.m., RFK received news that a CBS poll had predicted his victory over McCarthy in the California primary—49 percent to 41 percent, a prediction that was spot on. The turnout at the polls in the Mexican-American districts had been large that day, boding well for Kennedy.

Wearing a blue pullover and flowered beach trunks, RFK spoke with Ethel about whether the result was good enough and whether South Dakota, which held its primary on the same day, had any early returns of voter preferences. He knew that victories in urban California and rural South Dakota would give him the momentum to persuade key politicians and Democratic Party delegates that he was the candidate who could win the presidency. Richard Goodwin and Fred Dutton joined Kennedy and discussed the impending victory. Tired, RFK left to take a short nap before going to the Ambassador for what now looked like a victory celebration. RFK had considered staying in Malibu but relented to go to the Ambassador when the press said they would not go out to Frankenheimer's house to interview him.[11]

Around 7:15 p.m., Frankenheimer, with passengers Fred Dutton and RFK, headed for the Ambassador via Malibu Canyon along the Ventura Freeway, as crowds were beginning to assemble at the hotel. Frankenheimer took a wrong turn and ended up on the Harbor Freeway interchange. He quickly became upset and desperate to get out of heavy traffic. Kennedy told him, "Take it easy, John; life is too short."[12]

Traffic clogged the Ambassador's horseshoe driveway shortly after 6:00 p.m., as Kennedy supporters gathered at the hotel. RFK and senatorial candidates Alan Cranston and Max Rafferty had all booked the Ambassador for what they believed would be their celebratory parties. The hotel was also hosting several business meetings: the Bulova Watch Company, General Electric, and Pacific Telephone had booked rooms. Fifteen hundred guests occupied the Ambassador's 516 rooms, leaving no vacancies. Four hundred regular employees were working that night and because of the crowds 244 had been hired as extra help. RFK's entourage occupied eighty-eight rooms.[13]

The security arrangements at the Ambassador were sparse. The Los Angeles Police Department (LAPD), which later came under severe criticism for its policing of the victory rally, explained its policies of protection for political candidates in its summary report:

> The Department assumes a position of neutrality toward personalities and political issues and the policy provides that the Department takes enforcement action wherever necessary. It further provides that Los Angeles Policemen are not assigned to public gatherings or crowd control situations for non-enforcement or extra-enforcement purposes. This includes the

screening of visitors at events, acting as guards at private parties, or providing dignitaries with personnel for nonpolice purposes.[14]

According to police officer Daryl Gates, who later became Los Angeles chief of police,

> Had we been [at the Ambassador that night] I have no doubt we would have pre-planned Kennedy's route from the Embassy ballroom . . . to the Colonial Room . . . and we would have had enough officers on hand to protect him . . . but Kennedy's people were adamant, if not abusive, in their demands that the police not even come close to the senator while he was in Los Angeles. . . . I think Bobby always had an affection for the LAPD because of the help we gave him [fighting organized crime]. But this was different. This was politics, Kennedy-style people politics. And in his bid for the presidency Kennedy had taken the side of the 'peaceniks' and the flower children—which, from a political standpoint was . . . very wise. . . . He wanted no uniforms around at all.[15]

Gates said that, in retrospect, the LAPD should have insisted on security for RFK. However, Gates was worried that, had the LAPD assigned plainclothes officers inside the Ambassador without RFK's knowledge, Kennedy's aides would have accused the police of spying.[16]

The LAPD deployed eight officers, in four cars near the hotel in anticipation of the large crowds. A Ramparts police car arrived at the Ambassador before the shooting in response to an earlier call about an illegally parked car.[17] William Gardner, the head of hotel security, said he received no request to provide personal security for Robert Kennedy but he had anticipated security problems and hired eight guards in addition to the ten plainclothes hotel security staff. Gardner said that Kennedy had been a guest at the hotel on previous occasions during the 1968 campaign and that it was made clear to him that "the Senator did not want any uniformed security guards in his presence nor did he want any armed individuals as guards. Mr. Gardner said that this is one of the reasons why he did not have any guard assigned to escort the Senator through the hotel during the visit."[18] The total security force was eighteen guards, and six uniformed fire inspectors were assigned to the hotel for the evening to enforce fire and occupancy regulations.[19] Rosey Grier and Rafer Johnson assisted Bill Barry with RFK's personal security.

On the first floor, RFK aides James Lowe, Pierre Salinger, and Frank Mankiewicz checked newspaper credentials and issued press badges at a desk inside the foyer behind the Embassy Ballroom, where RFK planned to give his victory speech. Aide Judy Royer was in charge of the area behind the stage—the Embassy Ballroom anteroom and the kitchen/pantry; her responsibility was to keep the area clear of people who weren't supposed to be there. In the fifth floor presidential suite, California Democratic Party boss Jesse Unruh and the California delegation were assembled.

Kennedy arrived at the hotel at approximately 8:15 p.m., and went immediately to his suite of rooms, 511 and 512. His aides, family, and friends joined him as he settled down to begin a night of campaign discussions, interviews with the media, and watching the voting returns on television with Fred Dutton; his brother-in-law and campaign manager Stephen Smith; Adam Walinsky; journalist Warren Rogers; Budd Schulberg; Charles Evers, brother of assassinated civil rights leader Medgar Evers; Rosey Grier and Rafer Johnson; and Bill Barry.

By 8:30 the Embassy Ballroom downstairs was reaching its occupancy limit. Officially, only people with Kennedy badges were allowed to enter, but there were many unsupervised routes to the room and guards had trouble restricting the flow of people into the ballroom. Many people were able to circumvent the guards by using the unguarded entrances. At 9:30 p.m., a fire department inspector ordered that the main doors be closed to all entry except on a one-in, one-out basis. This measure proved futile.[20]

The crowd was beginning to smell victory by 10:00 p.m. Upstairs, the corridor between the Royal and Presidential suites on the fifth floor was rapidly filling with television equipment, news reporters, and photographers. RFK had already completed four interviews: one on the fourth floor with NBC's Sandy Vanocur, a family friend; two in the CBS/ABC fifth floor suite; and one for Metromedia in the Royal Suite, where he had invited the press for drinks. Plans were in place for a celebration party at The Factory, a downtown nightclub part-owned by Pierre Salinger and RFK's brother-in-law Peter Lawford. The party was expected to draw the Hollywood elite.

CBS declared victory for RFK at 11:00 p.m., and the crowd in the ballroom responded enthusiastically. A mariachi band entered the room and moved toward the stage, where The Sounds of Our Times band was playing "This Man Is Your Man" to the tune of "This Land Is Your Land." Millions watched the victory celebrations on television, and the crowd responded by singing, dancing, and cheering. Security guards blocked the entrance to the ballroom. People screamed at each other through the din. The crowd chanted, "We want Bobby! We want Bobby!" loud enough so that Jesse Unruh on the fifth floor could hear it. Unruh came down to calm the crowd and promised them RFK would be arriving soon. He sent his aide, Jack Crose, to tell the senator that the crowd was anxiously awaiting his arrival.

Meanwhile, Kennedy volunteer Susan Harris had befriended reporters Jon Akass and John Pilger. She delivered drinks to them and, to avoid the crowd in the ballroom, found a shortcut through the pantry. Returning to talk to the reporters she told them, "There's a little guy in there [the pantry] who keeps looking at me kind of funny, just staring as if he's waiting around for something." She later identified "the little guy" as Sirhan Sirhan.[21]

The crowds were now convinced that their candidate would arrive at the Democratic Convention in Chicago in August with enough momentum to secure the party nomination for president. By winning both the California and South Dakota primaries, Kennedy had moved into a position to challenge Vice President Hubert H. Humphrey for the nomination. Eugene McCarthy, Kennedy's other Democratic Party opponent in the primaries, now had little to no chance of winning. Kennedy's victory in California gave him 174 delegate votes and his victory in South Dakota gave him another twenty-four votes. He now had 393½ convention votes to 258 for McCarthy and 561½ for Humphrey. Although Humphrey had the most delegate votes, many political commentators believed only Kennedy could provide the Democratic Party the leadership necessary to defeat the likely Republican candidate, Richard Nixon.

RFK, Frank Mankiewicz, Fred Dutton, Dick Tuck, and Bill Barry left RFK's fifth floor suite at 11:45 p.m., to take a service lift to the kitchen area. They were followed by Rafer Johnson, Rosey Grier, union organizers Dolores Huerta and Paul Schrade, and Budd Schulberg. On the way to the lift Kennedy told a *LIFE* magazine reporter to meet him in the Colonial Room after his speech. A vice president of the Ambassador Hotel, Uno Timinson, led RFK and his entourage to the Embassy Ballroom. RFK told Mankiewicz he didn't want to go through the crowd to get to the stage so Timinson showed the men to the freight lift. Reporter Constance Lawn ran down the stairs and through the kitchen. As she passed through the pantry, which was lit by three blue fluorescent tubes slotted in the ceiling, someone called out asking if RFK was coming that way. Lawn answered in the affirmative and also remembered catching a glimpse of a swarthy looking young man who she later identified as Sirhan Sirhan.[22]

John Frankenheimer was standing behind the stage watching the speech on a television monitor when Sirhan brushed past him. He felt a "shaking" inside himself. He was supposed to stand next to Robert Kennedy on the podium but instead went out to his car to wait for him. Frankenheimer said, "I was standing there in the archway feeling like someone in 'The Manchurian Candidate.' I can see Bobby's face on a big television monitor . . . and I can see his back for real. As I stood there a figure went by me and it was as if there was electricity coming out of his body. I've never felt anything like it before or since. Of course, it was Sirhan Sirhan."[23]

As he walked through the kitchen corridor Kennedy stopped to shake hands with a few cooks and waiters. Then he moved through the pantry double doors to the anteroom behind the Embassy Ballroom before walking up to the curtained stage at 12:02 a.m. The corridor he had walked through was a narrow lane with steam tables. Trellis fences with artificial leaves, which had been used to fence the dance band off from the floor, had been stacked up against them. As Kennedy reached the anteroom, he briefly stopped to sign a Kennedy campaign poster for supporter Michael Wayne. As RFK approached the lectern to give his victory speech, a roar of cheers swept the room and supporters chanted "We want Bobby!" Kennedy, unable to begin his speech until the cheers subsided, had to wait a minute after he arrived on the podium. Finally a hush descended on the ballroom, and RFK began to thank his friends and supporters for giving him the final and most important primary victory of the campaign. It was now approximately 12:13 a.m., on June 5, the first anniversary of what the Arab world called the Second Battle of Palestine and what the West referred to as the Six Days' War.

Following his speech, RFK heard a voice say, "This way, Senator."[24] As he left the podium, radio news reporter Steve Bell shouted at him, "Senator, Senator, is there anything you would like to say to Senator McCarthy?" Kennedy turned, looked at Bell and gave an "Are you kidding?" look.[25] According to the original plan, RFK was supposed to leave the Embassy Ballroom and go down a back stairwell to a room where another group of supporters was waiting. The plan was changed. *Look* journalist Warren Rogers had arranged a question and answer session with members of the print media. RFK's advisers agreed to the session, saying that, because it was already so late, the East Coast reporters might miss their deadlines if Kennedy didn't first meet with them in the Colonial Room, situated at the far end of the kitchen pantry. Kennedy made his way behind the stage to the anteroom, where he shook hands with waiters Martin Patrusky and Vincent DiPierro and supporter Robin Casden. The hotel's assistant maitre d', Karl Uecker, took the senator's hand to guide him along the route to the Colonial Room.

Mel Stuart and Vilis Lapenieks had been filming RFK for a television special, "The Making of the President 1968." Stuart and Lapenieks had been upstairs with Kennedy and filmed him coming down through the kitchen and out into the ballroom. If they had gone before him into the pantry, they would have been able to block any potential assassin.[26]

Kennedy had asked Bill Barry, who always led Kennedy through the crowds, to take Ethel back to the hotel room. Barry had entrusted Ethel to another aide and was fighting his way back through the crowd to join the senator. A surge of people surrounded RFK. Timothy Rich handed Kennedy an envelope of photos he had taken of the senator in April, hoping RFK would autograph one for him. RFK didn't stop but proceeded through the double doors leading to the pantry.

RFK entered the pantry, where a line of kitchen workers stood on his left side. As Uecker led Kennedy by the right arm, Kennedy girls shouted, "We love you!" RFK proceeded to shake hands with kitchen employees. As Jesus Perez shook RFK's hand, he said to the senator, "Señor Kennedy, mucho gusto!"[27] Kennedy moved on to shake hands with some cooks and busboy Juan Romero. At that moment, a young man moved from the vicinity of the ice machine toward the steam table where Kennedy was shaking hands.

Concurrently, the young man brushed past photographer Virginia Guy, his gun chipping one of her teeth. He had pulled the pistol from the waistband of his jeans and begun firing rapidly at the senator.[28] RFK was hit in the head and collapsed reaching out and grabbing security guard Thane Cesar's clip-on tie. RFK fell on his back as the seventy-seven-strong crowd that surrounded the senator began to scream and panic, pushing and shoving one another as they tried to make sense of the chaos that followed the first shots. Bullets were sprayed around the room as Kennedy aides jumped on the assailant. Juan Romero bent down to Kennedy, who was laying in a small pool of blood seeping from the wound on the back of his head, and told the senator, "Come on, Mr. Kennedy, you can make it." Kennedy replied, "Is everybody all right?" The first doctor on the scene was Dr. Abo, who gently moved in between Kennedy and a distraught Ethel, who had been led from the back of the crowd to her husband by Richard Tuck. Kennedy's breathing was sparse. Groping to find a wound, Abo discovered a hole behind and below the right ear.

Earl Williman, an electrician at Desilu Studios, jumped onto the steam table and stomped on Sirhan's hand, releasing the gun from his grip. As Bill Barry exhorted Grier to "Take him!" Sirhan retrieved the dropped gun and continued firing. Johnson grabbed the gun by the barrel; Grier held the butt. Incredibly Sirhan still had his finger on the trigger housing and eventually managed to squirm away from Grier. "That's when I ran into him," recalled Warren Rogers. Rogers was headed for the kitchen to escort Kennedy to the Colonial Room when he heard five shots. Rogers "pushed open the doors, ran smack into [the assailant]. I got him under his right leg, and he had the gun in his left hand. His face was against mine."[29] Finally, Johnson and Grier managed to pry the gun from Sirhan's hand.

Bullets struck five others in the crowd but none of the resulting wounds were fatal. Paul Schrade, forty-three, who had been standing behind Kennedy, was shot in the forehead; Irwin Stroll, seventeen, was shot in the left leg; ABC TV unit manager William Weisel, thirty, was shot in the abdomen; Ira Goldstein, nineteen, was hit in the right rear buttock; and Elizabeth Evans, forty-two, was struck by a bullet in the forehead. Eventually the assailant was subdued and taken to a nearby police station.

The shock of the second Kennedy assassination in five years had a profound effect on the American people; across the country the response was immediate. Congress called for approval of stiff gun control measures that Kennedy had favored. Senate Democratic leader Mike Mansfield proposed the creation of a special committee to find ways and means to cope with the growing violence across the United States. Presidential candidates Humphrey, Rockefeller, Nixon, and McCarthy halted their campaigns as word of the shooting spread. Senator Eugene McCarthy was at his headquarters in the Beverly Hilton at the time. At noon he arrived, appearing haggard, at the hospital where Kennedy was being treated. He was met by Kennedy aide Pierre Salinger and surrounded by the Secret Service agents ordered by President Johnson for all presidential candidates following the shooting.

Seventy-seven-year-old Rose Kennedy heard about her son's accident after she awoke to attend 7:00 a.m. Mass at St. Xavier's Church in Hyannis. Casually she turned on the television set and heard the words "Senator Kennedy lies in critical condition . . . shot in the brain." Joseph Kennedy Sr., who was wheelchair-bound after having suffered a stroke in 1961, learned the news when he inadvertently overheard part of a conversation about the details of the shooting between his youngest son, Senator Edward M. Kennedy, and Rose. Richard Cardinal Cushing of Boston called and offered his sympathies.

Robert Kennedy died at 1:44 a.m., on June 6, an agonizingly long twenty-five hours and twenty-nine minutes after he had been wounded. He failed to rally from a three-hour operation that had sought to remove .22-caliber bullet fragments from his brain and died in a bare cubicle in the fifth-floor intensive care ward of the Good Samaritan Hospital. Curtains had been drawn around the glass and metal walls of the cubicle to give some privacy. Reverend Thomas Pecha administered Kennedy the last rites of the Roman Catholic Church. His last breath came as his family gathered around the bed. His wife Ethel; brother Edward Kennedy; JFK's widow, Jackie Kennedy;

sisters Jean Smith and Patricia Lawford; and brother-in-law Stephen Smith were all in the room with him. Close friends sat in the hospital's paneled board of director's room.

Outside the hospital Kennedy's press secretary, Frank Mankiewicz, gave a short simple statement to the press: "Senator Robert F. Kennedy died at 1:44 a.m., today, June 6, 1968. He was 42 years old."

As investigators and reporters learned about the tragedy shortly after it occurred, they discovered that the young Arab whom police had arrested for the shooting had been trying to explain his actions during the melee. A *Newsweek* reporter said Jesse Unruh had heard Sirhan shout, "I did it for my country!" Unruh accompanied police when they took the assailant to the police station. Unruh asked Sirhan, "Why him?" The young man replied, "It's too late."[30]

2
RFK AND ISRAEL

"Let us make it clear that we will never turn our backs on our steadfast friends in Israel, whose adherence to the democratic way must be admired by all friends of freedom."
—JOHN F. KENNEDY, SPEECH AT EASTERN OREGON COLLEGE OF EDUCATION, SEPTEMBER 11, 1959

"[If Israel is attacked] we will stand by Israel and come to her assistance."
—ROBERT F. KENNEDY, 1964

"My father covered the war here in 1948, and he was always a great supporter of Israel, and for that support he died."
—KATHLEEN KENNEDY TOWNSEND, DAUGHTER OF SENATOR ROBERT F. KENNEDY

Cape Cod has been the center of Kennedy family life since 1925, when Joe and Rose Kennedy first rented a summer cottage there. Each year at Hyannis Port, Massachusetts, the Kennedy family gathered in the summer for an annual reunion, the beginning of the clan's tradition. There the Kennedys spent summer days sailing the *Victura*, and later John F. Kennedy's *Marlin* cruised in the port for three presidential summers between 1961 and 1963.

Robert Kennedy spent the summer of '64 in Hyannis Port, still brooding over his brother's assassination the previous autumn but fired with enthusiasm for his coming senatorial campaign in New York State. Kennedy planned to return to Hyannis Port in the summer of 1968, following his expected victory in the California presidential primary.

By 1926, when Hyannis Port was already being referred to as the leading summer resort of Cape Cod, financier and banker Joseph P. Kennedy and his wife Rose bought the old Malcolm Cottage, a rambling white clapboard house with green shutters located at the end of a lane near a private beach and Nantucket Sound. Refurbishment and remodeling doubled the house's size to fourteen rooms and nine baths and provided a children's playroom and a theater in the basement. The house still stands, a monument to the Kennedy family's remarkable triumphs and tragedies.

Each morning during the summer months, Rose Kennedy attended Mass at St. Francis Xavier Church on South Street in Hyannis. A devout Catholic, she was deeply committed to her faith and passed this commitment on to her son Robert. Rose taught her children that God and religion should be a central part of their lives, while Joe sought to imbue them with ambition and purpose. As the Kennedy children grew into adulthood and began their independent lives, Hyannis Port remained the venue for family reunions.

As time passed Joe's sons Jack, Bobby, and Ted and his daughter Jean acquired properties nearby. Bobby's and Jack's were adjacent to the original house. Although the group of houses was not gated, it became known as the "Kennedy Compound." At the main house Joe and Rose learned that their oldest son, Joe Jr., had died in a bombing mission during World War II. And there they learned that their second son, Jack, president of the United States, had been assassinated. Finally, there they learned that their son Bobby had been assassinated in Los Angeles by a Palestinian fanatic angry at the presidential candidate's support for Israel.

Robert Kennedy was born in Brookline, Massachusetts, an elite suburb of Boston, on November 20, 1925. His family seemed to have the good fortune Americans were admired and envied for. His father, Joseph Kennedy, had accumulated considerable wealth. His mother was the daughter of a man who had been twice elected mayor of Boston. Politics was in Bobby's blood.

The only doors that had not opened for Joseph Kennedy were those to the homes of the exclusive Boston Brahmins, which consisted of old families like the Cabots and Lodges. The Kennedys were Irish and Roman Catholic, which made them doubly unacceptable to the proper Bostonians. Joseph Kennedy was determined to open the doors for his sons. He also wanted them to be secure enough financially that they would not have to enter the business world to make a living. He gave each of his children a trust fund and encouraged them to enter some kind of public service. For his sons that meant politics.

At first Robert, slight in build, shy, and uncoordinated, was considered the family runt. However, he more than compensated for these disadvantages by trying the hardest in sports and throwing himself into every enterprise he was engaged in. His father recognized that Robert was more like him than the others were. "Bobby," as he was known within the family had a steely, tough character and was also fearless. These characteristics came to the fore when RFK, as he was known during his political career, managed his brother's presidential campaign, battled for civil rights, and tackled the problem of organized crime.

Throughout his life, Robert Kennedy was a devout Catholic, and for a time, he considered the priesthood. His father did not encourage him to follow a religious vocation but urged him instead to seek a career in government service. When Robert was twelve, the family moved to England after Joe Kennedy was appointed ambassador to the Court of St. James as a reward for his help in getting Franklin D. Roosevelt elected president. While in London, Bobby, Jack, and the other children attended parties with the royal family. In 1940, when the family moved back to the United States, Bobby attended private schools, then spent a period of time in the U.S. Navy, stationed in the Caribbean. He went to Washington, D.C., in 1945 to persuade Navy Secretary James Forrestal to assign him to a destroyer named after his brother Joe. Demobbed, Robert worked on his brother Jack's congressional campaign in 1946, then enrolled as a student at Harvard. He received his bachelor of arts degree in March 1948. Later in the year, he enrolled at the University of Virginia Law School and graduated with a juris doctorate in 1951. Prior to enrollment in law school, he spent time traveling abroad, including a stint as an accredited reporter for the *Boston Post*, an arrangement made possible by his father who wished his son to have some experience of the world at large.

Kennedy covered the Arab–Israeli war of 1948 for the *Post*. Twenty years later, the war between Arabs and Jews continued to rage and again Kennedy involved himself in the conflict. As James Reston wrote in the *New York Times* the day after RFK's death, "In many ways the personal characteristics of Robert Kennedy were very much like the dominant characteristics of the American people. We are an ambitious, strenuous, combative, youthful, inconsistent, abrupt, moralistic, sports-loving, non-intellectual breed and he was all these things. He was an all or nothing man and he lost everything in the end. . . . He was prepared to choose between defeat at home and defeat in Vietnam, and between Israel and the Arabs, as few politicians and few Americans have, and this cost him not only the leadership of his party but his life."[1]

Palestine and the United States

The conflict between Israel and its Arab minority and Arab neighbors became one of the most intractable international problems of the twentieth century. It was a problem that Western governments and American politicians could not ignore. From the time of his first visit to the Middle East as a war correspondent, RFK developed his knowledge and opinions about the conflict, decisively siding with the Israelis. Later, as a politician, he rejected the Arab argument that Israel was an illegitimate nation.

The first steps of the founding of Israel, a watershed event in Middle East–Western relations, began in the aftermath of World War I. Victors in the war, Britain and France were allowed to establish mandates over areas previously controlled by the newly defunct Ottoman Empire, an ally of the defeated Germany. While France was rewarded with Syria and Lebanon, Britain took control of Iraq, Jordan, and the poisoned chalice of Palestine, where Zionists, expecting the establishment of a Jewish homeland, had already begun settling.

After World War I, and for the rest of the first half of the twentieth century, Arabs and Jews struggled for control over Palestine. Violence became commonplace during the 1920s and 1930s, but the more pressing concerns of World War II brought it to a hiatus. European Jews, especially German Jews who were being persecuted by Hitler's Third Reich, called for the establishment of a Jewish state within the borders of Palestine throughout the interwar period, but Britain and France were too concerned with Europe's stability to concentrate on a small Middle Eastern colony.

The movement for the establishment of a Jewish homeland was called Zionism, and its religious roots lay in the Old Testament prophecies that the Jewish people should "return" to Zion, i.e., Jerusalem. Theodore Herzl, an Austro-Hungarian Jew, was the first to articulate the Zionist political agenda, in his book, *The Jewish State*, published in 1896. Initially many Zionists, especially Russian Jews seeking refuge from the tsar's pogroms, were prepared to consider a number of proposed sites for the Jewish nation. However, as the religious elements of Zionism began to predominate in the post–World War I era, the movement sought to persuade Western nations that Palestine was their homeland.

As Jews began to immigrate to Palestine from Europe, violence erupted. Arabs resented the new Jewish settlements that grew during World War I. The British came down on the side of the Jews with the Balfour Declaration of 1917, which committed the British government to a "Jewish National Home." The effort was two-pronged. Britain would support the institution of a Jewish state once enough Jews had entered Palestine, and Zionists would be responsible for trying to secure for Britain, rather than the United States, France, or another European state, the mandate for Palestine from the League of Nations. In a world of geopolitical bargains, Britain was aware that an

Israeli state would be important in helping protect British imperial interests in the Middle East and the Suez Canal.

However, throughout the 1920s Jewish immigration into Palestine did not increase as Zionists had forecast. Not until Hitler began his program of solving "the Jewish problem" within Germany did immigration take off. By 1942 the Jewish population in Palestine had increased to 30 percent of the total population. To deal with the Arab population's growing resentment, especially following the Arab Rebellion of 1936–1939, Britain sent more than one hundred thousand troops to keep the peace. Concomitant to this action, the British government began to curb Jewish immigration. However, Jewish opposition to this policy was muted because of the outbreak of World War II in 1939.

Following the outbreak of war, a number of Arab leaders expressed support for Hitler's policy of exterminating Jews, believing that Hitler could deal with as many potential colonists as possible at the source. One of the Arab leaders, the Grand Mufti of Jerusalem, spent time in Berlin urging Hitler to quickly facilitate his plans for the Jews. The Grand Mufti was encouraged not by the Koran but by a tsarist forgery, "The Protocols of the Elders of Zion," which provided "scientific proof" that the Jews were an inhuman and evil force in the world and influenced Arab leaders in propagating the idea that inhumanity was endemic to the Jewish race. According to Alan Dershowitz, "The Palestinian leadership, with the acquiescence of most of the Palestinian Arabs, actively supported and assisted the Holocaust and Nazi Germany and bears considerable moral, political . . . culpability for the murder of many Jews."[2]

When the Labour Party came to power in the United Kingdom at the end of World War II, British government ministers decided to abide by the 1939 policy of curbing Jewish immigration to keep both sides happy. In response the Jewish settlers initiated a campaign of violent resistance and looked to the United States for support.

While President Roosevelt appeared to be sympathetic to the Jewish cause, his assurances to the Arabs that the United States would intervene to prevent bloodshed without consulting both parties caused uncertainty about his position. When Truman acceded to the presidency upon Roosevelt's death, he made clear that his sympathies were with the Jews and that he accepted the Balfour Declaration. Truman believed the promise of a Jewish state was in keeping with President Woodrow Wilson's principle of self-determination. The new president initiated several studies of the Palestine problem that supported his belief that, as a result of the Holocaust and the murder of six million Jews in German-occupied Europe, Jews were an oppressed people and also in need of a homeland. Throughout the Roosevelt and Truman administrations, the Departments of War and State, recognizing the possibility of a Soviet–Arab connection and the potential for restriction on oil supplies to the West, advised against U.S. intervention on the Jews' behalf.

Britain and America, in a joint effort to find solutions to the Arab–Israeli problem established the "Anglo-American Committee of Enquiry." In April 1946 the committee submitted recommendations that neither Arabs nor Jews dominate Palestine. It concluded that attempts to establish nationhood or independence would result in civil strife; that the United Nations should establish a trusteeship agreement aimed at bringing Jews and Arabs together; that full Jewish immigration into Palestine be allowed; and that two autonomous states with strong central governments be established to control Jerusalem, Bethlehem, and the Negev. However, Winston Churchill believed that the Arabs, who had sided with Hitler, were "owed . . . nothing in a postwar settlement."[3] As Dershowitz observed, "It is quite remarkable that the Palestinians were offered anything after the Second World War, considering the fact that their leadership actively sided with the losing Nazis. Supporting the losing side generally does not result in the offer of statehood. The Jews got the Balfour Declaration for supporting the right side in World War I. The Palestinians got a generous offer of partition after siding with Hitler."[4]

Britain referred the problem to the United Nations in February 1947. The UN General Assembly voted 33 to 13 (with 10 abstentions) to partition Palestine into separate Jewish and Arab states. Jews were a substantial majority in those areas of Palestine partitioned by the UN for a Jewish state.[5] During the half year preceding the British retreat, a civil war took place within the boundaries of Mandatory Palestine and the British were not willing to expend lives to stop it. The Jewish armed groups won this round of fighting with ease, which startled them almost as much as it startled the Arabs. They won because of their greater military capabilities and the vast infrastructural superiority they enjoyed.

When Britain announced it's intention to withdraw from Palestine by May 15, 1948, Jewish organizations united to create their own state. Israeli leader, David Ben-Gurion, was ready to accept a partition of Palestine even though the resulting Israeli portion would be tiny. When he realized that Arab states would not recognize a Jewish state no matter what size, he announced a unilateral formation of an independent Jewish state. At midnight, on May 14, 1948, the provisional government of Israel proclaimed a new state of Israel. On that same date, the United States recognized the provisional Jewish government as the "de facto" authority of the Jewish state (de jure recognition was extended on January 13, 1949). The response from the Palestinians and Arab nations was immediate. The surrounding Arab states, within the Arab League, moved troops to the Palestine border.

With their actions, the Arab nations rejected the idea of a two state solution, the same policy proposed today. As JFK's secretary of state, Dean Rusk, observed, "It is ironic that the Palestinians are now demanding an Arab state in Palestine; they could have had an Arab state in Palestine had they accepted the partition resolution in 1947, which provided for an Arab state in Palestine and for a Jewish state in Palestine. But they went to war to prevent any part of the partition resolution from taking effect, including the creation of the state of Israel."[6]

The second round of fighting began with the May 15 invasion of Arab armies, which were bent on "exterminating the Jews."[7] Those armies were almost as ill-prepared for fighting as the Palestinians had been. Consequently they were roundly defeated. What remained of the UN-proposed Palestinian state after the fighting was quickly absorbed by Jordan and Egypt, without protest from the UN. Neither Arab nation wanted a Palestinian state.[8]

Despite continual claims that Israel's victory in the 1948 war left over a million refugees, many argue that the facts are in disagreement. Arabs who left their homes during the fighting, critics say, include those whose relatives entered Israel from 1946 onward, and their numbers were closer to four hundred thousand. Most of the refugees took it upon themselves to flee despite Jewish assurances that they would not be harmed. Palestinian claims that they were removed at gunpoint are spurious, critics allege, citing research by the Arab-sponsored Institute for Palestinian Studies in Beirut, which found that "the majority of the Arab refugees in 1948 were not expelled and 68 percent left without ever seeing an Israeli soldier."[9]

This view was held by the young congressman Jack Kennedy when he visited Israel in 1951 with his brother Bobby. Jack Kennedy believed the Arabs left on their "own accord."[10] Notwithstanding these facts Alan Dershowitz argues that it is impossible to reconstruct the precise dynamics of the 1948 war: "No one will ever know . . . whether most of the Arabs who left Israel were chased, left on their own . . . [or both]."[11] What is certain, according to Dershowitz, is that "the story of Jewish displacement of local Palestinians was a fictional one."[12] Furthermore, Dershowitz argues, "Instead of integrating the refugees into the religiously, linguistically and culturally identical society, they were segregated into ghettoes called refugee camps . . . while being fed propaganda about their glorious return to the village down the road that had been their home for as little as two years."[13]

Dershowitz is supported in his views by Jean Peters, a former State Department employee, who initially sympathized with the Palestinians' plight but came to see the conflict in a different light following years of research. Peters argues that the conflict between Jews and Arabs is not the fate of the Palestinian Arabs but the product of an "institutionalized enmity," a hatred of Jews brought down from generation to generation that makes the existence of a Jewish state intolerable. Peters argues that, following the 1948 war, the Palestinian Arabs were generally not absorbed by the racial and national entities they joined because Palestinian refugees kept alive a very visible grievance, i.e., masses of Palestinians in wretched refugee camps helped justify the uncompromising anti-Israeli stand of Arab countries. The Arab position was a smokescreen for the real Arab agenda: the elimination of Jews and the Jewish state. Peters quotes a former UN Relief and Works Agency official Ralph Galloway to the effect that the Arab states did not want to solve the refugee problem. They instead wanted to keep it as an open sore, as an affront to the UN, and as a weapon against Israel. As Arab-American journalist Joseph Farah observed, "You have to give the Arabs credit. This Palestinian fiction is the most effective propaganda campaign that the world has ever seen."[14] Farah also noted that, "There is no language known as Palestinian. There is no distinct Palestinian culture. There has never been a land known as Palestine governed by Palestinians. Palestinians are Arabs, indistinguishable from Jordanians, Syrians, Lebanese, Iraqis, etc. . . . Keep in mind that the Arabs control 99.9% of the Middle East lands. . . . Greed, pride, envy, covetousness. . . . No matter how many land concessions the Israelis make, it will never be enough."[15] Furthermore, what few westerners realized was that Palestinians were (and are to this day) hated throughout the Arab world.

As Dershowitz and Peters demonstrate, after Israel managed to secure its borders in the 1948 war, the Arab nations refused to recognize its legitimacy or sign a peace treaty. Jordan, Egypt, and Syria governed the remaining portions of Palestine until the Israelis took possession of them after the 1967 war—a war in which the goal of the Arab League was the "destruction of Israel and its inhabitants."[16]

Between 1948 and 1967, Jordan and Egypt occupied the West Bank, the Gaza Strip, and the Old City of Jerusalem. The Palestinian Arabs never attempted to establish an independent state in the territory allotted to them by the 1947 United Nations Partition Plan. They cooperated with its unilateral annexation by Jordan, thereby becoming part of Jordan's political system. During this time, Jews were driven from the Old City and denied access to holy sites.

The goal of Palestinian nationalism, according to pro-Palestinian academic Edward Said, "was based on driving all Israelis out."[17] Until 1967 virtually no Palestinian leader called for a Palestinian state, instead arguing that Palestine should be merged with Syria and Jordan.[18] And Dershowitz said, "Accordingly, the Palestinians rejected the independent homeland proposed by [the UN] because it would have entailed a tiny Jewish homeland alongside it. The goal has always remained the same: eliminating the Jewish state and transferring the Jews out of the area."[19] Palestine Liberation Organization (PLO) executive committee member Zahir Muhsein told journalists in 1977, "The Palestinian people do not exist. The creation of a Palestinian state is only a means for continuing our struggle against the state of Israel for our Arab unity. . . . Arab national interests demand that we posit the existence of a distinct 'Palestinian people' to oppose Zionism."[20]

In 1964 the PLO was founded with the goal of "liberating Palestine in its entirety," and later in the decade Yasser Arafat became its leader. Historian Efraim Karsh has persuasively argued that Arafat was less interested in the establishment of a Palestinian state that could coexist with Israel than with Israel's destruction. Arafat pursued his policy of terrorism, argues Karsh, in an effort to destroy the Jewish state, and his organization has propagated these ideals from the beginning.[21]

Despite America's continual support for Israel, U.S. leaders have usually defined American interests and tried to implement policies in the Middle East in a way most closely in accord with winning support from the widest possible group of Arabs and Muslims. U.S. policies from 1948 onward did not become "anti-Arab" or "anti-Muslim" but instead opposed radical Arab regimes against their moderate counterparts while throwing their support to Israel. U.S. leaders avoided antagonizing or insulting Arab regimes, and during the 1940s and '50s American leaders wanted to play an anti-imperialist role in the Middle East. They opposed continued British and French rule in the region and voiced support for reform movements. For example, when Abdul Nasser took power in Egypt in 1952 the U.S. government welcomed the coup.

Still, the cold war between the United States and the Soviet Union had the greatest influence on policy toward the region. By the mid-1950s, the United States believed that Arab governments, especially in Egypt, which was drawn into the Soviet camp, were taking sides. Egypt was soon joined by Syria and Iraq. During the Eisenhower administration, the United States feared that the Iranian government was also being taken over by communists. However, this did not prevent Eisenhower from opposing the British, Israeli, and French plot to overthrow Nasser during the Suez Crisis of 1956. Eisenhower's administration believed the action would antagonize Arab nations and push them further toward the Soviets. The American governments from the 1950s to the 1980s also supported some Arab countries that were under assault from other Arab nations that were allied with the Soviet Union.

Following JFK's assassination, President Lyndon B. Johnson gave his support for Israel to such an extent that one adviser described him as having "Jewish corpuscles in his blood."[22] During the Johnson administration Palestinians became convinced that the United States had irrevocably committed itself to the Israeli state.

JFK and Israel

The United States at first tried to pursue a careful course designed to persuade Arab nations that it was in their interests to ally themselves with the West. By the 1960s, however, the Kennedy administration decisively positioned Israel as a leading ally of the United States. Kennedy did not start out his presidency with an emotional attachment to Israel. He had his differences with the new nation in part because Israeli leaders wanted to acquire nuclear weapons. He managed to get inspections teams into Israel's Dimona Plant to see if they were producing bomb-grade fissile material and settled for a weak inspection arrangement. Israel secretly continued its efforts to build a bomb.

In the 1950s JFK argued in favor of independence for Algeria, and his 1957 speech criticizing the French government for suppressing the Algerian Nationalist Movement was favorably met in the Arab world. According to Warren Bass, Kennedy did not have any strong ties to the Jewish communities in his constituency when he was a congressman and senator, and it was unlikely that Jewish influence in the United States drove his decisions later in his presidency. The American Israel Public Affairs Committee and other pro-Israel groups in the United States did not have any real political influence at the time. It can be argued that both Eisenhower and Kennedy sought an alliance with Israel not to satisfy domestic political concerns but as an investment in Israel's growing strength and political stability.[23]

As a potential presidential candidate, John Kennedy addressed the Middle East conflict in a speech given on March 17, 1958:

> Quite apart from the values and hopes which the state of Israel enshrines—and the past injuries which it redeems—it twists reality to suggest that it is the democratic tendency of Israel which has interjected discord and dissension into the Near East. Even by the coldest calculations, the removal of Israel would not alter the basic crisis in the area. For, if there is any lesson which the melancholy events of the last two years

or more taught us, it is that, though Arab states are generally united in opposition to Israel, their political unities do not rise above this negative position. The basic rivalries within the Arab world, the quarrels over boundaries, the tensions involved in lifting their economies from stagnation, the cross pressures of nationalism—all of these factors would still be there, even if there were no Israel.

In 1960 Kennedy said that friendship with Israel was not "a partisan matter. It is a national commitment."[24]

As president, Kennedy adopted these sentiments toward Israel, but because American society was dominated by the cold war, his foreign policy centered on realities. In his search for allies around the world, allies that would counter Russia's subversive efforts, he turned to the Middle East. At first he considered making alliances with Nasser's Egypt, and the two leaders engaged in a rich personal correspondence.[25] Kennedy was making chess-like moves to adequately arm the Israelis and maintain rapport with the Arabs, while keeping the Soviets out, the Suez Canal open, and the oil flowing. However, the rapprochement with Nasser was cut short by the Egyptian leader's impulsive intervention in Yemen's civil war, which led Kennedy to deploy fighter jets to Saudi Arabia as a warning to Nasser not to go too far in his efforts to promote Arab Nationalism. The Kennedy administration was also frustrated by the Palestinians' refusal to recognize the Israeli state.[26]

In 1961 Kennedy sent an adviser on Jewish affairs, Myer Feldman, on a secret mission to Israel. Feldman told the Israelis that President Kennedy had pledged his support of the Sixth Fleet in the event of any Arab attack on their nation. Late in 1962 the president and the Israeli Foreign Minister, Golda Meir, held a meeting in Palm Beach and discussed a possible invasion of Israel by its Arab neighbors.[27]

JFK was the first president to sell major arms to the Israelis, a move which marked the origins of America's strong alliance with the Jewish state. The U.S. sale of arms to Israel was a momentous event and may not have happened had JFK listened to advisers who advocated that the United States remain neutral, according to historian Warren Bass. (Some historians believe Eisenhower, fearful of an intensifying crisis in Jordan in 1958, reevaluated Israel's strategic potential and was the first U.S. president to give whole-hearted support to the Jewish state.) When RFK first met Deputy Defense Minister Shimon Peres during negotiations over the Hawk antiaircraft missile purchase, the memory of RFK's first visit to Israel was the first topic of conversation.

Warren Bass maintains that JFK, for the brevity of his time in office, made a tremendous difference. The weapons systems he sold to Israel were defensive in nature, but they set a precedent. As Israeli prime minister Ben-Gurion foresaw at the time, the two nations eventually moved closer, once U.S. policy focused on which armaments to sell rather than whether or not to sell any at all. Before the end of Kennedy's presidency, Israel had begun asking for F-104 fighters, tanks, and ground-to-ground missiles. The founding generation of Israeli leaders was eager to lessen reliance on France and Britain for arms in favor of the United States, which they considered a more reliable and more powerful ally. And, according to leading Israeli diplomat Mordechai Gazit, "When Kennedy met with Golda Meir he said, 'Madame foreign minister, let me tell you, we have a special relationship with Israel.' Since when did we have a special relationship? Only when he [JFK] opened his mouth at that meeting in December 1962. So the special relationship was born then and there. Then he said, 'We will have the will and the capacity to come to Israel's assistance, if attacked.'"[28]

However, the Kennedy administration was also successful in maintaining relations with the Arab states. According to Deputy Special Assistant to the President for National Security Affairs Robert Komer, "I think that Arab–Israeli relations, which are often characterized as one of the great failures of American foreign policy, are actually one of the greatest successes; we actually managed to carry water on both shoulders. We increased our aid to Israel, increased our aid to the Arabs, and maintained tolerable relations with both. That was pretty surprising; it was not easy."[29]

RFK and the "Young and Tough Nation"

RFK's father, Joseph Kennedy, arranged for his son to be accredited as a correspondent for the *Boston Post* and for Cardinal Spellman and James M. Landis to supply him with letters of introduction. RFK began his journey to the Middle East on the *Queen Mary* on March 5, 1948. George Terrien, RFK's friend from college, accompanied him. After a few days in London they went to Cairo, where RFK became impressed by the strength of Arab nationalism. He wrote in his journal, "Everyone hates the British . . . who, they believed, kept them subjugated without advance in order to keep their own prominence. . . . No middle class at all. The lower class are absolutely peons. . . . Poor children have a terrible existence with flies crawling in their eyes and nose and it seems to bother them not one iota. . . . They know no better. . . . Beggars everywhere and all want American dollars. Will not take English hard currency. . . . Honking of horns incessant . . . men go around holding hands like mad."[30]

In Cairo, an RKO Radio Pictures representative warned Kennedy not to journey to Palestine. Kennedy ignored the advice, and on March 26, Good Friday, he flew with his companion to Lydda Airport and traveled with a Jewish Defense League escort by armored car to Tel Aviv. Along the road the travelers were menaced by armed Arab guerrillas. Arriving in Tel Aviv, RFK and his friend were taken to Haganah headquarters in order for their credentials to be checked. Released, they took a walk around the city but were picked up by security police. "A large crowd gathered," RFK wrote, "[we] were blindfolded and put in [a] car and again taken to headquarters to be interrogated by Security Police. Advised us to stay off streets unless with someone."[31]

By choice Kennedy lived with Israeli soldiers, and once he narrowly escaped death when an Israeli tank convoy, on its way to Jerusalem, was attacked by Arabs. He turned down the chance to journey to Jerusalem with his hosts. Kennedy reached Jerusalem with the help of a different Israeli tank captain who offered him a lift. When he arrived in the city, he learned that Palestinian fighters had wiped out the convoy he had been traveling with earlier.[32] In Jerusalem, he interviewed everyone he could find including Haganah soldiers who blamed the British for everything. RFK also spoke to a British soldier who was sympathetic to the Jewish cause. According to RFK, the Jewish soldier "admitted British had been responsible for much of the terrorism but said officers had tough time controlling men who had seen some of their buddies blown to hell." RFK also interviewed members of the Jewish resistance group Irgun, a group that had recently bombed the King David Hotel in Jerusalem. He described Jerusalem as a city in which "firing is going on at all times. Still impressed by vehemence of all parties. More and more horrible stories pouring in. . . . Correspondents all very jumpy. As much shooting is going on . . . things very nervous."[33]

As Robert Kennedy roved around Jerusalem, he could not have known that in the mixed Arab-Jewish neighborhood of Musrara lived a four-year-old boy named Sirhan Sirhan.

RFK and his friend left Jerusalem and visited a kibbutz to talk to kibbutzim, who spoke of their strong commitment to the coming Jewish state. Kennedy left the Middle East on April 15 but not before he had sent back reports to the newspaper in a series that was published on June 3–6. In his first report RFK gave an ambiguous and balanced view of the plight of both Jews and Arabs. He wrote, "It is an unfortunate fact that because there are such well-founded arguments on either side each grows more bitter toward the other."[34] His second report praised the Israelis for their unparalleled courage, determination, strength, and dedication to securing a homeland. The Jews in Palestine, he wrote, "have become an immensely proud and determined people. It is already a truly great modern example of the birth of a nation with the primary ingredients of dignity and self-respect. . . . The Jews who have been lucky enough to get to Palestine are hardy and tough . . . [have] an undying spirit that the Arabs, Iraqi, Syrians, Lebanese, Saudi Arabians, Egyptians and those from trans-Jordan can never have."[35]

In his third article, RFK criticized the British role in Palestine:

> Our government first decided that justice was on the Jewish side in their desire for a homeland, and then reversed its decision temporarily. Because of this action I believe we have burdened ourselves with a great responsibility in our own eyes and in the eyes of the world. We fail to live up to that responsibility if we knowingly support the British government who behind the skirts of their official position attempt to crush a cause with which they are not in accord. If the American people knew the facts, I am certain a more honest and forthright policy would be substituted for the benefit of all.[36]

In the original draft for his fourth article, RFK wrote that "hate" was the underlying cause of the problems in Palestine. But he was also optimistic that Jews and Arabs could work together after having observed them working side by side in the orange groves outside Tel Aviv. He believed that if a Jewish state could be formed it might be "the only stabilizing factor" in the Middle East.[37] According to Kennedy biographer Margaret Laing, "The Jews had the qualities he admired most. And, as time passed, his emotional commitment to them was to grow."[38] Throughout his life Kennedy remained sympathetic to the Israeli cause.

Kennedy understood too well the problems that held the Palestinians back, problems that would be repeated time and again until the turn of the century. Although pro-Jewish he had sympathy for the Palestinians and commented on one occasion, "The people of the Arab world are largely illiterate, wracked by disease and poverty, without the education and organization to enrich their harsh desert lands . . . victims of irresponsible leadership."[39]

Following his brother's death, Robert Kennedy knew he could not work with the new president, Lyndon Johnson, so he resigned his position as attorney general. In early 1964 he considered running for governor or senator and accepted the offer of party activists to fight the election for senator from New York, a state that had 2.5 million Jews, 15 percent of the state's population. Larger numbers of Jews were concentrated around New York

City. No Democrat could win without their support, and Kennedy's appeals for their help were sincere; he genuinely supported the Israeli state.

Prominent Jews like Abraham Ribicoff, who was in JFK's cabinet; David Dubinsky, the trade union leader; and the humorist Henry Golden gave their support to RFK's senatorial campaign. Other Jewish leaders, however, were suspicious of the candidate and thus cited his father's alleged anti-Semitism and RFK's close working relationship in the 1950s with Senator Joseph McCarthy, who was disliked by liberal Jews. During the campaign, RFK criticized Soviet treatment of Russian Jews, advocated more aid for Israel, and was photographed in a Jewish synagogue wearing a yarmulke. But he also tried to be balanced in his approach by advocating continued shipments of surplus food to Egypt. At one point in the campaign, he disavowed Arab support, a decision that firmly placed the Democratic politician in Israel's corner.

On September 18, 1964, the *New York Times* reported, "the Democratic candidate recalled that as a newspaper correspondent he had become involved in Israel's War of Independence. He said he had ridden a tank from Tel Aviv to Jerusalem when Jerusalem was besieged by the Arabs. Mr. Kennedy contended that he had been among the first to see that the Jews were going to defeat the Arabs in Palestine. . . . He said the United States should make it clear that in case Israel were attacked, 'we will stand by Israel and come to her assistance.' . . . He backed Israel's plan to use Jordan river water in the Negev, and [said] that he favored a joint United States–Israel attempt to desalinize Mediterranean water for use in the desert."[40] In later speeches during his campaign, Kennedy told his audiences that Israel had received more American aid during his brother's administration than at any other time and reminded his audiences he had participated in the administration's decision to send Hawk missiles to Israel.

RFK ran against Republican Senator Kenneth Keating, who had also given his support to the state of Israel. The *New York Times* opposed Kennedy's candidacy and a number of liberal-minded celebrities, including Gore Vidal, Paul Newman, and James Baldwin, threw their support behind Keating, conveniently forgetting the Republican senator's conservative positions on wiretapping and opposition to U.S. Supreme Court civil liberties decisions. Those who opposed him accused Kennedy of being a carpetbagger. Kennedy dismissed this accusation, as he had been a resident of New York for part of his childhood. The backlash against Kennedy was unsuccessful, and New York voters, perhaps influenced by memories of his brother, elected him as their new senator in November 1964.[41]

In 1966 RFK's brother, Senator Edward M. "Ted" Kennedy, chairman of the Special Senate Subcommittee on Refugees and Escapees, visited

Palestinian refugee camps in Jordan and Lebanon. At the end of his visit, Ted called for the repatriation or compensation of Palestinian refugees who had fled Palestine from 1948 onward. Aware that his brother was taking a liberal line on the issue of Palestinian refugees, Robert Kennedy worked hard to maintain the trust of the Jewish community in New York State, a group he would need to solicit if he ran for president or reelection as senator.

In Senate speeches in 1965–67 Kennedy made numerous references to Israel, raising the issues of the Jewish state's nuclear program and support for arms from America to maintain its military balance with the Arab states. He often quoted his brother who said that "friendship for Israel is not a partisan matter—it is a national commitment."[42]

In October and November 1966 terrorist activity against Israel rose, with attacks originating in Syria and Jordan. There were also continued Syrian artillery attacks on kibbutzim in the area below the Golan Heights. In April 1967 Israel decided to respond by attacking, via air, the Syrian emplacements on the Golan Heights. On April 7 Israel shot down six Syrian aircraft in an air battle. Following the April attack, the Israeli government warned its neighbors that it would be forced to take further action unless terrorism from Syria was terminated. The Soviets then passed false intelligence information to the Egyptians, claiming that Israel was massing troops to strike at Syria. Israel denied these claims and UN ground observers confirmed the Israeli assertions. On May 18 Egypt requested that UN forces stationed on the Egyptian-Israeli border since the 1956 Suez Crisis be withdrawn. UN Secretary General U Thant complied, allowing the Egyptians to blockade the Straits of Tiran, effectively cutting off Israeli shipping access to the Port of Eilat.

On May 30 Egypt, Syria, Jordan, and Iraq signed mutual defense agreements designed to facilitate a combined attack on Israel. Israelis feared a second Holocaust and at first attempted to diffuse the crisis with diplomacy. When the United Nations failed to accomplish anything, it was clear that Israel would be forced to act. On the morning of June 5, the Israeli air force launched a preemptive attack against Arab airfields. Israel warned King Hussein to stay out of the war, but the king attempted to penetrate West Jerusalem. Jordanian troops opened a heavy artillery barrage on West Jerusalem and also targeted the center of the country. Israel counterattacked, surrounding the Old City of Jerusalem. On June 7 Israeli troops entered and secured the Old City, reunifying Jerusalem for the first time since 1948.

During the period of crisis and following the Six Days' War, May–June 1967, RFK suggested that America supply Israel with "whatever food or economic assistance she requires . . . to repair the ravages of war within her borders." He spoke of Israel as "a tiny outpost of Western culture and ideals . . . a gallant democracy [possessing] arms and courage." He mentioned the verbal guarantees President Kennedy had given to Meir and Ben-Gurion and wanted these secret guarantees revealed in order to place the U.S. commitment to Israel on more official footing.

In 1967 he also discussed the problems in the Arab nations whose people were "largely wracked by disease and poverty, without education and organization to enrich their harsh lands." While he was aware of the exploitation that Western nations had engaged in, Kennedy also blamed irresponsible Arab leaders who had used the oil wealth of Arab nations to construct palaces, purchase Cadillacs, and indoctrinate their peoples to turn against the West.[43]

In January 1968 Kennedy made pro-Israeli statements, reported by the *New York Times*, in which he recommended arms sales to Israel. On January 8 he said, "The US should supply Israel with whatever weapons it needed to offset whatever Russia was supplying the Arabs so that Israel 'can protect itself.'" He specifically included the fifty Phantom jets the Israelis had requested.[44]

Shortly before he announced his intention to run for president, Kennedy proposed a five-point peace plan at a United Jewish Appeal dinner. All the points were consistent with Israel's own positions on the issues. Shortly after Kennedy announced his intention to run for president, on March 16, 1968, messages were sent to Israeli leaders through an intermediary saying, "Israel could not have a better friend than the Senator."[45] The intermediary also told Israeli leaders that Kennedy was contemplating a visit to their country later in the year.[46] The American Israel Public Affairs Committee invited the leading presidential contestants, including Republicans Nixon and Rockefeller and Democrats Humphrey, McCarthy, and Kennedy, to debate Middle Eastern problems. All of the candidates expressed support for Israel, both militarily and economically, and called for Arab-Israeli negotiations.

During the primary campaigns, Kennedy continued giving his expressed support to Israel, competing with his rival Senator McCarthy in emphasizing that America's Jewish community could depend on him to support the embattled nation. In fact he admitted to one of his aides that he had pandered to voters who continued to regard him as an anti-Semite.[47] Kennedy knew he had to sway two important constituencies to win the final round of the 1968 Democratic primaries: the Mexican Americans and the Jews. He had the support of the Hispanic communities, but the Jews were still uncommitted. They were vitally important because a higher percentage of them voted in primary elections than any other ethnic group.

RFK especially needed the support of the Jewish community in Los Angeles. In his attempt to win one of the primary campaigns' largest blocks of delegates to the Chicago Democratic Convention, he visited Los Angeles on May 20 and spoke at the Temple Isaiah wearing a yarmulke. He advocated assistance to Israel "with arms if necessary."[48]

On June 1, in his televised debate with Senator McCarthy, Kennedy said, "I do think we have some commitments around the globe. I think we have a commitment to Israel, for instance, that has to be kept. But what I don't think is that we can be the policemen of the world."[49] Both McCarthy and Kennedy said that the United States should send Phantom jets to Israel, but McCarthy was in favor of replacing only the eighteen jets that Israel lost in the 1967 war on a one-to-one basis. Kennedy advocated sending fifty jets. On June 1 he had also spoken at the Temple Isaiah, again wearing a yarmulke and again giving his support for the sale of fifty Phantom jets to Israel. The speech was carried over the radio on station KFWB and was heard by Pasadena resident, Mary Sirhan, who reported it to her son, Sirhan.

However, more important than any of the pro-Israeli comments Kennedy made during the primary campaigns was the speech he gave at Temple Nevel Shalom in Portland, Oregon, on May 26. A photo of RFK giving his speech to the congregation appeared across two columns at the top of page three of the May 27 edition of *The Independent*, a Pasadena newspaper. In the accompanying photo RFK is again seen wearing a yarmulke. The caption reads, "Bobby Says Shalom." In this speech, Kennedy went further than the other candidates in support of Israel by stating the United States "must defend Israel against aggression from whatever source. Our obligations to Israel, unlike our obligations towards other countries, are clear and imperative. Israel is the very opposite of Vietnam. Israel's government is democratic, effective, free of corruption, its people united in its support. The Soviets have sent supersonic fighters to the Arabs. Soviet planes and pilots they have trained are on Arab soil. Forty Soviet warships are in the Mediterranean, and their advisers are in Arab nations. . . . The U.S. should without delay sell Israel the fifty Phantom jets she has so long been promised." RFK called for ending U.S. economic aid to Arab countries, which was used in support of aggression against Israel.[50]

The Sirhan family members were avid readers of *The Independent*. In the May 26 edition of the newspaper, columnist David Lawrence had argued, in an article entitled "Paradoxical Bob," that RFK had taken a contradictory position in his approaches to the Israel and Vietnam problems. Lawrence pointed out that RFK paradoxically supported disengagement in Vietnam and engagement and commitment in Israel:

Presidential candidates are out to get votes, and some of them do not realize their own inconsistencies. Just the other day, Senator Robert F. Kennedy of New York made a speech in Los Angeles which certainly was received with favor by Protestant, Catholic and Jewish groups which have been staunchly supporting the cause of Israel against Egypt and the Arab countries. . . . Lots of people . . . think the situation in the Middle East is not nearly as dangerous as the situation in South-East Asia. Also there are many members of Congress who feel that it is proper for the United States to render military support to Israel in the Middle East, it is just as necessary to protect the countries of South-East Asia against aggression. . . . A large number of people in this country are deeply concerned with the events in the Middle East, particularly with the fate of Israel. Hence the political candidates see a big advantage in proclaiming their support of American intervention in the Middle East.

Sirhan Sirhan, a young Palestinian immigrant, had this clipping in his pocket when he was arrested for Robert Kennedy's murder.

3

SIRHAN AND PALESTINE

"I and the public know
What all schoolchildren learn
Those to whom evil is done
Do evil in return"

—W. H. AUDEN

Jerusalem

Sirhan Sirhan, whose name means "one whose attention is wandering," was born on March 19, 1944, in Jerusalem, the capital of Palestine per a 1922 British mandate. At the time of his birth, his parents, Bishara and Mary Sirhan, Christian Arabs, lived in the new city, which later became part of the new state of Israel.

Bishara's ancestors were originally from Taibeh, a small town with a Greek Orthodox and Roman Catholic population built on several hills about thirty miles north of Jerusalem. Three stone Orthodox and Roman Catholic churches stand on three of the hills. On a clear day the Jordan Valley and the Dead Sea are clearly visible. Bishara's father owned land in Taibeh that was rich with olive trees and wheat fields. He bought it from savings he accumulated while working in South America. The family was not popular with the townspeople, partly because they always kept to themselves and also because Bishara's father was a moneylender.[1] In June 1968 Bishara's eighty-nine-year-old mother was still alive.

Bishara Sirhan married Mary in 1930. He was a mechanic working for the British government in Palestine, repairing water pipelines—pipelines that were blown up by the Palestinian Arab population during the campaign of rebellion between 1936 and 1939. By the time of the 1948 war, Bishara had attained the position of foreman and held testimonials as a good worker. He built his own house and did his best to look after his family.[2]

49

During the 1930s and 1940s the Sirhan family increased to six children—five boys and a girl, Aida. At the time of Bobby Kennedy's assassination, Sharif was thirty-eight, Saidallah thirty-six, Adel thirty-three, Sirhan twenty-four, and Munir was the youngest at nineteen. Mary gave birth to thirteen children, but six of her babies died shortly after birth or in early childhood. The Sirhans' daughter Aida survived into adulthood but died in 1965.[3]

Sirhan's father, Bishara, was a small man with a strong-boned face. At the time of Robert Kennedy's assassination he was fifty-two, but he looked much older. At the time of the 1948 war the family lived in the Musrara Quarter outside the walled city in a rented, traditionally Arab three-story house—Number 82, Rehov Shivtev Yisrael. The house was situated near the Damascus Gate, in an area that, before 1948, had a mixed Arab–Jew population. It had a red-tiled roof, a courtyard, elegant arched windows set in thick stone walls, and a garden of eucalyptus trees. Water was drawn from a cistern, but the house had electricity. The Sirhans lived on the ground floor apartment for seven years.

St. Paul's Street was one of the many streets in Jerusalem that divided the Jewish and Arab sections of the city. The sections were separated by barbed wire. A British radio station was positioned above the Sirhan home. During the 1948 war, a Jewish organization took over the house in a raid on the station. The family retreated to the basement in fear.

The Sirhans were thrifty and lived modestly comfortable lives. Young Sirhan lived in Jerusalem until he was four years old. The family was forced to flee the city when fighting broke out. During one violent incident, the Jewish group, Irgun, bombed the Damascus Gate. Eleven Arabs and two British policemen were killed in the attack. Sirhan and his father, who were about to go through the gate when the bomb exploded, narrowly escaped injury. According to Bishara,

> I was going to the store to buy coffee and a few other things for the house and took Sirhan with me. We were just about to go into the Gate when I heard people shouting. I looked back and saw something black being thrown out of a car. It began to roll down the slope and then it exploded with a great bang. I picked up Sirhan and ran into the gate and then to the left. He seemed to have fainted. I was mad with anger. I laid Sirhan down on a shelf. He wasn't hurt anywhere but his eyes were shut. I rubbed his face and his hands. After a few minutes his eyes opened and I asked him, 'Sirhan, do you feel any pain?'

And he answered, 'No, Daddy.' I kept on rubbing his hands
and his body. Then he got up and asked, 'Why do the Jews do
this thing? Don't they believe in Christ?'[4]

The violent incident had a psychological effect on the young Sirhan.
After the bombing, he remained in bed for two days and stayed in the house
for two weeks. According to his parents the four-year-old witnessed five other
separate incidents of violence and death during the rest of the family's stay in
Musrara. After one incident, Mary said, Sirhan "was pale for some time.
Wouldn't move for some time. Couldn't move. Fainted. After a truck full of
dynamite exploded near our home Sirhan wouldn't go out of the house for
days. . . . Sometimes he would talk in his sleep. . . . One night, living in Old
Jerusalem, I felt him and he was cold like a stick. More than any of his brothers, he had less blood and more fear." Mary also said Sirhan would go into
trancelike states.[5] Later, when he was eight years old, Sirhan witnessed the
death of his brother Munir (after whom the Sirhans' youngest child was
named) when a runaway Army truck, trying to avoid a sniper, struck the
child in St. Paul's Street.[6] Sirhan remembered an Arab military checkpoint at
Jerusalem's Zion Gate and an Arab soldier there who let him look through
binoculars at the Jewish part of the city. The Arab soldier told Sirhan that all
the land he could see belonged to them.[7] Following the shooting of Robert
Kennedy, psychiatrist Dr. George Y. Abe discovered that Sirhan suffered from
a number of neuroses as a child—he wet his bed, bit his nails, was fearful of
walking into a dark room, and felt shy and sensitive about his body.[8] Sirhan,
in later years, said that neither of his parents expressed affection for him
through hugs and kisses.[9] A boyhood friend of Sirhan's, Ziad Hashimeh, said
Sirhan grew up in the midst of murder, filth, and terror. He was continually
beaten by his father and affected by scenes of warfare on his doorstep.
    At the end of the 1948 war, Jerusalem was split in two. The Arabs
had been expelled from the western quarter and the Jews had been expelled
from the eastern side. Because of the fighting and the growing hatred and
animosity between the Jewish and Arab populations, the family fled east.
For a few weeks the Sirhans lived in the Greek Orthodox Convent of St.
Nicholas, which had been converted to accommodate hundreds of Arab refugees. The space was used as a school and hospital. Later the Sirhans were
allotted a rundown house at the corner of Suq el Husroor and Al Malak
Street inside the city. They lived in one room measuring 15 feet by 30 feet
until they immigrated to America in 1957. They had the bare essentials of
life, a tiny kerosene stove, and a small stipend from UN welfare workers.
According to Mary Sirhan, "We tried to [go back to the house] but how can

we? We didn't have it. We didn't have . . . They drove us from our homes. They drove us out of our land which we called home. We didn't have anything, where to go or what to do, where to eat, where to sleep."[10] The family was reduced to the misery of refugee status.

For most of the nine years between 1948 and 1957, Bishara was unemployed; he found a few small jobs and received financial assistance from relief organizations. The family was registered as refugees with the United Nations Relief and Works Agency for Palestine Refugees (UNRWA). Mary Sirhan ran a crèche and Sunday school. The Sirhans' house did not have electricity, and they collected water from a cistern. A total of fifty people lived in the two-story house.

The young Sirhan, together with his brothers and sister, played in the streets outside his home. A favorite game was "aseer," a form of tag using a ball. Sometimes the children would rent a bicycle, as the family was too poor to purchase one. According to accounts of those who knew the family at the time, Sirhan preferred reading to outdoor activities. His parents were anxious that violence could erupt in the streets at any time, and they may have discouraged their son from playing outdoors.[11]

A Christian Palestinian, Sirhan was taught at the Martin Luther School, which was attached to the Lutheran Church of the Savior, which stood facing the door leading to the courtyard of the Church of the Holy Sepulcher. The majority of the school's students were Palestinian Arabs. Sirhan was taught by Arab teachers who instilled in him the principles of the Palestinian cause. They promoted Palestinian nationalism and made continual references to the great Arab warrior, Saladin, who had expelled the foreign crusaders from Jerusalem. Teachers tried to inspire the children in their care to fight for the Palestinian cause.[12] At the tender age of seven, Sirhan was intrigued by the assassination of King Abdullah of Jordan at the Aksa Mosque, a ten-minute walk from the Sirhan home. King Abdullah had been murdered because militants viewed him as a traitor to the Palestinian cause. According to his father, Sirhan "was very much interested in this event."[13]

As the children grew, strains developed between Bishara Sirhan and his two elder sons, Saidallah and Sharif. According to neighbors who knew the family in Jerusalem, the older boys were aloof, displayed weak characters, and took money from the family finances to spend on themselves. They also took out debts in their father's name. In response Bishara threw the boys out of the family home. The elder sons maintained contact with their mother, who frequently sent them food and money. After a while Bishara reconciled with his sons but did not allow them back in the family home. The two older boys remained in Jerusalem when the family immigrated to America.[14]

A neighbor in Jerusalem said that Bishara beat Sirhan frequently, sometimes with his hands and sometimes with a stick. According to Ziad Hashimeh, who was the same age as Sirhan and was a close friend, Bishara Sirhan beat his wife Mary and also struck Sirhan, "on the back . . . everywhere."[15]

In December 1956 the Sirhan family secured the sponsorship of missionary Haldor Lillenas, who had met Bishara while visiting Israel. Bishara asked Lillenas to help his family immigrate to the United States. Lillenas agreed and organized assistance from the U.S. government for the family. According to Bishara, the family decided to move to America because it was "a wonderful country where one could always find work and make money. . . . One day I saw one of my friends talking to a foreigner. I stopped to greet him and he introduced me to the person he was talking to. From his accent I knew he was an American so I said to him directly, 'You are an American, I want to go to your country, will you sponsor my family?' And the American said that he would try to help and later he did arrange to sponsor us."[16] The Sirhans were sponsored by two families belonging to the First Nazarene Church in Pasadena. When the family secured sponsorship, Sirhan was two months away from his thirteenth birthday.

Although the family saw the move as beneficial, Sirhan became sullen and ran away from home. Even at this young age he knew, having listened to broadcasts by the Voice of America on the radio and gauging the anti-Arab sentiment, the United States was the enemy of the Arabs.[17] According to Sirhan, "I didn't want to leave; I wanted to stay in my own country with my own people. I know that the US was against the Arabs and was friendly with Israel, and a friend of my enemy is my enemy. I knew about US policy because I did a lot of listening on the radio to the Voice of America."[18]

The young Sirhan was gone all day and spent his time in a park in Ramallah, fifteen miles north of Jerusalem. When he returned to the family home later that evening his father was angry, prepared to mete out punishment. However, Adel Sirhan stepped in and asked his father to show forgiveness. Over a meal of tabbouleh, a cold mixture of cucumbers, tomatoes, and grain, the family united in their desire for a new life in America and an escape from the Arab–Israeli conflict.[19]

Pasadena

The Sirhans journeyed to the United States, first from Amman to Beirut and then by ship to Naples and on to New York. They traveled by train across America to Pasadena. On arrival in the United States, Sirhan was treated for a minor parasitic condition of the small intestine. The family entered the country with "permanent resident status" and remained citizens of Jordan. Saidallah, who remained in Jerusalem when the family emigrated, was the only member of the family to apply for citizenship after his arrival in the United States in 1960. At first Sirhan was not impressed with his new life, but he was hopeful that his position as one of an "oppressed" minority would improve. The twelve year old asked his mother if by becoming a U.S. citizen he would get blonde hair and blue eyes.[20] From an early age he referred to himself as a "Palestinian Arab" even though he was, technically, a Jordanian citizen.[21]

Although Pasadena was a separate city, it was, essentially, part of the Los Angeles conurbation. Apart from a dozen or so skyscrapers in central Los Angeles, the area consisted of car-jammed freeways and single-story houses, stores, and businesses. The residential areas were clean and pleasant but monotonous in their grid-like patterns. When the Sirhans arrived in Pasadena, they stayed with their sponsor, Haldor Lillenas, and they maintained contact with their sponsoring organization, the First Nazarene Church, for a year after their arrival. In 1958 they were attracted to the First Baptist Church run by Dr. Charles Bell. Only Mary and Munir attended services regularly, however. Eventually, the family was housed in a modest apartment on Lake Avenue.

By 1958 Bishara had had enough of the United States. He found it difficult to fit in, disliked the culture, and thought American society was immoral. The socio-political divide was too much for him. He became disturbed that American women had so much independence and was afraid his wife, Mary, was adopting their ways. The couple also clashed frequently, as they had in Jerusalem. They were temperamentally unsuited to one another. Bishara was especially concerned because his position as *pater familias*, head of the family, had been eroded by the newly acquired Western attitudes his wife and sons displayed. About six months after the family's arrival in Pasadena, Mary and her sons began to challenge Bishara's authority. Bishara was also upset because his wife had maintained contact with the two elder boys in Jerusalem, further undermining his authority.

Following a family feud whereby Mary sided with her sons, Bishara asked his wife to choose between him and the children. She chose the children and Bishara left, taking the family savings of approximately $500. The young Sirhan Sirhan felt "no sense of loss" when his father abandoned the family.[22] Bishara traveled to New York, where he worked as a maintenance mechanic. After his mother became ill, he returned to Jerusalem. Following his arrival in Jordan, he wrote to his wife demanding that she and the children join him in East Jerusalem. However, Mary Sirhan had grown accustomed to the freedom American women enjoyed. The Reverend Haldor Lillenas sided with Mary and wrote to the Department of Immigration, describing Bishara Sirhan as an "undesirable alien," suggesting he be refused reentry into the United States.[23] However, Bishara made another two trips to New York to work before he returned home to Jerusalem for good and settled in his ancestral village, Taibeh. In all he spent five years in the United States with no contact with his family in Pasadena.[24] Mary Sirhan, embarrassed by her husband's departure, lied about his leaving, telling neighbors and friends that Bishara had left to care for his aged mother in Jerusalem.

Sirhan, who became known to his friends as "Sol," entered the sixth grade at Longfellow Grammar School in the spring of 1957. He was placed two grades below his actual age. His teacher was Mrs. Floyd Fraley, who later could not remember anything outstanding about her pupil except for his double-barreled name. Comments on his school record for January–June 1957 describe him as "trying hard" to overcome his language difficulties and "showing improvement." He was also described as "co-operative, well-mannered and well-liked." He achieved a C + , a barely above-average score, in his tests.[25]

In the autumn of 1957 Sirhan transferred to Marshall Junior High School in Pasadena for one year until September 1958 when he moved to Eliot Junior High School. The transfer was made when Sirhan's mother bought the house at Lake Avenue. Sirhan maintained his C + average grades and secured a newspaper delivery route for the Pasadena *Independent Star-News*. At thirteen Sirhan took the Pintner Test for General Ability and achieved a test level of eight years and eight months. He took the Terman-McNemar Test when he was fourteen years and ten months and achieved a test level of twelve years and eight months mental level. His scores for verbal reasoning, abstract reasoning, and the ability to see objects in three-dimensions were very low. When he was seventeen, he took the Stanford Binet IQ Test and scored 89—slightly below average.[26] He had not yet expressed any radical political or nationalistic views when he entered junior high school, but he continued to describe himself as a "Palestinian Arab." Most of the people he came in contact with during this period in his life described him as "polite" and "normal."[27]

Sirhan spent two years at Eliot Junior High School, and during this period he left impressions with his teachers and fellow students. Samuel Soghomonian, Sirhan's English and social studies teacher, described him as a boy who was bullied because he was "dark complected" and "a foreigner." Soghomonian was Armenian, which led him to empathize with the young Palestinian. A fellow classmate described Sirhan as always arguing with his teachers and "attention-seeking." Some reported that the young Palestinian began to criticize the United States and become more outspoken about his Arab origins during this time.[28]

In 1960 Saidallah and Sharif joined the Sirhan family in Pasadena. Munir and Sirhan were in school. Mary had secured a position as a housekeeper for the Westminster Presbyterian Church on Lake Avenue for five mornings per week and also worked in the nursery. Their only sister Aida worked as a secretary and Adel had part-time work as a painter. Sharif secured work in accountancy having had experience working as an accountant for Mobil Oil in Amman, Jordan. The family pooled their money.[29] However, central to their lives was the hope that the family could one day return to live in "Palestine," in particular, Jerusalem.[30]

In September 1960 Sirhan enrolled at John Muir High School, a large establishment housing three thousand students with a mixture of socioeconomic backgrounds representing the Pasadena population. Although Sirhan was not bright, his behavior and attitude in school gave his teachers the impression that he was a slightly above-average student.[31] He seemed intelligent and articulate because he had a verbal IQ of 109, an above-average score—but his reasoning level was far below at 82.[32]

Seeing students from wealthy backgrounds socializing among themselves had an impact on Sirhan, an impact long recognized by educators who have understood how school populations, differentiated by social class, material possessions, and social groupings can cause resentment and bitterness. Sirhan began to recognize that, for him at least, America was a society of the haves and have-nots. He identified with the have-nots and characterized the haves as students with blonde hair and blue eyes. Sirhan was beginning to identify himself along racial lines.[33] At this time he was described by friends and fellow students as "taciturn," "surly," "hard to get to know," "withdrawn and alone" but also "pleasant and well-mannered."[34] He dreamed of getting an important job in Jordan after he studied at a university in America.[35]

At John Muir High, Sirhan became interested in learning Russian and German. At first he wanted to be a doctor, but then he decided that life as a diplomat in the foreign service was his ultimate goal.[36] He became enamored of the military, joined the California Cadet Corps (138 Battalion, B Company), and, for three years, attended the corps' meetings and drill practice. His CCC courses involved firearm safety and target shooting.[37] He told author Dan Moldea, "I was familiar with guns because of my Cadet Corps training in high school, which was a state-sponsored program. I've fired M-16's, M-14's, .45's, .22's. I could tear a gun apart and put it back together. We used to have competitions."[38] On completion of his high school education, Sirhan showed signs that his Arab heritage remained an important part of his life. On graduation he signed his name in Arabic, and he was fascinated with the famous Arab singer Umm Kulthum, a supporter of Egyptian president Abdul Nasser. Kulthum's songs registered with Sirhan on two levels. In times of crisis she sang songs with a patriotic theme, but she also sang about unrequited or lost love.

Sirhan made friends with two students, Walter Crowe and Tom Good. Sirhan had known Crowe since Crowe was eleven or twelve because they had both delivered newspapers. Crowe remained friends with Sirhan two years into college, at which point they drifted apart. Crowe transferred to the University of California–Los Angeles and finished there with a degree in history. Sirhan went to work at the racetracks. In March 1968, upon prompting by his mother, Crowe called Sirhan, and they met at Bob's Big Boy restaurant near Pasadena State College. After dinner they went to topless bars. In an initial interview with the FBI, Crowe said Sirhan "was never violent," but later he told the Bureau the truth: Sirhan was moody and had expressed violent hatred for Israel.[39] The friends saw themselves as antiestablishment intellectuals who took positions on issues that were the antithesis of those adopted by the majority. Crowe gave Sirhan C. Wright Mills's *The Power Elite* and books by Paul Goodman and Albert Camus, authors who argued that Western society was bourgeois and corrupt. Sirhan described these books as "Terrific. . . . It opens your mind. What a contrast to the bourgeois stuff around here."[40] Later Crowe said it had been difficult rebuilding their friendship; he believed Sirhan resented Crowe's superior education.

By 1963 the Sirhans had settled into their new home at 696 East Howard Street, a modest frame cottage with a large magnolia tree in the front yard. The house had a value of $15,000 in 1968 and was in a "white" neighborhood. Further east the area along Howard Street became racially mixed, and then, eventually, it became a black neighborhood. The family was not house proud: the area around 696 East Howard was untidy, and the backyard was overgrown with weeds. Rubbish collected near the garage. The neighbors described the family as "aloof" and "superior" in their attitudes.[41] One neighbor described Sirhan as "just a funny sort of a person. He made you feel uncomfortable when he was around . . . never talked to you."[42]

The Sirhans resisted acculturation. At home they spoke Arabic and they listened to taped Arab music, especially the music of Umm Kulthum, all day long. They read Arab newspapers and observed Arab customs. Despite his all-English education Sirhan's mother tongue remained Arabic, although Sirhan claimed to think in English.[43] All of Sirhan's brothers described themselves not as "Christian Arabs" but as "Palestinian Arabs."[44] The brothers also strongly disapproved of their sister Aida's marriage to a non-Arab.[45]

There is very little evidence that Sirhan was successful in wooing girls when he was developing as a young man, despite his claims to the contrary. A police report indicated that he was so shy he used to drive around a girl's home for days at a time without stopping to say hello.[46] Sirhan told Robert Kaiser that his first sexual experience was with a girl who visited the gas station where he worked. She arrived late at night, and Sirhan used to take her to the back of the gas station. As he finished work at four in the morning, he bought her breakfast. Later, he said, he made love to her in his 1949 Cadillac at a drive-in showing a Burt Lancaster movie. Sirhan confessed he had not experienced "sex with love" too much, only sex for sex's sake. He said he used to pick up girls at Sunset Boulevard, and he remembered a particular "conquest" the night before his sister Aida died.[47]

The family had their share of problems and trouble with the authorities. Adel and Munir lived at home along with Sirhan and their mother. Sharif and Saidallah had their own homes but visited the Sirhan family home frequently. Mary Sirhan, now a single parent, had little or no effective control over her sons and often asked Arab-American friends to intervene in disputes. The sons felt no inclination to obey her, as was Arab custom. Gradually, a wall built up between the mother and her sons.[48]

The Pasadena police were called to the Sirhan home on August 4, 1963, when an argument erupted between the nineteen-year-old Sirhan and his mother. Sirhan approached Officer R. D. Cannow while he was sitting in his police car and told the officer he was afraid to return home. Cannow took Sirhan home and another argument occurred. Cannow advised Sirhan to leave the house for a cooling off period, and no further action was taken by the Pasadena police.[49]

Mary's daughter, Aida, like her mother and brothers, adopted American mores. Aida was a small woman with a pleasant disposition. She moved to Palm Springs in 1963 to take a job as an accountant at a candy store. There she met and married Herbert Mennell. Knowing the family would disapprove of her marriage to an "outsider," she kept the marriage secret from her brothers. Mary likely knew about the marriage but never brought the subject up in conversation. Aida returned to Pasadena when she developed leukemia, and her illness grew progressively worse. Sirhan helped nurse his sister in her last days. Not until the funeral did the family meet Aida's husband.[50]

Sirhan's oldest brother, Saidallah, was a surly and bitter young man and a virulent anti-Israeli who claimed the Jewish state "did not exist." He made no effort to seek American citizenship and was self-conscious about his English skills, which were poor compared to those of his brothers. He liked Middle Eastern music and the music of Ravi Shankar and played the oud, an instrument of the lute family. In 1962 he was arrested for drunk driving and also for "drunkenness and disturbances."[51] By 1963 Saidallah had become a problem for the family. He was unsettled in America, drank too much, and argued with his brothers. He went to work for Michael Ganguin Incorporated in Pasadena as a machinist in April 1966. Saidallah was arrested for disturbing the peace and drunkenness on August 17, 1966.[52] On November 1, 1968, Saidallah went to his mother's house to ask for money. He told her he knew she had received some funds from several Arab church groups. Mary Sirhan denied she had received the money, but Saidallah refused to leave the house, insisting she give him some money. He threatened to hit her.[53]

During a confrontation with Sirhan, Saidallah threatened his younger brother with a can opener. The threat of violence was so serious that Sirhan called the police. According to the official police report, "It was learned that [Sirhan] is at the stage where he does not want advice or will not listen to his elders, and when spoken to, he flies off the handle and an argument starts. The complainant [Sirhan] would not listen to the undersigned . . . and kept arguing with his family." Sirhan's mother wanted him out of the house for a short period so things could settle down. The police advised Sirhan to escape the household for a while, and he went to live with William Beveridge, who had hired Sirhan as a gardening assistant. For a short time Sirhan lived in Beveridge's camper at the rear of the gardener's house.[54]

Following RFK's assassination, Saidallah took every opportunity to cash in on the family connection to the murder. In fact, the whole family expected to benefit financially from the tragedy. They expected to get $100,000 from a deal that involved selling Sirhan's story to a major media outlet. Robert Kaiser asked Adel Sirhan why the family expected to make money off Sirhan's misdeed. Adel replied, "Look, as long as there is money to be made."[55]

Saidallah invented stories in hopes of selling them for "big money." He said that once a *Life* magazine reporter and photographer sent two men to his apartment to beat him up and that sinister-looking people followed him and tried to shoot him as he drove his car north on the Pasadena Freeway. In response to his claims, the police examined his car and discovered a number of discrepancies in his story concerning the trajectories of the bullets allegedly fired into the vehicle. The police gave Saidallah a lie-detector test; his answers to the important questions were "unsatisfactory."[56]

During the period before Sirhan's trial, Saidallah was hit by a car and was in the hospital with serious injuries. When asked about his brother's accident, Sirhan said he felt nothing. At the hospital, while visiting Saidallah, Sirhan's brother Sharif became violent with one of the nurses and the police were called. On hearing the story of Sharif's troubles, Sirhan complained that the incident might have harmed his image in the eyes of the American public.[57]

As the hospital incident indicates, Saidallah was not the only brother to display violent, criminal behavior. Sharif, the accountant, once dated a student from Pasadena City College (PCC), and for him at least the relationship was serious. The girl ended the relationship because she felt Sharif and his brothers were "sexist."[58] Upset at the end of the affair, Sharif became desperate and made threatening phone calls to the girl. He also made two attempts to cut the fuel lines in the girl's car and an attempt at tampering with the car's brakes. Sharif was put under surveillance by Pasadena police and, following his third attempt at sabotaging the girl's car, was arrested on December 18, 1963, for attempted murder.

On reading about his arrest in a Pasadena newspaper, Sharif, who had been released on bail, became angry and arrogant. He believed the newspaper had no right to describe him as an "attempted murderer." Sharif's behavior at the time was eerily similar to his brother Sirhan's five years later when he was arrested for the murder of Senator Kennedy. Sharif did not accept nor believe he had attempted to murder his ex-girlfriend, and the prosecutors believed he was a seriously disturbed young man, a belief that undoubtedly allowed Sharif to escape imprisonment. He was sentenced to one year's probation and ordered to seek psychiatric treatment.[59] Sharif's crime also had repercussions on his employment and his family. He was fired as an accountant for the Baptist Convention, and his brothers were ridiculed by neighbors. Still, the family united behind Sharif. In a response that she repeated following Sirhan's crime five years later, Mary Sirhan became blind to her son's guilt, blamed the local pastor Dr. Bell for Sharif's dismissal, and stopped attending the church.[60] After RFK's assassination, she expressed the view that her son Sirhan had committed a patriotic act.[61]

Following his arrest for attempted murder, Sharif's life took a downturn. He could not find further employment, began to borrow money from friends, and spent his time gambling at the racetrack. Sharif's love of the racetrack probably prompted Sirhan's earlier efforts to become a jockey. During Sirhan's trial for the Kennedy assassination, Sharif threatened Sirhan's lawyer Russell Parsons and defense investigator Michael McCowan. McCowan knocked Sharif unconscious, believing that his client's brother had been tampering with his car. Sharif also caused trouble for the family by telling Sirhan's lawyers that Sirhan had told his brother Adel, a few days before June 4, that he (Sirhan) would soon become famous. Adel denied that this had happened.[62] Following the assassination, Sharif told investigators that he had not spoken to his brother, Sirhan, in five years.[63] In 1973 he was convicted in a federal court of writing a letter threatening Israeli prime minister Golda Meir.[64]

The Sirhans' youngest son, Munir, known as "Joe," also had a troubled history and conflicts with the law. He was a disciplinary problem in school, and as early as 1959 a neighbor complained to the police about Munir's malicious mischief. In November 1963 Munir was involved in a high-speed pursuit with the California Highway Patrol. In 1964 he was involved in a juvenile investigation of a "sex and homosexual party."[65] On April 8, 1966, he became a suspect in a "marijuana possession and sales case" after the police were tipped off by informant John O'Hanian. Munir ran away from home and was arrested for vagrancy in Flagstaff, Arizona, on May 26. Returning home, he began smoking marijuana and was arrested on June 10, 1966, for selling the drug to a state narcotics agent. He was tried as an adult and convicted on October 13, 1966. On December 1 of that year, he was placed on five years' probation with the first year to be served in county jail. However, he served only nine months, and on May 15, 1967, his conviction was set aside when the judge revealed that Munir had been a juvenile at the time of the crime.[66] In June 1968 Munir worked at Nash's Department Store in Pasadena as a sales assistant.

Adel was different from the other brothers. He had a quiet nature, loved music, made picture frames, and was seen as a polite, gentlemanly character around Pasadena. Adel was also a musician who played the oud at various Arab clubs around the Los Angeles area. When working, he earned up to $150 per week. When not working as a musician, he turned to picture framing. The family trait of gambling did not bypass Adel, although his game of choice was poker. He was no more successful than his brothers and frequently borrowed money to pay off his debts.[67] Adel, by temperament, had been best placed to settle in to American society. According to The Fez supper club's Arab-American owner, Lou Shelby, "The two elder sons were fairly pragmatic and not too idealistic. They were beginning to adjust to America and of them, Adel was best adjusted to the conflicting cultures. It's true they retained their old nationality but Adel, at least, allowed his Jordanian passport to lapse, and I had quite a job getting it renewed in a hurry when he had an engagement in Mexico."[68]

Following high school, Sirhan enrolled at PCC, an impersonal institution with thousands of students. He began to attend regular meetings of the Organization of Arab Students. Fellow members recalled his virulent Arab nationalism and hatred for Jews.[69] After March 1963 he became a part-time student and held down a number of part-time jobs. The entire length of his stay at PCC was only one year and five months. In his fourth and last semester, he earned five F grades. He was dismissed on May 18, 1964, for poor attendance, but Sirhan begged the college authorities to keep him on, arguing he had missed classes because of his sister Aida's illness. The authorities were unrelenting.[70] Sirhan lied about his dismissal from college, telling one acquaintance that he had been asked to leave because he was having an affair with a math teacher.[71]

In March 1964 Sirhan found work at John Davies's service station in Pasadena. He attended the gas pumps and cleaned the station and the restrooms. He worked the night shift from 8:00 p.m. to 4:00 a.m., and when Davies decided to close down at midnight, Sirhan worked 4:00 p.m. to midnight. According to Davies, his new employee was always polite, courteous, and hardworking. Sirhan worked at the service station for ten months but left because he felt one of his managers was too severe in his criticisms.[72] Sirhan moved to another service station nearby, this one managed by Ivan Milicic, but soon left after a win on the horses at Santa Anita Racetrack.[73]

Sirhan's next job was as an assistant to gardener William Beveridge, but he was fired for not tending to his duties on an estate. By mid-1965, following two years of low-income meager jobs, Sirhan set his sites on becoming a jockey and secured employment at Santa Anita Racetrack as a stable hand. The stewards at Santa Anita said Sirhan, twenty-two, was too old and, at five feet five inches and 120 pounds, too big to be a jockey, but Sirhan believed he could eventually master the skills and reflexes of a jockey. According to Adel, "[Sirhan] always went to the heart of everything. If he got interested in something, he read everything he could get his hands on."[74] The job Sirhan had with Gordon Bowsher was not to his liking, however. He began by mucking out and grooming the horses. He did manage to get his "hot-walker" license, which allowed him to walk horses to cool them off following a race.

Sirhan eventually grew tired of the job at the stables, which held no future for him. He set his sights on a position available at a horse-breeding ranch in Corona. According to Sirhan, "At Corona they bred horses. I had seen a note on the bulletin board at Santa Anita, offering a position as an exercise boy. I responded and met Frank Donnarauma, who was the trainer. . . . I didn't know that 'Frank Donnaraumer' was an alias. . . . I didn't know anything about criminals."[75] Conspiracy advocates later claimed that Sirhan was connected to organized crime through Donnarauma. (Note: Robert Blair Kaiser spells the name as "Donnarauma"; Sirhan spells the name as "Donaruma"; Moldea spells it "Donnarumma.")

Sirhan was excited to have a job working on a ranch, the Granja Vista del Rio Thoroughbred Horse Farm. He later told NBC News that he "loved it. . . . That was the most enjoyable experience of my life . . . horses. . . . They're easy to be with. I love to be with them."[76] Bert C. Altfillisch, the owner, hired Sirhan on June 2, 1966, and told him he would be doing "everything," including working as an exercise boy.[77] Sirhan produced his hot-walker license from the California Horse Racing Board, and he told Altfillisch he had five months experience at the Santa Anita Racetrack. As Corona was too far from Pasadena to commute, Sirhan found lodgings at the Highlander Motel, where one of the lodgers, Van Antwerp, offered him a couch for the night after Sirhan failed to locate the manager.

At the Huddle, a poolroom in Corona, Sirhan made friends by purchasing drinks for a group of men while he waited to play pool. One of the men in the group was Terry Welch, a fellow employee at Granja Vista who described Sirhan as a man "who wanted to know everything. He read everything. He could talk about everything like an expert: art, music, electronics, law, the manufacturing of glass, metal. You name it, he knew about it. He was like a geisha girl."[78] Welch further described Sirhan as neat, clean, and intelligent. He also said that Sirhan was an avid reader of law and frequently discussed cases that he had read about in the newspapers.[79]

Sirhan was not the mild-mannered, obsequious young man that conspiracy writers like to portray, although he could adopt this personae if it suited his purposes. Munir Sirhan said his brother was stubborn and had tantrums.[80] William A. Spaniard, a twenty-four-year-old Pasadena acquaintance of Sirhan, said the young Palestinian was "a taciturn individual."[81] Not only did Sirhan frequently display a quick temper, but he also was considerably adept at forcefully putting his arguments forward and stubbornly standing his ground. He said he was always "a good listener, but I'm very hard to persuade."[82] At the Granja Vista del Rio Ranch Sirhan put himself forward as the spokesperson for an exercise boy strike. The exercise boys complained they were overworked and took their complaint to Altfillisch. Sirhan's aborted education at PCC stood him in good stead as he articulated the exercise boys' grievances. Altfillisch was impressed by Sirhan's "big words" but refused to give in to the employees' demands.[83]

Sirhan also became enamored with a girl, Peggy Osterkamp, who he saw at the ranch. Sirhan said she looked "beautiful on a horse."[84] He made no effort to ingratiate himself with her apart from casual greetings. Investigators believed the beautiful Osterkamp would never have been interested in a short and unattractive man like Sirhan. However, he was so taken with her he wrote her name in his notebooks and in one entry identified her as "Peggy Sirhan." There is evidence that in the days before the shooting Sirhan traveled to Corona where Osterkamp lived. He told his lawyers he had gone there every day—including the Saturday and Sunday before the assassination—since he had his car fixed.

At the Granja Vista, Sirhan received an injury to his head that, according to his family, affected his personality. After the injury, his family said, he became increasingly moody, possibly indicating brain damage, which would be a mitigating factor in the crime he committed two years later.

On a foggy day, September 25, 1966, Sirhan led his horse, Hy-Vera, for a workout. The fog had the same effect on a horse as a blindfold. One trainer, Millard Sheets, was frightened enough to withdraw his horse from the workout. Another, Lynn Wheeler, complained it was just too foggy. But trainer Larry Heinnemann told the owners, who had come all the way from Los Angeles to see their horses run, that the fog had lifted sufficiently to take the chance. At first the horses began to jog very slowly, almost a canter. Then the riders brought them into a gallop. As Sirhan took the lead the fog returned. Suddenly the owners heard a crash and a scream. When they arrived at the scene of the accident, Sirhan was semiconscious and blood trickled from his ear. He was covered in mud and blood, and he thought he had gone blind. After fifteen minutes an ambulance arrived and took Sirhan to Corona Community Hospital, where he was treated by Dr. Richard A. Nelson.

According to Nelson, "Sirhan questioned all of the medical applications and all the medicines administered to him and appeared unduly frightened of the various treatments. He was one of the most reluctant patients I ever had."[85] Dr. Paul Deeb, head radiologist, reported that X rays of Sirhan's head were "negative" as to "concussion, fracture, or serious internal injury."[86] Sirhan suffered two deep wounds over his left eye and under his chin, which required stitches. He was discharged the following day. A few weeks later, on October 8, he fell off his horse a second time and received a slighter injury that also required treatment at a hospital.

Sirhan was examined twice after the accidents, on November 8 and December 20, 1966, by Dr. Milton Miller, a Corona ophthalmologist. Dr. Miller said that his examination showed there were no abnormalities, and he believed Sirhan had been exaggerating his injuries. When Miller refused Sirhan a letter supporting his claim for compensation, Sirhan telephoned the doctor and threatened him.[87] On July 10, 1967, Sirhan filed a claim and it was adjudicated on October 2, 1967, and February 7, 1968. Sirhan's doctor, Dr. Maurice Nugent, and the insurance company's doctor, Albert Tashma, an ophthalmologist, reported that Sirhan had 20/15 vision and did not have "any permanent disability as a result of the accident."[88] However, a consultant neurosurgeon said that a complaint of head injuries could not be accurately checked and advised that the adjudicator err on the side of caution. Sirhan was awarded $2,000 and bitterly complained that the award was too small.[89] He also believed the claim had been delayed because he had mistakenly retained the services of a Jewish lawyer and because he was an "Arab."[90]

Sirhan worked at the ranch until November 13, 1966, when he was fired. Altfillisch lost confidence in Sirhan after the would-be jockey, whose skills were less than competent, had his accident. Sirhan's last pay check was on December 6, 1966. Altfillisch believed that the young rider had a lot of ambition but that the accident made him lose his nerve. Sirhan's ambitions to be a jockey were now lost. He became bitter and bent on vengeance. Blaming Altfillisch for his problems, he wrote in his notebooks, "I believe I can affect the death of Bert C. Altfillisch."[91]

After Sirhan left the Granja Vista Del Rio, he went to work for owner-trainer Bob Wheeler at the Del Mar Race Track, starting on November 16, 1966. He lasted only a few weeks. Sirhan failed to qualify as a rider. He was fired after he argued with the foreman, Larry Peters. Peters had seen Sirhan kick a horse in the belly, and when he remonstrated with Sirhan, he was taken aback at the young employee's vitriol. Peters said Sirhan's temper was unusually violent when he was told he would never be a jockey.[92]

Following the loss of his racetrack job and facing the prospect of a life of unskilled and lowly employment, Sirhan became bitter and angry. He believed he was fit for better employment. Christian Ek, a twenty-three-year-old Swede who was a classmate of Sirhan, said, "[He] dreamed of being something big in Jordan after his studies in the United States."[93] Holding unrealistic expectations, he waited for a professional-type job, made excuses in rejecting work he felt was unfit for him, and spent the next nine months unemployed. According to friends Patricia and John Strathman, Sirhan became "depressed" and fascinated with "magic." He told them he could see "mystical bodies." The Strathmans became embarrassed at Sirhan's obvious fantasies.[94]

Sirhan was asked numerous times by friends and acquaintances why he had not applied for American citizenship. He always replied that he was an "Arab" and felt there was no freedom in the United States. He also resisted American citizenship because of U.S. support of Israel.[95] Sirhan came to believe that he could have more freedom in Russia and China and that stories of refugees fleeing from those countries were products of American propaganda. When it came to political discussions, Sirhan adopted a closed-minded attitude. No one could convince him his arguments were wrong, and he always dug his heels in if the conversation became polemical.

In January 1967, despondent that his career ambitions had faded away, Sirhan began drinking. He was introduced to the Tom Collins at The Fez. During the following months, his life centered around going to the race-track and dabbling in mysticism. He frequently visited Broughton's Used Book Store near Colorado on Lake Street and began reading books on Rosicrucian philosophy. The sect had originated in Europe during the up-heavals of the sixteenth and seventeenth centuries. Rosicrucians claimed to have acquired the ancient secrets of Middle Eastern mathematics, medicine, and alchemy. Over time they inculcated their members with the belief they could create gold and medicines that could cure every disease. As the move-ment grew the Rosicrucians abandoned many of their medieval practices in favor of more modern ideas about the power of the mind. In the early 1900s an occultist named H. Spencer Lewis founded a Rosicrucian order in San Jose, California. For a modest fee a member of the order would receive a membership card, the secret password, instructions on how to execute a secret handshake, and a promise that the applicant would develop greater will power, an improved memory, and the ability to influence others. Mem-bers also learned about cosmic powers and reincarnation. Sirhan sent in his $20 fee and misleadingly stated on his application form that he had been a student of psychology, philosophy, and metaphysics for three years.[96]

Sirhan's mother began to worry that her son spent too much time in his room. He had become so fascinated with the ideas propagated by the Rosicrucians that he began to practice some of their theories, including "white magic," by, for example, staring intently at lit candles, trying to develop his mental powers. Sirhan used a hypnotic technique that had been around for centuries: he began with relaxation to make his central nervous system pas-sive and then regulated the heartbeat, inducing intense concentration. The kind of trance he used varied in depth, and experts argue that it is impos-sible to enter a deep trance state using this method. Believing strongly in the power of thought projection, Sirhan even tried to influence the performance of horses at the racetrack. Two incidents convinced Sirhan he had succeeded: once he believed he had made his mother get out of her bed in the middle of the night to go to the bathroom and once he believed he had made a horse fall down. Sirhan became enamored of this newly found way of improving his failing life. According to Sirhan, he "always asked the question . . . 'What is this life about? What is this reality, this world?' I always wanted to know what was behind it."[97]

During this period of unemployment, Sirhan frequently visited the Pasadena Public Library on Catalina Street, especially during the summer of 1967 when he read everything he could get his hands on about the Six Days'

War. He avidly read *B'nai B'rith Messenger* keeping track of "Zionist intentions."[98] Angry and bitter at the Arab defeat, Sirhan frequently railed against the pro-Israeli television news and the "bias" of magazines like *Time, Newsweek*, and *U.S. News and World Report*.[99] The war had an intense effect on him. Sirhan had seen photographs of Israeli soldiers triumphantly taking control of the Suez Canal. Later he remarked, "If I had seen those guys personally, I would have blasted them. . . . I would have killed them."[100] His anger against Israel provoked him to write in his notebooks, "2 June 1967, 12.30pm—A Declaration of war against American Humanity when in the course of human events it has become necessary for me to equalize and seek revenge for all the inhuman treatments committed against me by the American people." Another entry declared, "Long Live Nasser. . . . Long live the Arab Dream."

In July 1967 Sirhan went to the Pasadena City College, the institution he had recently left, to look at job vacancies. A retail stock clerk position paying $135 a week looked attractive, and he visited the placement bureau to apply for the job. It was the first attempt Sirhan had made to find a job since he was fired in December 1966. According to the PCC employment counselor, Jeanne Herrick, "When he handed me the application, he hadn't filled it out. . . . He wouldn't put his work experience. The job he was asking for, he had no qualifications for. It said a man five foot ten inches tall and he was five foot two. . . . He wouldn't give me any further information . . . so I tried to tell him that we had to have further information. . . . He was a foreign student. . . . He [had to] have a permit from Dean Lewis." Angry, Sirhan went to see Lewis to complain about Herrick. When Herrick proceeded to interview Sirhan again, with Dr. Lewis present, Sirhan began to lie about the first interview. Herrick said, "He said I told him that he should go back to his own country, he didn't have any right here, and he ought to go back where he came from. . . . He was extremely touchy."[101]

After requesting and then tearing up his second application, Sirhan "came back, all alone," according to Herrick, "at the very end and leaned way over the desk and shook his finger in my face, and said, 'Now, this will teach you to underestimate jockeys.'"[102] Over the following weekend Sirhan seethed at the perceived injustice meted out to him, and he returned to the college demanding to see the president. The president's secretary told Sirhan that he could see the vice president instead as the president was at a meeting. Placated by the vice president, Sirhan calmed down and filled out a new application. He did not get the job.

To his mother, Sirhan seemed to be a friendless young man.[103] Marilyn Hunt, a cocktail waitress at the Hi-Life Bar in Pasadena said she saw him a number of times over the year preceding the assassination and he always seemed to sit very quietly alone at the bar.[104] Sirhan also frequented Shap's Bar, where he placed his horseracing bets. One of his few ventures outside the house was playing Chinese checkers with two elderly ladies, Anna Sylvan and Olive Blackslee, who lived down the street. Mary Sirhan began to encourage him to look for work and eventually secured a job for him, at a health food store at 1380 North Lake Avenue, which belonged to John Henry Weidner, a Seventh-Day Adventist who was always willing to help down-trodden people like the Sirhans. The store described itself in its advertising as "Pasadena's largest natural foods center—Certified raw milk, fertile eggs, unsulphured dried fruits, live food juices, fresh organically grown fruits and vegetables." Weidner was a former captain in the Dutch Army, and during World War II he had organized resistance to the Nazi occupation. His organization received Jews, airmen, and many others who were victims of the Nazis.

Sirhan worked with Weidner from September 1967 to March 1968. According to Weidner,

> His mother presented him to me as "Sol." . . . His sister was a customer in my store, and I became friends with her—I became close to the mother. I am a 7th Day Adventist . . . so sometimes when we had a special meeting at the church I invited her, and she came several times, and she had no car, so I took her from the home to the church—sometimes in the evening, sometimes on Sunday morning . . . so we became quite close, and at the same time, even before I became so much close, her boy, Munir, came to my store . . . I gave a job, and I think he worked for one week. . . . One night in the car, she say, "Can you find something for Sirhan? He's without work actually." So I told her he could see me, starting 17th September, he could come every Sunday.

On November 19 Weidner hired Sirhan full time. Sirhan worked in the stockroom, waited on customers and delivered orders.[105] According to Weidner, "he had to take orders . . . but he found it hard to take my orders and he didn't like to have things explained to him. His attitude seemed to be 'I'm as good as you are.'"[106] Sirhan's Arab pride also caused difficulties. He would not wear an apron, believing it was a garment worn only by women, and he also felt shame that his mother had asked for the job at Weidner's.

Sirhan discussed politics, religion, and philosophy with his boss. One of Weidner's assistants said Sirhan was "a fanatic when it comes to a discussion of religion or politics."[107] According to Weidner, Sirhan believed he was "an Arab . . . till the end." Weidner quoted Sirhan as saying, "They [the Jews] have stolen my country. They have no right to be there. It belongs to Jordan and they have taken it." Weidner said Sirhan believed "The Jewish people were dominating, they had a lot of wealth, a lot of power, and he say [sic] there is no freedom in America. . . . He always had the attitude of resenting authority. . . . He could be very nervous and arrogant. . . . He was thinking alone . . . knowing his hate of the Jews . . . and knowing his complex of inferiority, seeing in Kennedy a man who has a big name, rich, successful life, happy—now Sirhan, you have got to do something big."[108] Weidner engaged Sirhan in many discussions about the problems of the Middle East. According to Weidner, "he hated the Jews because of their power and their material wealth, they had taken his country from his people who were now refugees. Because of Israel, he said, his family had become refugees, and he described to my wife how he himself had seen a Jewish soldier cutting the breast off an Arab woman in Jerusalem." He told Weidner, "There is no God. Look at what God has done for the Arabs! And for the Palestinians! How can we believe in God?"[109]

It was Sirhan's "touchiness," arrogance, and feelings of inadequacy and inferiority that caused friction between the employer and employee. Weidner said he sometimes "felt that [Sirhan] had turned against the whole American way of life, and that he was an anarchist in revolt against our society. And yet he had beliefs and principles. Personal honor and his self-respect were important to him. And second only to that he esteemed patriotism. He had strong patriotic feelings for his country [Palestine]. Yes, I would say he loved his country."[110]

Following a mistake in a delivery order, Weidner remonstrated with Sirhan. Sirhan insisted Weidner's poor communication skills were to blame for the error. He fled the store in a rage but returned later to put in his two weeks' notice. The following two weeks were fraught with conflict between the two men. Finally, on March 7, Weidner told Sirhan he had to listen to him without complaint or leave the store immediately. Sirhan refused, sat down, and demanded Weidner give him a further two weeks' salary because he was being fired. Sirhan threatened to take his case to a labor tribunal. Weidner was forced to call the police, and when they arrived Officer R. E. Reinek questioned Sirhan about his citizenship. Sirhan exploded, insisting they had no right to question him on that subject. He showed them his immigration card and said, "I am a Palestinian."[111] Officer Reinek told Sirhan to leave the store and no further action was taken by the Pasadena Police Department. On April 24, 1968, Sirhan took Weidner to a labor board, but the board decided in Weidner's favor.

During Sirhan's long period of unemployment, from March until his arrest in June 1968, he busied himself by looking after the garden at 696 East Howard, cooking, making repairs around the house, and fixing small mechanical problems on his beloved De Soto car. Sirhan paid $410 for the pink and white 1958 vehicle. He raised the money through odd jobs. During this period of unemployment, on one of his visits to the Santa Anita Race-track, he expressed hatred for Robert Kennedy. John Shear, an assistant to trainer Gordon Bowsher, was visited at his barn by a young man who called himself "Sol." "He didn't know anything about horses, but he said he was willing to learn and to help out in any way he could," Shear said. One morning at the barn, shortly after Sol had been hired, a coworker was reading aloud a newspaper account of Robert Kennedy recommending the allocation of arms to Israel. "Sol just went crazy," Shear said. "He was normally very quiet, but he just went into a rage when he heard the story." After the assassination Shear immediately went to the security people at the track, who subsequently informed law enforcement officials.[112]

On Easter 1968, Adel's boss Lou Shelby visited the Sirhans. He had known Adel for seven years, but it was the first opportunity he had had to talk to his younger brother. According to Shelby,

> We had a really big argument on Middle East politics. . . . We switched back and forth between Arabic and English. Sirhan's outlook was completely Arab nationalist—the Arabs were in the right and had made no mistakes. I tried to reason with him and to point out that one could be in the right but still make mistakes. But he was adamant. According to him, America was to blame for the Arabs' misfortunes—because of the power of Zionism in this country. The only Arab leader he really admired was Nasser and he thought Nasser's policies were right. The Arabs had to build themselves up and fight Israel, that was the only way. The only outside friend the Arabs had was Russia, but, according to Sirhan, Russia had not proved a good enough friend during last June's fighting [the Six Days' War].[113]

In April 1968 Sirhan became fascinated with the circumstances surrounding the assassination of Martin Luther King. He had been at the racetrack the day King was shot, and he remembered a horse, Pink Pigeon, was racing that day. He said an African American, who had been holding a portable radio, approached him crying and shouting, "They shot him! They shot him!" Sirhan heard someone ask, "They shot who?" And the reply was, "Brother Martin Luther King."[114] Sirhan was empathetic to the plight of African Americans and believed the only way they could attain equal rights was through violence.[115]

On April 5 Sirhan received his insurance check for $1,705 from the Argonaut Insurance Company. As he already had $200 saved, he thought he might purchase a Mustang car if he could win some money at the racetrack. Within a week he had lost a few hundred dollars at Hollywood Park.[116] Thereafter his "investments" worsened, and he was left with only a few hundred dollars. Luck also seemed to escape Sirhan in the months leading up to the assassination of Robert Kennedy. As he fixed a bent axle on his De Soto, the jack he was using slipped and bruised his shoulder. Thinking he had mended the car correctly, he took it for a test run on the San Bernadino Freeway. But the back wheels seized up bringing the car to a halt. Sirhan was experiencing one bit of bad fortune after another. He was out of work. He had lost most of his money. And he had no luck with girls.

On May 15, 1968, according to Godfrey Jansen, Sirhan watched a CBS documentary, "The Story of Robert Kennedy," on television. He took notice halfway through the program when the narrator told of how Kennedy had visited Palestine as a war correspondent in 1948. The narrator continued, "Living with Israeli troops, seeing war and death at close hand for the first time . . . seeing the Jordan River red with blood of Jews and Arabs . . . he wrote his dispatches and came to his decision." The program ended there with an Israeli flag waving in the breeze. "Bob Kennedy decided his future lay in the affairs of men and nations." The program, paid for by the Kennedy for President Committee, did not overtly say RFK supported Israel. But in Sirhan's mind the Israeli flag said it all.

4
THE SHOOTING

"Sirhan looked like Satan himself, Sirhan looked like the Devil. As long as I live I will never forget those utterly cold, utterly expressionless eyes of his."

—AUTHOR GEORGE PLIMPTON

The Stalking

The idea of assassination had been with Sirhan many years before he shot Robert Kennedy. The idea formed in his mind when he was a young student, and it was expressed when he underlined passages in his school textbooks that made reference to previous presidential assassinations. It was also revealed in numerous entries in his diaries and notebooks. As an Arab forced to live in a society that Sirhan believed saw him as a member of an aggressive and anti-Semitic nation of people, he began to formulate political ideas that supported his view of the world. He became disillusioned with American society and its principles of government, and he began to make entries in his notebooks that referenced his hatred for American political leaders and the American system of government, which, he believed, had made him impoverished, a second-class citizen in American society.

In 1968 he began to stalk Senator Kennedy. A former employee of the Ambassador Hotel, Danny G. Bobbitt, told police detectives that he had seen Sirhan at the Ambassador "two or three weeks earlier asking about RFK's whereabouts."[1]According to Joseph and Margaret Sheehan, Sirhan attended the Los Angeles Sports Arena Kennedy rally on Friday, May 24, 1968. Following RFK's speech the Sheehans waited outside the arena to catch a glimpse of the presidential candidate. In the crowd they saw Sirhan, who looked "completely out of character with that crowd . . . very quiet, intent and purposeful in a frightening way." Margaret Sheehan thought Sirhan was "intense and sinister."[2]

Five days later, Saturday, June 1, Sirhan drove to the Corona Police Department Shooting Range. The shooting range roster indicates that he started firing at 12:50 p.m., and finished at 3:00 p.m. On the way home he stopped at the Lock Stock 'N Barrel gun shop situated at 8972 East Huntington Drive in San Gabriel, part of the Los Angeles sprawl, to buy more mini-mags and regular westerns.

On Sunday, June 2, Sirhan drove his mother to church and picked her up after the service. Later, police checked gun ranges in the Los Angeles area but could not confirm that Sirhan had practiced his shooting skills that day. Sirhan's whereabouts that afternoon remained a mystery. However, on Sunday night he was seen at the Ambassador Hotel at approximately 7:30 p.m. Sirhan had discovered that Kennedy was due to give a speech at the Ambassador. At first Sirhan denied he had been at the Ambassador that evening. Later he said, "Maybe I was there," after defense investigator Robert Kaiser implied that television news teams may have caught him on camera. This claim by Sirhan revealed a conscious effort to hide the fact that he had been stalking Kennedy.[3]

Sirhan had taken an advertisement with him to the Ambassador that night that read, "You and your friends are cordially invited to come and see and hear Robert Kennedy on Sunday, June 2, at eight pm at the Cocoanut Grove, the Ambassador." "A guy like me," Sirhan said later, "a nobody getting a personal invitation to go down to the Ambassador! Too much out of my class!" Sirhan believed if he took the newspaper cutting with him, "they couldn't throw me out of the place."[4]

He elbowed his way to the front of the crowd waiting for RFK to give his speech. Sirhan stood in front of Susan Reading, who observed that he had his hands clasped behind his back and was looking "sullen." Suddenly, Sirhan grabbed a piece of paper out of the hands of a woman standing nearby and said, "Let me see that!" Sirhan had been in a front position in the aisle RFK was due to walk down toward the stage. However, he had left the vicinity before Kennedy had arrived. The senator was late arriving at the Ambassador because he had taken his children to Disneyland that day.[5] Later in the evening Sirhan caught a glimpse of RFK standing on the Ambassador's outdoor terrace. At his trial he explained how this sighting had changed his opinion of the man he wanted to "blast": "My whole attitude toward him changed. Before I had pictured him as a villain. . . . But when I saw him that night, he looked like a saint to me." This impression might have lasted, he intimated at his trial, had his old enmity not been resurrected by a newspaper advertisement two days later.[6]

Following Kennedy's speech in the Palm Terrace Room, RFK passed through the kitchen area. Miriam Davis, a hostess for the event that evening, walked around the hotel for twenty minutes following the senator's speech. She saw Sirhan sitting in the pantry area. Either Sirhan had missed Kennedy's journey through the pantry or he had lain in wait but was unable to either observe him or shoot him. William Blume said he recognized Sirhan. Blume had worked in the liquor store next to Weidner's health food store, where Sirhan had worked. He observed Sirhan in the lobby area adjacent to the Palm Terrace Room.[7]

Sirhan drove his mother to work at approximately 8:00 a.m. on June 3. Around 11:00 a.m. he stopped at the Richfield gas station at 2529 E. Foothill Boulevard in Pasadena and filled his car with gas. John Davies, the garage owner who had employed Sirhan as a part-time worker from March 1964 to June 1965, recognized him. According to Mary Sirhan her son was at home watching television between 11:00 a.m. and 4:30 p.m., and he stayed at home all evening.[8] Sirhan said he had been at home all day raking leaves, sleeping, and reading the newspapers, and in the evening he drove out to Corona, possibly to see Peggy Osterkamp. He later told Michael McCowan, however, that he had put 350 miles on his car's odometer that day. Sirhan might have driven 260 miles to San Diego, where RFK was due to speak at a campaign rally that evening. RFK collapsed from exhaustion at the El Cortez Convention Center, though, and the rally was cancelled.

On Tuesday, June 4, at 8:00 a.m., Sirhan bought a newspaper at Washington Boulevard and Lake Avenue in Pasadena. He returned home at 9:30 a.m. As he read the paper, he began making decisions about which horses to bet on in the afternoon races. Sirhan abandoned the idea of going to the races that day after he decided that none of the horses running looked like good bets. Sirhan said, "I was losing all the time and that day I did not like those horse entries. . . . I decided to go target shooting instead of going to the races, I think."[9] In fact, Sirhan had planned to go target shooting all along. After his arrest and while awaiting trial, Sirhan was asked by prosecuting psychiatrist Dr. Seymour Pollack if the horses were running on election day. Sirhan didn't know. Later Sirhan asked a defense investigator to find out.[10]

At 11:00 a.m. Sirhan drove to the San Gabriel Valley Gun Club in Fish Canyon in Duarte, a Los Angeles suburb, and was one of the first to arrive, at 11:30 a.m. He registered using his real name and correct address. Sirhan rapid-fired his gun using a small screwdriver to remove the shells after he emptied the gun's chambers. He purchased more boxes of bullets from Everett C. Buckner, the range master, and insisted he have a box of shells that would not misfire. Buckner later observed Sirhan rapid-fire shooting, expending between three hundred and four hundred bullets.[11] Michael Soccoman, a member of the club, handled Sirhan's gun. He said that Sirhan was a good shot and that the young Arab fired the best two shots on Soccoman's target that day. Sirhan told Soccoman he was going hunting. When Soccoman questioned the legality of the bullets Sirhan was using, Sirhan said he didn't know if they were legal but they were certainly lethal enough to "kill a dog."[12]

Two other visitors to the club that day, student Henry Carreon and his friend David Montellano, said Sirhan shot very fast rapid fire and used mini-mags with hollow points. Sirhan told them the mini-mags "spread a lot more on impact."[13] Later, a young woman asked Sirhan for advice about shooting, and he showed the girl how to aim and shoot. He told her the gun was firing to the left, and she had to stand properly then squeeze the trigger slowly with even pressure. Sirhan stayed with her for about twenty minutes until the range master shouted cease-fire, as the range closed at 5:00 p.m.

Leaving the shooting range Sirhan drove to the Pasadena City College (PCC) campus and called in at Bob's Big Boy restaurant, where he caught sight of an Indian student he knew by the name of Gaymoard Mistri. Mistri was sitting at the counter drinking coffee. Mistri and Sirhan talked about the horse races and horses in general. They also discussed a news item about recent clashes between Israel and Jordan. Sirhan became angry, hitting the *Herald-Examiner* with the back of his hand and telling Mistri how bad the situation in the Middle East was.[14] Sirhan ate a hamburger, drank his coffee, and left Bob's Big Boy at approximately 7:00 p.m. He walked with Mistri to the nearby PCC campus and met three Arab students, including two he knew, Marouf Badren and Anwan Sayegh, who were members of the Organization of Arab Students. As the students were due to attend 7:00 p.m. classes, the two friends parted after some small talk.

Mistri had bought a newspaper for the classified advertisements. He handed the reading sections to Sirhan, who noticed an advertisement for a parade celebrating the first anniversary of the Six Days' War.[15] The ad said the parade would be "tonight," and Sirhan took that to mean the evening of June 4. However, the paper was an early edition of the next morning's newspaper, and the parade had been organized for the evening of Wednesday, June 5. Mistri and Sirhan walked back to the parking lot of Bob's Big Boy, where they parted company after Mistri turned down Sirhan's offer to play pool.

The Victory Parties

The evening of June 4, Sirhan drove into Los Angeles to watch the "Jew" parade. The ad had given him a "burning feeling inside."[16] Sirhan said, "[I went] to see what those goddamned sons of bitches were up to. I was driving like a maniac."[17] Finding no signs of any victory celebrations on Wilshire Boulevard or Miracle Mile, Sirhan noticed a storefront campaign party for Republican primary election candidate for senator, Thomas Kuchel. He stopped in and overheard that several large parties were being held that night at the Ambassador, a short distance away. At that point, he said, he decided to go to Republican Max Rafferty's primary election night party at the Ambassador, in part because he knew Rafferty's daughter, Kathleen, from college. It is likely this statement was self-serving and constructed to avoid suspicions that he had known about the Kennedy victory party at the Ambassador. At the Rafferty party he drank several Tom Collins drinks as if they were "lemonade." Sirhan told Dan Moldea, "I didn't know anything about beers or liquors. I was a square. The Tom Collinses tasted just like lemonade. I was tired. It was late. I was an early-to-rise, early-to-bed person. I was out of my element."[18]

Sirhan had illegally parked his pink and white De Soto Firelite a couple of blocks from the Ambassador. The following day an FBI agent parked on New Hampshire Avenue found it. Inside the car agents found two spent .22 cartridges on the front seat and a book in the back titled *Healing: The Divine Art* by Manley Palmer Hall. Items later recovered from the car were:

- Two bullet slugs on the front seat and an unfired bullet
- A black leather wallet containing Sirhan's driver's license and other ID cards in the glove compartment
- A Canadian dollar
- A key ring with six keys and a tag with the De Soto's license number
- An empty box, labeled mini-mag .22 long rifle, HP
- One hundred and fifty Blue Chip stamps
- A number of cashier's receipts
- A raffle ticket from St. Elizabeth's Western Fiesta May 20, 21 (grand prize: a 1967 Pontiac Firebird)
- Two photos of a man on horseback and one of several sheep
- Some matchbooks from Shelby's Pizza Parlor, Foothill Boulevard, Pasadena
- A paper bag labeled "Jack in the Box"
- Four newspapers
- The *Los Angeles Times*, June 4 and 5, 1968
- The *Christian Science Monitor*, June 2, 1968
- A business card for "Lock Stock 'N Barrel. Fine Guns. 8972 East Huntington Drive, San Gabriel"
- A sales receipt for $3.99 from the same gun shop dated June 1, 1968

Sirhan put his wallet in the glove compartment before he tucked his gun under the waistband of his denim jeans. His blue velour shirt concealed the gun from view. Later, Sirhan said he took the gun with him because he was afraid "Jews" would steal it.[19]

At the Rafferty party, which was held in the Venetian Room of the Ambassador, Sirhan spoke to two young men, a Mexican and a Puerto Rican. Sirhan criticized "the rich Rafferty people who step all over the poor." When one of them said that Kennedy might help, the poor Sirhan angrily responded, "Kennedy! He should never be president. You think that he really wants to help the poor? Kennedy helps himself. He's just using the poor. Can't you see that?" At about 8:45 p.m. Sirhan struck up a conversation with Hans Peter Bidstrup, and they both sat down. According to Bidstrup, Sirhan had a drink in his hands. Sirhan asked Bidstrup which floor RFK was on and if the senator had bodyguards. Bidstrup did not know anything about Kennedy's security arrangements and before he could continue the conversation Sirhan jumped up to ask a fire inspector, Michael Wherton, about his job.[20]

Between 9:00 and 9:30 p.m. Sirhan engaged in conversation with Humphrey Cordero and Enrique Rabago. Rabago began talking to Sirhan in Spanish but, on realizing that the short swarthy young man was not Hispanic, began speaking in English. Rabago asked if "we," meaning RFK supporters, were winning. Sirhan answered they were but then turned "arrogant . . . acting like a big shot," according to Rabago. Sirhan expressed disdain for Kennedy. "Don't worry about him if he doesn't win," he said, "that son of a bitch. He's a millionaire and he doesn't need to win. He just wants to go to the White House, but even if he wins he's not going to do anything for you or for any of the poor people."[21] During the conversation Sirhan referred to Kennedy as a man who "did not care about poor people and merely sought to gain the presidency for personal reasons" and said that Kennedy was going to buy the presidency.[22] When Cordero suggested that they go back into the hotel, Rabago hesitated because they were both wearing casual clothes. Cordero asked Sirhan for his opinion. Sirhan replied, "Why shouldn't we go in there, we are voters; we're putting them in office."[23] Sirhan later gave his description of the meeting with the two young men: "In the garden I met two Mexican boys," he said, "dressed as I was. We talked about Robert Kennedy. They were afraid to go inside. [I said,] 'If he doesn't like the way we're dressed, the hell with him.' The younger fellow convinced the older one about this. I agreed with the younger fellow."[24] Sirhan also complained he had just spent twenty dollars for a drink at the Rafferty headquarters to show off to a hostess who had "looked down on him."[25]

Sirhan moved to the Colonial Room, situated between the ballroom and the serving pantry that led through a passage right into the Embassy Ballroom. The Colonial Room was almost empty, had a small private dining area, and had been designated as the next call for RFK following his expected victory speech in the Embassy Ballroom. It was fitted up as a small, extra-writing pressroom, and about a half dozen female telegraph operators and a dozen or so people were hanging around. It held three teletype machines, which were situated against the long north wall of the room. The reporters watched RFK's speech from a television monitor in the northwest corner of the room. The main exit and entrance on the south wall opened on to the lobby. No security guards were posted on the swinging entrance door to the Colonial Room. Western Union operator Mary Grohs, who was stationed in the room, was startled to see Sirhan staring over her shoulder at her teletype machine.

At 9:30 p.m. fire inspector Cecil Lynch decided the Embassy Ballroom had reached its capacity and told security guards Albert Stowers and Jack Merrit to begin letting people in according to a one-in, one-out system. Supporters in the lobby complained as the doors were shut. Disappointed at not being able to secure a place in the ballroom to watch Kennedy give his speech, some decided to gain access by surreptitiously going through the kitchen pantry.[26]

Teresa Christian saw Sirhan at the Embassy Ballroom bar. She said he looked "nervous," and she chastised him for pushing his way to the front of the crowd.[27]

At around 10:30 p.m. Dr. Marcus McBroom saw Sirhan in the pantry area. Sirhan had been leaning against a steam table. McBroom at first believed he was a hotel worker but then noticed he was not wearing a white uniform. According to McBroom, Sirhan looked "out of place."[28] Minutes later Sirhan attempted to enter the anteroom behind the stage where RFK was due to give his speech. Kennedy worker Judy Royer approached him and asked if he had a pass. Later, she asked him again to leave the pantry area. Sirhan told her he didn't and then returned to the pantry area where he asked a hotel busboy, Jesus Perez, "Is Kennedy coming through here?" Perez told him he didn't know and observed that Sirhan seemed nervous and was twisting a piece of paper in his hands.[29] Sirhan had entered the pantry from the Colonial Room and followed a girl he had seen drinking coffee. Robert Klase, another Kennedy helper, asked Sirhan to leave the anteroom behind the stage at about 11:00 p.m.[30]

The kitchen staff had suspected RFK might go to the Embassy Ballroom stage through the pantry because the passageways there had been lined with trellis-covered green and white wooden barriers and some of the counters had been covered with white tablecloths. Also, a three-man television crew had set their equipment up in the anteroom just beyond the pantry. Both Jesus Perez and twenty-eight-year-old waiter Martin Patrusky saw Kennedy when he passed through the pantry on his way to give his victory speech. They both observed Sirhan in the pantry area. Sirhan remained in the pantry standing close to Perez at the corner of a serving table.[31]

According to a United Press International (UPI) report Perez said Sirhan waited in the kitchen area for about thirty minutes and asked "three or four times" if Kennedy would pass through the pantry. Perez said Sirhan looked "worried" but "not nervous" and the waiter "did not see anyone with [Sirhan]."[32]

Some hotel staff, unaware of the change in plans, thought RFK was going to go to the downstairs ballroom. However, to accommodate the new plan, Kennedy aides Fred Dutton and Bill Barry mapped a route to the Colonial Room. An Ace guard suggested Kennedy and his entourage move through the crowd in the Embassy Ballroom, but RFK had asked to go the "back way."[33] Security guard Thomas Perez was stationed in the anteroom behind the podium. The anteroom led to the pantry. Two guards were assigned to escort RFK through the pantry: Stanley Kawalec, who was ahead of the senator, and Thane Eugene Cesar, who was behind.

Before RFK had finished his speech, aides Fred Dutton and Bill Barry checked the shortcut to the Colonial Room. Walking across the pantry, which was less crowded than any other passageway, they both agreed it would be the safest route. Barry and Dutton returned to the stage from the Colonial Room through the swinging pantry doors to the anteroom and up the inclined hallway at the back of the stage. They stepped through the stage drapes to the senator's retinue, which surrounded RFK as he finished his victory speech.

Following the speech, security guard Thane Cesar approached Kennedy as he came through the swinging doors. He began pushing people back away from Kennedy as he was having difficulty moving forward. RFK and Cesar reached the ice machine shortly before Karl Uecker, who was holding Kennedy's right hand, leading him through the pantry. Cesar moved behind Kennedy and took his right arm at the elbow. He let go as Kennedy shook hands with a kitchen worker, eighteen inches from the first steam table.

The Assassination

At 12:15 a.m. on June 5, as Kennedy moved through the pantry, Sirhan approached from the area of the tray rack and ice machine. About twenty people were in front of Kennedy, and the senator was in the midst of a group of about fifty people. Perez and Patrusky both saw a "smirk" on Sirhan's face as he fired his gun.[34] Vincent DiPierro remembered the "stupid smile [Sirhan] had on his face. . . . It was kind of like an envious smile, like, you know, villainous."[35] George Plimpton's wife, Freddie, said, "His eyes were narrow, the lines on his face were heavy and set and he was completely concentrated on what he was doing."[36] Sirhan had darted out, leaned against a steam table, and extended his hand with the revolver toward RFK. The first two shots were deliberate with a slight pause between, followed by wild rapid firing. As he aimed his gun, witness Richard G. Lubic heard Sirhan shout, "Kennedy, you son of a bitch!"[37]

According to Rafer Johnson, "Once I saw . . . I thought it was a balloon, the first shot, because I didn't see anything. I looked, and then the second shot, I saw smoke and I saw something like . . . the residue from a bullet or cap, looked like a cap gun throwing off residue. And when I saw that, I started . . . I fought my way through, and . . . by the time I got there, he had—the fellow had—I don't know how many shots, I couldn't count them to tell you the truth, but I know it was like four or five. And when I saw the senator . . . I saw the senator down, and I saw someone else down there, but I really just glanced at them because I wanted to get the guy with the gun."[38] There were seventy-seven people in the pantry when the shooting occurred, and eighteen were later designated by police and investigators as "key witnesses."[39]

Patrusky described for reporters how Sirhan had come "out of the corner near the ice machine where Kennedy was standing. He had a kind of funny smile on his face and one hand was in front of the other. Then I saw him raise his hands. I didn't know this thing was real until I saw Kennedy sliding down in front of the ice machine. One of the [waiter] captains grabbed the guy by the neck. The guy was waving the gun and a couple more shots went off. I saw two other people fall."[40] According to Boris Yaro, a photographer for the *Los Angeles Times*, "Kennedy backed up against the kitchen freezers as the gunman fired at him *point blank range* [emphasis added]. He cringed and threw his hands up over his face. I turned around and saw Kennedy lying on the floor."[41] Security guard Thane Cesar said, "I saw a hand sticking out of the crowd between two cameramen and the hand was holding a gun." Seeing a flash from the muzzle of the gun, Cesar "ducked because I was off balance and fell back and when I hit [the floor] I fell against the ice boxes and the Senator fell right down in front of me."[42]

Edward Minasian, a hotel employee, was standing within five feet of Kennedy when the senator was shot. Minasian "could tell [Kennedy's] right shoulder was very close to my left shoulder. . . . In my peripheral vision I observed someone running in the direction . . . from east to west. . . . I saw a revolver extended. . . . I saw the arm extended with the revolver and he had reached around Mr. Uecker. . . . [Sirhan] reached between the steam table and Uecker, with his arm extended, and I saw the explosion of the shells and I saw the Senator raise his arm practically in front of his face and then the second shot went off."[43] Witness Valerie Schulte said, "The Senator turned something more than [a] 90 degree angle [and was] facing roughly something west of north where there were people standing."[44] She told investigators she saw Sirhan pushing a small gun toward the senator; the gun was to the side or back of Kennedy's head when Sirhan began firing.[45] Boris Yaro said, "The suspect appeared to be lunging at the Senator."[46] Los Angeles attorney Frank Burns testified that Kennedy was facing "directly west of north looking about that way."[47] Sirhan's firing position was to the right and to the rear of Kennedy,[48] and according to Karl Uecker, Sirhan was "right . . . standing next to me."[49]

Kristi Witker said, "People were running in all directions. . . . There were two very distinct series of pop-pop-pop . . . pop-pop-pop-pop-pop. Three pops, then five—eight in all. . . . I saw the gunman standing, pointing the gun and firing. I remember at least two people, Rafer Johnson and Rosey Grier, grabbing the gunman's arm but not succeeding in getting the gun away from him. . . . He just kept standing there and shooting." George Plimpton was a few yards behind Kennedy when the shooting began, "As the shots rang out," he remembered, "I acted on pure instinct. Somebody yelled, 'Get the gun, get the gun.' . . . I grabbed hold of his gun hand but I couldn't wrest the goddamn weapon out of it."[50]

Richard Lubic observed an arm and a gun pointed at Kennedy's head. According to witness Boris Yaro, "All of the sudden the firing stopped and some men jumped onto the suspect and there were cries of 'get him, get him, get the gun.'"[51] Uecker told the Grand Jury, "The arm [he] was holding the gun in, [I] pushed the arm down on towards the steam heater, and my right arm I took around his neck as tight as I could, and pressing him against the steam heater. The guy in front of me couldn't get loose. While I was holding the hand where he had the gun in, I was trying to get the point of the gun as far as I could away from the part where Mr. Kennedy was laying. From the left side, I was trying to push the gun away to the right side where I didn't see too many people, while he was still shooting. . . . The people behind me were pushing against the steam table."[52] Uecker's description held clues as to the dynamics of the shooting and was a jumping off point for assassination conspiracy theorists (see chapter 5).

In addition to Kennedy, five people in the crowd were wounded: Paul Schrade, head of the United Automobile Workers Union and friend of RFK;

William Weisel, an ABC unit manager; Ira Goldstein, a California news service reporter; Elizabeth Evans, a political supporter; and Irwin Stroll, a teenage bystander. Later, ballistics experts said that a bullet taken from the base of Kennedy's neck and bullets taken from victims Goldstein and Weisel were fired from the suspect's gun to the exclusion of any other gun in the world.[53]

Sirhan managed to get off eight shots before Karl Uecker, Rosey Grier, Rafer Johnson, and George Plimpton finally subdued him. George Plimpton thought Sirhan was "enormously composed." He added, "Right in the midst of this hurricane of sound and feeling, he seemed to be almost the eye of the hurricane. He seemed purged."[54] Plimpton would later describe Sirhan as "Satan himself . . . those utterly cold, utterly expressionless eyes of his."[55] Sirhan said, "I felt a choking in my throat and people were holding me and beating me and twisting my left knee, and pounding my head on the table. They hurt my left eye. . . . Two policemen dragged me out. . . . They told me later I was on television!"[56] Immediately following the shooting, Dr. Marcus McBroom told KABC reporter Carl George that he heard Sirhan say, "'I did it for the country,' 'I love my country' or something to that effect. . . . He was shouting like he'd done the right thing or was attempting to do the right thing. . . . He was trying to do something for the good of the country . . . I heard him say."[57] McBroom later told reporters that Sirhan said, "I did it for my country. I can explain everything!"[58]

Meanwhile, Kennedy lay dying on the pantry floor. Twenty-one-year-old student, Paul Grieco, told Kennedy that "everybody was okay" and "you are going to be okay—just lie still." Grieco then held Kennedy's head, "because I thought he shouldn't be lying down like that. I thought he would bleed less if I held his head up a little." Grieco said Kennedy was at "the height of his consciousness" when he asked, "Is everybody okay?"[59]

Kneeling next to Robert Kennedy was busboy Juan Romero, an eighteen-year-old whose stepfather, a waiter, had gotten him the job at the Ambassador. Romero was a Kennedy admirer and had persuaded a friend earlier in the evening to let him answer Kennedy's request for room service. When a Kennedy aide answered the door to the room, Romero pushed the food cart in and found himself standing next to Kennedy, who shook his hand. Later he observed Kennedy moving through the kitchen pantry following the speech in the Embassy Ballroom. Romero moved close enough to stick out his hand for the senator to shake once more. As Kennedy grabbed it, Juan heard a bang and felt a flash of heat against his face. He saw "the guy put out his hand to the Senator's head. . . . Then I see the guy put a bullet in the senator's head. I thought it was just firecrackers at first," Romero said thirty-five years later, "or a joke in bad taste."[60] But then he saw Kennedy sprawled on the floor. "He was looking up at the ceiling, and I thought he'd banged his head," Romero remembered, "I asked, 'Are you okay? Can you get up?' One eye, his left eye was twitching and one leg was shaking." Romero lifted Kennedy's head and felt warm blood spilling through his fingers. He said Kennedy was "chewing something and somebody said, 'Throw that gum away.' I was going to do it, then I changed my mind—I just couldn't do it." Ethel pushed the busboy out of the way but moments later allowed him to press some rosary beads into her husband's hands.[61]

Kennedy looked around and recognized his wife, who was awaiting the birth of their eleventh child in January; she was kneeling beside him. He called her name several times. Los Angeles doctor Stanley R. Abo attended to him and attempted to keep the head wound bleeding to prevent a clot from forming. Dr. Martin Esther, who also treated Kennedy, believed the senator had suffered cardiac arrest. His right eye was open with the eyeball slightly deviated to the right. Abo said Kennedy was "moving both legs, contorting his body from time to time and moaning. . . . He immediately recognized his wife. He looked up at her and reached out with his right hand. He said, 'Ethel, Ethel.' She murmured, 'It's all right, it's okay.' When they picked him up to put him on a stretcher, he said, 'No, No, don't,' he was obviously in pain. He said, 'Am I all right?' Ethel looked at me. I said to him, 'You're in good shape. Everything will be all right. An ambulance is on its way. Don't worry.'"[62]

Robert Kennedy had suffered three wounds:

- Wound 1—the fatal wound to the head. The bullet entered the brain and fragmented into two large and many tiny pieces. Fragments of the mastoid bone were scattered in the brain. Two wound tracks were visible in the X rays. According to coroner Thomas Noguchi, who performed the autopsy, powder burns on the right ear area indicated Kennedy had been shot from a distance of 1 to 1½ inches.

- Wound 2—a wound to the shoulder. The bullet entered from the back of Kennedy's armpit, through soft tissue, and traveled upward at an angle of 59 degrees to the vertical, moving back to front. It exited through the right front chest.

- Wound 3—a wound to the neck. The bullet entered from the back of Kennedy's armpit at an angle of 67–70 degrees to the vertical in a path nearly parallel to the path of the bullet that caused wound two. The bullet did not exit the skin and lodged near the sixth vertebrae, where the neck meets the back, 2 centimeters from the spine. According to Noguchi, both wounds in the area of Kennedy's armpit and right side were the results of shots fired at very close range.

All three bullets traveled back to front, right to left and upward. A fourth bullet passed through Kennedy's jacket without causing injury; it traveled the same path as the bullets that caused wounds two and three. Later, Noguchi said it was impossible to determine which bullet hit Kennedy first. There were five holes in Kennedy's coat: an exit hole at the right front of the shoulder—no nitrate; an exit hole three-quarters of an inch to the rear of the right shoulder seam—nitrate particles present; an entrance hole two inches below the shoulder seam in the right sleeve—nitrate deposits; and two holes in the rear right sleeve seven inches below the shoulder seam—nitrate deposits.[63] Noguchi later stated that despite his efforts he could not accurately trace the flight pattern of so many bullets.[64]

An ambulance was dispatched at 12:18 a.m. and took five minutes to travel the 2.2 miles to the Ambassador. Bill Barry and Warren Rogers rode in the cab with the driver. Ethel Kennedy, Fred Dutton, and one of Kennedy's sisters, Jean Smith, were in the rear with the attendant. As the attendant attempted to stop the flow of blood from the head wound Ethel shouted, "Don't touch him!" and slapped him. Barry tried several times to enter the back of the ambulance. He yelled, "Don't touch him, you son of a bitch, or I'll come back there and kill you." When Kennedy began gasping the attendant administered oxygen.[65]

The ambulance arrived at Central Receiving Hospital, eighteen blocks from the Ambassador, at 12:30 a.m. Ethel Kennedy watched as her husband was wheeled into treatment room no. 2. Kennedy was comatose and in shock. A doctor slapped his face to try and revive him as Ethel took the stethoscope proffered by a doctor. She heard for herself the beat of her husband's heart.[66]

As doctors connected the senator to a heart-lung resuscitator machine, a nurse suctioned his pharynx. Blood emitted from his right ear and his eyes were wide open, staring at the ceiling light. Adrenaline was injected into his heart to bring him out of shock, but he remained comatose even though his reflexes became hyperactive. He had lost a considerable amount of blood as a result of the bullet, which entered and passed through the mastoid bone on the right side of his head. Some of the fragments of bullet and bone went toward the brain stem.

After the initial diagnosis at Central Receiving Hospital, Kennedy was taken to the Good Samaritan Hospital, a few blocks away. The ambulance was met by resident doctor Paul Ironside and a team of doctors who began to prepare Kennedy for brain surgery.

At the Ambassador stark reminders of the tragedy that had just occurred remained. In the pantry lay a blood-soaked "Kennedy for President" hat. On the wall, five feet from where the senator fell, someone had already taken a crayon and scrawled "The Once and Future King." Mayhem continued in the hotel until well after 1:00 a.m. as between three and four thousand people were herded into the lobby, Embassy Ballroom, Gold Room, Dolphin Court, and Colonial Room. Kennedy supporters wandered aimlessly, unable to make sense of what they had witnessed. Some were crying, others screaming. All wondered what condition Kennedy was in.

The Arrest

Police officers G. W. Blishak and R. J. Velasquez were at the rear entrance to the Ambassador when they received the message that a shooting had occurred. At 12:21 a.m. Velasquez requested assistance and an ambulance. At 12:22 Officers Travis White and Art Placencia radioed in that they had reached the main entrance of the hotel, and at 12:27 fifteen police cars responded that they were en route to the Ambassador.

The men who had subdued Sirhan handed the assailant over to the police officers when they arrived. Sirhan was transported through a hostile crowd that was shouting "Kill him! Kill him!" He was bundled into a police car and taken to Ramparts Police Station. Jesse Unruh, who accompanied the accused to the station, asked the suspect why he shot Kennedy. "Do you think I'm crazy, so you can use it in evidence against me?" Sirhan replied.[67] At Ramparts, accompanied by police officers and Jesse Unruh, Sirhan was first taken to the breathalyzer room of the police station. His eyes were subjected to a light test, and on the basis of that test, as well as his appearance and movements, Officer White formed the opinion that the suspect was not under the influence of drink or drugs. Sergeant Jordan believed Sirhan was not intoxicated because he was able to identify an officer by his badge number and appeared rational.[68] However, Officer Placencia said Sirhan's pupils were dilated because he was under the influence of drink or drugs.[69]

At Ramparts Police Station, Sirhan was searched, and officers found on his person the following items:

- Four $100 bills
- One $5 bill
- $1.66 in change
- A comb
- A car key
- A newspaper clipping of David Lawrence's column titled "Paradoxical Bob" from the May 26, 1968, edition of the Pasadena *Independent Star-News*

- Two .22 unexpended cartridges
- One expended copper-jacketed slug
- A song sheet handed out to Kennedy supporters at the Ambassador
- A newspaper advertisement inviting readers to attend a campaign rally to hear RFK speak on Sunday, June 2, at 8:00 p.m.

The car key was given to Officers White and Placencia, who were ordered to begin a search in the vicinity of the Ambassador for the suspect's car. At 1:00 a.m. Police Sergeant Jordan was instructed to transfer the prisoner to the Parker Center, Los Angeles Police Department (LAPD) headquarters, situated at 150 North Los Angeles Street. Jordan, Officer F. R. Willoughby, and Sergeants Adolph Melendres and Frank Pratchett escorted Sirhan there in an unmarked police car. The suspect was taken to interrogation room 318 at 2:05 a.m.

Sergeant Jordan said that Sirhan never appeared irrational and that in his years on the force Sirhan was "one of the most alert and intelligent people I have ever attempted to interrogate."[70] According to LAPD records, Deputy District Attorney John Howard, Investigator George Murphy, and the suspect participated in the following exchange, with Sergeants Jordan and Melendres acting as observers:

Howard: You understand you have the right to remain silent?
Sirhan: Yes, sir.
Howard: You have the right to an attorney if you wish. Do you understand your rights, first of all?
Sirhan: Yes, I think I shall remain incognito.
Howard: You do not wish to make a statement. Is that correct?
Sirhan: I said yes, sir.
Howard: Okay . . . would you tell me your name?

Sirhan refused. Later in the interview he decided to converse with the police officers who were present but he would not give his name or discuss the shooting. According to Sergeant Jordan, the suspect had a keen mind and fancied himself as something of an intellectual.[71] He told officers, he had "got nothing out of life" and "they [i.e., American society] won't give it [success] to me."[72] Sirhan wanted to talk about the case of Jack Kirschke, a deputy district attorney who had been arrested for a double homicide the previous year, and also about the Boston Strangler case, thus revealing his interest in notorious criminal cases. He was evidently aware that both killers had received lenient sentences even though they had committed multiple murders.

Sirhan was held in an isolated second-floor cell in the remote hospital wing of the jail and continued to refuse to give police any personal details, including his name. He was booked under the name "John Doe." Sirhan was kept under constant surveillance by six uniformed guards. One deputy sheriff remained inside the cell with Sirhan for the duration of his captivity. The square cell was painted grey and contained a bed, wash basin, and toilet. Five teams of two deputies each patrolled the outer perimeter of the jail. When handed his jail clothing, Sirhan objected and was overly concerned about his appearance. He took a long, deliberate shower.[73]

Sirhan was incarcerated in the medical ward because he had a broken left index finger and a sprained left ankle, injuries he sustained as he was being restrained during his shooting spree. He had also suffered a hematoma of the forehead, a minor abrasion on the face, and an upset stomach. Kennedy's bodyguard, Bill Barry, had struck Sirhan twice in the face with his fists.[74]

The following morning LAPD police discovered the assassin's identity when two of his brothers, Adel and Munir, went to the police station after having seen their brother on television. Police confirmed Sirhan's identity through fingerprints that were taken when Sirhan applied for his hotwalker license.

Sirhan's motive was at the time a mystery. Years later, police officers and the public continued to question why Sirhan killed Robert Kennedy. One of the police officers involved in Sirhan's initial investigation and interrogation, however, had no doubts why the young Palestinian committed the crime. Sergeant Jordan said, "The only thing I can figure out is that one of the things I found in his pocket was an article about where Bobby had come out very pro-Israeli. In my mind, my theory has always been . . . is what it would be like if I was able to parachute into Germany in the middle of the war and shoot Hitler. To the German people I'd be the worst scumbag of all time. In my own mind, I'd say, 'Hey, I'm a hero. I did the right thing for the world.' That's the way he struck me. He really believed that he had done the right thing."[75]

In the days that followed Sirhan's arrest, investigators and lawyers began to learn more about Sirhan Sirhan. About ten hours after the shooting, LAPD officers went to Sirhan's home and conducted a warrantless search. Although the officers had no specific reason to believe that Sirhan had been part of a conspiracy to kill other political leaders, the California Supreme Court ruled the entry to the Sirhan property was justified because the potential threat was so serious. In this case, there were "exigent circumstances," defined by law as "a compelling need for official action and no time to secure a warrant."[76]

In Sirhan's bedroom officers found:

- Two large spiral notebooks
- One small spiral notebook with writing on only two pages
- A handbill about a rally in Pasadena for Senator Eugene McCarthy
- A May 23 issue of the *Christian Science Monitor*
- Rosicrucian literature
- An honorable discharge from the California Cadet Corps by reason of graduation from high school on June 18, 1963
- A brochure advertising a book on "mental projection" by Anthony Norvell
- An envelope on which was written, "RFK must be disposed of like his brother was."

When Sergeant Willis searched the garage he found, among other items, three .22-caliber bullets on the workbench. One bullet appeared to be mutilated. Two empty casings were also found.

The Los Angeles Police Department quickly formed a task force, named "Special Unit Senator" (SUS), comprised of several law enforcement agencies, to investigate the murder. The LAPD chief of detectives Robert A. Houghton chaired the SUS meetings. The team included Assistant Attorney General William Lynch, U.S. Attorney Matt Byrne, Assistant U.S. Attorney Robert Brosio, members of the Los Angeles District Attorney's Office, FBI agents, and a team of Los Angeles detectives. Houghton told the task force he did not want another Dallas. He said, "I want you to act as if there was a conspiracy until we can prove that there wasn't one." What Houghton didn't consider at the time he made this statement was the fact that it is virtually impossible to prove a negative.

5

THE TRIAL

"The abuse of the insanity defense has led to what may be called the alibi of abnormality. Instability is not insanity, maladjustment not psychosis.... It seems that every abuse has its apologists.... A defendant in a murder case in whom nobody ever saw any signs of abnormality before his arrest, may be declared insane, spend some time in an institution, and then be [released].... He has acquired a psychiatric hunting licence to kill."

—DR. FREDERIC WERTHAN, AUTHOR OF *A SIGN FOR CAIN: AN EXPLORATION OF HUMAN VIOLENCE*

Grant Cooper [Sirhan's lawyer]: Let me ask you this. You felt [RFK] should be dead?
Sirhan: I didn't like him at all. So whatever in hell happened to him, I didn't give a damn.
Grant Cooper: Well, obviously you felt you were the one to stop him.
Sirhan: Yes, I did.

The Defense and the Prosecution

Sirhan's official trial opened on January 7, 1969. The prosecution article charged that "on or about the fifth day of June 1968, the said defendant, Sirhan Bishara Sirhan, did wilfully, unlawfully, feloniously and with malice aforethought murder Robert Francis Kennedy, a human being." The trial lasted until April 14 and involved fourteen weeks of testimony by ninety witnesses.[1] Four days after the jury was sequestered it returned a guilty verdict on the charges of first-degree murder and five counts of assault with intent to commit murder.

The trial was held in the seventy-five-seat capacity courtroom on the eighth floor of the Hall of Justice, 210 West Temple Street, a large gray building on a small hill on the southern side of the Hollywood Freeway. It was typical of most criminal courthouses in cities across the United States. It stood in the center of downtown Los Angeles near the *Los Angeles Times* building, the Music Center complex, and City Hall. Built in 1925, it is the oldest structure in the civic center. It has remained empty since the 1994 Northridge earthquake. For a half century, until the Criminal Courts Building was opened across the street in 1973, it was the sight of many famous trials, including the Manson family murder trial.

Each morning of the trial, Sirhan was taken down a secure staircase from his six-foot-by-eight-foot cell on the thirteenth floor, where he had been incarcerated since the shooting. He appeared in court dressed in a pale blue tie and blue-grey suit that his mother had bought for him. As he walked into the court, he would invariably smile and wave at his mother and brothers, Adel and Munir, who sat in the back row of the courtroom. According to a number of reporters present, he "had an air of unremorsefulness."[2] During his time at the Hall of Justice, Sirhan smoked ten cigars a day and read books on the occult and paranormal philosophy.

In the beginning it looked as though there would be no trial as the defense offered a plea bargain: Sirhan would plead guilty in exchange for the promise of a life sentence instead of execution. Los Angeles District Attorney Evelle Younger supported the deal in hopes of avoiding a long and expensive trial and also because the prosecution's psychiatrist had discovered that the defendant showed signs of mental illness. Younger urged Judge Herbert V. Walker to accept the plea bargain arrangements.

Sixty-nine-year-old Judge Walker was known for being unscrupulously fair and had a strong belief in the law.[3] He disagreed with the plea bargain arrangements in the Sirhan case because "[We] have a very much interested public [who] continually point to the Oswald matter, and they just wonder what is going on, because the fellow wasn't tried." Walker wanted to prevent accusations of a government cover-up and knew that the public would not be satisfied with anything less than a full public exposure of the evidence in the case. He also believed that the knowledge gained from the trial would help to prevent similar future crimes.[4] Walker was aware of the likely cost of a trial but believed the expense necessary as it was in the public interest.[5]

At first Judge Walker proposed a compromise, and another plan was worked out in which Sirhan would plead guilty but stand trial in the penalty phase so that the basic arguments of both sides could be heard. Following a *Los Angeles Times* story about the secret plea bargain, however, Sirhan and his defense team changed their minds about the compromise. Sirhan, the defense lawyers now argued, had a right to tell his story in support of Palestinian rights. The defendant had been encouraged in this view by an attorney named Abdeen Jabara who consulted with the defense team. Jabara represented a group of rich Arab Americans who wished to use the trial as a political platform. Accordingly, the full trial went ahead.

The defense team consisted of Grant B. Cooper, sixty-five; Russell Parsons, seventy-three; and Emile Zola Berman, sixty-seven. Cooper was the most experienced of the lawyers; he had worked for four decades in law and had learned the California Criminal Code and procedures incisively. At the time of the Sirhan trial he was experiencing law problems of his own, however. He had represented defendants in the famous Friar's Club gambling case, which involved mobsters who had swindled gamblers at the club's gaming tables. Cooper was found to have in his possession "secret documents" relating to the case, and a criminal case was being prepared against him at the time of the Sirhan trial.

Russell Parsons was a Palm Springs resident whose age was causing him to lose his effectiveness as a lawyer. Although the Sirhan family trusted him and he had become a father figure to Sirhan, he relied on his defense colleagues to handle most of the burden of the case.

Emile Zola Berman was Cooper's friend and assisted with the case because Cooper asked for his help. He was Jewish and one of New York City's most respected lawyers. Berman accepted no pay for his part in the defense. He steered the defense lawyers away from hatred of Jews as a motive and instead persuaded the lawyers to argue for diminished capacity as a primary defense. Berman strongly opposed any attempt by his colleagues to portray Sirhan as a political assassin.

The chief prosecutor was Lynn Compton, a former University of California–Los Angeles football player, who had worked in the District Attorney's Office for seventeen years. Compton believed in the death penalty. Forty-seven-year-old David Fitts and forty-four-year-old John Howard assisted him. Fitts was a brilliant courtroom orator, was soft-spoken, and worked hard at overcoming a slight speech impediment. Howard worked mostly at research.

The jury was made up of a cross-section of middle- and working-class Los Angeles citizens. After examining fifty-nine prospects in nine days of questioning, seven peremptory (unexplained) challenges by the prosecution, and five challenges for the defense, eight men and four women, including four Mexican Americans and one Jew, were selected. Seven were Republicans; five were Democrats. Three had mathematical backgrounds—a

math teacher, an IBM computer programmer, and an aerospace systems analyst; two were employees of the Department of Water; and the other seven
were a clothing store owner, a gas company employee, a mechanic, a switch-
board installer, a telephone service supervisor, a plumber, and a service representative for Pacific telephone.

Court personnel had a great deal of respect for the jury, which was
led by Foreman Bruce Elliot, a systems analyst for TRW Systems Inc., who
held a doctor of philosophy degree. The jurors were a friendly and cooperative group who accepted their sixty-four sequestered days and nights, over a
period of sixteen weeks, without bitterness or complaint. They spent week-
ends with their spouses. Most Fridays they were bussed to Paramount Studios to see special movie screenings, including *The Odd Couple* and *Barefoot
in the Park*, and they organized chess and Scrabble tournaments and outings
to the beach. They were attentive to the complex testimony of ninety witnesses, which resulted in 107 volumes of transcript. Weighing this massive
accumulation of evidence, they had to decide whether Sirhan was completely
responsible for his act.

The defense lawyers were pleased with the jury selection as they
had wanted an educated group of people able to understand the complicated
psychiatric defense of diminished responsibility.[6] At the time of the trial no
one doubted who pulled the trigger—Sirhan shot Kennedy and then was
instantly disarmed in a roomful of witnesses. Grant Cooper said, "There
will be no denial that our client, Sirhan Sirhan, fired the shot or shots that
killed Robert Kennedy."[7]

Sirhan's lawyers didn't try to prove that their client did not know
what he was doing but rather argued that he had lacked the capacity to "maturely and meaningfully reflect upon the gravity of his contemplated act."
They tried to save Sirhan from the gas chamber by showing him to be mentally incapable of premeditating the shooting—a partial defense that could
have reduced the charge from first-degree murder (which involves premeditation) to second-degree murder or manslaughter (which do not). They enlisted no fewer than two psychiatrists and four clinical psychologists in their
argument. If Sirhan was judged to be suffering from diminished responsibility at the time of the shooting, he would not receive the death penalty but
instead be given a maximum term of life imprisonment. In support of their
effort to reduce the charge to manslaughter, defense lawyers pointed to
Sirhan's blind Arab rage at his victim's oft-expressed sympathy for Israel.[8]
Sirhan thought this demeaning and embarrassing. At every stage he insisted
his act was "political," and he argued with his lawyers over their efforts to
show he was mentally ill.

The prosecution argued its case throughout February and called to the stand forensic scientists, eyewitnesses to the shooting, handgun experts, the arresting police officers, and people who had known Sirhan in the years and months preceding the shooting. They argued that Sirhan was not, essentially, "psychotic." He knew right from wrong and was fully able to judge the seriousness of his act. Prosecuting attorney David Fitts told the court, "In this case the People suggest to you that this cold and calculated decision to take the life of Robert F. Kennedy had been arrived at substantially in advance of the defendant's appearance at the Ambassador Hotel, and that the actual act of assassination was simply the culmination of a series of preparatory events, mental processes on the part of this defendant which had been at work over a substantial period of time."[9]

Prosecutors called a number of witnesses to the assassination, beginning with California Democratic Party Chief Jesse Unruh and the two famous African-American sportsmen who had served as Kennedy's unofficial bodyguards, Rosey Grier and Rafer Johnson. Each told his poignant story of accompanying RFK to the kitchen pantry on their way to the Colonial Room.

The prosecution set out the facts of the case to suggest premeditation on Sirhan's part:

- Sirhan "clandestinely" purchased a pistol from a friend.
- Sirhan purchased "hollow-nosed" ammunition.
- Sirhan visited the Ambassador Hotel on Sunday, June 2; this, the prosecution alleged, showed Sirhan had been "stalking" RFK.
- Sirhan went to the San Gabriel Valley Gun Club on June 4 to practice "rapid-firing" of his pistol; the prosecution argued that this showed he was preparing for the shooting at the Ambassador.
- Sirhan deliberately left his wallet in his car; this, it was alleged, was the sort of precaution a reasonable assassin would take if he believed he had only the slightest chance of escape.
- Sirhan inquired about Kennedy's security.

Sirhan's "Diminished Capacity"

In support of their thesis that Sirhan was mentally ill, the defense lawyers called to the stand five of their six expert psychiatric witnesses in an attempt to show that Sirhan acted under diminished capacity and was incapable of premeditating murder. They also called witnesses who testified that Sirhan had grown up in a war zone and was the son of a man who administered regular beatings. His lawyers highlighted Sirhan's injuries when he worked as a hot walker and suggested his fall from the horse might have resulted in brain damage. Emile Zola Berman argued that because Sirhan could not, allegedly, remember either writing in his notebooks or shooting RFK he must have been "without premeditation or malice, totally the product of a sick, obsessed mind and warped personality."[10]

The answer to Sirhan's level of guilt or whether he was guilty or not under California law would turn on how the jury viewed Sirhan's state of mind at the moment he pulled the trigger—on whether he was then capable of "mature, meaningful reflection" on what he was doing. Accordingly the trial centered on psychological assessments of Sirhan. In fact psychologists and their ability to safely diagnose diseases of the mind were on trial. "The medical testimony," said Grant Cooper, "is the guts of our case."[11] The prosecution stressed Sirhan's private notebooks with their oaths to kill Kennedy as proof of premeditated murder, while the defense interpreted the same writings as the work of a demented misfit.

Not until 1843 was society sufficiently mature to find a man not guilty of murder by reason of insanity. The McNaughton Rule, which holds that a defendant may be convicted of a crime if he could distinguish right from wrong at the time the crime was committed, was central to Sirhan's trial.[12] The rule had always been controversial. Some states and federal jurisdictions adopted the Durham Rule, which held that a defendant was not responsible for a criminal act if that act was the result of a mental disturbance or defect. Many rejected this rule because it seemed to place the role of the judge in the psychiatrists' hands. The McNaughton Rule prevailed in California at the time of the Sirhan trial, and California had established a legal precedent that ruled that a person charged with murder could be found guilty of a lesser degree of murder if he had a mental disorder that affected his ability to "maturely and meaningfully premeditate and deliberate" upon the gravity of his act. This precedent was referred to as "diminished responsibility."[13]

In 1968 the rule stated, "The jurors ought to be told in all cases that every man is to be presumed to be sane and to possess a sufficient degree of reason to be responsible for his crimes, until the contrary be proved to their satisfaction; and that, to establish a defense on the ground of insanity, it must be proved that at the time of the committing of the act, the party accused was laboring under such a defect of reason, from disease of the mind, as not to know the nature and quality of the act he was doing; or, if he did know it, that he did not know he was doing what was wrong."[14]

Grant Cooper prepared the way for the psychiatrists' and psychologists' testimony by putting Sirhan on the stand the week before the experts

were called in. Sirhan told of his passionate beliefs regarding his Palestin-
ian/Arab heritage, his troubled early years as a refugee amid the carnage of
the 1948 Arab–Israeli war, his virulent hatred toward Israel and the Jewish
people, his ambivalent attitudes toward Kennedy, and his blackout at the
crime scene. His courtroom behavior on and off the stand—a volatile mix of
anger, supercilious smiles, and inappropriate comments—served to demonstrate the defense's contention that their client was a disturbed young man.
Cooper told the jury, "But what was the motive? Not gain for him. Because
of an immature mind, he believed he was right. How stupid! He believed he
shouldn't be punished for it. How stupid! How immature! . . . He thought it
would start a third world war . . . a state of anarchy. . . . Ladies and gentle-
men, in all honesty, is this the thinking of a mature, healthy mind?"[15]

The defense made a psychiatric case that Sirhan was a manic "Jekyll
and Hyde" character incapable of premeditating anything and coming apart
under stress. Sirhan was in such a state of "disassociation" when he killed
Kennedy. By varying degrees Sirhan was described as a paranoid, a paranoid
schizophrenic, and, simply "mentally ill."[16] Emile Zola Berman told the jury,
"The evidence in this case will disclose that the defendant, Sirhan Sirhan, is
an immature, emotionally disturbed and mentally ill youth."[17]

Dr. Martin Schorr, who tested Sirhan and testified for the defense,
believed the defendant was a paranoid schizophrenic, "guided by inner beliefs that did not match the realities of the outer world."[18] He also described
Sirhan as "not a raving maniac. . . . He's not wild. . . . He's got a keen sense of
justice, which comes from his private [mental] world. . . . The paranoid is
most anxious to convince you how right he is and how wrong everyone else
is."[19] Schorr's testimony was later discredited when prosecution lawyers
discovered that the psychologist had copied parts of his assessment report
from another psychologist's published textbook.[20]

Sirhan's lawyers placed most importance on their client's Rorschach
test. Sirhan was shown ten cards and asked what he thought the blots suggested. Sirhan's responses, according to two defense psychiatrists, suggested
paranoia, schizophrenia, or both, as well as hostility and aggression. In a
related test, Schorr testified, he had asked Sirhan to stare at a blank piece of
paper. In the blank paper Sirhan saw "the figure of that arrogant self-as-
sured bastard with the victorious smirk on his face. It's that minister in
Israel, Moshe Dayan, and he's looking down at people, but there's a bullet
that's crashing through his brain at the height of his glory."[21] Schorr said he
then asked Sirhan where the defendant was in relation to the scene. Sirhan
replied, "I am the scene. I'm the one who's killing him."[22]

Defense psychiatrist Dr. Bernard Diamond, a full professor in the
University of California law school, medical school, and school of criminology,

testified that he believed Sirhan had hypnotized himself to commit the killing, although he admitted his thesis sounded "absurd and preposterous . . . a script which would never be acceptable in a class B motion picture."[23] Diamond disagreed with Sirhan's lawyers that the killer was too sick with paranoia or paranoid schizophrenia to plot the assassination rationally. He suggested that the lights and the mirrors had thrown Sirhan into a "trancelike state," transforming him from a harmless bystander into an automaton wired to kill. Diamond testified,

> The Embassy Room lobby was crowded, the lights were hot and blinding, and Sirhan Bishara Sirhan—transfixed by his own image rebounding to infinity in the walls and mirrors— slid from a half-drunk high into some hypnotic twilight all his own. And suddenly he was in the serving pantry between ballrooms at the Los Angeles Ambassador Hotel, with a triumphant Bobby Kennedy bearing down on him at the head of a crowd of followers. He wants to shake hands, Sirhan thought dimly. But when Kennedy got close enough to touch, Sirhan— too entranced to know what he was doing or why—yanked a pistol from his belt and yelled, 'You son of a bitch!' and fired again and again.[24]

Diamond hypnotized Sirhan six times and spent a total of twenty to twenty-five hours with the alleged assassin. He also interviewed Sirhan's family and came to the conclusion that Sirhan's trances began in childhood. Sirhan's mother told him her son had a history of "spells" dating back to his boyhood in Jerusalem during the 1948 war. Diamond also discovered that Sirhan had been practicing mind control, staring into candle flames until he hypnotized himself. Diamond believed that Sirhan was a good subject for hypnotism. He claimed that Sirhan "went under" easily, and he also believed Sirhan had been hypnotized before.[25]

Diamond hypnotized Sirhan to experience a psychic reenactment of the murder. Sirhan did not say anything about why he had been in the pantry, but he did act out the moments before he pulled the trigger. Jumping up from his prison cell bunk Sirhan "pulled an imaginary gun out of his belt . . . and he fired it convulsively. . . . It was very dramatic, very real. . . . 'You son of a bitch.' A momentary pause and then he started to choke. He was actually re-experiencing the choking when they took away the gun. . . . He was gasping for breath, actually turned blue a little bit. I became fearful myself."[26]

Diamond concluded that Sirhan's boyhood trances, his self-taught hypnotism, and the mirrors at the Ambassador came together to provoke Sirhan into killing Kennedy. He believed Sirhan had unknowingly programmed himself "for the coming assassination. . . . The mirrors in the hotel lobby, the flashing lights, the general confusion—this was like pressing the button which starts the computer. He was back in his trances. . . . Only this time it was for real and this time there was no pistol in his hand. This time there was no loaded gun."[27]

The Prosecution's Case

Prosecution lawyers centered their case on Sirhan's statements, actions, and movements immediately preceding the murder. They also recounted Sirhan's hatred of Israel and the Jews and also his hatred of Kennedy, who had given his wholehearted support to the Jewish cause. Lawyers told the jury how Sirhan had practiced with the murder weapon and how he had stalked Kennedy in the weeks before the assassination. Some years later John Howard described the Sirhan case: "If you strip everything away, it looks like a guy in there with a gun, shot a guy, shot five other people. . . . You arrest him and he says, 'I shot the son-of-a-bitch.' That's as cold turkey a lawsuit as I've seen in 28 years. We have a lot of guys up for life with a lot less evidence. . . . Sirhan is guilty. Sirhan said he was guilty."[28]

The prosecution had a star witness in the form of African-American garbage collector Alvin Clark. Clark used to engage Sirhan in conversation when he called at the family home to collect the week's garbage. He also met Sirhan every Wednesday at the Orange Julius stand for a drink.[29] Clark said Sirhan had been looking for a gun larger than his .22.[30] During his trial testimony Clark also related how the two men talked about Martin Luther King's death in April 1968. Clark reminded Sirhan how Kennedy had paid to bring King's body back to Atlanta and said, "[Sirhan] was upset somewhat about the death of Luther King. He asked how the Negro people were going to react. I told him I didn't know—there wasn't but one person responsible for his death. He asked me what did I think the Negro people were going to do about it. I said, 'I mean what CAN they do about it?'"

Clark also told the court that Sirhan had made threats against Robert Kennedy's life: "He asked me about the upcoming election, and I said I was going to vote for Senator Kennedy. And Sirhan said, 'Whatever do you want to vote for the son-of-a-bitch for, because I'm planning on shooting him.'" Clark responded by telling Sirhan, "You would be killing one of the best men in the country."

Clark said he got along well with Sirhan and "thought much of him," but he also admitted under cross-examination that he had told the FBI he hated Sirhan and would do anything to see him convicted. In David Fitts's follow-up to the cross-examination, Clark clarified that he had told Fitts the truth when he told the court about Sirhan's threats on RFK's life.[31] Defense psychiatrist Dr. Diamond could not explain away Clark's testimony and implied that Clark had been lying to the court about Sirhan's threatening statements.[32]

The prosecution team called on psychiatric expert Seymour Pollack, a forensic psychiatrist in charge of the division of psychiatry and law at the University of California, to testify regarding his examination of the defendant. Pollack had interviewed Sirhan for a total of twenty-five hours during January and February 1969. During his testimony he systematically rebutted every major defense argument. Pollack agreed that Sirhan had a substantial mental illness and that he had some clinical signs and symptoms of psychosis but insisted that Sirhan was not psychotic and that his mental state did not come under the California law of diminished responsibility.[33] Diamond and Pollack agreed on Sirhan's specific intent, but they disagreed on whether or not Sirhan had the capacity to "meaningfully and maturely reflect on the gravity of his contemplated act."[34] Pollack said some evidence suggested that Sirhan was psychologically disturbed at the time he shot Kennedy and that he was probably drunk and knew right from wrong when he committed murder. However, Pollack argued that hallucinations (or in layman's terms "a voice from God") was not present when Sirhan pulled the trigger. David Fitts summarized, "Sirhan is not normal but no man is normal who commits murder. . . . The question is whether or not, given his degree of mental impairment or, if you will, diminished capacity, Sirhan yet had the ability to harbor malice against a human being, to premeditate murder."[35]

Pollack dismissed as "extremely remote" and "very illogical" Diamond's theory that Sirhan was in a trance when he shot Kennedy. Pollack believed Sirhan had a political motive for killing Kennedy and said Sirhan had committed murder simply because he hated the senator. Even Sirhan agreed with Pollack's assessment saying, "That guy [Pollack] understands me."[36]

Pollack acknowledged that Sirhan might indeed have been suffering from some form of psychosis and that he likely suffered from "substantial mental illness." Pollack said Sirhan suffered from

> clinical signs and symptoms of psychosis. He has, for example, many delusions [but] there was nothing whatever that . . . indicated at any time that Sirhan was clinically psychotic. . . . It's

my belief that Sirhan's ideas, attitudes . . . were not evidence
of psychotic delusional thinking. . . . I believe that Sirhan focused on Senator Robert Kennedy as an individual who should
die not only because of the Kennedy promise to give Israel the
jet bombers that would cause death to thousands of Arabs, in
Sirhan's opinion, but also because Sirhan wanted the world to
see, he wanted the world to see how strongly our United States
policy was in the pro-Israel/anti-Arab movement in the face
of, in spite of our government's professed interest for the underdog, and world justice.[37]

Pollack believed Sirhan's ideas were "bizarre," "but they are not bizarre to many people who believe in them, just as many people believe in
astrology; just as many people believe in . . . cults."[38] Pollack thought Sirhan's
political ideas were "not delusional" and that psychosis was not present in
his expression of them. He believed Sirhan "felt that it was his duty, that he
would be looked up to by the Arab world and that he would be considered a
hero."[39] Pollack argued that Sirhan was not mentally ill enough under California law to be absolved of first-degree murder.[40] He said Sirhan's "motivation in killing Senator Kennedy was entirely political, and was not related to
bizarre or psychotic motivation or accompanied by peculiar or highly idio-
syncratic reasoning."[41]

Sirhan's "Diminished Capacity" Defense

Defense psychiatrist Schorr, on the basis of interviews, said Sirhan's responses to the Rorschach Inkblot Test, the Bender-Gestalt Test of Intelligence, the Thematic Apperception Test, and the Minnesota Multi-Phasic
Personality Inventory indicated that the defendant suffered from "paranoid
psychosis, paranoid state." Sirhan's lawyers, although puzzled by Schorr's
description of Sirhan's purported motives—Sirhan had apparently killed a
father figure—nevertheless supported any testimony that would point to
diminished responsibility. Assistant District Attorney John Howard attacked
the validity of the tests Schorr administered to Sirhan, which were controversial within the psychological community[42] and conducted under ridiculous conditions (the test conditions were not discussed during the trial).
According to Robert Blair Kaiser, Sirhan's lawyers, who were in the room
during Schorr's sessions with their client, made jokes as the tests were administered. At one point, Kaiser said, Parsons joked about whether Schorr,
not Sirhan, was the crazy one.[43] The jurors were also not told that Grant
Cooper had difficulty believing anything Sirhan said to him.[44]

The jurors soon realized that insanity, like culpability, was a highly controversial and elusive subject, imbued with opposing lines of explanation. They became contemptuous of the psychiatric evidence in the case because the defense and prosecution experts had such divergent opinions. The problem of expert testimony with regard to a criminal's mental condition was no more acute then than it is today. Psychiatrists have been known to slant their findings toward the side that hires them, which gives juries every right to suspect corrupted testimony. Psychiatrists often explain criminal behavior by making reference to contorted clinical definitions. And because psychiatrists frequently disagree with each other's diagnoses, the profession has been devalued in the public's eyes and this has lessened the impact of psychiatrists' testimony in court. Furthermore, few medical problems are more difficult to differentiate between than conversion and dissociative disorders (or shell shock) and malingering (the intentional production of the signs of a physical and mental disorder so as to deceive others).

From the start Sirhan's family did not want their lawyers to pursue a defense of diminished responsibility. To Arabs, mental instability brought profound shame to the family. Sirhan also objected to the defense strategy, and in the period before the trial he had set his mind on pleading guilty as charged. He told Dr. Diamond he did not want them portraying him as "some stupid person or something like that. I'd rather die and say I killed that son-of-a-bitch for my country, period."[45]

However, Sirhan's lawyers believed the diminished responsibility approach best guaranteed that the accused would not go to the gas chamber. Defense lawyers and doctors called to testify for the defense refused to acknowledge that, in the context of Sirhan's genuine political beliefs, his actions were as rational as those of any terrorist. Sirhan had gone along with his lawyers in the mistaken belief that they had centered their arguments around the mitigating *political* circumstances of the crime rather than any ideas about mental illness.

Sirhan wanted to plead guilty to the first-degree murder charge if there was a "guarantee of life and having a chance to tell my story on the witness stand, plus another guarantee of parole after seven years. I absolutely want a guarantee of that."[46] Although Sirhan protested throughout the trial that he was sane, he nevertheless acceded to his lawyers wishes, hoping that if he escaped execution, Palestinian terrorists would one day take measures to secure his release, perhaps in a prisoner exchange.[47] Russell Parsons confirmed this idea for Sirhan.[48] At one point during the trial proceedings, Sirhan whispered to Robert Kaiser, "Better a live dog than a dead lion."[49]

In fact Sirhan did not have to wait long for a prisoner exchange offer. In 1973 Palestine Liberation Organization chairman Yasser Arafat ordered the kidnapping of three American diplomats and offered them in exchange for Sirhan. When President Nixon refused the offer, Arafat ordered that the diplomats be tortured then murdered. Arafat took credit for these murders during a private dinner with Romanian President Nicolai Ceausescu two months later. The U.S. government kept this attempt to free Sirhan and the subsequent murders of the three diplomats a secret for fear of creating an obstacle to any future diplomatic settlement of the Arab-Israeli conflict.[50]

The Verdict

On April 17 the jury reached a verdict in the case. The jurors rejected the testimony of the psychologists and psychiatrists who said that Sirhan had some form of mental illness. During their deliberations, they took the same inkblot tests and other psychological tests that had been administered to Sirhan. The tests backfired on the defense lawyers' position when several of the jurors found some of their responses remarkably similar to Sirhan's "paranoid reactions."

The evidence presented at the trial suggested that psychological testing is as much an art as a science and even experts can disagree about their findings. As *Life* magazine editorialized,

> What does seem in doubt is the adequacy of courtroom proceedings which sometimes appear to become scripts written by psychiatrists and, in the candid opinion of Sirhan's own star psychiatrist witness, "too illogical even for the theatre of the absurd." . . . Prosecution and defense psychiatrists often agree in their medical diagnosis of a defendant's mental condition and motivation. The disagreement usually occurs when psychiatrists are asked to go beyond giving and analyzing such information and to offer their judgments of whether a defendant is "responsible" for a criminal act or legally "sane" when he commits it. The difficulty is that these are not really objective medical or scientific terms but moral and legal ones; in a courtroom they can be practically synonymous with innocence or guilt. . . . This obviously will not resolve the fundamental philosophic differences between psychiatry and the law— which, we suspect, have a great deal to do with our collective inability to decide whether criminal behavior is socially caused

or individually willed. But it will confirm that wrestling with this conflict in court is a task that society has delegated to a jury of the defendant's peers, and to them alone.[51]

Prosecutor Lynn Compton believed that the psychiatric defense in a criminal case took culpability away from the defendant. Compton said, "The whole reason for their [the psychiatrists'] discipline is finding something wrong with somebody. . . . [Diamond is] a walking lie detector, handwriting expert, gun expert. . . . Anybody who didn't agree with him was a liar."[52] Frederic Wertham, MD, author of *A Sign for Cain: An Exploration of Human Violence*, concurs with Compton's observations and believes the psychiatric defense has been used far too widely and often skews any moral considerations. Wertham wrote, "Psychiatry is a potent weapon. The danger is that it is sometimes applied to explain brutal and sadistic acts in a way that actually amounts to condoning them. We are apt to use psychiatry the way a drunk uses a lamppost: not for the light but to lean against." Wertham believes that many psychiatric excuses, if successful in court, often lead to a psychiatric hunting license to kill.[53]

The defense psychiatrists' objectivity was challenged numerous times during the trial. As the prosecution suggested, Sirhan's inkblot test could be explained by common sense. His reference to blood and body parts might have come from his childhood memories of war torn Jerusalem, rather than a psychosis. It became obvious as the psychological testimony progressed that personality could not be measured quantitatively like body temperature and that no real standard for a "normal" personality was available. *Newsweek* magazine asked some psychologists to comment on the tests used in the Sirhan trial. They said that some of the tests, in which the patient is asked to agree or disagree or give their own responses, presented an oversimplified picture of personality. As the Sirhan jurors discovered, some statements could be misinterpreted and because of the tests' limitations the assessor's judgment and interpretative ability affected any result.[54] Furthermore, the defense's case did not benefit when their psychiatrists opined that Sirhan's act was not rational and described his political act of violence as the product of a deranged mind.

The four days of deliberation leading to the first-degree murder verdict were not without disagreement between jurors. At first eight agreed to a first-degree verdict with two arguing for a second-degree conviction on the grounds of diminished mental capacity and two undecided. Following discussions about the psychiatric testimony, ten jurors agreed to the first-degree charge with two undecided.

As they neared the end of their deliberation the first-degree jurors had only one juror left to convince: sixty-two-year-old Susan J. Brumm, who felt sorry for Sirhan. Brumm finally capitulated, reasoning that since Sirhan had never been in trouble before the murder he must have had the mental capacity to control himself.[55]

When the jurors returned to the courtroom, Sirhan, surrounded by three security guards, entered the jury box. Judge Walker asked whether the jurors had reached a verdict. The foreman replied, "We have, your honor." He handed a sheaf of papers to the bailiff, who took them to the judge. Judge Walker quickly looked over them, then handed them to the county clerk to read the verdict: "We the jury find the defendant guilty of murder in the first degree." Sirhan reacted impassively when the verdict was read and was quickly led back to his cell to await sentencing.

Mary Sirhan heard the verdict at home on her television set. Adel Sirhan told a caller, "We didn't expect this verdict. My mother is so depressed she can't talk to anyone." Mary and Adel Sirhan did not mention Robert Kennedy's death or say whether they empathized with the Kennedy family's suffering.[56]

The penalty hearing—the final phase of the trial required by California law, in which the jury determines whether a convicted murderer should be sentenced to life imprisonment or death—was short. The defense recalled Sirhan's mother to the stand in the hope she might be able to arouse sympathy for her son. She testified for less than a minute. Then the summation began with prosecutor John Howard calling for the death penalty, and Grant Cooper urging that the defendant's life be spared as "a kind of posthumous tribute" to Robert Kennedy, who, he said, abhorred all violence.

The jurors retired to their deliberation room and it quickly became clear that many jurors had come to loathe the defendant. Speaking to reporters later, some referred to Sirhan as a "conniving brat" and "an animal."[57] The jury decided the death penalty was the just punishment for Sirhan's crime. The jurors agreed to the death penalty because Sirhan lacked remorse, his crime had political implications, and his victim had been the father of eleven children.

Judge Walker had the power to overturn the jury's sentencing verdict. Few people expected the judge to change the verdict to life imprisonment; he had set aside only one death sentence in nineteen capital convictions. But at the last minute the Kennedy family entered an unexpected plea for clemency, raising the possibility that the judge might keep Sirhan from the gas chamber. The plea came in the form of a handwritten letter from Senator Edward M. Kennedy addressed to District Attorney Evelle Younger, who read it aloud in court: "My brother was a man of love and sentiment and compassion. He would not have wanted his death to be the cause for the taking of another life. . . . If the kind of man my brother was is pertinent, we believe it should be weighed in the balance on the side of compassion, mercy and God's gift of life itself."[58]

After listening to a lengthy review, Judge Walker said, "It is the feeling of this court that the jury was right and I have no reason to change my view now. . . . It is the judgment and sentence of this court that for the crime of murder in the first degree you are to die in the manner prescribed by law." Mary Sirhan burst into tears. Sirhan fiddled with his cigar, shrugged, and smiled slightly. He told his lawyers, "The real battle has begun."[59] Sirhan was taken to San Quentin's death row and put in a cell isolated by a wire mesh barrier from other prisoners. Two floors beneath his cell was the gas chamber.

Sirhan knew it was unlikely he would be executed. California had placed an unofficial ban on executions after Aaron Mitchell's death in 1967. Eighty-one prisoners were on death row in San Quentin Prison. On February 18, 1972, the California Supreme Court ruled that the death penalty as practiced in California violated the state constitution's prohibition against cruel and unusual punishment. In June the Court reduced Sirhan's sentence to life imprisonment.

Sirhan's trial suggested that the law is an imperfect instrument for laying ghosts to rest and for fully investigating all aspects of a crime. Many questions regarding the circumstances of the Robert Kennedy assassination remained, and as the years passed the case became highly controversial.

Following the trial, researchers into the assassination found much to criticize. They faulted Sirhan's lawyers for not questioning much of the evidence put forward by the prosecution and the Los Angeles Police Department for not following up reports that co-conspirators might have accompanied Sirhan. As the years passed the RFK case, like the JFK assassination, was picked apart to reveal a number of highly controversial discrepancies in the evidence. The Los Angeles Free Press, in an article written by Lillian Castellano and Floyd Nelson, said "photographic proof" showed that two extra bullets were lodged in the wooden divider between the sets of swinging doors at the western end of the Ambassador Hotel pantry. Others pointed to alleged eyewitness evidence that a second gun had been used in the assassination and that co-conspirators had accompanied the assassin. Despite repeated reinvestigations over the years, the critics refused to accept the conclusion that Sirhan alone had committed the murder.

6

CONTROVERSIES: THE PHYSICAL EVIDENCE

> *"Lessons learned? Placing into a new context what I had known all along about the case, I now realize that even law-enforcement officials—who possess the training, qualifications and experience to determine the significance of crime-scene evidence—do make mistakes if their abilities are not put to the test under the proper circumstances and conditions. In other words, if one does not account for occasional official mistakes and incompetence, then nearly every such murder could appear to be a conspiracy, particularly if a civilian investigator—like me, with limited access and resources—is looking for one."*
>
> —DAN MOLDEA, *THE KILLING OF ROBERT F. KENNEDY*

In the years following the assassination, critics of the investigation identified issues that persuaded them that Robert Kennedy had likely been killed as the result of a conspiracy. They also accused the Los Angeles Police Department (LAPD) and the FBI of covering up the true circumstances of the shooting. Important questions were raised about the scientific analysis of physical evidence in the case centering on the gun used by Sirhan, the position of RFK when he was shot, the possibility that a second gunman had fired the fatal shots, the discovery of purported "bullet holes" in the pantry doors, and the allegations that the LAPD had falsified and/or destroyed some important physical evidence. The critics of the official investigation raised questions about the crime that were subsequently widely reported in the U.S. media:

- How could Sirhan have shot Kennedy from 1 to 1.5 inches away (according to the coroner) if eyewitnesses had placed the assassin's gun no closer than 1.5 and 5 feet from the senator?
- How could Kennedy's wounds angle sharply upward if witnesses said Sirhan's gun was pointed horizontally?
- Why didn't the police check security guard Thane Cesar's weapon? Cesar had held anti-Kennedy sentiments and was standing behind the senator at the time of the shooting.
- Why couldn't all of the bullets recovered at the scene of the crime and from the victims' bodies be positively identified as coming from Sirhan's gun?
- Were bullet holes or bullets found in the pantry doorway divider, as eyewitnesses claimed? There is a famous photograph showing police officers and Dr. Thomas Noguchi pointing to two apparent bullet holes. The presence of extra bullets in the door divider meant that more than one gunman was involved.
- Were there differences in the cannelure design and rifling angle of the bullet lodged in RFK's neck when compared to the bullet that entered shooting victim William Weisel? If there were, this would indicate two guns had been used in the shooting.
- Why did the Los Angeles police destroy the pantry door dividers and ceiling tiles that allegedly showed bullet holes?
- Why did the LAPD destroy thousands of photographs of the crime scene?
- Why did the LAPD destroy photographs taken of the shooting by fifteen-year-old Scott Enyart?
- Why did the 1975 firearms panel fail to match Sirhan's gun with the three intact bullets recovered from the victims?
- Why did the LAPD destroy a second gun that had been used to test ballistics evidence?

The Gun

Sirhan used a .22-caliber Iver-Johnson cadet model with a snub-nosed 2.5-inch barrel in the assassination. The serial number was H-53725. It had a dull blue steel finish with an eight-bullet chamber, double action. After Sirhan was subdued at the Ambassador Hotel, Rafer Johnson took possession of the gun and handed it over to LAPD officers at Ramparts Police Station. Sergeant R. L. Calkins examined the gun, removed one spent shell from the chamber; the remaining seven empty shells were left in the cylinder.

Albert Leslie Hertz, a resident of Alhambria, a small town south of Pasadena, had purchased the gun at the Pasadena Gun Shop on August 10, 1965. Hertz was a retired civil engineer who had worked on projects in Argentina, Saudi Arabia, and Korea. He purchased the gun for protection during the 1965 Watts Riots but had never used it and kept it in its original wrapping paper and box. Hertz's wife decided the gun was too dangerous to have around the house and gave it to her daughter, Dana Westlake. Westlake was living in Pasadena when her mother gave her the gun. She hid it in the attic away from her small children. In December 1967 she decided she no longer wanted the gun around the house, so she gave it to her next-door neighbor's son, George Erhard, a gun collector.

Erhard told investigators he sold the gun to a person he knew as "Joe," who worked at Nash's department store at the corner of Arroyo and Colorado in Pasadena. Joe was twenty-two-year-old Munir Bishara Sirhan, Sirhan Sirhan's brother. Erhard said he needed the money from the gun sale to finance some work on his car.

In an interview by the LAPD, Munir said Sirhan asked him to obtain a gun because he wanted to visit a rifle range. When Munir explained that rifle ranges rented guns, Sirhan said, "I don't want to get involved. I don't want a signature."[1] Sirhan then asked his brother if he knew anyone who sold guns. Munir told him about Erhard and later told investigators, "I don't know why my brother wanted it, you know, wanted anything to do with guns."[2] Munir said that Sirhan had asked him, "See if you can see that guy to get me a gun." Munir spoke to Erhard in the parking lot of Nash's store, and Erhard showed him the pistol. William Price, a friend of Erhard, witnessed the incident. At this point, Munir said he asked Erhard to bring the gun to the Sirhan house, since his brother was interested in buying it. When Munir brought Erhard to the family home to listen to some records, they met Sirhan, who was in the dining room. Sirhan told them about his time in the California Cadet Corps. Munir said he told Sirhan that it was illegal for a noncitizen to own a gun. Sirhan insisted they buy it. At first they haggled over the price. When the three agreed to a sale price, Munir produced $19 and Sirhan paid the $6 balance.[3]

According to the LAPD Summary Report, however,

> On June 25, 1968, a polygraph examination was administered to Munir Sirhan to determine his truthfulness regarding the gun and whether or not Erhard had ever been in the Sirhan home. Munir Sirhan's responses to questions indicated he was being untruthful. . . . Munir . . . admitted that he was lying

when he said Erhard had been inside his home. . . . He corrected himself and stated he had asked Erhard if he had any guns for sale and that eventually Erhard showed him the .22-caliber revolver. He examined the gun in the parking lot of Nash's Department Store. . . . After examining the gun, he told Erhard he did not have sufficient money to purchase the gun at that time. He asked Erhard to bring the gun to the corner of El Molino and Howard Streets in Pasadena later that evening and told him that he would have the money to purchase the gun. Munir stated that he and Sirhan were together when Erhard came to deliver the gun. Munir Sirhan then stated that Sirhan Sirhan had been the one who bought the gun. Munir was again informed that the polygraph test showed that he had actually purchased the gun. Munir Sirhan refused to change his story.[4]

It is likely that Munir and Sirhan purchased the gun in such a clandestine manner because they were both aware that it was unlawful for aliens to own handguns.

Sirhan first shot the gun in March 1968 and practiced with it about a half dozen times between March and May 1968. He said he "liked guns."[5] Munir said Sirhan kept the gun in the glove compartment of his De Soto. Munir often heard Sirhan playing with something that made a "click, click" sound, and he believed it was the gun.[6] Munir had been "frightened" by the look in Sirhan's eye when his brother handled the gun. In fact Munir was so worried he made Sirhan swear on their dead sister, Aida, that he would not use the gun in a "bad" way.[7]

Sirhan had violated three California laws merely by possessing the pistol he used to kill Robert Kennedy. Thus, if Sirhan were simply an unwitting patsy involved in a conspiracy, the conspirators must have knowingly chosen a man who had been risking the whole conspiratorial venture by possessing an illegal weapon and firing it at a police range. Had Sirhan been caught with the illegal weapon, the purported conspiracy would have collapsed.

The Dynamics of the Shooting

The LAPD reenacted the crime on film, twice in 1968 and a third time in 1977. Based on the reenactments and LAPD criminalist DeWayne Wolfer's trajectory analysis, investigators concluded that Sirhan could have moved his gun to within one to three inches from Kennedy's head and fired four bullets at an upward-leftward angle. (Investigators made this conclusion without considering RFK's possible change in posture when he was hit.)

Many researchers dismissed the police reports and instead relied on eyewitness testimony to reach a contradictory conclusion. The researchers argued that information provided by the witnesses indicated that Sirhan's position in the pantry made it impossible for him to shoot the senator in the back of the head from a distance of an inch or so. No witness testified that the assailant had been less than a few feet away from Kennedy. Criminalist William W. Harper, a critic of the LAPD investigation, concluded there had to be at least two firing positions to account for all of the bullets and all of the wounds.[8] According to conspiracy writer Lisa Pease,

> As you will recall five people were shot besides Kennedy, one
> of whom was shot twice; Kennedy himself was shot four times.
> Doesn't that add up to ten bullets? Not if the LAPD could come
> up with some magic ones. The bullet that pierced Kennedy's
> coat without entering him took a path of roughly 80 degrees
> upwards. The bullet was moving upwards in a back to front
> path (as were all of Kennedy's wound paths). But the LAPD
> figures this must be the bullet that hit Paul Schrade. Had
> Schrade been facing Kennedy, he would still not be tall enough
> to receive a bullet near the top of his head from that angle. But
> he was not standing in front of Kennedy. He was behind him
> by all eyewitness accounts, and as shown by the relative posi-
> tions where the two fell after being hit.[9]

A number of explanations can account for the trajectories of the shots with-out introducing a second gun or second shooter. Some of these explanations are contrary to the official version of events. As Los Angeles attorney Vincent Bugliosi said, "If [Wolfer's] report is in error, for whatever reason, then there might be an explanation for some of these things: ricochets, parts of bullets, fragments. This whole notion of a second gun is premised on the assump-tion [Wolfer's] report is correct."[10] The following scenario is entirely plau-sible, although other scenarios could account for the eight shots:

BULLET 1 missed Kennedy and struck Paul Schrade in the forehead.
BULLET 2 passed through RFK's jacket and exited through his shoulder pad
    as he raised his arm. This bullet then likely hit one of the other four
    victims after continuing its upward trajectory and then ricocheting
    off of the concrete ceiling after passing through the ceiling tiles. The

main candidate for this shot is Elizabeth Evans. Evans believed she was bending down at the time of the shooting; she could have been pushed over in the commotion while she tied her shoelaces so that the bullet lodged in her forehead in an upward direction. We have only Elizabeth Evans's guesses about her positioning when the first shot was fired. We do not know if her head was tilted or if she was pushed backward following the first shots. Any number of positions could have allowed the bullet to go "upward" through her scalp. This bullet may account for two of the ceiling tile holes, entry and exit.

BULLET 3 hit Kennedy in his right armpit and lodged in the back of his neck. This bullet was recovered.

BULLET 4 hit RFK in the mastoid. This was the fatal shot. Bullet fragments were recovered.

BULLET 5 went through Ira Goldstein's left pant leg without striking him. This bullet could have hit Irwin Stroll. A bullet was recovered from Stroll during surgery.

BULLET 6 hit William Weisel in the abdomen and the bullet was recovered near the spine during surgery. (This bullet could have first entered, then exited RFK's shoulder pad if RFK was stooped.)

BULLET 7 was lost in the ceiling interspace. This may very well have been the bullet that entered RFK's armpit one inch above the other armpit wound, then exited his chest and traveled upward.

BULLET 8 hit Goldstein in the thigh and was recovered.

As RFK was turning, raising his arm, bending a little to protect himself, and reacting to the shot fired, he might then have been hit in the right armpit. This bullet traveled through his shoulder and lodged in his neck. RFK might then have been hit again in the armpit by the bullet that exited through his chest, traveling upward to the ceiling, where it was lost in the interspace. In this scenario, the next bullet would have gone through Kennedy's shoulder pad without harming him. This bullet purportedly went in an upward angle but, depending on the positioning of the victims, the angle of Sirhan's gun when it was fired, and whether RFK was bent over and turning at the time, it may have hit another victim, possibly William Weisel.

Obviously RFK's posture changed quickly as he, having been hit twice, began to collapse. In Sirhan's intense struggle with Uecker and others, his gun could have come within point-blank range of RFK's head. Also, Sirhan's gun was still firing as his hand was slammed on the serving table, after he had been grabbed by RFK's friends. The gun was therefore positioned low. No witness actually saw RFK being shot.

If you factor in all of these possibilities, the eight shots are still accounted for.

Three ceiling tile holes are accounted for in the above scenarios. The alleged bullet holes in the pantry door divider were too small to be made by .22-caliber bullets. In fact, they were not made by bullets at all, as Moldea discovered.

Conspiracy advocates use the confusion surrounding the number and direction of the bullets to make a case for conspiracy. Critic H, in an article for a website dedicated to exposing a conspiracy in the JFK assassination, criticized Dan Moldea for adding extra shots to his inventory of the bullets.[11] Critic H alleged that Dan Moldea was mistaken in his conclusion and wrote that one of the victims [Paul Schrade] was struck in the forehead by a bullet that struck nothing else. Critic H clearly misunderstood Moldea's hypotheses. Moldea did not accept the LAPD's bullet accounting, which stipulated that the shot that hit Schrade had gone through Kennedy's shoulder pad. Moldea wrote that the LAPD's official bullet inventory, "which has contributed heavily to the second-gun theories, is wrong. . . . I believe that the first shot missed Kennedy, and hit Paul Schrade in the forehead . . . which contradicts a major conclusion by Wolfer but also helps to provide a better explanation for how Sirhan shot Senator Kennedy at point blank range."[12]

Moldea believes that no one can say with absolute certainty what happened to the four stray bullets—the bullet that passed through Kennedy's jacket without striking him, the bullet that went through Kennedy and exited his chest, the bullet that struck the ceiling and exited through one of the ceiling tiles, and the bullet that was supposedly lost through the ceiling interspace. Moldea believes that the shoulder-pad bullet probably struck one of the other four shooting victims, not Schrade. Moldea's scenario accounts for eight bullets.

Critic H further maintains that RFK's autopsy proves conspiracy. Critic H said that a close inspection of RFK's autopsy report revealed that the description of the shot to the head represented a pathologic impossibility and ruled out Sirhan's gun as the weapon responsible for the head wound. Critic H alleged that these so-called discrepancies in the autopsy report reveal that RFK was killed by a bullet larger than a .22.

Critic H's work, however, is fatally flawed. According to ballistics expert Larry Sturdivan, who wrote the majority of the casualty criteria for bullets, fragments, etc., used by the United States and the North Atlantic Treaty Organization (NATO), consulted and testified on wounds ballistics to the House Select Committee on Assassinations in 1978,

[Critic H's] whole essay hinges on [his allegations that] . . . the 2 x 2 cm rim of raised tissue (and the 2 x 2 cm wound tract in the cerebellum) [shows] . . . that the original entry hole was 2 x 2 cm. No, it doesn't! It tells us that the bullet damaged tissue out to about a centimeter around its trajectory. The stretching and shearing of soft tissue abruptly pushed apart by the bullet tears cell membranes and capillary walls. The infusion of blood and cellular contents causes the tissue to swell and the back pressure prevents blood flow. This is the tissue that is already dead or will die due to lack of oxygen. It would eventually become necrotic if the patient lived. It is the tissue removed by the surgeon in the process called debridement. This effect is completely independent of the size of the hole in the skull and, with an expanding bullet, it is maximal at the entry site on the brain. Thus, all of [Critic H's] major conclusions in this essay are baseless, because he has no means of determining what the size of the hole in the skull was.[14]

Critic H's analysis is typical of a conspiracy writer's work. He has relied on "experts" who do not have the relevant training to reach sound, scientific conclusions. Sturdivan researched Critic H's work on this subject and found it to be simply wrong. The experts Critic H had chosen, Sturdivan stated, had no real knowledge of physics:

The surgeons and medical examiners whose work [Critic H] refers to, do not know physics and thus do not understand the "ballistics" part of wound ballistics. They speak in non sequiturs like "wound profile" in a gelatin block. The same is true of most medical examiners and forensic pathologists. Reading papers by these writers would not help [Critic H] to understand what's going on. Only a few medical examiners, like Vince DiMaio, know physics well enough to realize what causes the tissue damage. However, I sent [Critic H] a write-up explaining the physics of tissue damage about the path of a projectile. He either didn't understand it or prefers not to acknowledge the findings because they invalidate the conspiracy he wants to build.

Sturdivan also took issue with Critic H's characterization of Thomas Noguchi's autopsy work. Critic H's allegations, Sturdivan said, is the typical conspiracy theorist's diatribe against everything written by an objective witness on the case. For instance . . . he complains that Noguchi repeated an estimate of the size of the missing scalp wound that he evidently got from the surgeon standing next to him. Then about 3 pages later he complains about Noguchi not giving an estimate of the size of the bone wound that was also missing. There was nothing that Noguchi could do to avoid [conspiracy theorist] carping. . . . [Critic H] makes blunders that should not be made by even the novice. He speaks of the bullet used as an "expanding" bullet then speaks of it as a .22 inch projectile in penetration (it expands to a larger dimension that varies from case to case, depending on velocity at impact, depth and thickness of any bone encountered, etc. and, in this case, evidently fragmented). . . . The important concept is the amount of stretch to which the tissue is subjected. Imagine a point on the center of the trajectory of the approaching bullet. At one instant, two particles (molecules or structures) are in contact with each other, at the next instant they are on opposite sides of the bullet. As your point of view moves laterally off this trajectory, the stretch decreases continuously until it reaches a point within the elastic limit of the tissue. At this point the tissue remains undamaged, though it will stay somewhat stretched because of the swelling of the badly damaged tissue closer to the bullet path. It is this stretched tissue that puts back-pressure on the swollen area, preventing blood flow to any cells that might still be alive. When reading the attached keep in mind that with low velocity handgun bullets the final cavity is very little larger than the (expanded, if applicable) diameter of the bullet.[15]

(For a detailed examination of RFK wounds ballistics and Critic H's conspiracy claims, see appendix A.)

Responding to Critic H's allegations that he presented a scenario in his book that "proved" more than eight shots were fired, Dan Moldea said,

Nobody I know can say with absolute certainty what happened to the four stray bullets at the crime scene of Senator Kennedy's murder. . . . In its official inventory of the bullets fired by Sirhan, the LAPD claimed that Paul Schrade was wounded by the bullet that went harmlessly through the shoulder pad of Senator

Kennedy's suit coat. Some people clearly believe the LAPD's flawed and widely discredited bullet count. I do not. Instead, I believe that the shoulder-pad bullet probably struck one of the other four shooting victims—someone other than Schrade. So, regardless of how much some critics try to twist and torture the crime-scene evidence, my explanation does not add a single bullet to the final bullet count.

Moldea also criticized Critic H's diagrams, which characterized "the people at the crime scene, including Senator Kennedy and the other five victims, as being stick figures, standing tall and upright throughout the incident." Moldea also criticized Critic H for his failure to recognize the "kinetic movement of the crowd, that everyone in that room must have been in motion after the first or second shot."[16] As wounds ballistics expert Larry Sturdivan told this author, "If anybody . . . tells me he can reconstruct the location and posture of each person in that room at the time of each shot, I would conclude that he was delusional. If I were there, I would guarantee that my location and posture would change continuously between shots and there would be no way I could remember exact locations or postures at any given moment. Photographs help, but one cannot pinpoint the time of the photograph to the millisecond and that's what one would need to do to reconstruct a trajectory from gun to entry point."[17]

Dan Moldea believed the anomalies in the ballistics evidence could be explained logically without resorting to tortuous theories. Moldea discussed how the pantry crowd's reactions to the shooting could account for the divergent angles of bullet entries and the fact that none of the eyewitnesses placed Sirhan's gun next to RFK's head.

Ambassador Hotel maitre d' Karl Uecker led Kennedy through the pantry, and Ace security guard Thane Cesar met the entourage at the double swing doors. Uecker led Kennedy by the right wrist through the crowd that filled the pantry passageway. Cesar moved directly beside Kennedy. He was on his right side all the while pushing people away from the senator. He took Kennedy's right arm at the elbow while Uecker held RFK's right wrist. Both let go as RFK shook hands with the crowd.

Kennedy moved through the pantry shaking hands with excited supporters and hotel workers, occasionally breaking loose from his guides. Uecker said, "I took the Senator behind the stage. I was going to turn left to go to the Ambassador Ballroom and somebody said, 'No. We're going that way. We're going to the press room [the Colonial Room].' I said, 'This way, Senator.' It was a last-minute decision. I don't know who made it. . . . The

Senator was really happy, and he stopped again and again to shake hands. . . . I got his hand, his right hand and I said 'Senator. Let's go now.' [A split second later I] felt something, somebody, moving in. . . . The next thing I heard was a shot. It sounded like a firecracker. Then I heard a second shot. Senator Kennedy's right arm flew up and *he was turning* [emphasis added]. . . . It looked like the Senator saw what had happened."

Uecker, in his testimony, has hinted that conspiracy advocates were wrong to use the assistant maitre d' to establish that Sirhan could not have fired from within inches of RFK's body. Uecker, saying that he "felt something, somebody, moving in," confirmed that he and RFK were very close to Sirhan. Key witness Edward Minasian also gave a clue as to how Sirhan was able to move past Uecker when he said, "I saw an arm extended with a revolver and he [Sirhan] had reached around Uecker."[18] The shot that killed Kennedy was fired from a distance of approximately one inch.

About twenty people were in the pantry in front of Kennedy. Kennedy was in the midst of about fifty people. As Cesar approached Kennedy as he walked through the pantry doors, people began pushing and shoving toward the senator. Cesar began to push them away, as they made it difficult for the senator to move forward.

Cesar's account is crucial because he was certain about how Kennedy was standing at the moments shots rang out. Cesar told Dan Moldea, "A lot of people testified that [Sirhan] was standing this way [with Kennedy facing his assailant]. I know for a fact [that's wrong], because I saw him [Kennedy] reach out there [to shake hands with a busboy] and which way he turned. And I told police about that."[19]

Although Cesar did not see any bullets hit Kennedy or see him fall, he knew the senator's head was turned away from Sirhan's gun, exposing the right rear of his head, the part of his body hit by the fatal bullet. Cesar dropped, with Kennedy, to the floor to avoid being hit by bullets. He pulled his gun out of his holster for only about thirty seconds as he began to stand up.

Cesar was in shock. He also had powder burns in his eyes. He ran out of the pantry when he saw Sirhan struggling with Kennedy's aides and returned with other Ace guards, Jack Merrit and Albert Stowers, who had been in the Embassy Ballroom. Merrit entered the pantry with his gun drawn.[20]

The official LAPD version of the shooting concluded that the sequence of shots was as follows:

BULLET 1 hit Kennedy in the head.
BULLET 2 went through Kennedy's shoulder pad, did not harm him, exited, and hit Paul Schrade.

BULLET 3 entered Kennedy's right armpit and lodged in his neck.
BULLET 4 entered Kennedy's back and exited through his chest, traveling
       upward to the ceiling, where it was lost in the interspace.
BULLETS 5–8 hit the other victims, one as a ricochet off the ceiling.

     The reliable witnesses to the shooting all said the distance from
Kennedy to Sirhan's gun was between one and a half and three feet. Boris
Yaro, a photographer for the Los Angeles Times, said "Sirhan *lunged* [emphasis added] at Kennedy, he was stabbing at Kennedy and pulling the trigger. Kennedy was backing up, he turned and he twisted and he put his hands
up over his face." Yaro also said that the gun was within "a foot" of Kennedy's
head and that Sirhan "held the gun at arm's length and fired down."[21] Therefore the first bullet could not have hit Kennedy because his wounds displayed "scorch marks," which could have resulted only from the gun having
been placed an inch or so from his head.
     And, as Moldea explained,

> All twelve of the eyewitness' statements about muzzle distance
> are based on—and only on—their view of Sirhan's first shot.
> After the first shot, their eyes were diverted as panic swept
> through the densely populated kitchen pantry. The seventy-
> seven people in the crowd began to run, duck for cover, and
> crash into each other. . . . No one saw the muzzle of Sirhan's
> .22 get that close—but no one saw the Senator get shot either.
> All of the eyewitness testimony is based on Sirhan's location,
> relative to Senator Kennedy's, at the moment of the first shot—
> which, I believe, missed the Senator and struck Paul Schrade,
> who was standing several feet in back of him. Therefore, in
> my opinion, the issue of muzzle distance for that first shot is
> moot. After the shooting started, the crime scene became cha-
> otic. The eyewitnesses were busy covering up and falling all
> over each other. Yet, we know from Noguchi's excellent au-
> topsy—not from any of the eyewitnesses—that the Senator was
> hit three times by contact or near-contact shots, along with a
> fourth shot that went harmlessly through the shoulder pad of
> his suit jacket.[22]

     One of the most reliable witnesses, Lisa Urso, who was able to see
both Kennedy and Sirhan, saw Kennedy's hand move to his head behind his
right ear. As the distance from Kennedy to the gun after the first "pop" was
three feet, it is likely he had moved his hand simply as a defensive reaction

to the first shot fired. Urso described Kennedy's movements as "[jerking] a little bit, like backwards and then forwards." Moldea believes the backward and forward jerking occurred when Kennedy recoiled at the explosion of the first shot. RFK was then accidentally bumped forward, toward the steam table, which was bolted to the floor, and into Sirhan's gun, where he was hit at point-blank range.[23]

Moldea believes the first shot hit Paul Schrade because the labor activist's last memory was of the senator smiling and turning toward the steam table. Furthermore, in support of his thesis that the first shot hit Schrade, Moldea quotes Edward Minasian as saying, "I saw the fellow [Schrade] behind the Senator fall, then the Senator fell."[24] Kennedy probably saw Schrade hit because when he himself lay dying on the floor he asked, "Is Paul all right?" If Kennedy had indeed been hit by the first shot he would not have been standing, observing Schrade. The injury to Kennedy's head was so severe he would not have been able to observe anything once the bullet struck.

Moldea's thesis is supported by eyewitness Vincent DiPierro, who told investigators,

> I stuck my hand out and he shook my hand and I tapped him
> on the shoulder and said, 'Congratulations Mr. Kennedy.' And
> I walked with him as far as I could . . . I stayed as close as I
> could to him . . . into what is the kitchen more or less . . . and
> this guy . . . he was in a kind of a funny position because he
> was kind of down . . . like if he were trying to protect himself
> from something. . . . He tried to push the people away from his
> hand . . . and then he . . . swung round and he went up on his
> . . . tiptoes . . . and . . . he shot . . . and the first shot I don't know
> where it went, but I know it was *either his second or third one
> that hit Mr. Kennedy* [emphasis added] and after that I had blood
> all over my face from where it hit his head, because my glasses
> . . . [Martin Patrusky] saw the blood all over my face.[25]

Moldea's thesis is further supported by key witness Frank Burns, who was identified as one of the six in the group closest to the senator (the others were Karl Uecker, Thane Cesar, Juan Romero, Jesus Perez, and Martin Patrusky). Although Burns insisted the gun was never less than a foot or a foot and a half from Kennedy, he nevertheless described the dynamics of the shooting in such a way to make it entirely feasible that Sirhan's gun moved to an area inches away from the senator. Burns suffered a burn on his face that he thought was caused by a bullet passing near his cheek. It was likely a powder burn from Sirhan's pistol. Burns said,

> I had just caught up with him [in the pantry], and was a step or so past him. And I'd turned around facing the same way as he toward the busboys—I was just off his right shoulder, a matter of inches behind him. . . . The noise [from Sirhan's gun] was like a string of firecrackers going off, it wasn't in an even cadence. In the process, a bullet must have passed very close to my left cheek because I can remember the heat and a sort of burn. I remember an arm coming towards us, through the people, with a gun in it. I was putting together the burn across my cheek, the noise and the gun and I was thinking, "My God, it's an assassination attempt." I turned my head and saw the gun and quickly looked back to the Senator and realized he'd been shot because he'd thrown his hands up toward his head as if he was about to grab it at the line of his ears. He hadn't quite done it. His arms were near his head and he was twisting to his left and falling back. And then I looked back at the gunman, and at that moment he was almost directly in front of me. He was still holding the gun and coming closer to the Senator, *pursuing the body so that the arc of the gun was coming down to the floor as the body was going down.* (Emphasis added.)[26]

Burns's description of the shooting may be the key to understanding how the angles of the bullet paths in Kennedy's body were not consistent with the LAPD's conclusions that Sirhan's gun was extended horizontally.

Following the first shot, which hit Schrade, Kennedy was struck by a bullet that passed through his jacket and entered his shoulder pad as he raised his arm to defend himself. Then two shots hit his right armpit—one bullet lodged in the back of his neck. Finally, according to coroner Thomas Noguchi in an interview with Moldea, the fatal shot to the head occurred. Noguchi said he based part of his analysis on the fact that had Kennedy been hit in the head on the first shot he would not have been able to stand. The shot to the head would have taken him off his feet immediately.[27] Noguchi told journalist Douglas Stein in 1986,

> The senator had three gunshot wounds—a head wound behind his right ear and two through the right armpit. To recon-

struct a scenario of the shooting, the gunshot wound to the head wouldn't tell us much, except how close the assailant may have been. We must remember the body is constantly moving, with arms especially changing position. When you examine a body, it's in a horizontal state, so I had to physically and mentally place his body in an upright position to interpret the wound configurations. When a bullet penetrates the skin, it generally leaves a round hole. But the wound to the senator's armpit was not round. To make it round, I had to move the arm fifteen degrees forward after raising it to ninety degrees. I had to do that to understand the relation of the bullet corridor within the body to the body's movement. The senator's head wound came from a back-to-front direction; the second wound was on the side, and the third was slightly shifted, indicating he was turning clockwise. . . . We know that the three gunshot wounds were at close range.[28]

Moldea believes much of the misunderstanding about the shooting is the result of a general lack of knowledge about how crowds react during violent incidents. Both conspiracy advocates and official investigators did not factor in the dynamics of crowd movement and how crowds can rapidly change direction and positioning in an instant. Crowd dynamics are especially relevant in the Kennedy case because after the first shot people reacted with fear, shock, and perhaps defensiveness. People in the pantry were also turning their heads to look for the source of the sounds; on realizing a gun had been fired, some would have stumbled, fallen, and crashed into objects around them and clashed with others in the crowd. In such circumstances it is easy to see how only a few witnesses placed Sirhan's gun within a foot or two of Kennedy's head. It should be remembered that none of the LAPD's "most credible" witnesses actually saw Kennedy shot.

Dr. Marcus McBroom supported Moldea's conclusion about the crowd's movement in a statement he made to KABC TV Los Angeles reporter Carl George immediately following the shooting: "I was five or six people behind him [RFK]. He was moving and then stopping. Apparently a little . . . if I'm not mistaken . . . a man who was in a work shirt, his hair was all tossled. He sort of approached the senator from the front and he was sort of smiling and then suddenly it seemed like there was one shot and then five shots in quick succession. I do know the crowd panicked and I was thrown back into the ballroom."[29]

Furthermore, as Moldea points out, the estimates for the distance of the gun were based on when the first shot was fired. The estimates ranged from one and a half feet to eight or nine feet. In an instant, following the first shot, the whole dynamics of the crowd changed. As one LAPD detective told Moldea, "Eyewitness testimony? You talk about seventy-seven people in a room and twelve actual eyewitnesses to the shooting. These are people who were in the wrong place at the wrong time. You're expecting accuracy in their statements? Twelve different eyewitnesses will generally give you twelve different versions of a story."[30] As Noguchi observed, "I believe that the Kennedy assassination must go down in the history of forensic science as a classic example of 'crowd psychology,' where none of the eyewitnesses saw what actually happened."[31]

It is unlikely that other shooters in an elaborate conspiracy would have remained undetected. In addition, conspirators could not have known which route Kennedy was to take when he left the Embassy Ballroom stage and entered the kitchen pantry. An aide directed him along that route. A number of other routes could have been taken. Sirhan had been stalking Kennedy. As this was likely his third attempt to shoot the senator, he simply got lucky and likely deduced that as RFK had used this route on his way to the ballroom stage he would return this way. Conspiracy advocates find these facts irrelevant. They believe that multiple assassins might have been waiting at various locations on the possibility that RFK chose another route. However, there is a central weakness in their thesis: no evidence has surfaced to support it.

The Doorframes

The morning after the shooting the Associated Press published a photo of two police officers near the doorframe of the pantry's swinging doors. A photographer had asked them to pose showing purported bullet holes in the frames. The frames were destroyed by the LAPD one year after the shooting and some months after Sirhan's trial ended. During the 1970s a number of conspiracy writers and investigators interviewed witnesses, including police officers and shooting eyewitnesses, who also testified to having seen bullet holes and/or bullets in the door frames of the pantry's swinging doors. These additional bullets or bullet holes would have indicated that more than eight shots had been fired in the pantry and, accordingly, that more than one shooter had been involved in Senator Kennedy's murder.

The issue became controversial in 1975 when the coroner, Noguchi, told attorney Vincent Bugliosi, "He [LAPD criminologist Wolfer] pointed, as I recall . . . to several [circled] holes in the door frames of the swinging doors leading into the pantry. I directed that photographs be taken of me pointing to these holes."[32] Years later Noguchi put his comments into the proper perspective when he stated that he simply believed he had been pointing at bullet holes but he did not know whether they were actual bullet holes or not. Others with him when the photo was taken believed Noguchi was identifying bullet holes. He was directed to them by Wolfer, who had only been exploring the possibility that bullets had created the holes in the center divider.[33]

Bugliosi also interviewed Los Angeles police officer Robert Rozzi, who told him he had also observed what he believed to be bullet holes in the doorframes. According to Rozzi, "Sometime during the evening when we were looking for evidence, someone discovered what appeared to be a bullet a foot and a half or so from the bottom of the floor in a doorjamb on the door behind the stage. I also personally observed what I believed to be a bullet in the place just mentioned. What I observed was a hole in the doorjamb, and the base of what appeared to be a small-caliber bullet was lodged in the hole."[34] Noguchi's and Rozzi's comments were supported by ex-FBI agent William Bailey, who told Bugliosi that he had actually inspected the two bullet holes in the center divider and found the base of a .22 slug in each hole during his fifteen- or twenty-minute pass through the crime scene on the night of the shooting

Wolfer was the LAPD official in charge of the crime scene. On Sunday, June 9, 1968, he told Special Unit Senator (SUS) investigators, "We've been over the kitchen area twice, and we're going at least one more time. It's unbelievable how many damn holes there are in that kitchen ceiling. Even the doors have holes in them, which can be mistaken for bullet holes. At any rate, we have three bullets that definitely come from the gun taken from Sirhan, one from Kennedy's sixth cervical vertebra, one from [victim] Goldstein and one from Weisel."[35]

Wolfer recovered the bullets (except for one lost in the ceiling interspace) that were expended by Sirhan's gun, and he made reports accounting for all the bullet holes. "There were many holes and we explored all the holes in the door and were never able to find any bullets or even any indication that there was a bullet. . . . There were many holes in the woodwork on the swinging doors that were caused by some other object. All of the holes were explored and no bullets were ever found."[36] In a September 20, 1971, sworn deposition Wolfer said, "Well, these objects, the holes in the door, as I recall here today, were caused by something that went through and didn't spread them, but punched a hole there. You could see the impression of the wood pushed into the hole. It wasn't a typical bullet hole, but there were many of those holes in the door. In fact, when I arrived they had several of them circled."[37]

Wolfer's partner, Sergeant William Lee, a ballistics firearms expert, concurred with Wolfer. On December 15 Lee was interviewed by the LAPD, and the interview report stated, "[Subject states] . . . this examination was visually conducted and it was, and is, his opinion that there were no bullet holes. Subject does recall examining holes, but none of these in his expert opinion were caused by bullets."[38] Furthermore, according to Moldea, "Independent firearms experts, even those critical of the LAPD's investigation, who have studied the LAPD's photographs of the 'object,' have insisted that the object is simply too small to be the base of a .22-caliber bullet."[39]

A 1975 LAPD report stipulated that "[Wolfer] recalls that portions of wood were removed from the right hand side of the doors. . . . Subject examined these pieces of wood at the scene and found no holes he could attribute to a bullet. The wood was taken to SID [Special Investigation Division] where it was further examined by fluoroscope. This examination determined there was no bullet in the examined wood."[40] SID man Bob Druley said, "I know that there were holes there that people thought were bullet holes that were not. They were just places where somebody had driven a nail out and chipped the plaster and then repainted over it. There was no wiping ring on the holes or anything. You know, when you shoot a bullet through something—lead or otherwise—the trash on the bullet wipes off on the entry where it goes through. It's called 'the wiping ring.' And it leaves a little dark area around the hole."[41] Furthermore, the frames were taken back to the police laboratory and analyzed for gun metal residue; none was found. Nor were any spent rounds found at the end of the hole. A hole is a bullet hole only if a bullet made the hole.

Conspiracy advocate Greg Stone revealed in 1976 that FBI personnel Al Greiner and Richard Fernandez had photographed four "bullet holes in Sirhan's line of fire." Los Angeles deputy FBI chief Roger "Frenchy" LaJeunesse countered,

> If a police officer or detective is on the scene, and he's not with SID, he wouldn't know a bullet hole from a nail hole! The average working detective, he just wouldn't! He's not trained! His job is to isolate the scene! Don't touch it! Don't move anything! I know that SID conducted the forensic crime scene search because that was entrusted to them. . . . I think that [FBI agent Al Greiner] should not have said "bullet holes." He should have said "reported bullet holes" or "alleged bullets" . . . he didn't say [bullet holes] to me. I'm speculating that he probably wishes now in retrospect that he would have said, "Somebody told me

they were bullet holes, so I called them bullet holes." . . . Honestly, Al wouldn't know bullet holes from nail holes.[42]

Ex-FBI agent William Bailey continues to insist to this day that two .22 bullets were in the center divider. However, as Moldea has indicated, if this were true Wolfer must have repeatedly perjured himself when he claimed that bullets had not been removed from the doorframe. According to Moldea, Bailey, like many another crime scene witnesses, was simply mistaken. "To continue to suggest that Wolfer lied," Moldea wrote, "is also to suggest that Wolfer, the officers in the SID, and the LAPD wittingly engaged in a conspiracy to permit the escape of Sirhan's co-conspirators. And that defies the evidence, as well as all logic."[43]

Moldea discovered the origins of the doorframe controversy. According to him, before the police removed the crowd on the night of the shooting, a souvenir hunter was observed trying to pry what he believed to be a bullet from the doorframes. The souvenir hunter was stopped and the incident was reported. Los Angeles Sheriff's Office deputy Walter Tew then marked what he believed to be bullet holes in the frames. Because he circled them and added his name and badge number more people began to notice them. Thus the myth began that the door divider "definitely held bullets" or had bullet holes. None of the people, including police officers, who identified the holes as bullet holes had any experience in criminalistics or firearms identification. None (with the exception of Walter Bailey) had seen bullets in the holes or the recovery of bullets from the holes. This erroneous identification caught on in the days following the shooting and led to photographs of purported bullet holes. In fact independent firearms experts have since stated that, after examining the photographs, they believe what was identified as the base of a bullet was in fact too small to be the base of a .22 bullet.[44] X rays of the frames also did not reveal any bullets.

As former Los Angeles Police Chief Daryl Gates observed, "the officers [who identified holes in the divider] were not ballistics experts but patrolmen who had come on the scene for crowd control. A photographer asked them to pose and, wanting only to be cooperative, they did. But the holes were not bullet holes. We dismantled the doorframe and determined that it contained no bullets. Eventually we threw away the doorframe—an obvious act of covering up according to some."[45]

The destruction of the frames and the ceiling tiles a year after the shooting did indeed lead many conspiracy advocates to accuse the LAPD of covering up a conspiracy. A police attorney, Dion Morrow, said in 1975, "There was no place to keep them. You can't fit ceiling panels into a card file."[46]

Further in response to allegations by conspiracy advocates who accused the LAPD of destroying evidence, falsifying evidence, and coercing witnesses, SUS Chief Robert Houghton said, "After the trial was over [someone] came to me and asked whether or not it would be proper to destroy or get rid of those doorjambs. . . . I presume they asked . . . about the ceiling tiles, to store them for, as we intended to do, in perpetuity, without taking up a lot of space . . . so I told them if they had the adequate evidence . . . from those doors . . . then go ahead and destroy them, as long as that evidence was maintained in the file."[47] SID criminalist David Butler said, "It's a matter of routine, because you cannot physically hold all the evidence that the department takes in."[48] Thomas J. Miller, who authorized the destruction, said, "We determined through SID that the holes in those items were not bullet holes. So when it was time to dispose of them, we put a disposal card through."[49] Furthermore, it is logical to assume that, if the LAPD were part of a cover-up, it would not have waited a year to rid itself of incriminating evidence.

Dave Butler, an LAPD firearms expert, put into perspective the mistakes made during the collection of physical evidence in the crime. According to Butler,

> I know there's been criticism of the way evidence was handled [in the RFK case]—but the criticism was coming from people who have probably never been in a major crime scene—and had all of the weight of all of the responsibility of that crime scene on his shoulders. The manual of the department gives exclusive authority to the technician. It gives us sole jurisdiction to exceed the chief of police. And that is an awesome responsibility because if you do something wrong, it's going to affect the whole investigation. Witnesses lie, witnesses are [biased] by prejudice—but physical evidence is not. That's as close to pure as you can get. Of course, the fault comes with the interpretation. The collection, the preservation, and the interpretation of that evidence. That's a subjective analysis. And that's where the problem comes in, and that's where the dispute between various examiners and experts arise on these issues. But, as to the handling of it, I don't think that I could have done any better. And I don't know of anybody else that would've done things differently or better.[50]

The Ballistics Evidence

Bullets and bullet fragments were removed from Robert Kennedy's body during surgery at the hospital. The neck bullet was left in place as it was not deemed to be life-threatening. During the autopsy it was removed and used to identify the weapon used in the shooting. The bullet that actually killed RFK had fragmented on impact and thus could not be used to link the murder bullet to Sirhan's gun.

DeWayne Wolfer said he made a positive match between all of the bullets in Bobby Kennedy, excluding the fragmented fatal bullet, and the bullets subsequently test-fired from Sirhan's gun. Wolfer made striation comparisons using a comparison microscope. Striation is the process that causes a bullet to become scratched as it passes along a gun's barrel. While Wolfer was unable to identify the bullet that caused Kennedy's mortal head wound, he did confirm that it had been mini-mag ammunition and had the same "rifling specifications" as other bullets fired from Sirhan's gun. Unfortunately, Wolfer offered no supporting documentary evidence at Sirhan's trial and this only fuelled claims by conspiracy advocates in later years that Wolfer had been part of a cover-up.

In 1970 ballistics expert William Harper examined the bullets removed from Kennedy's neck and William Weisel. Harper said the bullets could not have been fired from the same gun as their cannelure designs and rifling angles were inconsistent. However, it was discovered that Harper had misrepresented his education and work experiences and an investigation found the "expert" was judged by criminalists with "recognized qualifications" to be "not one of their peers."[51]

In 1975, as the controversies surrounding RFK's assassination became widely publicized, Paul Schrade and CBS, Inc., petitioned the Superior Court of California, County of Los Angeles, requesting that the firearms evidence be reexamined. The court granted the petition and ordered that a panel of experts be formed to conduct a reexamination. The American Academy of Forensic Sciences (AAFS) and the Association of Firearm and Tool Mark Examiners (AFTE) were contacted and asked to submit names of firearms experts to the attorney general of the State of California. A panel was constituted with leading firearms experts recommended by the AAFS, AFTE, and other interested parties. After a thorough examination of the firearms evidence by each panel member individually, the members collectively reported that William Harper had been wrong. They also informed the court that their examination of the evidence revealed that three victim bullets (the Kennedy neck bullet, the Weisel bullet, and the Goldstein bullet) could be matched with one another, but they could not say which gun had fired them. While their investigations and tests could not establish that Sirhan's gun fired the three victim bullets, they said, "there is not evidence to indicate that more than one gun was used to fire the items examined."

One of the experts, Lowell Bradford, ruled out the possibility of a second gun because "there was no significant differences in the general characteristics of all the bullets that were found on the scene" and "specific characteristics on the victim bullets enabled an identification of all the victim bullets as being fired from the same gun."[52] Furthermore, in his report, Thomas Kranz, Los Angeles County Board of Supervisors special counsel who had been appointed to independently investigate RFK's assassination, stated, "[Experts] Garland, Cunningham, Biasotti and Berg were of the conclusion that they were within one step away from linking the individual characteristics of the bullets to the Sirhan gun. Such a phase mark process would have defined the individual characteristics of the bullets when they were in a better condition to be examined in 1968."[53]

Sirhan's gun was damaged by "heavy leading" (barrel fouling), which compromised further tests following those carried out by Wolfer shortly after the assassination. The 1975 ballistics panel guessed that they could not positively match the victims' bullets because the gun had been repeatedly fired. Moldea settled the issue by interviewing police officers who confirmed that the heavy leading was caused by numerous test firings of Sirhan's gun by Los Angeles police officers who were, in effect, "souvenir hunters." "Thus, Wolfer, and only Wolfer, could have positively matched the three victim bullets," wrote Moldea, "before the leading of and permanent damage to the barrel of Sirhan's gun. Wolfer legitimately made these matches and testified honestly. His analysis could not be confirmed by the firearms panel or anyone else because the barrel became damaged immediately after he conducted the tests."[54]

Damaging the gun was not the only mistake made with regard to the pistol evidence. Wolfer matched the bullets recovered from Robert Kennedy and two other victims with seven bullets that were test-fired from Sirhan's gun. On June 7, 1968, Wolfer presented the seven test bullets to the grand jury along with Sirhan's H53725 gun. Wolfer testified that he had made a positive match between the bullet lodged in Kennedy's neck and the test bullets with his comparison microscope. Wolfer said that Sirhan's gun and "no other gun" fired the neck shot that hit RFK. Because Wolfer wanted to test the slugs removed from the other victims with the test bullets, he asked to keep three of the seven test bullets.

Four of the bullets were then placed into evidence before Sirhan's Grand Jury along with the gun and the bullets taken from the victims. Because Sirhan's gun was no longer available to him, Wolfer found a similar .22 gun (serial number H18602) to conduct sound level and pattern tests. He did not retain any of the bullets from these tests, but later, when the original gun and bullets became available, he put the test bullets fired from Sirhan's gun that he had retained into an evidence envelope and mistakenly wrote the identification number for the weapon he had used for the sound tests. Wolfer had asked for the number from a colleague when he was writing on the manila envelope. The mistake was not noticed during Sirhan's trial, but when it was discovered, it led to cries of a cover-up and the allegation that two guns had been used in the assassination. Further cries of cover-up continued when it was revealed that Wolfer's test gun, which had been taken from the police property section, had been returned and, following normal procedure, destroyed. According to Moldea, "The H18602 was originally scheduled for destruction in July 1968, a year after the gun had been booked as evidence in a 1967 robbery case, as per standard operating procedure. After the gun had been used as a test weapon in the Kennedy case and returned to the Property Division, a new date for destruction, superseding the former, was imposed. The problem was that no one bothered to change the original date of destruction on the property report."[55]

The LAPD also came under criticism over the years because its files and the physical evidence were kept secret and barred from public scrutiny until the 1980s. Former Police Chief Daryl Gates sought to explain why the files were kept under wraps:

> By now [the 1980s] everyone was demanding to see our files. Personally I had no objection to opening them up. The problem was the files contained information given to us on a confidential basis. We had all kinds of information from people who were around the Senator, what they were doing, who they were with, private information. I didn't think we had any right to disregard a confidential relationship. This only added more fuel to the conspiracy theories, 'If the police weren't hiding something, they'd let us into that file. So they're hiding something, they know there's a conspiracy, and that's why they don't give us that file.' Finally, I got so sick of this, I recommended the files be placed in the hands of our archivist, pointed out what we thought was confidential, and let him worry what to do about it.[56]

The evidence in the case clearly establishes that victims Kennedy, Weisel, and Goldstein were shot by the same gun, and together with eyewitness testimony, it also indicates that Thane Cesar was unlikely to be "the second shooter." As the Kranz Report stated, "the ballistics examination and test results conducted by the ballistics panel in 1975 proved that for a second gunman to have shot any of [the Kennedy, Weisel, and Goldstein bullets], the second gunman would have had to have shot a weapon with the exact same imperfections, same muzzle defects, same leaded barrel conditions and same individual characteristics as the weapon used by Sirhan. Additionally, this second gunman would have had to use the same type of ammunition, firing at approximately the exact same moment as the Sirhan weapon was being fired."[57] As the report makes clear,

> Assuming for the sake of argument that the second gunman was standing directly behind Senator Kennedy and slightly to the right. The three bullets recovered from Kennedy, Goldstein and Weisel . . . all were identified by five of the seven experts as having come from one gun, and the other two experts testified under oath that they found no evidence that these three bullets had come from a second gun. Therefore, assuming a second gunman, he would necessarily have had to have fired into a north-west-north position to hit Senator Kennedy from the right, rear, and then conversely and almost simultaneously, this second gunman would have had to have made a substantial turn to his left and have fired directly behind the Senator, into a western direction, striking victims Goldstein and Weisel.[58]

Since the LAPD files were made available to the general public, no "smoking gun" or credible evidence has been found that would indicate a second gunman murdered Robert Kennedy.

The "Missing Photographs"

The LAPD destroyed 2,410 of more the 2,700 investigation photos when their usefulness was deemed to be nil. The photos included shots of the crime scene, photos of witnesses, and the prints and negatives taken by the Fire Department's photographer on duty on the night of the assassination. The list of photos destroyed also included pictures taken by newsmen and film shot by amateurs. According to Lt. Roy Keene, who authorized the destruction, "To control the confidentiality of . . . documents . . . we tried to work with a minimum of . . . copies. . . . They would not be souvenirs. And this has happened: scraps of clothing, threads of clothing, photographs ended up with souvenir hunters' collections. So in determining the exact number of sets of autopsy photos required for court preparation, we destroyed more than the copies necessary. That's all. That's all that was about." Robert

Houghton said, "If there was anything funny going on, those DA guys [district attorneys Dave Fitts, Buck Compton, and John Howard] would have spotted it immediately."[59]

It was also claimed that photographs taken in the pantry that night by fifteen-year-old Scott Enyart disappeared. This disappearance provoked conspiracy theorists to hypothesize that Enyart's photos would have revealed a second shooter had they not been destroyed. Critics concluded that the police confiscated the photos to hide evidence of a conspiracy.

On June 5, 1968, Enyart was taking photos for his school newspaper, the *Fairfax High School Gazette*. When RFK finished his speech in the hotel ballroom, Enyart followed Kennedy into the kitchen pantry. He said he raised his camera over his head and pressed the shutter repeatedly, then climbed up on a steam table and took even more photographs. Minutes later he returned to the ballroom to record the chaos there. Enyart claimed police confiscated his photographs—on three thirty-six exposure rolls—as evidence and said he was interviewed at Ramparts Police Station.

Enyart said he received about two dozen prints/Xeroxes back from the police, all of which showed either the speech or the ballroom after the assassination. None of what he considered the important ones were returned to him. Told that the evidence in the case had been sealed for twenty years, Enyart waited until the late 1980s to request that the police return all of his photos. At first the authorities said they did not have the negatives, saying they destroyed them in August 1968. They later said they had been misfiled and would be returned to him. Enyart hired a lawyer and sued the LAPD for $2 million in damages for the loss or destruction of his photographs. Following years of legal battles his case finally came to fruition in 1996 when a jury ruled in his favor. However, the negatives were stolen as a courier delivered them to Enyart. He was awarded damages.[60]

The verdict in the Enyart case was a blow to the LAPD, which had come under constant accusations that they had covered up an RFK conspiracy. Skip Miller, who argued the case for the district attorney's office, however, said that Enyart's claim that he took important photographs in the hotel pantry at the time RFK was shot "was just wishful thinking." Miller said that Enyart took only one roll of film and, more important, he was not in the pantry in the first place.[61] To prove his allegations, Miller called as a witness one of Enyart's two friends who had been with him on the night of the shooting. Brent Gold, who later became a psychotherapist, said Enyart never walked in the pantry following RFK's speech but instead was with him in the hotel lobby when the shooting occurred. Gold said, they both "walked out to the front" of the hotel "to the lobby" and then they both responded to screams and commotion indicating something was wrong inside. Gold said both of them went back inside the Embassy Ballroom and insists, "I knew we were both outside in the lobby area when Kennedy was shot and he [Enyart] wasn't in the pantry." Furthermore, said Miller, Bill Eppridge, a *Life* photographer, said Enyart's claim that he was the person in his photographs was untrue and that the person standing on the steam table was instead Harry Benson.[62]

According to the District Attorney's Office, Enyart (today, a committed JFK and 9/11 conspiracy advocate) was awarded damages because the jury was allowed to hear witnesses who had misled it with allegations of a purported conspiracy. Miller also believed that jury misconduct occurred and that some jurors expressed hatred of the LAPD and a belief in conspiracy theories jarred their deliberations.

The Acoustics Evidence

Many years following the assassination, critics of the official version of the RFK case said some audio recordings provided evidence that more than eight shots were fired in the Ambassador Hotel pantry. If more bullets than Sirhan's gun could hold were fired, then the existence of a second gunman could be proved. The claims of extra shots fired originated from two audio recordings made of the events in the hotel's pantry and Embassy Ballroom: the "ABC News tape" and the "Pruszynski tape."

Dan Moldea identified ABC News as the only television network broadcasting when the shooting began. Its equipment was recording from the back of the Embassy Ballroom. Both Andrew West of Mutual Broadcasting and Jeff Brent of Continental Broadcasting were also recording, but they switched on their microphones only after the shooting began. Moldea wrote,

> In November and December 1982, these three audio sound recordings were subjected to scientific, but controversial, acoustical analysis, in an attempt to determine if a distinctive gunshot "audio signature" can be identified and the number of gunshots counted. According to Dr. Michael H. L. Hecker—an electrical engineer with the Stanford Research Institute in Menlo Park, California—who conducted the tests, 'On the basis of auditory, oscillographic and spectrographic analyses of these three recordings, it is my opinion, to a reasonable degree of scientific certainty, that no fewer than 10 gunshots are ascertainable following the conclusion of the Senator's victory speech until after the time Sirhan Bishara Sirhan was disarmed.'[63]

The alleged "discovery" that ten shots were heard on the ABC/Brent/ West recordings of the shooting has not withstood close scrutiny. Experts have disagreed as to the reliability of the tests conducted on the tapes.[64]

In the 1980s Steve Barber was given an opportunity to examine an audio copy of the ABC tape that purportedly contained the sounds of the gunshots. Barber was famous for having discovered that the acoustics evidence used by the House Select Committee on Assassinations (HSCA) investigation into the JFK assassination was flawed. Subsequent examination of the Dallas Police dictabelt recordings by the Ramsey Panel confirmed Barber's research. Barber worked on the tapes with Nobel Prize–winning physicists Luis Avarez and Norman Ramsey. They both praised Barber's contribution.[65]

Writer Robert Cutler had sent Steve Barber the RFK assassination tape in the 1980s and asked him to determine if the gunshots were audible. Barber stated, "I think that I was told I would hear balloons popping, and not to confuse this with gunshots, as I recall. I seem to remember this because [Cutler] told me that the shots may not appear on these, since the news reporters had possibly turned off their [microphones] and may not have captured the shots. I remember that I had written Cutler back and told him that I [couldn't] hear anything except what would possibly be balloons being popped and that I [could] hear where the recorder was turned off and then back on in spots, but that I thought that I heard zero gunshots."[66]

The present author sent Barber an audio tape recording of live broadcasts compiled by JFK researcher and author Larry Sneed. The tape is a collection of the live news broadcasts on the night RFK was shot; none of the recordings were made in the pantry. Part of the recording contains the broadcast made by ABC News, which was stationed in the Embassy Ballroom. After examining the tape Barber concluded,

> This recording was obviously made AFTER the shooting. The vocal contents of the pandemonium that is going on during the segment of the tape proves this, for one thing. The screaming and shouting of people are those of panic stricken individuals, reacting to something wrong. . . . For another thing, the so-called shots that narrator, Howard K. Smith, indicates that we could possibly hear, in NO WAY bear any resemblance at all to the sounds of gunfire heard clearly on the "Pruszynski Tape." The sounds that I hear that they suggest may be gunfire may be nothing more than the sounds of the microphones . . . bumping either into things . . . or [the person] fumbling

around with it, or something of that nature. They do not re-
semble gunfire at all, to me, and most certainly not the sounds
as captured on the "Pruszynski" recording. . . . The ABC tape
is absolutely worthless.[67]

At the request of this author, Michael O'Dell, a technical analyst
who worked with the Ramsey Panel when it examined the acoustics evidence in the JFK assassination, examined the same tape recording. O'Dell
stated, "I don't believe any shots were captured on the ABC tape. . . . I think
[the ABC tape] is worthless. . . . And the timing of [the purported shots] is
not in agreement with [the Pruszynski tape]. . . . People are already screaming on the ABC tape."[68] One of the major problems in finding the shots on
the tapes is the fact that there were hundreds of balloons in the ballroom,
some of which were popping before, during, and after the shooting.

In 2005 another "acoustics controversy" arose: the "Pruszynski tape"
mentioned earlier. A CNN journalist approached Dan Moldea and told him
about a tape recording that supposedly captured the sounds of more than
eight shots fired in the Ambassador Hotel pantry. Stanislaw Pruszynski had
made the recording. He had told the LAPD that he was in the pantry at the
time of the assassination and claimed his cassette recorder was running all
through the shooting.

The LAPD files state, "Pruszynski, Stus—At Ambassador Hotel on
June 4th; tape is his recording of events at the hotel. Includes end of RFK's
speech, possible shots being fired, post-shooting hysteria in kitchen, and
interviews with a man who claims Sirhan was not alone. Pruszynski nar-
rates what he is seeing." The tape was eventually lodged with the California
State Archives.[69] It is the only recording in existence that was taken in the
pantry and records all of the shots fired from beginning to end.

In 2006 the present author requested a copy of the Pruszynski tape
from the California State Archives. Steve Barber and two associates, Dr. Chad
Zimmerman and Michael O'Dell, examined the tapes. After examining the
tape Barber concluded,

I have counted nothing more than seven shots. I hear [what
may be] the [eighth] shot just a millisecond before [a] woman
screams what sounds to me like "Aahhhhhhhhhh! I think my
husband's been shot!" . . . Whoever she is, she is standing VERY
close to the microphone, as her voice is terribly distorted, and
the last shot is fired just as she begins to scream. . . . I hear a
"pop" sound that is deeper in tone just before Sirhan begins

shooting his weapon. . . . There is a clear distinction between this first "pop" or explosion than the sound of those from the gunfire. . . . It is definitely NOT gunfire. . . . It could be a thumping noise in the background. . . . I am listening with earphones and it is quite apparent [the thumping noise is] not explosions from weaponry or gunshot.

After further analysis Barber concluded,

[The deeper tones] . . . have somewhat of a knocking sound in one sense, or, a balloon bursting in another. Compared to the gunfire, which has more of a popping sound, these two tones are sort of a "muffled" sound. There seems to be no "blast" to them. . . . [The] "mysterious thump" [is possibly] that of a door being opened, then the sound that I described as sounding like someone running their finger up the lowest string on a guitar which, in reality, would be the door squeaking as it is opened and then the door bumping into something, like the wall or whatever, as it has completely reached the extent of how far it can be opened. . . . If one of those two thumps is supposed to be Cesar's .38 going off, then, we should hear the crowd reaction to the gun blast, as well as RFK falling to the ground. Instead, we hear absolutely ZERO crowd reaction until after Sirhan unloaded his gun, nearly 5 seconds later.

In other words, from the time the last of the two thumps are heard, until the woman screams "Aahhhhhhhhhh! I think my husband's been shot!" I count nearly 5 seconds. . . . I think the woman screaming is Mrs. Kennedy. I can make out her saying what sounds very much like "Get back!" during the seconds following the shots. In conclusion, I hear a total of 7 "pops" from what would be the rapidly fired gunshots. I hear two deeper toned sounds, that to me sound nothing like the known shots.[70]

Michael O'Dell said, "I still have a lot of uncertainty about how many shots are clearly identifiable on the Pruszynski tape. Right now I'm willing to identify six for certain. But of course the real question is whether there is solid evidence for more than eight. I certainly don't see how anyone can use it to claim more than eight and that's the main point."[71]

Following a thorough examination of the tape using computer software Dr. Chad Zimmerman stated,

I ran the audio through an analysis program, which provided [an] audio analysis. I took two different graphs and split them apart, enhanced the second to a different color then overlayed them with 50% opacity [see photo insert]. You can see eight spikes that correlate to the audio gunshots. The last occurs just before the scream. However, I don't think one can necessarily say that more shots couldn't have existed after that point, but that they would have been drowned out by the scream. However, in my opinion, there are only eight, .22-caliber gunshots heard on that tape. Now, preceding these eight, I hear one deeper audible "pop" just prior to the eight shots in rapid succession. However, this is a bit longer and deeper, which sounds more like a balloon pop than a gunshot. . . . My only real contribution here is the spectrographic run that I did, which showed 8 spikes. According to those with better credentials, it only shows 7 shots. Either way, I'd say that . . . 8 or fewer shots are heard and none would be a .38.

With regard to the possibility that RFK could have been shot by security guard Thane Cesar, who carried a .38-caliber pistol, Zimmerman said, "there certainly isn't a .38 shot on [the] tape."[72]

Steve Barber described the "deeper tone sounds" as,

the first two sounds we hear, which Chad [Zimmerman] and I agree sound more like balloons exploding, or something of that nature. Then a very, very slight pause, and then the 7 popping sounds that show up on [Zimmerman's] graph which can easily be identified as gunshots. . . . I might add that, after listening to the two thumping sounds more carefully, it is my conclusion that these sounds are not in the same location as the shooter who fires the 7 gunshot sounds. They seem to have less volume than the actual gunshots. This, to me, lends more support to the conclusion that if a .38-caliber weapon was fired from within the same location as Sirhan, the volume of the shots should be much higher—not softer—since it was suggested it was a higher caliber weapon, which would then cause a higher level of sound, than that of a .22-caliber. . . . [Furthermore] while listening to a gentleman talking with Pruszynski, he actually stated that the shots "weren't very loud," and he thought the sounds were . . . Chinese type fireworks of some sort. This, to me, certainly adds to the fact that no .38-caliber weapon was fired![73]

The researchers thus ruled out the possibility that Cesar had fired his .38 revolver.

After Barber, O'Dell, and Zimmerman studied the tape, the present author solicited the assistance of an independent expert to examine their research results. Philip Harrison, a forensic analyst and consultant for J. P. French Associates, an independent forensic speech and acoustics laboratory based in York, England, examined a digitized version of the Pruszynski tape (see appendix B). Professor Peter French confirmed the outcomes of Harrison's research.

Harrison analyzed the material using three different methods, both independently and simultaneously. These involved (1) listening analytically to the recording via high quality headphones, (2) examining visual representations of the recording's waveform (oscillographic displays), and (3) analyzing spectrograms (plots of sound energy across frequency over time), all using specialized computer software.

Harrison agreed with Barber, O'Dell, and Zimmerman that there could be no more than eight shots on the tape and that the "thumping" sounds could not have been made by a .38 pistol. Harrison stated, "It is generally accepted that Sirhan's gun held eight bullets and that all eight of them were fired. This leaves the sound of an eighth shot unaccounted for. Assuming that the shot was fired and since the sound cannot be readily identified it must be masked to some extent by other sounds."

Harrison went on to explain how there were

several other impulse sounds surrounding the shots and many others across the thirty-five minutes of recording. Determining the actual source of these sounds is not viable as the quality of the recording is not adequate and there are no reference sounds with which to compare them. It is, however, possible to state that there is no evidence to support the claim that there are shots from a .38-caliber gun in the recording. There is no trace of a sound which has the characteristics of such an acoustic event. [Furthermore] the sounds preceding the shots do not bear any resemblance to a .38 shot or the other seven .22 shots. It is not possible to determine their source but this is not necessary as the important question is whether another gun was fired, not what is the source of all sounds in the recording. . . .

[Supporters of a second gunman theory] could happily claim
that the impulses before the shots start are the sounds of other
shots but I cannot see how they could support their claims
with any acoustic evidence from the recording. The sounds
bear no resemblance to the other .22 shots and a shot from a
higher caliber weapon would produce a much louder sound
with a different acoustic quality which is not consistent with
anything found on the tape.[74]

Accordingly, this new acoustics research by Barber, Zimmerman,
O'Dell, and Harrison proves, to a high degree of probability, that when Sirhan
shot RFK he was unaided and that a "second shooter" who purportedly
fired extra shots was not present in the Ambassador Hotel pantry. This new
evidence also invalidates claims that extra bullets were found in the pantry
doorframes.

Furthermore, allegations made by the Discovery Channel in 2007
that up to 13 shots were fired in the pantry has proven to be flawed by
Harrison and Barber. (http://hnn.us/articles/44466.html)

Additionally, earwitness testimony had never established a scenario
in which 13 shots had been possible. FBI files show that the majority of
pantry witnesses never heard such a large number of shots fired. The FBI
files, furthermore, show that no one who had been in the pantry when Robert Kennedy was shot told the FBI or LAPD that 13 shots had been fired.
Only one witness gave this number but she never said this at the time she
made her original statement in 1968. In 1992 Nina Rhodes told conspiracy
authors that she heard from 10-14 shots.

Most of the pantry witnesses described the gunshots in terms of a
'number of shots', 'a series of firecrackers', 'several shots' or 'a number of
shots in rapid succession'. Suzanne Locke said she heard '8 or 10' shots. Most
witnesses could not remember how many shots had been fired. However, of
those witnesses who ventured an opinion about how many shots had been
fired the vast majority put the number of shots at 8 or less, including:

Barbara Rubin – '3 shots followed by 5 quick shots'.
Lon Bruce Rubin – '6 shots'.
Charles Bailey – '5 shots'.
Jimmy Breslin – '4 or 5 shots'.
Stanley Kawalac – '4 shots'.
Robert Ray Breshears – '4 shots'.
Thomas Perez - '7 shots in about 3 seconds'.

Uno Timanson – '3 or 4 shots'.

Rafer Johnson -'I don't know how many shots, I couldn't count them to tell you the truth, but I know it was like four or five.'

There is also a fair amount of consistency amongst a number of witnesses as to the grouping of the shots – first one, two or three shots then a pause followed by a rapid succession of shots. Kristi Witker said, "People were running in all directions. . . . there were two very distinct series of pop-pop-pop . . . pop-pop-pop-pop-pop. Three pops, then five -eight in all. . . . I saw the gunman standing, pointing the gun and firing."

Bill Eppridge said that when he got to 'some doors that seemed small for the crowd' he heard two shots in very rapid succession–"Eppridge at first thought these were fireworks as they had been in Chinatown, San Francisco, the day before and there were many fireworks there. There was a pause after the second shot and people were scattering. Eppridge realized that what he thought were fireworks were actually shots. He ran forward instinctively thinking he had better count the shots. He counted a total of six shots."

(FBI interview with Bill Eppridge 19 June 68)

It is also clear from eyewitness testimony that, incredibly, no one saw this purported 'second shooter'. The pantry was small and the positioning of the people around RFK was well established by the investigations. Therefore the Discovery Channel expert's claim that Sirhan did not shoot the fatal RFK bullet, which was fired at point blank range, leaves only one suspect for the second gun - Thane Cesar - an innocent man.

7

CONTROVERSIES: THE WITNESSES

" ... time dissipates the shining ether, the solid angularity of fact."

—RALPH WALDO EMERSON

Numerous leads were followed during the Robert Kennedy assassination investigation, especially those that indicated conspiracy. The LAPD assassination investigation team, Special Unit Senator (SUS), was inundated with information from individuals and members of political groups claiming to have knowledge of Sirhan's conspiratorial activities prior to the assassination. Information suggesting a Mafia tie-in was anaylzed. Many men of Middle Eastern appearance, and who bore a slight resemblance to the assassin, were reported to the authorities. All leads and tips had to be tracked down, and this caused numerous cases of mistaken identity. However, nagging questions remained:

- How was Kennedy hit at point-blank range when not a single eyewitness saw the barrel of Sirhan's gun get closer than a foot and a half away from Kennedy's body?
- Why did witnesses see Sirhan with a mysterious girl in a polka-dot dress?
- Did co-conspirators meet with Sirhan in the days before the shooting?

The SUS had to investigate many reports by witnesses in the pantry and Embassy Ballroom who claimed to have seen Sirhan accompanied by co-conspirators. According to Lieutenant Higbie, who interviewed 433 people who had been connected in some way to the events of June 5, "Various individuals . . . made strong statements indicating that they saw Sirhan at the hotel accompanied by [others]. . . . Each individual was reinterviewed in depth and has either retracted . . . statements after they had been proven false, or . . . voluntarily modified . . . previous statements."[1] In hindsight the SUS realized they had contaminated their witnesses by gathering them together in a single room before questioning so that the witnesses were able to discuss the shooting among themselves. Many witnesses alleged they had seen things that they later admitted "they only heard."[2]

It became clear to the SUS investigators that further mistakes had been made in the initial period following the shooting:

- Police failed to rope off the crime scene area. This may have resulted in the loss of bullet fragments to souvenir hunters.
- Police failed to test fire the weapon held by Ace Security guard Thane Cesar, which could have conclusively proved that he did not shoot Kennedy as some conspiracy advocates alleged. Cesar volunteered to go to the Ramparts Police Station for questioning on the night of the shooting. Police checked his gun but did not retain it for ballistics testing.
- Kitchen employees were allowed to mop up the blood from the kitchen floor. This resulted in a loss of evidence that might have helped determine the direction of the shots.
- Special Investigation Division (SID) personnel were not called in immediately to take control of the crime scene.
- Police interrogators had not been adequately briefed. Some officers conducted interviews without having seen the pantry or an accurate floor plan.
- Key witnesses were not kept separate from the other witnesses, and many were interviewed by the news media before they talked to investigators.
- Vigorous investigations of former criminals who had a remote association with Sirhan, especially mob-connected Frank Donnarauma, who had met Sirhan when he was working as an exercise boy, were not conducted. Sirhan was accused of having been "a Zionist agent" and "a mafia-linked assassin"; the Los Angeles Police Department (LAPD) investigations into these connections were less than adequate.

Because many conspiracy writers have accused the LAPD of covering up a conspiracy, conspiracy advocates have concluded that Sirhan was used as a patsy. Some have accused the Central Intelligence Agency (CIA) of leading the conspiracy and have alleged that the LAPD and the Federal Bureau of Investigation (FBI) supported the Agency. Other conspiracy advocates have pointed the finger of guilt at the mob. As former LAPD Chief Daryl Gates observed, "The LAPD were [supposedly] a bunch of right-wingers. Other right-wingers [it was alleged] whom the police wanted to protect killed Kennedy. THAT was why we weren't at the Ambassador. We KNEW something was going to happen. Talk about being caught in a no-win situation. We're specifically asked to stay away, something happens, and we're accused of being part of it because we're not there."[3]

It was inevitable that the RFK assassination would be linked to conspiracy. After all, no assassination of a major U.S. political figure in the previous one hundred years had escaped suspicion that something more than the official version of the crime seemed likely. John Lawrence, who fired shots at President Andrew Jackson, was considered at the time to be part of a wider Whig conspiracy. Conspiratorial theories surrounding President Abraham Lincoln's assassination, which claim that Booth and his companions had assistance from leading figures in Lincoln's administration, still exist. Charles Guiteau, President James Garfield's assassin, was called innocent by his sister, who insisted that a member of the Stalwart faction of the Republican Party fired the fatal shot. Leon Czolgosz, President William McKinley's assassin, was widely believed to have been part of an anarchist conspiracy. In fact, leading members of anarchist groups were arrested at the time of McKinley's assassination because the authorities believed they conspired with the assassin. Giuseppe Zangara freely admitted he had intended to kill President Franklin Roosevelt but missed and killed Chicago Mayor Anton Cermak instead. Still, rumors persist that Chicago mobsters hired Zangara to kill Mayor Cermak. At the turn of the century, books and television documentaries persist in presenting "evidence" proving that the assassins of John F. Kennedy and Martin Luther King Jr. were innocent.

Almost from the start conspiracy advocates alleged that various individuals had been involved in a conspiracy to assassinate Robert Kennedy. The list of conspirators included:

- Thane Cesar, who allegedly fired the fatal shot as he stood behind RFK in the pantry. Cesar admittedly harbored anti-Kennedy sentiments and initially lied to investigators when they questioned him about a .22 pistol he owned.
- A girl wearing a polka-dot dress and two accomplices, who allegedly accompanied Sirhan at the Ambassador Hotel. The main source for

this allegation was Sandra Serrano, a Kennedy supporter present at the Ambassador who testified to observing three people, including the girl in the polka-dot dress escaping from the hotel and shouting, "We shot Kennedy!"

- Jerry Owen, an ex-convict who said his horse trailer was to be used as the conspirator's get-away vehicle.

- A "security guard" who Don Schulman said had fired shots at Kennedy.

- Photojournalist Khalid Khawar, who was identified as "Ali Ahmand," an Iranian secret agent, by conspiracy writer Robert Morrow.

- Khaiber Khan, who was described by Philip Melanson as "a CIA-linked Iranian espionage master working in the RFK campaign in Los Angeles."

Thane Eugene Cesar

At a Coalition on Political Assassinations (COPA) conference in 2002, Lawrence Teeter accused Ambassador Hotel security guard Thane Cesar of having assassinated Robert Kennedy. Teeter stated, "[Cesar] acknowledged that he led Senator Kennedy into the pantry—by the arm, he had hold of his arm, so he was in direct physical contact with him—and when Senator Kennedy turned to his left to shake hands with a busboy—Mr. Cesar grabbed his arm and pulled him back around, before bringing him forward. When the shooting began, Cesar acknowledges he dropped to the ground—which put him in a position to [fire at an upward angle]—and he pulled his gun drawn. Rosey Grier ordered him to put it away, so he did. What was he planning to do to Sirhan?" One witness saw Cesar fire his gun, Teeter said.[4]

Allegations that Cesar was involved in the shooting surfaced in the mid-1970s as conspiracy writers speculated about multiple assassins. The conspiracy theorists based their theories on a number of factors. The investigation of the shooting placed Sirhan in front of RFK at the time of the shooting. Because the fatal shot had been fired into the back of Kennedy's head, conspiracy advocates reasoned that a second shooter had to be firing from the rear. As the only person in the pantry who was known to have carried a weapon, Cesar became a prime candidate for the second shooter. According to conspiracy advocate Ted Charach, "The presidential candidate was murdered by a second gun—a uniformed unidentified gunman, firing four distinct shots from the rear at contact range. . . . The second gunman was a professional, functioning at the time as a private guard. . . . He fell down backwards, simultaneously with Kennedy, his double-action revolver out of his holster even as they fell."[5]

Twenty-six-year-old Thane Eugene Cesar worked on the assembly line at Lockheed Aircraft. Early in 1968 he had applied for the position of security guard at Ace Guard Service because he was desperate to earn extra money and the additional $3 an hour wage was enticing. He worked part time for Ace on occasion, and in the late afternoon on June 4 he received a call to report to the Ambassador Hotel for duty. Cesar said that he was called late because another guard had called at the last minute to say he could not show up for work and that he was not there as a "bodyguard" but for "crowd control." At 11:15 p.m. he was assigned to check credentials at the Colonial Room doorway and clear the way for the Kennedy entourage en route. As the crowd entered through the kitchen pantry food service area, he took up his duty and followed Senator Kennedy closely behind and to the right. Seconds later, when the shooting began, Cesar hit the floor and drew his weapon only as he began to get up. He insisted he did not fire it.

When Cesar was interviewed during a reinvestigation of the assassination by the Kranz committee in the mid-1970s, he was asked why he did not draw his gun to protect Senator Kennedy. Cesar replied, "I was a coward."[6] He also told investigators that he could have left the Ambassador without talking to anyone about the incident as no one seemed to be interested in taking his statement. He told LAPD officers that he had been inside the pantry at the time of the shooting, and they took him to Ramparts Police Station, where he was questioned. However, officers failed to examine his .38 pistol. Cesar also told the Kranz team that Ted Charach, who had filmed him for a documentary, *The Second Gun*, had taken his statements out of context and exaggerated them.[7]

Conspiracy advocates alleged that the only armed man witnesses saw close enough to Kennedy to fire and cause powder burns was Cesar. Did Cesar shoot RFK point-blank behind the ear while they were both standing, then fall to the floor and fire three more times?

For more than thirty-five years Cesar has had to live with the accusation that he was Robert Kennedy's real killer. Every anniversary of the assassination produced more allegations and "conclusive proof" that Cesar had lied about his involvement in the "conspiracy" and that he had been hired as the second gunman. Over time Cesar consulted two lawyers who both said he had an excellent case for libel action. However they refused to represent him as there was "no money in it." According to one lawyer, "The case you've got is with people who have no money."[8]

Dan Moldea researched Cesar's background thoroughly and found no sinister connections with groups or organizations that had an animus toward Robert Kennedy. Cesar was initially evasive when LAPD investigators questioned him about his political views. He was a supporter of 1968 presidential candidate George Wallace after the Watts Riots of 1965. He held radical right-wing views and disliked the Kennedys. He told Dan Moldea in 1987 that he had "no use for the Kennedy family. . . . I've read a lot of books on the Kennedy family and I think they're the biggest bunch of crooks that ever walked the earth."[9] However, Moldea found no evidence that Cesar had worked for the Mafia, the CIA, or billionaire Howard Hughes, and he had not worked as a freelance hit-man or been a member of a right-wing political organization—as conspiracy advocates alleged.[10]

Moldea also discovered that Cesar had never been a wealthy man, and there was no evidence that he had received any funds from conspirators. According to Moldea, "At the time of my first interview with him, Cesar had only $2,500 in his bank account and still owed the bulk of the $88,000 mortgage on his house. He owed $8,000 on a truck and $5,000 for another personal loan. Also, on December 9, 1986, Cesar married his third wife, Eleanor, a Filipino woman, and began taking care of her and helping to support her family."[11]

According to Thane Cesar, "No matter what anybody says or any report they come up with, you know, I know, I didn't do it. The police department knows I didn't do it. There're just a few people out there who want to make something out of something that isn't there—even though I know that some of the evidence makes me look bad."[12]

Moldea arranged for Edward Gelb, a former president and executive director of the American Polygraph Association who had over thirty years experience in the field, to give Cesar a polygraph test. According to Gelb, "Based upon the polygraph examination and its numerical scoring, Thane Eugene Cesar was telling the truth when he answered [questions about his alleged role in the shooting]. . . . In other words, Cesar did not fire a weapon the night Robert Kennedy was killed nor was he involved in a conspiracy to kill Kennedy."[13]

Accusing Cesar of being the second gunman seems ridiculous at the outset. He would have had to put his gun very close to Kennedy's head at the same time Sirhan was firing rapidly in his direction, and he would have ran a considerable risk of being shot. The Cesar-as-second-gunman theory is thus rendered highly improbable.

The Girl in the Polka-Dot Dress

At his trial Sirhan testified to feeling "quite high" (that is, intoxicated). He said that he had been afraid that he would've found himself in trouble if he had had any more liquor because no one at the Ambassador would have taken care of him. He decided to go home and walked to his car, which was parked a few blocks from the hotel. However, as Sirhan reached his car he decided he was too drunk to drive, so he returned to the Ambassador to "drink some coffee" and "sober up." He said he didn't remember picking up his gun, which was in the car's glove compartment. "I was in search of coffee. . . . I don't know where I found it, but eventually I found some coffee." He also later remembered that "somebody referred me to the kitchen for coffee." He poured coffee for a "beautiful girl" who wore a plain white dress, and "the next thing I remember . . . I was being choked."[14] Sirhan said, "This girl kept talking about coffee. She wanted cream. Spanish, Mexican, dark-skinned. When people talked about the girl in the polka-dot dress, maybe they were thinking of the girl I was having coffee with." Sirhan said he had wanted to take her on a date.[15]

For decades conspiracy theorists have posited that Sirhan was accompanied in the hotel by a pretty girl who wore a polka-dot dress and who might have been Sirhan's "controller" or "co-conspirator." Judith Groves, a political consulting firm employee who was in the lobby when the shooting occurred, heard three shots and saw a woman splattered with blood run out of the ballroom and a wounded man being carried through the lobby. She described going into the Embassy Ballroom through the Lautrec Room with the help of a "strange" man. She said that the man spoke to two women in a foreign language and that one of the women was wearing a polka-dot dress.[16]

Security guard Jack Merrit said he saw a girl in a "polka-dot dress" immediately prior to the shooting. Richard Houston, who was in the pantry at the time of the shooting, said he had seen a "girl in a black and white polka dot dress with ruffles around the neck." Houston said he heard the girl say, "We killed him," as she ran from the pantry.[17] Nurse Gloria Farr described seeing a man who bore a resemblance to Sirhan next to a woman wearing a "polka-dot scarf."[18]

George Green stated he had seen Sirhan standing near a woman wearing a polka-dot dress before he went to the Embassy Ballroom bar for drinks. Green gave two differing descriptions of the girl's dress—in one description he said it was a "white dress with black polka dots." In another description he said the girl was wearing a "dark dress, which may have had some type of white dots."[19]

A similar description of the girl was provided by Darnell Johnson and Booker T. Griffin. Johnson claimed to see the woman in the Embassy Ballroom both before and after RFK was shot. Griffin said he saw Sirhan standing eight to ten feet away from him in the Embassy Ballroom next to a woman who was wearing a dress "described by the media as polka dot. I can't say for sure but it had some color in it other than white." Griffin said the two "seemed out of place."[20]

Other witnesses said Sirhan had been in the Embassy Ballroom next to a "girl wearing a dress with polka dots." Lonny L. Worthy said he saw Sirhan during the evening in the Ambassador standing next to a woman and he thought they were together. Kennedy volunteer Susan Locke said she had observed a "suspicious-looking" woman wearing a polka-dot dress in the Embassy Ballroom prior to RFK's speech. Locke said the woman seemed "out of place" and "expressionless" in the midst of the celebrations for RFK's California primary victory. She said the woman wore a "white dress with blue polka dots."[21]

The SUS spent some considerable time trying to track the mysterious girl down and searched the news film archives in their attempts to find photographic evidence of her existence. None was forthcoming.

Some of the accomplice-related reports might have originated with a couple who were filmed in the Embassy Ballroom shortly before the shooting. The present author recently discovered the one-second still from news broadcast film footage taken that night. It clearly shows a girl in a polka-dot dress accompanied by a man who looks like Sirhan. The girl is definitely "pretty" as some witnesses described her. And she has dark hair that fits the description given in a number of reports. Some reports refer to "Sirhan and the girl" looking "out of place" and appearing rather "grim" at the time the crowd around them was cheering. While the film clip shows the girl in the polka-dot dress looking joyous, the man who shows some resemblance to the young Sirhan does indeed look rather "grim." Further film footage reveals this same man to be in the Embassy Ballroom immediately following the shooting. (See photo insert.)

The allegations that the girl in a polka-dot dress was Sirhan's accomplice mainly arose, however, from statements made by a Kennedy campaign supporter, Sandra Serrano, who was sitting on an external staircase outside of the Ambassador's Embassy Ballroom. This story of a girl with Sirhan was also supported by pantry eyewitness Vincent DiPierro and Police Sergeant Sharaga who said a couple, "the Bernsteins," also observed a girl shouting, "We shot him!" DiPierro, the son of the Ambassador's maitre d', said he saw a pretty girl wearing a polka-dot dress standing next to Sirhan seconds before the shooting. DiPierro later identified the girl as Valerie Schulte.[22] Schulte had been wearing a bright green dress with yellow polka dots, was pretty and blonde, and as DiPierro stated, had a "pug-nose."[23]

On June 7, 1968, FBI Special Agent Richard C. Burris interviewed

Serrano at her home, 2212 North Marengo Street, Altadena, California. Serrano said she left the Embassy Ballroom at 11:30 p.m. and went outside to sit on a stairway that led to the ballroom. She sat on the fifth or sixth step. Two or three minutes after she took a seat she said a woman and two men, one of whom she later identified as Sirhan, started up the stairs. The woman, as she approached Serrano, said, "Excuse us," and Serrano moved to the side so the three could pass. Approximately half an hour later, she heard noises that sounded like a car backfire, and one of the men and the woman ran down the stairs shouting, "We shot him! We shot him!" Serrano asked, "Who did you shoot?" and the woman replied, "Senator Kennedy."[24] Serrano immediately returned to the Embassy Ballroom and asked an unidentified guard if Kennedy had been shot. The guard told her she must have been drinking. She next phoned her parents who lived in Ohio. She said she was crying and hysterical. After telling a few close friends what she had witnessed, she was asked by a television crew if she would like to tell her story. Later, Agent Burris took Serrano to the Embassy Ballroom and told her, "On television, with Sandy Vanocur, you didn't say anything about seeing a girl and two men going *up* the fire stairs. You only said you saw a girl and a man coming *down*. And later you told the police you saw two men and a girl going up together *and one of them was Sirhan Sirhan.* That was the most significant thing you had to tell the police and yet you didn't say anything about this in your first interview, your interview on television." Serrano said, "I can't explain why."[25]

On June 8, 1968, the FBI questioned Serrano's parents, Manuel and Amparo Serrano, who said their daughter did not say anything to them about a girl saying, "We shot Kennedy." Her mother recalled that Serrano had said, "Why would they do anything like this?"[26] When asked why she did not mention her story to her mother, Sandra Serrano gave the weak excuse that she had always had trouble talking to her mother.[27]

When Sander Vanocur interviewed Serrano on television shortly after the shooting, she reported that she had heard shots. This prompted the LAPD to conduct sound tests. The sound tests proved that Serrano could not have heard shots fired in the Ambassador's pantry from where she sat on the outside steps.[28] The distance from the pantry to the stairs, which were situated on the outer wall of the opposite end of the Embassy Ballroom, was approximately one hundred yards. There were a number of doors, curtains, and walls between the two points. Serrano, although initially implying the sound of "backfires" were likely shots, said she had been misquoted and insisted she heard only "backfires."[29]

For thirty-five years conspiracy advocates have used Serrano's story as proof of a conspiracy. Although the LAPD maintained that she retracted her story under intense questioning, conspiracy theorists said she had been bullied into saying her story was false. LAPD Sergeant Hernandez gave Serrano a polygraph test on June 20, 1968. Asked if she was sitting on the stairway at the time of the shooting, she replied, "Yeah, I think I did. . . . People messed me up . . . stupid people . . . just in all the commotion and everything. . . . I was supposed to know more than I knew. . . . I told [District Attorney staffer John Ambrose] I heard the people say 'We shot him' or 'They shot him' or something. And I remember telling him that I had seen these people on the . . . on the stairway."[30] According to the LAPD Summary Report, "Polygraph examination disclosed that Serrano has never seen Sirhan Sirhan in person; further, that Miss Serrano fabricated, for some unknown reason, the story about the girl in the polka-dot dress. Responses to relevant questions indicate that no one made statements to Miss Serrano telling her that they had shot Kennedy or that she heard any gunshots during the late evening of June 4 or early morning of June 5, 1968. Miss Serrano was informed of the results of the polygraph examination."[31]

Hernandez's methods of interrogation during the polygraph examination were indeed forceful and intimidating, but they were not designed to cover up the possible involvement of conspirators in RFK's shooting. Police Lieutenant Emmanuel Pena, Hernandez's superior officer, said, "[The interrogation by Sergeant Hernandez] was a necessary move on my part. We tried every way in the world to find this gal in the polka-dot dress to see if we could substantiate her [Serrano's] story. And we couldn't do it. I wasn't about to leave the case hanging there."[34]

Furthermore, Hernandez's intense methods were not confined solely to witnesses who suggested conspiracy. He used the same approach with Munir Sirhan, who did not say anything in his interviews that indicated conspiracy. Hernandez simply tried to make Munir understand the gravity of his answers and to coax him to tell the truth about the purchase of the gun. "Let me tell you something now," Hernandez told Munir, "what has happened here is a tragedy to your family as well as the family of Senator Kennedy. . . . Please don't fabricate anything. Please tell me the truth . . . because the truth will be found out. . . . And I know that you are fabricating right now [about your involvement in the purchase of the gun]. . . . Now Munir, I want you to be aware that this investigation, 20 years from now . . . that somebody's going to be reading about Senator Kennedy. So please, I'll ask you again . . . don't become involved in this thing by telling something that you know is not the truth."[33]

Despite this evidence to the contrary, conspiracy advocates claim that both Hernandez and Pena had close connections to intelligence agencies, thus implying that the LAPD officers conspired to cover up a conspiracy to murder RFK. Pena's response to this allegation was, "I didn't come back [to the LAPD] . . . as a sneak to be planted. The way they [the conspiracy writers] have written it, it sounds like I was brought back and put into the [Kennedy] case as a plant by the CIA, so that I could steer something around to a point where no one would discover a conspiracy. That's not so."[34] Furthermore, to suggest that Sergeant Hernandez and Lieutenant Pena were involved in a cover-up would also implicate Robert Houghton, who had recommended the appointment of Hernandez to the SUS team.[35]

Hernandez asked Serrano during the polygraph test if, sometime following the shooting, when she heard "a kid" mention something about a white dress and polka dots, she replied "right." Asked if she got the idea of the girl in a polka-dot dress from this interaction she answered, "I don't know." Her responses to test questions about the girl indicated deception.[36] Serrano and DiPierro were together at the police station before they were interviewed by police. When DiPierro was interviewed by Sergeant Hernandez during a polygraph examination, he admitted he probably got the idea of a girl in a polka-dot dress from Serrano. DiPierro said, "She stated that there was this girl that was wearing a polka dot dress came running down, I guess it was the hallway, saying that 'We shot him,' and . . . she . . . you know, we started asking each other questions about the girl, and evidently I went along with what she said as being a person that I imagine that I saw."

DiPierro admitted that he saw "one girl [during the night] . . . that was in there that night with a pug-nose." This girl was likely Valerie Schulte, who had been standing five feet behind RFK when the shooting occurred. She said she was also standing near the tray stacker that Sirhan crouched by before he began shooting. In the chaos that followed the shooting—camera flashes, bright TV lighting—it would have been easy to mistake the color of Schulte's dress. "There was so much confusion that night," DiPierro said.[37] At the trial defense lawyer Grant Cooper asked DiPierro what caused him to notice Sirhan. DiPierro replied, "There was a girl standing in the area [of the pantry]." He said the girl was pretty, and when shown a photograph of Valerie Schulte, he confirmed that she was the girl in question.[38]

Serrano eventually admitted that she fabricated her story for "two reasons, so I didn't look like a fool, which I look like now. Another reason, because everybody figures . . . you know . . . I was sitting there [in the police station] hearing . . . descriptions of these people. Oh God, no, maybe that's what I'm supposed to see . . . more than I did. It messed me up, that's all, and I figured, well, they must know what they're doing—I mean, they are police, after all. They have to know what they're doing."[39]

Serrano's story involved inherent implausibilities from the beginning:

- Serrano's account was contradicted by fire department captain Cecil R. Lynch, who was on duty at the Ambassador checking fire escapes and exits. He had inspected the stairs Serrano claimed she had been sitting on. He said no one was on the stairs at the time she indicated. And, incredibly, she said she had sat on the stairway for fifty minutes.[40]

- Serrano was a Kennedy campaign worker who would have been naturally thrilled at the prospect of her candidate claiming victory in the most important primary of the election campaign. Yet she did not remain in the Embassy Ballroom at a crucial time, a time when nearly every campaign worker was awaiting the arrival of Kennedy to give his victory speech. No one could predict when Kennedy would appear in the ballroom to give his speech, but election officials knew it would be at some point between 11:30 p.m. and 12:30 a.m.

- It is illogical that someone who has been part of a conspiracy would immediately afterward shout out about their involvement. How would they be sure members of the public wouldn't take them seriously and have police apprehend them before they could escape the scene?

Serrano's story that Sirhan was accompanied by a young woman seemed to gain credence when investigators interviewed barman Albert LeBeau. On May 20, Kennedy visited Robbie's Restaurant in Pomona, a town that is part of suburban Los Angeles. Hundreds turned up for the event, and LeBeau was assigned to take tickets at the foot of the stairs leading to the second-floor restaurant. LeBeau said a person he identified as Sirhan had appeared with a woman that night and asked if he could enter even though he did not have tickets for the event. He let them go up. However, no one else in the restaurant who was interviewed by police could recall seeing Sirhan. A Latin-looking man who was similar in appearance to Sirhan appears in some photos taken that day. When LeBeau was asked to look at a photo lineup he failed to identify Sirhan. When investigators asked him if he could swear that the man he saw was Sirhan, he said he could not be certain.[41]

Defense investigator and author Robert Blair Kaiser believed LeBeau was telling the truth and that the young restaurant worker had correctly identified Sirhan standing with a female accomplice. Kaiser believed LeBeau's account because it was partly corroborated by two others at the restaurant.[42] However, Kaiser did not consider the alternative implications of LeBeau's story, assuming LeBeau was correct. Sirhan might have met the girl in the hours before the rally began and invited her to join him. He might not have mentioned this to his lawyers because he denied being there in the first place as his presence would have been more evidence of his stalking of Kennedy. Second, he might not have wanted to involve an innocent girl, whose acquaintance he had made just that night. It seems illogical for a conspirator to risk exposure in a place where newspaper photographers are present. Had the woman appeared in any of the photographs taken that night and had Sirhan succeeded in shooting Kennedy there and then, her relationship to Sirhan would have endangered the purported conspiracy.

As the years passed, discussion about the girl in a polka-dot dress refused to die down as Serrano stuck by her original story when she was interviewed by conspiracy writers, claiming she had been forced to retract her original statements. The girl's association with Sirhan could neither be proved nor disproved, as it rested on Serrano's word alone.

Yet a few possible explanations for Serrano's story do not rely on a conspiracy theory. Michael Wayne, a young man who bore some resemblance to Sirhan, asked RFK to autograph a poster he was holding when the senator made his way to the stage for his victory speech. Wayne ran out of the pantry with the rolled up poster when the shooting started and was mistaken for an assailant. Dennis Weaver, an Orange County Democratic registration drive coordinator, later told police that friends who accompanied him said Wayne had a gun.[43] A security guard handcuffed Wayne and turned him over to the police. A crowd of people assumed he was the assassin or an accomplice. As it turned out, Wayne was running for a telephone.[44] Cathy Fulmer, who was in the pantry at the time of the shooting, also became scared when Sirhan started firing and ran out of the pantry. She cried out, "Kennedy was shot!" Fulmer also said she had a conversation with a "stranger," later identified as Sirhan, shortly before the shooting began.[45] She wore a white dress with a polka-dot scarf,[46] and she may be the girl Richard Houston allegedly saw running from the pantry shouting "We shot him!" Fulmer was likely also the girl standing next to Sirhan whom Nurse Farr described.

There is certainly some evidence in the FBI files that confirms Serrano may have been telling the truth after all—or at least a version of the truth. Serrano told investigators that the emergency fire stairs she had sat on were located on the south side of the Ambassador Ballroom. Large double doors opened on to the stairway from a hallway adjacent to the Ambassador Room. From this doorway the stairs went down to ground level and up to double fire doors leading into the Embassy Room, which was located directly above the Ambassador Room.

According to the FBI files Geraldine Agnes McCarthy, a Kennedy supporter, had given a statement to FBI agents, which described her activities at the time of the shooting. She had been with members of her family in the Ambassador Ballroom. The party consisted of Geraldine McCarthy, Margaret McCarthy, Winnie Marshall, Mary Towley, Eileen Anderson, Phil Litroh, Chris Marshall, and Paul Benedict. They were waiting for the final election results and the victory speech by RFK. McCarthy said she and her family had been participating in the festivities and had been singing and dancing on the stage in the Ambassador Ballroom with the other celebrants. Shortly after midnight on June 5, 1968, she and several members of her family left the stage of the Ambassador Ballroom and went to a small alcove to the left of the stage and near the rear of the ballroom. This alcove had access to a stairway leading up to the Embassy Room and also had access to an outside door opening onto the Wilshire Street parking lot of the hotel. She stated that immediately outside this doorway to the parking lot there was a fire escape leading down from the floor above.

McCarthy and several members of her family were in this alcove attempting to get a breath of fresh air when several people came down the stairway from above and a girl in an orange dress stated "Kennedy has been shot." Shortly after that a girl in a "beige dress with black dots" came down the outside fire escape and exclaimed, "Oh my God, Kennedy's been shot." Geraldine McCarthy told FBI agents that at no time did she hear anyone make the statement, "We've shot Kennedy." She stated that several more people came down the stairway of the fire escape and she asked them questions, attempting to verify what they had heard, and it became apparent to her that RFK actually had been shot. She said that things became very confused and that within a short time the police began to request all those who were not directly involved to leave the building very quickly and calmly. She stated that at this time she and her family left the building and returned to their home in Sherman Oaks. (FBI interview with Geraldine Agnes McCarthy 24 June 1968, RFK-LA-56-156-SUB X-03-VOL 10)

McCarthy's story was confirmed by a family member, Mrs. Winnie Theresa Marshall, who lived in Hollywood. Marshall told FBI agents the family were on the stage most of the evening singing Kennedy songs and generally mixing with the crowd. She stated that at about "11:50 p.m. or midnight" her husband Chris had left the stage and moved to a smaller sideroom. She stated that while he was going to this other room he passed a fire escape area. She stated that while he was near the fire escape either her husband or Geraldine McCarthy, who had accompanied him, observed a girl and a young man come down the fire escape shouting, "They've shot him."

Marshall stated that Geraldine McCarthy had told her the girl had worn a polka dot dress and had been saying, "Kennedy has been shot." (FBI interview with Winnie Theresa Marshall, 27 June 1968 RFK-LA-56-156-SUB X-03-VOL 10)

Given this "new" evidence it is clear that if indeed Serrano had been telling the truth she had clearly been mistaken in alleging the girl in the polka dot dress shouting "We shot him."

Plus, there had been considerable opportunity that night for alcohol-fueled friction between thousands of liberal RFK and Alan Cranston supporters and thousands of right-wing Max Rafferty supporters. This might have led some Rafferty supporters to express momentary joy at the attack on Senator Kennedy. An FBI report reveals that, on the night of the shooting, a group of young people were handing out redish-orange bumper stickers with black lettering in the hotel lobby. According to Ambassador Hotel security chief William F. Gardner, the stickers made reference to JFK's death. New York reporter Jimmy Breslin believes the stickers said, "Expose the Kennedy Death Hoax." Moldea believes the bumper sticker report is crucial as it shows that anti-Kennedy activists were at the Ambassador that night and might have been the source of the gleeful cries that Serrano said she heard.[47] Serrano might also have been witness to an innocent cry of "We [i.e., the American people] shot Kennedy!" a natural response reflecting the intense concern Americans had at that time to the growing senseless violence that had become a societal phenomenon during the 1960s. Furthermore, the reports of a girl shouting "We shot him!" might be explained by comments made by a pantry witness, Los Angeles Schools employee Ralph Williams, who was outside the kitchen door at the time of the shooting. Williams described a girl who left the kitchen saying, "We've got him, we've got him," followed by another woman who described the first woman as "her crazy daughter."[48]

Jerry Owen

The most complicated and time-consuming allegations of conspiracy came from Oliver Brindley Owen, aka Jerry Owen, a former boxing prize fighter turned "minister," whose conspiracy allegations were promoted by William Turner and Jon Christian in their 1978 book *The Assassination of Robert F. Kennedy: The Conspiracy and Cover-Up*. At a Coalition on Political Assassinations conference in 2002, Turner stated,

> After the shooting, a fundamentalist preacher named Jerry Owen, who billed himself as the "walking Bible" because he

had memorized all 3,600 verses, surfaced to say that he had picked up Sirhan hitchhiking the day before [the assassination], arranged to sell him a horse, and was told to be at the back entrance of the Ambassador Hotel the following night at 11:30 with the horse for delivery. I interviewed Owen and concluded his story was fictitious, that he was telling it to put an innocent face on a pre-existing relationship with Sirhan. Our investigation verified that Owen and Sirhan had been seen together at the preacher's ranch. One of these witnesses reported Owen as saying RFK had to be killed because he would stop the Vietnam War and God would be angry.[49]

Owen was fifty-five at the time of the assassination. He volunteered his story about Sirhan to police after he saw Sirhan's photo in a newspaper the day after the assassination.

Oliver Brindley "Jerry" Owen was born in Ohio, and after leaving University of California–Los Angeles he became a sparring partner for ex-heavyweight boxer Max Baer. He claimed he had been an ordained minister since 1937 yet retracted this statement when interviewed by the SUS at the San Francisco Police Department headquarters. He told the police that his "ordainment" had consisted of living in a hotel room for a couple of days during which time he "prayed." Police discovered he had a history of "various suspicious and illegal activities." He was arrested on suspicion of robbery in 1930 but was released. He was involved in several paternity and extramarital investigations and had made insurance claims for six fires in his "church" properties. One insurance claim was denied because of fraud. In 1963 he was arrested in Cosa Mesa, California, on a fugitive warrant from Tucson, Arizona, for arson with the intent to defraud an insurance company. He was convicted of three counts of arson and sentenced to serve eight to ten years in prison. His case was successfully appealed in 1966. Several police informants called him a "confidence man," and he had used his evangelical position to seduce a number of women over the years.[50]

Jerry Owen volunteered information to the LAPD that he had met Sirhan and "another Mexican-looking kid" as they were hitchhiking for a ride in downtown Los Angeles at 6:00 p.m. on Monday, June 3. Owen said he took them up Wilshire Boulevard to Vermont, where they got out of the car and spoke to a tall dark man and a nineteen- or twenty-year-old girl with long dirty blonde hair. Sirhan purportedly returned to the vehicle and asked for a ride to Hollywood. Sirhan allegedly told Owen he was an exercise boy and wanted to buy a horse. Owen then purportedly offered to sell him one and agreed on a sale price of $250.[51]

Owen dropped Sirhan off at the Ambassador for ten minutes before they headed for the Hollywood Ranch Market. Sirhan promised to pay Owen for the horse, but Sirhan's "friends" turned up instead to give Owen a down payment. Sirhan told Owen he would give him the rest of the money at a meeting behind the Ambassador Hotel the following night, Tuesday, June 4. In interviews with police officers in San Francisco and Los Angeles, Owen lied about his prison record and failed to identify Sirhan in a group of ten photographs.[52]

Apart from lying about his prison record, Owen made frequent embellishments to his story, including telling police that his horse trailer was to be used as the conspirators' "getaway vehicle." According to SUS member Gordon McDevitt, "When Owen said 'I picked Sirhan up,' we couldn't ignore a statement like that. We had to run it down. Time and again, we picked away at every detail of everything Owen said, and anyone who saw him or said they saw him. The investigation of his story finally petered out. We just concluded that this guy was full of bullshit. He was a terrible waste of time that we couldn't ignore, because he was saying sensational things. We couldn't just say, 'This guy's a nut' and then ignore him."[53]

The SUS eventually found witnesses who challenged Owen's story. According to the LAPD Summary Report, the police proved that Owen had not only been inconsistent with his story but had also lied about many events that allegedly occurred. The SUS finally concluded that Owen, for one reason or another, was a confabulator, liar, and publicity seeker.[54]

Don Schulman

Don Schulman worked for KNXT-TV in Los Angeles as a news runner and was present in the pantry when the shooting started. Immediately following the shooting he was interviewed by Jeff Brent of Continental Broadcasting:

BRENT: I'm talking to Don Schulman. Don can you give us a halfway decent report of what happened within all this chaos?

SCHULMAN: OK I was ... ah ... standing behind ... ah ... Kennedy as he was taking his assigned route into the kitchen. A Caucasian gentleman stepped out and fired three times ... the security guard ... hit Kennedy all three times. Mr. Kennedy slumped to the floor.... They carried him away. ... The security guards fired back. ... As I saw ... they shot the ... ah ... man who shot Kennedy ... in the leg. ... He ... ah before they could get him he shot a ... it looked to me ... he shot a woman ... and he shot two other men. They then proceeded to carry Kennedy into the kitchen and ... I don't know how his condition is now.

BRENT: Was he grazed or did it appear to be a direct hit? Was it very serious from what you saw?

SCHULMAN: Well . . . from what I saw . . . it looked . . . fairly serious. He had . . . he was definitely hit three times. Things happened so quickly that . . . that . . . there was another eyewitness standing next to me and she is in shock now and very fuzzy . . . as I am . . . because it happened so quickly.

BRENT: Right. I was about six people behind the senator. I heard six or seven shots in succession. . . . Now . . . is this the security guard firing back?

SCHULMAN: Yes . . . a . . . the man who stepped out fired three times at Kennedy . . . hit him all three times . . . and the security guard then fired back . . . hitting . . .

BRENT: Right.

SCHULMAN: Hitting him, and he is in apprehension.[55]

Minutes later Schulman was interviewed by KNXT's Ruth Ashton Taylor. In this interview he said, "Well, I was standing behind him, directly behind him [RFK]. I saw a man pull out a gun. It looked like he pulled it out from his pocket and shot three times. I saw all three shots hit the Senator. Then I saw the Senator fall and he was picked up and carried away. I saw the—also saw the security men pull out their weapons. After then it was very very fuzzy."[56]

In 1971 Schulman said he did not see Sirhan shoot Kennedy, but he insisted that he saw the "security guard" fire his gun. He also saw wounds erupting on Kennedy's body but refused to make any connection to the two events. In subsequent years Schulman never again said he saw a security guard fire his weapon.

In the mid-1970s Thomas Kranz questioned Schulman. Schulman told Kranz that immediately following the shooting he was "tremendously confused" and that the words he used to describe the shooting to reporters in 1968 were the result of "confusion." Schulman reported that he meant to tell reporters that "Kennedy had been hit three times, he had seen an arm fire, he had seen the security guards with guns, but he had never seen a security guard fire and hit Robert Kennedy."[57]

From Schulman's original reports conspiracy advocates began to construct a second-gun scenario, a scenario built on confused statements made just upon emerging from the chaos that enveloped the pantry area the night of the shooting. The scenario gained merit when filmmaker Ted Charach said that Cesar pulled his gun before he fell to the ground during the shooting, thus giving Schulman's original statement that a guard had fired his gun some credibility. Yet Thane Cesar never said he had pulled his gun at that time. Cesar had drawn his pistol only after he had gotten off the ground. Further, Ace Security guard Jack Merrit entered the pantry, with his gun drawn, immediately after the shooting, thus adding to the confusion. Merrit had been in the hall outside the Embassy Ballroom when the shooting began, and when he entered the pantry, he could see Kennedy aides apprehending Sirhan, against a metal table, and RFK lying on the floor.

To further add suspicion to Schulman's "sightings," the news runner might not have even been in the pantry area at the time of the shooting. According to Dan Moldea, Robert Blair Kaiser has stated that KNXT-TV employees Frank Raciti and Dick Gaither said Schulman was standing with them, inside the Embassy Ballroom.[58]

Khalid Iqbal Khawar

In its April 4, 1989, issue, *Globe* magazine published a story that implicated Khalid Khawar in Robert Kennedy's assassination. The article gave an abbreviated summary of Robert Morrow's book *The Senator Must Die* (1988) in which the author accused Khawar of being an Iranian intelligence agent and of being present at the Ambassador Hotel on the night of June 5 as a conspirator involved in the Kennedy shooting. The *Globe* article included a photograph from the Morrow book showing a group of men standing near Kennedy as the senator gave his victory speech in the Embassy Ballroom. *Globe* enlarged the image of these men and added an arrow to one of them identifying him as, in reality, the notorious assassin, Ali Ahmand.

When the *Globe* published its article, Khawar was a naturalized American citizen living with his wife and children in Bakersfield, California, where he owned and operated a farm. On reading the article, Khawar became angry that he had been implicated in the assassination. Shortly after the story appeared in the *Globe*, Khawar received threatening phone calls and his property was vandalized.

In August 1989 Khalid Khawar sued the *Globe* and Morrow, insisting he was not the person identified by Morrow as Ali Ahmand. The evidence at the trial showed that in June 1968, when Kennedy was assassinated, Khawar was a Pakistani citizen and a freelance photojournalist on assignment at the Ambassador for a Pakistani magazine. He stood on the stage near RFK in the Embassy Ballroom so that a friend could photograph him with Kennedy. When Kennedy left the podium, Khawar did not follow him, and he was still in the Embassy Ballroom when Kennedy was shot. Both the FBI and the LAPD questioned Khawar about the assassination, but neither agency ever regarded him as a suspect.

The trial revealed that Morrow's allegations against Khawar were false and that the *Globe's* article was not "an accurate and neutral report of the statements and charges made in the Morrow book." Khawar was awarded damages of $1.2 million.[59]

Khaibar Khan

Khaibar Khan was an Iranian playboy who had spent a lot of time in May 1968 at Kennedy's Los Angeles campaign headquarters. He offered his services and those of his many Middle Eastern friends to help Kennedy get elected. RFK campaign worker, Eleanor Severson, told investigators that Khan had come into Kennedy campaign headquarters on May 30, 1968, to register for campaign work. From that time he turned up every day until the California primary election. On June 2 he arrived with four Middle Eastern helpers to work as volunteers. Everson said Sirhan was one of the men who accompanied Khan. Campaign workers Larry Strick and Estelle Sterns confirmed this account.[60]

Later Strick retracted his identification of Sirhan, and the SUS team decided Sterns had been exaggerating her story, especially when she said that Sirhan and another one of Khan's Middle Eastern friends had been carrying guns. The SUS also concluded that Severson and others could have easily misidentified one of Khan's friends as Sirhan because the group of men had similar Middle Eastern features. No credible evidence exists to tie Sirhan in with this group despite the attempts by conspiracy advocates to brand Khan as a "CIA" ally and an Iranian agent.

Frank Donnarauma and the Mafia Connection

Allegations that Sirhan had been on the Mafia's payroll arose when investigators discovered that one of Sirhan's associates at the racetrack where he worked was Frank Donnarauma, formerly Henry Ronald Ramistella, who might have been connected to the Mob. Ramistella was at the scene of Sirhan's horse-riding accident in September 1966. The LAPD discovered that Ramistella had been involved in petty crime and had also had his jockey license revoked in New Jersey after he provided false testimony to track stewards.

Ramistella changed his name to Frank Donnarauma after having had his license revoked. Under his alias he had applied and been accepted for his hot-walker license at Santa Anita. However, when track officials discovered he had lied about his identity, his license was again revoked.

Sirhan admitted he knew Ramistella but did not know that the name Frank Donnarauma was an alias. Sirhan told Dan Moldea, "Frank always seemed to be having financial problems, which probably stemmed from his gambling. He was a heavy gambler. . . . I knew nothing about [his criminal record]."[61]

The FBI investigated Ramistella and found no connection to organized crime or any evidence that he had played a part in the Robert Kennedy assassination. Despite these facts some conspiracy writers have attempted to tie the Mafia to the assassination, providing a motive but no concrete evidence that RFK's Mob enemies were behind the shooting.

The Mafia had good reason to want RFK out of the way. As the U.S. attorney general in the early 1960s, Kennedy had vigorously prosecuted teamster boss Jimmy Hoffa as well as numerous leaders of organized crime. However, it is unlikely that the Mafia would have attempted to assassinate Kennedy because were it to fail in the attempt the consequences would have been devastating. This is precisely why the Mob does not go after judges, law enforcement officials, and other politicians: it knows that if it were implicated in a high-level assassination the government's whole strength would be released on it. When in the 1940s senior Mafia boss Albert Anastasia proposed the murder of Thomas Dewey, then a highly effective anti-crime prosecutor in New York and subsequently a Republican presidential candidate in 1948, the Mob opted to murder Anastasia rather than risk the troubles that Dewey's assassination would have brought upon its head. An even more effective prosecutor, Rudolph Giuliani, U.S. attorney for the Southern District of New York and then mayor of New York City, similarly remained unscathed throughout his career.

The mysterious would-be assassins in hypothetical conspiracies must realize that the odds are heavily stacked against them. Men intelligent and capable enough to plan and carry out Kennedy's assassination had to be aware that one slight mistake would cause the whole plot to come crashing down. Whatever benefits the conspirators gained, they must have made efforts to find some simpler, less risky path to the same goal. The plain fact is that criminal groups like the Mob can find much more effective and secure ways of dealing with politicians who become thorns in their sides. One can organize public campaigns, give money to opponents, or attempt "blackmail." As most Mafia bosses have, at one time or another, concluded: killing a politician who has become disagreeable is "suicidal."

■ ■ ■

The SUS, the FBI, and other government agencies involved in the investigation of Robert Kennedy's murder found that reports about others' involvement in the crime led nowhere. The agencies acknowledged some shortcomings in the investigations. However, they had to deal with the stories of liars, opportunists, adventure seekers, and publicity seekers; as in previous investigations in the history of law enforcement, the SUS was frequently led astray. As its summary report concluded,

> The notoriety which accompanied the assassination and the mystery surrounding Sirhan's character and background made the subject of conspiracy fertile ground for evoking unusual responses from the general public. Opportunists, political adventurers and publicity seekers came forward to volunteer that they had seen or spoken to Sirhan or that they had information which was valuable to the investigation. Investigations were made into each allegation with generally negative results. The majority of the persons making the allegations were found to be lying for one reason or another. Many were found to be using the assassination to further their own private cause or to enhance their position among their associates.[62]

The RFK assassination investigation was remiss in failing to rigorously pursue every allegation of conspiracy, without time limits. Despite these shortcomings, the passage of time has strengthened rather than weakened the position the LAPD took at the conclusion of their investigation. For thirty-five years no credible "plotter" or "credible witness" has come forward to show that a conspiracy was responsible for Kennedy's murder. In an era when thousands of people who have been connected to every imaginable scandal negotiate fees for their stories, it is logical to assume that no such plotter exists.

8

DISTORTED TRUTHS

"Conspiracy theories offer much to believers. If slippery in their logic and often careless of facts and assumptions, they order the random and make consistent the paradoxical. Theories find purpose in tragedy and clarity in ambiguity."

—ROBERT ALAN GOLDBERG

A child dies from some unexplained illness; fisherman sail off never to return; random violence takes the life of an innocent bystander. And always behind these tragic events lies the question, Why? Confusion occurs because it is human nature to find order in chaos and to seek truth. Where we cannot find truth, we must invent it because that too is human nature. Believing in conspiracies and rejecting coincidences is more comforting than facing up to the fact that some things just happen.

Genuine concerns about the integrity of the police investigation of the assassination surfaced after Robert Kennedy's murder. Some pieces of the puzzle simply did not fit, and thus it was inevitable that some concerned citizens would question why and how such a charismatic and popular politician was assassinated. And, because the shooting was followed by chaos and turmoil, reconstructing the events to make sense of what happened was extremely difficult. The RFK murder investigation was also made difficult by the voluminous amount of evidence in the case. Thousands of people followed the case and were able, through their collective consciousness, to select different pieces of the puzzle to construct numerous arguments rebutting the official conclusion. As William Buckley wrote, "If O.J. [Simpson] was found not guilty, why can't everybody be found not guilty?"[1] Despite the overwhelming evidence against Sirhan, some conspiracy advocates use tactics similar to those used by O.J.'s defense team—e.g., discrediting witnesses, pouring scorn on scientific evidence, and otherwise building a smokescreen to hide the assassin's guilt—to allege that Sirhan is innocent.

Some answers to the questions surrounding RFK's murder were never found, investigators made many mistakes, and the American public had unrealistic expectations that the case would be orderly, pristine, perfect. In the chaos of the moment, many Ambassador Hotel eyewitnesses gave conflicting stories about what occurred when Sirhan fired his gun. The Los Angeles Police Department (LAPD) did not secure the crime scene very well. Police officers did not handle the physical evidence in the case in the way they were supposed to. However, instead of concluding that all bureaucracies are fraught with imperfect methods, conspiracy advocates pointed the finger of suspicion at unknown "conspirators" and accused the LAPD and the Federal Bureau of Investigation (FBI) of a deliberate cover-up. Conspiracy theories about the Robert Kennedy assassination took off.

The faulty memories of eyewitnesses to the assassination compounded the problem of conspiracy theories. People are programmed to find patterns and solve mysteries, and this tendency increases when they are presented with danger. Observers of the Kennedy assassination tried to impose some sense of order on the chaos that followed Sirhan's first shot. When Sirhan began shooting, bullets ricocheted and bounced off ceiling tiles, creating echoes of the shots that reverberated throughout the pantry. Naturally, to explain the din, several observers suggested a second shooter was present. But, in this case, the only credible witness to a second shooter, out of approximately seventy-seven people in the pantry, was Don Schulman, who said he had seen Thane Cesar fire his gun. As we read in chapter 7, Schulman's memory was faulty, and he changed his story following his initial reports to the news media.

The U.S. Army first recognized the inaccuracy of eyewitness testimony in the midst of the chaos and turmoil of war. Many of its reports about battles have shown that it is extraordinarily difficult to make sense of a battle until the following day, after the soldiers have had a chance to experience a good night's sleep. Information from shell-shocked soldiers immediately after combat, the Army discovered, was notoriously poor because it had not yet been processed in such a manner that it could be retrieved. Many witnesses of the RFK murder who gave reports about the shooting immediately after the event formulated better pictures of what occurred in subsequent interviews.

Other witnesses discovered their memories of events connected with the assassination were not as reliable as they initially thought. Some came forward to give detailed information about Sirhan's activities in the weeks and months preceding the assassination and about how unidentified accomplices had accompanied Sirhan. When asked to say their stories were based on "positive identification," many balked.

Everett C. Buckner was one of many individuals who were interviewed by the Special Unit Senator (SUS) investigators and who later were found either to have been mistaken or to have deliberately constructed stories for their own reasons. Buckner was the range master the day Sirhan went to the San Gabriel Valley Gun Club in Duarte. He recalled how Sirhan had visited the club on the morning of June 4, signed the nonmembers register, and began rapid-shooting his pistol. Shortly after he started shooting Sirhan asked Buckner for a box of fifty, .22-caliber Imperial Brand long-rifle mini-mags. According to Buckner, Sirhan had been at the range with a young attractive blonde girl who arrived after Sirhan and with another man. The unknown man took his rifle to the other end of the range while the girl, who had brought with her the first gun she'd ever owned, was allegedly joined by Sirhan, who offered to show her how to shoot. Buckner said the girl became agitated with Sirhan and was worried that "someone will recognize us."[2]

Investigators eventually found problems with Buckner's story. Three others at the range that day, Michael Soccoman, David Montellano, and Henry Carreon, all agreed that Sirhan had been alone. Buckner later admitted to investigators that he had not really heard any conversation between Sirhan and the blonde girl and he did not hear her say "Goddamn it, get away" or any of the other phrases he reported to police. According to the LAPD Summary Report, Buckner likely had confused the interaction between Sirhan and the girl with an incident involving George Mioch and his wife, who came to the range at approximately 11:00 a.m. Mioch and his wife had an argument over the gun the woman had just bought. The couple remembered seeing Sirhan but did not speak to him.[3]

Conspiracy theorists seized upon the anomalies of Buckner's and other eyewitnesses' testimony, exploiting the LAPD's mistakes in collecting evidence. Above all, investigations into political assassinations, which go beyond the brief of a simple murder, require the public to make informed judgments about the way U.S. government agencies work and also their ability to comprehend complex reports about ballistics, forensic pathology, etc. But the public cannot usually form such a judgment because it glimpses only fragments of the covert picture. Because the world of conspiracy is essentially one of duplicity, the public has no way of knowing who is telling the truth or whom or what to believe. How could the government disprove that the Central Intelligence Agency (CIA) was involved in the RFK assassination when the public did not believe any claims the Agency made? Thus an open season of claim and counterclaim, in which partial, out-of-context, or otherwise misleading "facts" have been put before a bemused public that is in no position to judge them, has ensued.

As Robert Houghton insisted in 1971, the police did the best they could the night RFK was shot.

> We were faced with a crime that would be examined every-where in the world, possibly for decades to come. There had never been one like it in Los Angeles history. Already it was under the public magnifying glass. Those who hated America as well as those who loved her were waiting for answers; Kennedy's enemies as well as his staunchest supporters were waiting, and patience could not be expected. There are people who mistrust all police, as a matter of principle, and others who admire the FBI but consider any local law enforcement agency, even a metropolitan one, basically bungling and in-competent. They were waiting, too. There were the clever people, as usual, standing by to profit by the cry of conspiracy, hooking their theories to journalistic wagons before the Ar-lington soil was tamped. Sooner or later—sooner, probably—they would all come running from everywhere to demand, "What *really* happened?"[4]

Sirhan trial prosecutor Lynn Compton also realized early in the in-vestigation that the Robert Kennedy assassination would inevitably, in some way, be linked to JFK's assassination: "As a case, it was rather a simple case. . . . We knew we were going to face the same thing [that is, JFK-type con-spiracy theories]. The left-wing is never going to be satisfied until they can lay the killings of Robert and Jack to the CIA or Barry Goldwater. They'll never be satisfied with this little punk Sirhan."[5]

As conspiracy theorists probe, they sometimes connect pieces of the puzzle that either don't really fit or fit as the result of mere chance. Because the LAPD made a number of mistakes in the collection and handling of the physical evidence and had difficulties in reconstructing the crime (because of the chaos that followed the shooting), it was automatically assumed that something sinister was afoot. But, as Police Chief Daryl Gates reasoned, con-spiracy advocates seek the least plausible explanation: "In my mind, only one question remains unanswered. . . . That is, how could you possibly get the police, the FBI, the Secret Service, prosecutors, courts and special com-missions ALL to engage in this cover-up conspiracy?"[6]

The way the LAPD mishandled particular pieces of evidence in the RFK assassination case was not at all unusual. Expert forensic scientist Michael Baden, who was called in to examine the JFK assassination medical evidence and the ballistics evidence for Martin Luther King's murder, explained how physical evidence in notorious cases has a way of disappearing—not because of any sinister motive, Baden insisted, simply because people wanted to collect memorabilia. As Baden explained, "Memorabilia of the famous have a way of vanishing into doctors' private collections. This is what happened to Einstein's brain. In the 1950s, Martin Luther King was treated at Harlem Hospital for a stab wound in the chest. In 1978, when we tried to get his medical records and X rays for the [HSCA] committee, they were missing. The administrator had put them in a safe, but somehow they had disappeared."[7]

Conspiracy advocates are further debunked by Sirhan's bravado. For example, why would conspirators have allowed a "hypnotized Sirhan" to outspokenly utter contempt for Robert Kennedy when the young Palestinian visited the Ambassador Hotel on June 2 and 4? Bringing attention to themselves in this manner is not the modus operandi for conspirators, who needed to act secretively. Had Humphrey Cordero and Enrique Rabago, among others, told police about Sirhan's hatred for Kennedy, Sirhan would likely have been detained and searched, thus putting the conspiracy in jeopardy.

Furthermore, Hans Peter Bidstrup, an electrician at the hotel, told police that he saw Sirhan with a drink in his hand on the night of the murder. Sirhan spoke to Bidstrup, asking him questions about Robert Kennedy, including, how long had RFK been at the hotel and what were his security arrangements? If plotters controlled Sirhan they likely would not have put their plans in danger of exposure by allowing their "patsy" to ask questions about the presidential candidate's security arrangements. This gross folly could have resulted in disaster for the plotters had Bidstrup informed RFK campaign officials.

Robert Kennedy, in the days before Secret Service protection, journeyed the length and breadth of the United States with very little protection. Plotters had endless numbers of opportunities to shoot the candidate from a distance while allowing a patsy to take the blame (as conspiracy theorists allege happened during the JFK and Martin Luther King assassinations). If the Robert Kennedy assassination was conspiracy-based, it would have to be the least planned of any conspiracy-type murder.

A new claim emerged in the fall of 2006 that perfectly illustrates the tortured logic of many conspiracy theories. A BBC news program, *Newsnight* (November 20, 2006), broadcast a report by Irish screenwriter Shane

O'Sullivan who purported to have proved that three CIA officers had been present in the Ambassador Hotel on the night Robert F. Kennedy was assassinated. The officers, O'Sullivan claimed, had been responsible for orchestrating the assassination. He identified the officers in film footage taken by several news organizations in the immediate aftermath of the shooting that was later edited into a single film for the LAPD's SUS. This film is now at the California State Archives.

O'Sullivan believed his discoveries were important because CIA officers could not have had legitimate reasons to work at the Ambassador that night. The CIA had no domestic jurisdiction, and some of the officers he named were based in Southeast Asia. So, if the alleged agents were in the Ambassador Hotel on the night of June 4, they could not have been there to provide protection or perform some other service for the senator.

O'Sullivan connected the officers to each other through their work in the CIA's secret war against Castro's Cuba during the Kennedy presidency. O'Sullivan named David Morales, the chief of paramilitary operations at the CIA's JMWAVE station in Miami; Gordon Campbell, chief of maritime operations at JMWAVE; and George Joannides, who had been involved in psychological warfare operations against Cuba. Joannides later was called out of retirement in 1978 to act as the CIA liaison to the congressional investigation into the JFK assassination.

Following research into the new allegations, this author has disproved O'Sullivan's identification of the men in the grainy film footage from the night of the RFK assassination. Friends and colleagues of the CIA officers that O'Sullivan claims to have identified have established that these men are not actually in the film footage.

The witnesses who identified these three CIA officers in the film for O'Sullivan appear to have a long-standing interest in connecting these men to alleged conspiracies. One witness who identified Morales, former diplomat Wayne Smith, has been convinced for many years that the CIA was involved in the purported JFK conspiracy. He told author Eric Hamburg, "The [JFK] assassination was carried out by the 'cowboys' of the CIA—men like Morales. Who I knew well from my days in Cuba."[8] Another O'Sullivan witness who says he can identify Morales—Bradley Ayers, a retired U.S. Army captain who was sent to the CIA's Miami base in 1963 to work with Morales—has written a JFK conspiracy book and has been involved with the conspiracy research community for years. The witness identifications by Smith and Ayers are therefore considerably weak.

O'Sullivan included in his report comments made by close friends of George Joannides and Gordon Campbell—Tom Clines and Ed Wilson.

Both of these former CIA officers denied that the men in the film were the men they knew. Clines and Wilson also failed to identify David Morales from the photographic evidence shown to them. In fact, both specifically said the man they were asked to identify was not Morales. Clines's and Wilson's conclusions were supported by statements made to this author by former CIA operatives Grayston Lynch, Luis Rodriguez, and Lt. Col. Manuel "Manny" Chavez.

Manny Chavez is a former U.S. Air Force intelligence officer who served in Venezuela as a military attaché during 1957–59 while Dave Morales was assigned to the CIA station there for a year (during the period 1957–58). After examining the same film footage used by O'Sullivan, Chavez stated,

> Dave Morales was not only a colleague in our office in Miami and Caracas but he and his wife were personal friends. No question Morales was very active as an operative and trainer in special operations, but he was an honorable and respectable person. It would be completely out of character for Dave to get involved in a personal vendetta against the Kennedys, he was too professional for that. . . . I was assigned to the CIA office in Miami from 1960 to 1964. Dave Morales worked in my office (we shared desks) during a four-month period (1961), until they moved to their own JMWAVE location in southwest Miami. We often socialized. . . . The tall dark man [in the LAPD film footage] does not look like Dave Morales. . . . [He] looks like a young, late 30s early 40s, Afro-American. . . . I worked on the photo to make it clearer and am more convinced that the person in the photos is not Dave Morales as I knew him up until 1963.

Manny Chavez's wife also knew Morales well. She also said the man in the film clip was not Morales.[9] Manny Chavez sent a copy of a photograph made from the LAPD film to Luis Rodriguez, the army representative in the Miami CIA office who worked side by side with Chavez and Morales. Rodriguez told Chavez, "That is definitely not Dave Morales."[10]

O'Sullivan's purported identification of CIA officer Gordon Campbell was made by Bradley Ayers and also by alleged freelance CIA operative David Rabern. Grayston Lynch, however, eliminates the possibility that the man observed in the film footage is Gordon Campbell. Lynch is a retired U.S. Army Special Forces captain and former CIA intelligence officer. His awards include three Purple Hearts, two Silver Stars, a Bronze

Star with V for valor, and the CIA's most coveted award, the Intelligence Star, for heroism at the Bay of Pigs "above and beyond the call of duty." When a force of U.S. trained Cuban exiles invaded Castro's Cuba in 1961, Lynch was the CIA's case officer, its point man, on the command ship, *Blagar*. He handled every communication between Washington and the beachhead and led the first combat team ashore. Investigative journalist Seymour Hersh described Lynch as the man who was "there at the Bay of Pigs and was in the perfect position to write the definitive ground-level account of what went right and what went wrong." Lynch says he "knew Gordon Campbell" and the man in the film footage is not Campbell.[11]

Ed Lopez, an investigator for the 1976–1979 House Select Committee on Assassinations who was authorized to examine JFK assassination documents at the CIA's Langley headquarters, made a positive identification of Joannides. Joannides was the CIA liason to the committee. Fellow HSCA investigator Dan Hardway, who had spent the same amount of time with Joannides as Lopez had, failed to identify Joannides from the LAPD film footage.

O'Sullivan's claims that David Rabern had been part of the Bay of Pigs invasion force and Rabern's identification of Morales, Campbell, and Joannides can now be seriously challenged. According to former *Miami Herald* reporter and author Don Bohning, no such "freelance operatives" were part of the invasion force. This knowledge is based on his own thorough research and his friendship with the late Jake Esterline, the CIA's project director for the Bay of Pigs, and Marine Col. Jack Hawkins, the paramilitary chief for the project. Don Bohning said, "This reference to David Rabern . . . intrigued me. I called Jack Hawkins, the Marine colonel in charge of the paramilitary side of the Bay of Pigs. . . . He said what I thought: the only two American CIA contract employees who even made it to the beach during the invasion—and then against orders—were Rip Robertson, now dead, and Grayston Lynch. . . . Hawkins seemed quite certain Rabern was not part of the invasion force itself." Bohning said he was "99.9 percent certain that David Rabern was not a part of the Bay of Pigs invasion force, as O'Sullivan identifies him." According to Bohning, "The only other Americans directly involved in the invasion were those contracted pilots from the Alabama National Guard. . . . If [Rabern] had a role in the Bay of Pigs invasion it is not part of the recorded history of the event. While a small thing, it does tend to discredit O'Sullivan's account; and Ayers, who presumably introduced Rabern to O'Sullivan."[12]

Bohning allows for the possibility that Rabern was involved in the Guatemala training of the invasion force, "but most if not all the trainers at the beginning were foreigners and later U.S. military personnel, led by Lt. Col. Frank Egan. I have never heard the name David Rabern associated with the Bay of Pigs in any context."[13] Grayston Lynch's wife told this author, "My husband said to tell you that the only two Americans involved in the Bay of Pigs invasion were he and his CIA partner William 'Rip' Robertson. Anyone else that tells you they were there, or says they can vouch for someone being there, is a . . . in no uncertain terms . . . liar. There have been, over the years, a whole raft of wanna be Bay of Pigs invaders both American and Cuban."[14]

It should also be pointed out that Rabern did not actually know David Morales, Gordon Campbell, or George Joannides. Lynch, Rodriguez, and Chavez did. It should be obvious to most historians and researchers that Chavez's, Rodriguez's, and Lynch's testimony must trump Rabern's.

This new evidence makes clear that O'Sullivan's witnesses are suspect at best and have been contradicted by more authoritative sources. However, it is the most incredible part of O'Sullivan's story that renders his theory suspect—the premise that CIA officers, bent on killing a political opponent, would allow themselves to be caught on camera at the crime scene. As RFK assassination expert Dan Moldea reasoned, "Why in God's name would these guys be there and allow themselves to be photographed if they were part of a plot to kill Senator Kennedy? That would make as much sense as a woman with a polka-dot dress running out of the crime scene, gleefully shouting, 'We shot him. We shot him.' It sort of defeats the goal of getting away after successfully executing a complicated conspiracy."[15]

A number of Kennedy aides present that night had been close to the senator when he was attorney general during his brother's administration. RFK oversaw the war on Castro during this period, and he paid a number of visits to CIA headquarters in Langley, Virginia, and at least one visit to the CIA's JMWAVE station in Miami accompanied by aides. Some RFK aides present in the Embassy Ballroom of the Ambasador Hotel were therefore in a position to recognize CIA officers, whom they might have come into contact with during RFK's trips to the CIA establishments. Any identification of agents at this time would have given grave cause for concern, particularly as this was just a year after the Jim Garrison New Orleans investigation, in which charges had been made that Cuban exiles and rogue CIA operatives had conspired to murder JFK. It thus becomes highly implausible that CIA officers would expose themselves at the risk that RFK or a Kennedy aide might recognize them or allow themselves to be photographed at the scene of a major crime they had purportedly organized.

Books written by conspiracy theorists are fraught with similar nonlinear logic. For example, it would be entirely irrational for conspirators to risk their enterprise by enlisting a patsy who owned an illegal weapon and who could have been arrested at any time in the weeks leading up to the shooting. Had Sirhan been challenged at the police shooting range and asked to show documentation for the weapon, the whole conspiracy would have collapsed. Conspirators could never have been certain they could avoid being photographed by the dozens of television reporters and photojournalists. Although photographers failed to catch Sirhan firing his gun on film the possibility of capturing a second assassin on film would always have been a problem.

In their efforts to promote sinister connections between Sirhan and nefarious actors in the RFK case, conspiracy writers frequently accept, unchallenged, statements by other conspiracy writers. In their book about the assassination of President Kennedy, Lamar Waldron and Thom Hartmann wrote, "Bobby Kennedy was assassinated on June 4, 1968, and many of the details of C-Day died with him. His convicted assailant, Sirhan Bishara Sirhan, was first represented by Johnny Rosselli's attorney. Sirhan had recently worked for a Cuban exile associate of Los Angeles mob boss Mickey Cohen. A frequent gambler who often lost, Sirhan had written in his diary about receiving money from 'a low-level mobster, prior to shooting Bobby.'"[16] Waldron and Hartmann give as the sources for this startling piece of information John H. Davis's *Mafia Kingfish: Carlos Marcello and the Assassination of John F. Kennedy* (1989) and David Scheim's *Contract on America: The Mafia Murders of John and Robert Kennedy* (1983). Davis wrote, "In his diary Sirhan repeatedly referred to Donnerroumas [*sic*] as a good friend who made him happy by paying him sums of money for various unspecified jobs."[17] Davis does not say where he found this information; in fact, Davis made it up. Nowhere in his diary does Sirhan make this claim. Sirhan actually wrote, "I shall begin realizing the sum of one hundred thousand dollars—as per the instructions of the bible." Sirhan's frequent scribblings about $100,000 were simply reflections of his obsession with wealth. He made no mention of Donnarauma, apart from one place where Donnarauma's name appears above a scribbling that reads "please pay to the order of Sirhan Sirhan the sum of 5." Scheim's comments about Sirhan's diary are more accurate. Scheim wrote, "Sirhan's notebooks: 'happiness hppiness Dona Donaruma Donaruma Frank Donaruma please ple please pay to 5 please pay to the order of Sirhan Sirhan the amount of 5.' Several other notations containing the phrase 'please pay to the order of Sirhan' were found in Sirhan's notebooks—references to Robert Kennedy or to 'kill' always appeared on these same pages."[18]

Only with leaps and bounds of the imagination could a reader connect Donnarauma with a payment to Sirhan. But this hasn't prevented conspiracy authors from muddying the waters by using flawed research, innuendo, and speculation to make their unconvincing thesis.

Other clues in Sirhan's notebooks mitigate against the idea of conspirators controlling and framing Sirhan. On June 6 Officer T. B. Young of the Pasadena Police found a crumpled piece of paper in the Sirhan family garbage can. Written in pencil it read, "RFK must be disposed of DDD Disposed of Disposed Disposed of properly Robert *Fitzgerald* [emphasis added] Kennedy must soon die die die die." It is difficult to imagine a group of sophisticated "conspirators," led by government agents, getting RFK's name wrong.

Conspiracy theorists did not simply use nonlinear logic to argue their theses. They also cleverly misinterpreted statements made by witnesses to create an aura of suspicion. Some writers have alleged that one or more of RFK's aides might have altered the route from the stage to the pantry to facilitate the murder.[19] However, as presented in chapter 4, Wayne Rogers, Fred Dutton, and Bill Barry, close aides or friends of the Kennedy family, were never suspected of having any conspiratorial reason for changing RFK's route.

As the decades passed conspiracy advocates began to insist that Sirhan did not fire the fatal shot. The only armed suspect positively identified as being in the pantry at the time of the shooting was Thane Cesar; therefore, conspiracy theorists said, Cesar must have fired the fatal shot. Sirhan, who had been set up as the patsy, fired only blanks. But why would conspirators have Sirhan firing blanks when they could have done a more thorough job by having him fire real bullets? If there had been a conspiracy to kill Robert Kennedy, the conspirators would have wanted to draw as little suspicion to themselves as possible. To that end, having multiple assassins in a crowded room, along with a visible assassin who was shooting blanks, would simply increase the chances that someone would suspect sinister forces at work. And how could the "team of assassins" have had foreknowledge of RFK's route to the Colonial Room? Conspiracy advocates can only fall back on the theory that either someone in Kennedy's retinue planned the route with the conspirators or multiple teams of assassins were stationed at various vantage points in the hotel.

Furthermore, if Sirhan shot blanks, how do we account for the bullets recovered? Conspiracy advocates maintain that the purpose of a second shooter was to kill Kennedy. Why would he risk his purpose by shooting others in the crowd? Conspiracy theorists can explain this anomaly away only by suggesting that yet another gunman was present.

To make their "patsy" arguments plausible, conspiracy writers rid Sirhan of a motive for the crime, making him more impressionable. Philosophers reason that any belief can be argued if enough assumptions are present and pertinent facts are forgotten. Philip Melanson's and William Klaber's books put this maxim to work: they selected portions of testimony and evidence from police files and ignored statements made by the many people who knew Sirhan to prove that the assassin did not have a political motive. According to Melanson and Klaber, Sirhan said he heard on the radio that Kennedy had promised to send jet bombers to Israel, "but [RFK's] statements there [at the Zionist Club in Beverly Hills] were anything but inflammatory. He spoke mostly about a negotiated settlement between Israel and her Arab neighbours."[20] Thus, Klaber and Melanson imply that Sirhan did not have any political motive in killing Kennedy because the senator spoke mostly of peace and only mentioned arms aid in the context of a Soviet build-up in the Middle East. Yet a wealth of evidence shows that Sirhan, from a young age, was fascinated with radical Arab nationalism, left-wing politics, and assassination as we shall read in chapter 11.

Similarly, Melanson selected only a part of the LAPD Summary Report to ostensibly show that Sirhan was not interested in politics. According to Melanson, "LAPD's Summary Report indicates that he was a member of the Organization of Arab Students at PCC. The head of the group, Kanan Hamzek [sic], told LAPD that Sirhan seemed very interested in school work but did not seem interested in politics. Another leader described the group as just 'a social organization' for Arab students—a far cry from 'radical Arab affairs.'"[21] With this truncated quote, Melanson failed to show the full context of Hamzeh's interview with LAPD investigators. The LAPD Summary Report said, "At that time Sirhan did not appear to be interested in politics. But, Hamzeh felt that Sirhan could easily have been influenced by any Arab nationalist cause since he had intense feelings against the Israelis."[22]

In 2004 author Peter Evans alleged that Palestine Liberation Organization (PLO) official Mahmoud Hamshari ordered Sirhan to kill RFK. Evans claims to have unearthed evidence that Aristotle Onassis gave Hamshari money to direct his PLO terrorists away from his Olympic Airways airlines at a time when planes were being hijacked, and that some of the money was used to hire Sirhan to kill RFK. Evans claims that Onassis was aware of the plot and, indeed, wanted RFK eliminated so the New York senator would not stand in the way of his marrying Jackie Kennedy. Evans supports the hypnotized assassin theory. However, he provides no evidence whatsoever that Hamshari, who was assassinated by Israeli intelligence agents in 1973 for his role in the murder of Israeli athletes at the 1972 Munich Olympics, gave the murder contract to Sirhan.

In fact, Evans's theory is fraught with inconsistencies. Although the author accepts the statements made by Onassis's friends and relatives that the shipping tycoon admitted he had been responsible for RFK's murder, Evans contradicts himself by quoting close Onassis aides as having had trouble sorting out their boss's "exaggerations, half-truths and lies." Evans is also unable to establish whether or not Robert Kennedy had an affair with his brother's widow, Jackie. Throughout the book he accepts this as a given, but he told reporters that it was only "entirely possible."[23] In fact there is no credible evidence to support the allegation.[24]

Central to Evans's thesis are entries in Sirhan's notebooks that purportedly connect Aristotle Onassis to the assassin. Evans wrote, "On the first page, Sirhan had written at the center of a roundel, amid Arabic writing, the single name, FIONA [Author's note: this is the first name of the girlfriend of Onassis's son whom Onassis hated]. And on another page: 2 NIARCHOS! [Author's note: Niarchos was Onassis's shipping rival.] On a third page, between the lines 'One hundred thousand dollars and Dollars—One Hundreds,' Sirhan had written in Arabic: 'They should be killed.' And next to that, the number THREE. Fiona, Niarchos and Kennedy—the names were startling by virtue of their very juxtaposition. But, as a lawyer, Georgakis [an Onassis aide] was always skeptical: he did not trust facts that were startling, and circumstantial evidence made him uncomfortable. But three names and a sum of money written in a killer's notebook—he had seen far flimsier evidence than that get a conviction in a court of law."[25]

What Evans does not inform his readers is that Sirhan had placed the name FIONA in a list of racehorse names, including Jet-Spec, Kings Abbey, and Prince Khaled. Bert C. Altfillisch, Sirhan's boss at the horse farm near Corona where Sirhan worked, said, "The FBI saw some names of women, which really turned out to be names of horses."[26] The entry "Niarchos" remains unexplained. However, the words in Sirhan's notebooks were the result of simple stream of consciousness ramblings he learned from Rosicrucian literature as ways to improve his life.

The original police and FBI investigators could find no connection between Sirhan and the PLO. And Evans's allegations that the PLO had been hijacking airplanes prior to Kennedy's assassination are spurious. The PLO did not begin to use the terrorist tactic of hijacking airplanes until July 1968, one month after RFK's murder. Besides, Fatah, which has always claimed responsibility for its terrorist actions, said the suggestion that it assassinate a prominent American leader was "counterproductive" if not "insane," according to author and lawyer Stuart M. Speiser.[27] Speiser also believed it would have been insane for Onassis to get involved with Fatah in such a way. "Why would Ari become involved in such a bizarre and risky plot?" Speiser wrote, "Bobby's distaste for the Onassis marriage did not furnish any motive for Ari to have him murdered. In fact, Ari would have been in a much more powerful position if Bobby had lived to become president." Speiser believes that Onassis's purported "confession" to friend Helene Gaillet was made at the time when the shipping magnate had lost his power and "Ari did not give up power gracefully. What more could he have done to restore the legend of that power than to make up a story that he had taken out a . . . figure like Bobby Kennedy?"[28]

There is also no evidence that Sirhan was paid to carry out the murder and no money transaction has surfaced to indicate that Sirhan or his brothers received large sums of money from a suspicious source. Sirhan's movements in the months prior to the assassination leave no unaccountable period when the assassin could have been hypnotized/indoctrinated or flown to the Middle East for terrorist training. Evans's claim that Sirhan spent a three-month period before the assassination being trained by terrorists or undergoing hypnotic indoctrination is absurd. As the reader will discover in chapter 9, conspiracy advocates have suggested that the person who hypnotized Sirhan was Dr. William Bryan Jr. However, Bryan himself maintained that certain conditions needed to be met to produce a controlled hypnotic assassin. In a 1974 broadcast two years before he died, Bryan said, "I am an expert in the use of hypnosis in criminal law, I sure as hell am. You have to have the person locked up physically, to have control over them; you have to use a certain amount of physical torture . . . and there is also the use of long-term hypnotic suggestion . . . probably drugs . . . whatever . . . and so on. . . . Under these situations where you have all this going for you, like in a prison camp and so on, yes, you can brainwash a person to do just about anything."[29]

Sirhan's movements were not unaccounted for or "in a blanket of white fog," as Evans put it. Evans quotes Los Angeles police officer Sgt. William Jordan, who told him that the special investigative team he worked on immediately after Kennedy's assassination could not account for Sirhan's movements in a three-month period in the year before the assassination. It appears SUS was relying on an FBI report about a Sirhan family friend who stated that Mrs. Sirhan had been worried "in late 1967" when Sirhan had not been home for "quite some time." The LAPD investigative team gave no credence to the idea that Sirhan was missing during any period from June 1967 to June 1968, despite the comments of Jordan and the statements of a family friend.

In the year prior to the assassination, waitress Marilyn Hunt had seen Sirhan frequently in Pasadena's Hi-Life Bar. Sirhan also was seen in Shap's Bar during this time. In July 1967 Sirhan filed a disability complaint for workmen's compensation. Between July and September 1967 Sirhan's mother and brother Munir said Sirhan often went to the Pasadena Library. Library records confirm he borrowed books during this period. Sirhan's mother said her son "stayed at home for over a year [*sic*] with no job" from October 1966 to September 1967. Also during this period, Sirhan, by his mother's account, often drove her to work. On September 9, 1967, Sirhan began work at John Weidner's health food store. Weidner reported no long periods of absence up to the time Sirhan left his employ in March 1968. So how did Sirhan "emerge from this 'white fog' in March 1968, [and] join the [Rosicrucians]," as Evans states? (Author's note: Sirhan became interested in the Rosicrucians in 1966.)

Sirhan discussed Martin Luther King Jr.'s murder with Alvin Clark, a Pasadena garbage collector sometime after April 4, 1968. This leaves only eight weeks unaccounted for before Kennedy was murdered. During most of that eight-week period, Sirhan was reported to be in Pasadena. Sirhan's friend, Walter Crowe, said he met Sirhan in Pasadena on the night of May 2, 1968, when they discussed politics. The last time he saw Sirhan was on the Pasadena College campus on May 23, 1968. Crowe said he was in a Denny's restaurant when Sirhan entered with a group of friends. Michael Haggarty, a former school friend of Sirhan's, said he last saw him on May 23, when they discussed Israel.[30] This leaves only a two-week period unaccounted for. In his conversations with Robert Blair Kaiser Sirhan referred to local newspaper and local radio reports throughout May. Besides, Sirhan was living at 696 East Howard Street, Pasadena. Family and friends have never suggested he was missing during this period.

Evans's scenario is fundamentally implausible. How could plotters, for example, be sure that Sirhan, after his arrest, would not suddenly remember his contacts, become evidence for the state prosecutors, and be kept in a safe house by the district attorney? If the plotters' plan was reliant on Kennedy's security to kill Sirhan in the chaos of the shooting, it couldn't have been a very well-thought-out plan. Furthermore, had Sirhan suddenly "remembered," he would not have thrown away the chance to save his own life by telling investigators of his involvement with Hamshari. His lawyers could also have built a strong case around the paid-assassin theory, arguing against the imposition of the death penalty that was eventually handed down.

Despite the overwhelming evidence that Sirhan harbored a hatred toward RFK, Sirhan's brother Adel, who believed his brother was innocent and part of a conspiracy, continued to appear on radio and television shows to expound the idea that Sirhan never hated Kennedy. Speaking on a California radio program, *Over the Shoulder*, Adel Sirhan stated that his brother never held any hatred for Kennedy.[31] Adel omitted to tell his radio audience that, prior to the assassination, Sirhan told him that Robert Kennedy was a "malevolent and dangerous person." Adel and his mother apparently didn't agree with Sirhan on this point at the time and argued with him about it.[32] Adel relied on the fact that the general public was unaware of a lawyer's comments at Sirhan's trial: "[During the second fortnight of May 1968, Sirhan] was disturbed that both his mother and brothers did not see, didn't perceive Senator Kennedy as the same destructive and malevolent and dangerous person as Sirhan perceived him to be; and I gather that he and his family, his mother and brothers, had some arguments about this."[33]

In the 1960s America was awash with anti-war and anti-government sentiment and the media was inundated with speculation about the JFK assassination. Given the mind-set of the public during this period, linking the RFK tragedy to suspicions about the JFK case was inevitable. As time passed conspiracy theories gained popularity; many seemed to believe that not everything had been explained about the assassination of JFK's brother, an outspoken politician who had also made many enemies on the road to the White House.

During the 1970s and 1980s American citizens were presented with a continual stream of books, television documentaries, and op-ed newspaper accounts that seemed to suggest that the assassinations of JFK and Martin Luther King had hidden histories, histories that would reveal the secret agendas and powerful dark forces that controlled American society. As Tony Tanner remarked in 1971, "The possible nightmare of being totally controlled by unseen agencies and powers is never far away in contemporary American fiction."[34] When logical answers were provided to explain some of the anomalies that existed in the RFK case, conspiracy advocates fanned the flames by finding patterns and connections where none existed or by connecting some parts of the story to speculation about hidden plotters and sinister forces who tried to hide the truth. Post-Watergate America became intensely susceptible to conspiracy arguments.

The American public also came to believe that conspiracy theories were far more coherent than simple explanations because they leave no room for the mistakes, ambiguities, and failures that are a prevalent feature in any human system. Allard Lowenstein, one of the first leading proponents of a conspiracy in the murder of Robert Kennedy, echoed these sentiments when he said, "Robert Kennedy's death, like the president's, was mourned as an extension of the evils of senseless violence . . . a whimsical fate inconveniently interfering in the workings of democracy. What is odd is not that some people thought it was all random, but that so many intelligent people refused to believe that it might be anything else. Nothing can measure more graphically how limited was the general understanding of what is possible in America."[35]

Conspiracy writers have been willing to accept Sirhan's denials at face value, yet they eagerly dismiss some reliable witnesses out of hand. Michael McCowan and Abraham Lincoln Wirin both revealed that Sirhan admitted to them that he killed Kennedy, yet they were both branded as liars by conspiracy advocates. Conspiracy theorists accepted Sirhan's declaimer that he never looked at previous pages in his notebooks when he sat down to write; thus he was unable to see the "RFK Must Die" entries that were purportedly written under a foreign "hypnotic spell." However, at the trial, his lawyer, Grant Cooper, called attention to the notebook entries, "RFK must die. . . . Robert F. Kennedy must be assassinated." Cooper asked Sirhan, "It appears in your notebook what might appear to be goals, did you have them in mind as goals when you wrote them down?" Sirhan replied, "Yes, sir, I did in reference to the assassination of Robert Kennedy."[36]

In fact the only time Sirhan might not have lied was when he described his hatred for Jews and the political motives that underlay his crime. He lied only when it came to "means and opportunity" and the issue of premeditation. Conspiracy advocates never mention Sirhan's numerous lies, including:

- He lied to Robert Blair Kaiser about having never read any books on the JFK assassination. In fact he had read William Manchester's *Death of a President: November 20–25, 1963* (1967) and numerous books dealing with assassinations.
- He lied about being at the Ambassador Hotel on the night of June 2.
- He lied about not knowing the contents of his notebooks. The day after the shooting he told American Civil Liberties Union (ACLU) representative A. L. Wirin to tell his mother to clean up his room. Wirin was startled to hear this incongruous request in the midst of a discussion about how the assassin was to be represented. It was damning evidence and proved that Sirhan did indeed remember what he had written in his notebooks, notebooks that proved premeditation.[37]
- He lied about concealing his identity at the Ambassador by leaving his wallet in his car. He told the police he always left it there. At his trial one of his employers said he had seen Sirhan pull his wallet from his pocket on several occasions.[38]

■   Sirhan faked his outbursts in court during his trial. He told his
    brother Adel he had planned them all along. At one point he asked
    Michael McCowan if he should "flip" as a way of demonstrating he
    was clever at fooling the court. He would "prove" that the outbursts
    were part of a clever plan.[39]

William Turner tried to connect Sirhan's notebook entries that made
reference to "Di Salvo" with the psychiatrist who purportedly hypnotized
Sirhan. Turner wrote, "But the one that stuck out was, 'Salvo Di Di Salvo
Die S Salvo.' It obviously alluded to the notorious Boston Strangler, Albert
DeSalvo. When I had talked with Sirhan in San Quentin, he insisted that he
had no idea who DeSalvo was. If that was true—the Boston Strangler case
was some years earlier—it stood to reason he had heard the name while in a
trance. It so happened that the DeSalvo murders had been cracked by the use
of hypnosis, and the hypnotist was a Dr. William Joseph Bryan Jr., who had
an office on the Sunset Strip of Los Angeles."[40]

Sirhan had been recorded on tape at Ramparts Police Station, following his arrest, and the tapes revealed that he was lucid, aware, and articulate at the time. He even refused to give his name but was willing to
engage in conversation with police officers about other matters. Sirhan talked
about Albert DeSalvo and said the killer's methods were "really cool."[41] And
it is hardly surprising that Sirhan had indeed heard about the Boston Strangler. The case had been highly publicized and the subject of a bestselling
book by Gerald Frank. The story was also made into a major Hollywood
movie starring Henry Fonda, George Kennedy, and Tony Curtis and was
released in cinemas in early 1968. Sirhan, a young man interested in criminal law and contemporary famous criminal cases, could not have failed to
have heard about Albert DeSalvo.

As historian Henry Steele Commager observed in the late 1960s,
"There has come in recent years something that might be called a conspiracy
psychology. A feeling that great events can't be explained by ordinary processes. We are on the road to a paranoid explanation of things. The conspiracy theory, the conspiracy mentality, will not accept ordinary evidence.
. . . There's some psychological requirement that forces them to reject the
ordinary and find refuge in the extraordinary."[42]

Conspiracy theories attract the attention of many Americans because their proponents have used age-old propaganda methods—exaggera-
tion, rumor, innuendo, guilt-by-association, and paranoia. Dr. Patrick Leman
of the Royal Holloway University of London conducted research on the phenomenon and concluded that conspiracy theories flower because people feel

Senator Robert F. Kennedy at the podium of the Ambassador Hotel's Embassy Room acknowledging victory in the California presidential primary election, just after midnight on June 5, 1968. This photograph was taken only minutes before Kennedy was shot in the adjacent pantry. To the left of Senator Kennedy is his wife, Ethel, and to the right is Jesse Unruh, Kennedy's California campaign manager. *AP Photo*

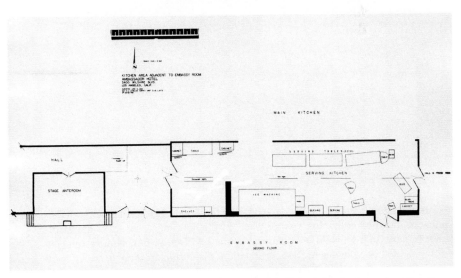

The Los Angeles Police Department's (LAPD) diagram of the Ambassador Hotel's serving kitchen, or pantry, and adjacent rooms. Bobby Kennedy was shot by Sirhan Sirhan in the serving kitchen. The survey for this diagram was made on June 6, 1968, the day after the shooting. *California State Archives*

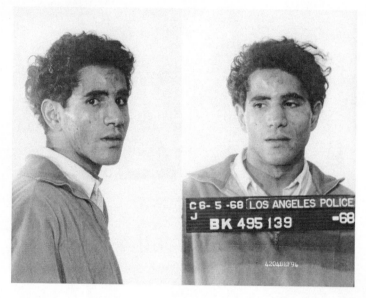

Sirhan's mug shot taken after his arrest at the Ambassador Hotel
by the LAPD. *California State Archives*

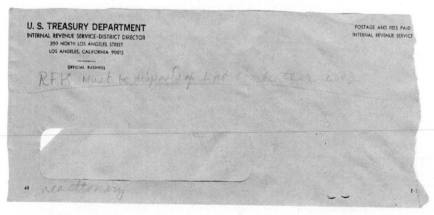

This photograph shows an envelope bearing the handwritten statement, "RFK
must be disposed of like his brother was." In the bottom left corner is the word
"reactionary." This envelope was found by the LAPD at Sirhan's house and was
used as evidence in the investigation. *California State Archives*

The .22-caliber pistol taken from Sirhan at the scene of the crime along with eight empty shells and three expended bullets that were recovered from the crime scene. *California State Archives*

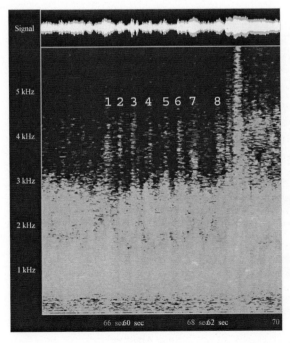

Dr. Chad Zimmerman's computer analysis of the Pruszynski audiotape. The graph shows eight spikes that represent Sirhan's eight gunshots. Notice that the sound spike beyond the eighth looks much different from the others; this indicates that it is a different sound. Both Chad Zimmerman and Steve Barber agree that the ninth spike is a woman, possibly Ethel Kennedy, screaming. (See pp. 135–136.) *Dr. Chad Zimmerman*

A series of LAPD photographs of Kennedy campaign worker Valerie Schulte in her polka-dot dress. Some eyewitnesses alleged that they saw Sirhan with a woman wearing this type of dress at the Ambassador Hotel on the night of the assassination. *California State Archives*

Sandra Serrano sitting on a staircase outside the Ambassador Hotel. She claimed that she heard loud bangs (similar to car backfires) inside the hotel while sitting in this very spot, and she claimed that a man and a woman fled the scene past her as she sat. She said that the woman, who was wearing a polka-dot dress, yelled, "We shot him! We shot him!" Serrano was given a polygraph test, and the results indicated that this story was not true. The LAPD also conducted acoustic tests that proved that someone sitting on these exterior stairs could not have heard gunshots inside the pantry. *California State Archives*

An image I captured from television news film footage. The image reveals a Sirhan look-alike standing next to a pretty woman in a polka dot dress in the Embassy Room during RFK's final speech.

Sirhan Sirhan.

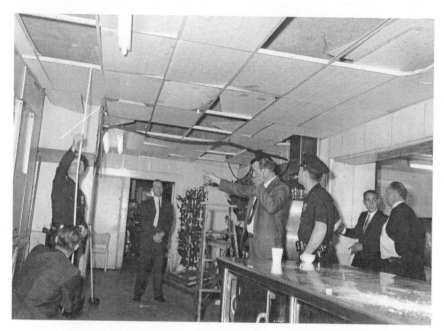

LAPD officers searching the interspace above the drop ceiling of the pantry at the Ambassador Hotel. They were looking for bullet fragments and assessing the angle of entry for the two bullets that went into the ceiling interspace. Only one of those two bullets was recovered. *California State Archives*

distanced from institutions of power and so are more likely to distrust official accounts. Furthermore, the rise of the Internet allows new theories to spread quickly and widely.[43] Leman pointed to September 11, 2001, as a striking example. In the Muslim world and in some parts of the West, conspiracy theories have grown around the tragedy. In France left-wing author Thierry Meyssan's book *L'Effroyable Imposture* (*The Horrifying Fraud*) was an overnight sensation, topping the bestseller lists. The book's central thesis is that the Pentagon and the World Trade Center were not attacked by Islamic terrorists but by a shadowy military-industrial cabal determined to provide an excuse for war against Iraq and Afghanistan. In the classic manner of conspiracy theorists Meyssan threaded together a number of discrepancies to create a near-plausible scenario. His evidence was based on inaccurate press releases and news accounts and photographs taken after the crash of American Airlines Flight 77 into the Pentagon. The Pentagon, apparently, showed no identifiable debris from a plane. Rather, he argued, the explosion occurred at ground level either by a cruise missile or a truck bomb set up by the American government to look like a plane crash. Similarly, the planes that crashed into New York's World Trade Center were not flown by Al Qaeda terrorists but were guided to their targets by remote control. Meyssan claimed that New York radio hams detected signals from navigational beacons within the towers. In the manner of most theorists, he fails to identify the hams.

Meyssan's thesis is important because it tangentially addresses how the public is only too ready to unquestioningly accept the most outrageous of conspiracy claims and how conspiracy writers deal with problematic facts. Meyssan claimed that witnesses who saw the American Airlines plane crash into the Pentagon were mistaken. As for the passengers on Flight 77, he believes they have simply disappeared. Meyssan's theories are not too far removed from those of RFK conspiracy advocates, who believe the U.S. government organized the plot.

The SUS investigated Sirhan's finances from when he was a thirteen-year-old newspaper delivery boy to his assassination of Kennedy. The unit investigated his bank accounts, earned income, and money he received from his injury insurance claim. It found no evidence of unusual amounts of money deposited in Sirhan's account, nor any evidence from family members that indicated he had come into funds beyond his normal earnings. Further investigations over the years, particularly the one conducted by Dan Moldea, have uncovered no credible evidence to suggest conspiracy in the murder of Robert Kennedy.

There was, however, highly controversial evidence in the Sirhan case that persuaded many that the conspiracy advocates had been correct all along.

This evidence centered on suspicions that Sirhan was hypnotized to murder Kennedy and then programmed to forget the crime.

9

THE MANCHURIAN CANDIDATE ASSASSIN

"The Embassy Room lobby was crowded, the lights were hot and blinding, and Sirhan Bishara Sirhan—transfixed by his own image rebounding to infinity in the walls of mirrors—slid from a half-drunk high into some hypnotic twilight all his own. And suddenly he was in the serving pantry between ballrooms at Los Angeles' Ambassador Hotel, with a triumphant Bobby Kennedy bearing down on him at the head of a crowd of followers. He wants to shake hands, Sirhan thought dimly. But when Kennedy got close enough to touch, Sirhan—too entranced to know what he was doing or why—yanked a pistol from his belt and yelled, 'You son-of-a-bitch!' and fired again and again."

—HYPOTHESIS PRESENTED TO THE COURT BY DEFENSE PSYCHIATRIST,

DR. BERNARD L. DIAMOND

The "Patsy"

At the trial Sirhan's lawyers tried to prove that their client had been in a "disassociated state" when he murdered Robert Kennedy and that he had possibly hypnotized himself to carry out the crime. Later, conspiracy advocates and some members of the medical profession trumpeted this theory, claiming conspirators had programmed Sirhan. The idea also took off with the public, which was introduced to programmed assassins through Richard Condon's novel *The Manchurian Candidate* (1959) and the 1962 hit movie based on the book.

Although by 1968 America had been saturated by mind control movies, documentaries, and ad hoc studies, the idea that Sirhan was hypnotized was first espoused by writer Truman Capote on NBC's *Tonight Show*. Capote, influenced by Madame Blavatsky's occult writings, speculated that Sirhan was "brainwashed" by "conspirators" and might have killed Kennedy as part of a plan to bring the United States to its knees by assassinating all of its leaders.

The issue of Sirhan's alledged hypnosis was particularly frustrating because it involved an area of scientific research that is difficult if not impossible to disprove. The Special Unit Senator's expert on hypnosis, Michael Nielsen, told author Dan Moldea in 1993 that "There is no such thing as mind control hypnosis. If a person were predisposed to do something like murder—well, you wouldn't even need hypnosis to convince him to do it. They would want to do it anyway. Say, if I hypnotized you and gave you instructions that you were going to kill somebody, there's no way in the world you would do that."[1] After Moldea published this interview, conspiracy advocates criticized him for dismissing the whole idea of hypno-programming without considering the opinions of the research community, some of whom believed that mind control was indeed possible.

Giving expert testimony at the trial, Dr. Bernard Diamond said that Sirhan shot Kennedy while in a self-induced trance brought on by the mirrors and lights in the Ambassador Hotel lobby. Diamond believed that Sirhan would not have shot Kennedy if the mirrors had not been present. Instead, Diamond argued, Sirhan entered a disassociated mental state. Diamond told the court, "I see Sirhan as small and helpless, pitifully ill with a demented, psychotic rage, out of control of his own consciousness and his own actions, subject to bizarre disassociated trances in some of which he programmed himself to be the instrument of assassination, and then in an almost accidentally induced twilight state he actually executed the crime, knowing next to nothing what was happening."[2]

Diamond, whom the defense team hired to ascertain Sirhan's mental state, hypnotized Sirhan to find out if he could remember what occurred on the night of the shooting. Diamond believed Sirhan was particularly susceptible to hypnotism and regarded him as a good subject. "Write about Kennedy," Diamond directed Sirhan while the subject was in his trance. Robotically, according to Diamond, Sirhan began writing down "RFK must die; Robert Kennedy is going to die." Diamond asked Sirhan if he had been hypnotized when he had written in his notebooks. "Yes, yes, yes," Sirhan wrote. "Who hypnotized you when you wrote in your notebooks?" Diamond asked. Sirhan responded, "Mirror, mirror, my mirror, my mirror."[3]

Under hypnosis Sirhan claimed he could remember giving a girl a cup of coffee, watching Kennedy come into the kitchen pantry, and being startled by mirrors in the pressroom where the teletype machine was situated.[4] He could remember nothing else. Sirhan's alleged memory loss led conspiracy advocates to suspect that the assassin had been programmed to commit the assassination and then forget the act. Even decades later Sirhan insisted he had no memory of the crime and told Dan Moldea, "I don't remember being in the kitchen pantry. I don't remember seeing Robert Kennedy. And I don't remember shooting him. All I remember is being choked and getting my ass kicked. . . . [The shooting] just isn't in my mind. . . . I don't remember aiming the gun and saying to myself that I'm going to kill Robert Kennedy. I don't remember any adrenalin rush."[5]

Diamond's ideas seemed to have some support from Sirhan's own lawyers even though they argued diminished capacity through mental illness. During the trial, Emile Zola Berman said, "He was out of contact with reality, in a trance in which he had no voluntary control over his will, his judgement, his feelings or actions."[6] In 1981, however, Diamond admitted his theories about Sirhan's hypnotic state were less than perfect in a speech he gave to the Northern California Hypnosis Society. Diamond also admitted that confabulation and fantasy were inevitable consequences and products of investigative hypnosis in the case of defendants, but not in the case of witnesses.[7]

Dr. Eduard Simson, a clinical psychologist when Sirhan was on San Quentin's death row, spent hours with the convicted assassin and also came to believe he had been "hypno-programmed" to carry out the murder. Eventually, though, Simson revealed himself to be extremely uninformed as to Sirhan's personality and character. The psychologist testified that "Sirhan rejected and disowned the notebooks. . . . I strongly suspect the notebooks are a forgery, for the thinking reflected in them is foreign to the Sirhan I carefully studied."[8] As we have seen, however, Sirhan's notebooks indeed revealed the assassin's true beliefs: his extreme nationalistic sentiments, his left-wing politics, his belief in the occult, and his anger toward American society.

Dr. George Estabrooks, who worked for the U.S. War Department after Pearl Harbor, also believed that a subject could be programmed through hypnosis to commit murder—but only as the result of intense programming. Estabrooks said, "Will the subject commit murder in hypnotism? Highly doubtful—at least without long preparation and then only in certain cases of very good subjects. . . . Yet, strange to say, most good subjects will commit murder. . . . For example, we hypnotize a subject and tell him to murder you with a gun. In all probability, he will refuse. . . . But a hypnotist who really wished a murder could almost certainly get it with a different technique. ... He hypnotizes the subject; tells the subject to go to [the victim's place], point the gun and pull the trigger. Then he remarks to his assistant that, of course, the gun is loaded with dummy ammunition [even though it is not]."[9]

Conspiracy writer Philip Melanson quoted Dr. Milton Kline and Dr. Herbert Spiegel in support of his theory that Sirhan was hypnotized by others. Kline said, "It [hypno-programming assassins] cannot be done consistently, but it can be done." Spiegel believed, "It is by no means simple, but under the right circumstances it is definitely attainable."[10] Spiegel submitted an affidavit to the California Supreme Court in support of an attempt by Sirhan's lawyer, Lawrence Teeter, to secure a new trial for the assassin. Spiegel testified, "Sirhan, being an outstanding hypnotic subject, was probably programmed through hypnosis to shoot Senator Kennedy and to experience a genuine amnesia of the shooting."[11]

Melanson has argued that Sirhan was

> definitely firing a gun and therefore should have been convicted of some kind of attempted murder if in fact they couldn't prove diminished responsibility. But I see Sirhan basically as a pawn in a conspiracy. My view is that while he was there shooting he didn't mastermind a plot to kill RFK. He was not a conscious participant with others when he was recruited into a plot. I see him as someone who is/was manipulated through his mind, through hypnosis, to shoot, firing a gun, to be a distraction for others who assassinated RFK. Unfortunately, Sirhan doesn't know enough about that to be able to provide leads or show leads on it for us and it is something that people other than Sirhan will have to try to figure out.[12]

Conspiracy writers also believe that a notorious hypnotist, Dr. William Joseph Bryan Jr., hypnotized Sirhan for the assassination. Bryan was famous for having hypnotized the Boston Strangler, Albert DeSalvo, and claimed to have discovered DeSalvo's motive under hypnosis. He also claimed he had worked for the CIA and bragged to two prostitutes that he had hypnotized Sirhan to kill Kennedy. Bryan's credibility as a source was damaged, however, when it was discovered he had a history of "bragging," consorted with prostitutes, and used unethical practices, including having sexual relationships with some of his patients. One associate described him as a "sexual pervert." In 1969 the California Board of Medical Examiners found him guilty of unprofessional conduct for sexually molesting four women patients who submitted under hypnosis. He was given five years' probation.[13] Shortly before he died, Bryan confessed to Hollywood reporter Greg Roberts that the Sirhan story was untrue.[14]

In 2002 Lawrence Teeter resumed propagating the theory that conspirators used Sirhan to commit murder. Teeter told reporters, "Have you seen 'The Manchurian Candidate'? It's the same thing with my client. He was the victim of hypnotic programming." Teeter claimed that Sirhan was the unwilling tool of some faceless conspirators in the CIA and the "military-industrial complex": "[New evidence] virtually proves that powerful branches of the U.S. government were behind the murder. . . . When a powerful branch of government commits such a murder it only makes sense if top people are involved. In the case of the programming of Sirhan those involved, either directly or indirectly, are the Los Angeles Police [LAPD], the FBI and the CIA together with the Pentagon."[15] In 2003, Teeter added, "There were a lot of powerful people who wanted him [Kennedy] dead and the truth never came out at the trial. At stake here is the integrity of the entire judicial system. There are peculiar subterranean things involved in this case but I can tell you this: My client is innocent."[16]

Conspiracy writers have gathered a wealth of evidence that they claim suggests Sirhan was likely in a mentally altered state on the night of the assassination:

- Not one person who was present in the Ambassador Hotel that night reported that Sirhan had been "drunk."
- Sirhan wore a "stupid" or "sickly" smile while he was firing his gun. Vincent DiPierro said what most stood out in his mind was Sirhan's "stupid smile. A very sickly-looking smile."[17]
- Mary Grohs, a teletype operator, remembered Sirhan standing and staring at the teletype machine of the Colonial Room in the hours before the assassination. Grohs said, "I'll never forget his eyes. . . . He just kept staring."[18]
- Sirhan showed incredible strength when he was being subdued following his shooting spree.
- Sirhan's eyes were enormously "peaceful," and he showed complete concentration on what he was doing.
- Sirhan remained silent about his identity when he was questioned by police officers following his arrest.
- Sirhan was unemotional and had complete self-possession.
- Sirhan got the "chills" following his arrest and exhibited similar symptoms at the end of his hypnosis sessions with Dr. Diamond.

- Sirhan's personality had changed after his fall from the horse at the racetrack. Lisa Pease speculates that perhaps one of the doctors who treated Sirhan saw him as a potential hypnosis subject and started him down a path that ended at the Ambassador Hotel.
- Sirhan's notebook entries showed certain phrases repeated over and over again, a sign of "automatic writing," which occurs when a subject is hypnotized.
- Sirhan's behavior during the trial indicated post-hypnotic behavior. He became enraged at the presence of two girls in the courtroom, for example. Pease also believes that Sirhan's outburst in court, when he confessed and asked the judge to sentence him to death, was the result of programming.

Lisa Pease wrote, "If the bulk of the witnesses [to the shooting] who gave matching stories are correct, then Sirhan couldn't have fired the shots and was in a disassociative state during the shooting. If he was under hypnosis and given amnesia-producing drugs such as the CIA [Central Intelligence Agency] was experimenting with for well over 14 years by that time, then Sirhan's claims of memory loss and innocence, while strange, may well be true."[19]

The Myths of Hypnosis

A number of myths about hypnosis have led most conspiracy writers to make grossly speculative conclusions about Sirhan Sirhan's purported hypnotic state.

Acclaimed psychologist M. H. Erikson has said that, although any tool can be misused, a body of acceptable scientific evidence that suggests hypnosis and the experience of trance is harmful in itself does not exist.[20] The subject retains the ultimate decision to comply with or refuse the suggestion. A 1979 study by Coe and Ryken indicated that hypnosis is no more bothersome to subjects than other activities, such as taking a college exam.[21]

Although hypnosis is a highly controversial subject and leading experts differ in their opinions and research, the scientific community has reached the consensus that the popular press has misled the public regarding the nature of hypnosis. The mass media have portrayed the myths of hypnosis with disregard to the actual facts. Countless movies and books have populated the idea that a human subject can be controlled. Hypnosis expert Robert Baker claims that what we call "hypnosis" is actually a form of learned social behavior. The hypnotist and subject learn what is expected of them and reinforce each other's behavior with their performances. The hypnotist provides the suggestions, and the subject responds to the suggestions. The rest of the behavior—the hypnotist's repetitive sounds and the subject's trance—are simply window-dressing, part of the drama that makes hypnosis intriguing. Strip away these dramas, Baker argues, and what is left are "psyched-up" states of suggestibility.[22]

No one really knows how hypnosis works, and scientists, including psychiatrists and psychologists, disagree about not only a definition but also how and why people react when in a trance. They do agree, however, that something unusual happens when a subject is put into a hypnotic state. Most psychologists agree that hypnotic techniques give the hypnotist access to the subject's subconscious and have value as a therapeutic technique in the treatment of mental disorders.[23]

Hypnosis experts fall into two categories: state and non-state theorists. State theorists argue that the hypnotic trance does exist and the phenomenon is characterized by increased suggestibility and enhancement of imagery and past memories. They agree that it may involve false memories, amnesia, and hallucinations and that the subject may lose control of his or her behavior. State theorists believe hypnotized subjects have entered a dissociative state and can be controlled by the hypnotist.

Non-state theorists dominate the research community in the United States and Europe.[24] Non-state theorists agree that the hypnotic state is less like a trance but more like imaginative involvement in a task. A hypnotized subject's abnormal behavior can be explained by normal human abilities, e.g., intense concentration, creative imagination, suggestibility, a willingness to act out inhibitions, and peer-group pressure (insofar as stage performances are concerned). Acts carried out by a hypnotized subject are the result of the subject's positive attitude, motivation, and expectancy. Non-state theorists argue that a subject's responsiveness to suggestions, like "raise an arm," "appear drowsy," etc., cannot be the result of a hypnotic trance because non-hypnotized subjects in control groups will respond to such suggestions in a similar manner.[25]

According to psychologist Dr. Graham Wagstaff,

> On the basis of such research . . . hypnotic subjects do not lose consciousness, control of their behavior, or their normal scruples, and are no more likely to engage in self-repugnant or anti-social activities than equivalently motivated non-hypnotic subjects. Indeed, the recent definition of hypnosis provided by the American Psychological Association clearly rejects the notion of the hypnotic automaton; thus it states, "Contrary to some depictions of hypnosis in books, movies or television,

people who have been hypnotized do not lose control over their behavior." . . . Notably also, in a further recent survey of ten experts on forensic hypnosis conducted by Vingoe (1995), all rejected the view that, "during hypnosis the control a person normally has over him or herself is in the hands of the hypnotist." A similar view is expressed by the editors of the contributors to what is probably the most important academic volume on hypnosis to be published this decade, *Theories of Hypnosis* . . . edited by Lynn and Rhue. . . . Thus Lynn and Rhue conclude: "Since the 'golden age' of hypnotism (the 1880s and 1890s), the view of the hypnotized subject as a passive automaton under the sway of a powerful hypnotist has faded in popularity. In fact, this rather extreme position is not endorsed by any of the theorists whose ideas are represented in this book."[26]

Among the many myths about hypnosis are the following:

- A subject is asleep when hypnotized.
- A subject is unconscious when hypnotized.
- Hypnosis involves domination and manipulation by the hypnotist.
- A hypnotist can make people act outside their own moral principles.
- People can be hypnotized over the telephone.
- People can be awakened by only the hypnotist, who has total power over the subject.
- Hypnosis can cause psychosis.
- Hypnosis can make a subject tell the truth.

Researcher and author Robin Waterfield, who has studied hypnosis for many years, believes the scientific community has established that "Hypnotism is not a truth serum; it cannot make you unwittingly reveal all the skeletons in your cupboard, your deepest and darkest sexual fantasies, your youthful dreams and misdemeanors. You can even lie when hypnotized, either deliberately or unconsciously in the sense that you might be recovering pseudo-memories."[27] Waterfield also discovered that "it is difficult to tell if a subject is fully hypnotized. There have been a number of cases where a hypnotized subject in a criminal case has lied to direct police away from the subject's culpability."[28] Hypnosis, therefore, does not undermine self-defense mechanisms; thus hypnotism is unreliable in helping to discover the veracity of a subject's thoughts.[29] Experts are clear in their belief that a hypnotized subject, including defendants in criminal trials, may lie, confabulate, or fantasize if there is motivation to do so.

Most experts agree that you cannot be hypnotized without your consent. Under hypnosis the hypnotist is merely a "facilitator" guiding a subject's own efforts. A hypnotized subject can break out of a trance at any time he or she chooses. But, while in a trance, the subject is in an advanced state of suggestibility—a suggestibility that does not negate the subject's own values, principles, and personal morals. His or her will is lowered but not removed. Furthermore, subjects undergoing hypnosis do not wake up, because they have never been asleep to begin with. Subjects consciously know what they have been doing under a hypnotic trance. The relaxed feelings they experience usually diminish their awareness of the outside world and allow them to focus on their inner feelings and thoughts and the words of the hypnotist, who suggests the direction the subject's thoughts will take.[30]

As far as post-hypnotic suggestion is concerned, the majority of experts believe that a subject can *always* choose whether or not to comply. When people appear in a hypnotist's stage show they act out foolishly because their inhibitions are lowered. Cases of criminals hiring hypnotists to assist in their criminal enterprises simply do not exist. Experiments that, at the outset, show that a hypnotized subject has obeyed a command to kill have all been proved to be flawed.[31]

Hypnotism, then, is effective in tapping into subconscious thoughts, which the subject may feel are too painful at a conscious level. The effects of hypnosis can be compared to the experience of a person who has had a night of heavy drinking and awakens in the morning with the thought, "What did I do?" Amnesia, in this case, has been self-induced so that subjects can cope with their embarrassing behavior. All people are able to hypnotize themselves to some degree; many people fall into hypnotic states spontaneously. Hypnotism is basically a form of relaxation.[32]

The CIA and Hypnotism

Conspiracy theorists frequently portray the Central Intelligence Agency as an all-powerful organization that is out of control. They suggest that the CIA successfully developed drugs and mind control techniques to manipulate their cold war adversaries or to get unwitting persons to do their bidding. Theorists also imply that the Agency often acted without political control and that it was in league with a cabal of powerful military-industrial interests that controlled the foreign and domestic agendas of post–World War II presidential administrations. Combined they were a powerful group that used assassination to eliminate those who opposed them, and to control U.S. citizens.

These theories are based either on half-truths or complete misperceptions. The CIA began its drug and hypnotism programs in reaction to Soviet methods of the time. In 1949 the Rand Corporation concluded that communist governments might be employing hypnotism as a tool for subversion and espionage. Reports also led the CIA to conclude that communist governments used drugs and hypnosis with counterrevolutionaries to force them to confess to trumped-up charges. The Agency was concerned that drugs and hypnosis played a major role in the 1949 trial of Hungarian dissident Cardinal Mindszenty, who had appeared drugged in court. The Agency was also concerned that American prisoners of war in Korea had been brainwashed. This idea was proved to be a myth. Evidence that North Korean torture, isolation, and sensory deprivation tactics were successfully used to control their captives is nonexistent. Only 22 out of 4,500 (or 0.5 percent) of those Americans captured by the Chinese defected.[33] It was also unlikely that "confessions" by American soldiers could be considered proof of brainwashing. U.S. soldiers had received specific instructions from their superiors to cooperate without giving away secrets if they were captured. Prisoners sometimes side with their captors because of their own low morale and the proclivities of a number of POWs rather than because they have been effectively brainwashed. It has been argued that the U.S. government knew the communists did not have any "magical tool," but it allowed the suspicions to remain public to alert U.S. citizens to the dangers of communism.[34]

Following the end of World War II, the CIA's hypnosis program, named BLUEBIRD, was initiated at a time when Americans began to appreciate the awesome power of the Soviet Union and China, including the threat of nuclear war that their power entailed. According to former CIA Deputy Director Ray Cline, "If the CIA had not tried to find out what the Russians were doing with mind-altering drugs in the early 50s, I think the then-Director should have been fired."[35]

The CIA understood the ethical implications of its own experiments. The chief of the CIA's medical staff advised his colleagues in 1952, "There is ample evidence in the reports of innumerable interrogations that the communists were utilizing drugs, physical duress, electric shock, and possibly hypnosis against their enemies. With such evidence it is difficult not to keep from becoming rabid about our apparent laxity. We are forced by this mounting evidence to assume a more aggressive role in the development of these techniques, *but must be cautious to maintain strict inviolable control because of the havoc that could be wrought by such techniques in unscrupulous hands.*" (Emphasis added.)[36]

The BLUEBIRD program was rechristened ARTICHOKE. Scientists who worked on the program have testified that they at no time intended to hurt any of their subjects. However, the general feeling in the CIA was one of patriotism, and CIA officers adopted the attitude that intelligence agents who operated against the United States did not have the same civil rights as the normal citizen and also that any interrogation methods, including the use of drugs, were acceptable. On the surface these attitudes appear to have an element of logic. As one intelligence agent said, "[There was a need for a truth drug] if someone planted an A-Bomb in one of our cities and we had 12 hours to find out from a person where it was. What could we do to make him talk?"[37] The U.S. research program included attempting to secure all supplies of LSD; experimenting with the drug BZ, which gave an eighty-hour "trip" with amnesiac effects; depriving subjects of sleep; and administering electro-convulsive, sensory-deprivation, or "white sound" therapy.

The CIA interrogated liars and deceivers in the course of its work, it sometimes needed to compel reluctant foreigners to spy for it, and it saw benefits to developing an amnesia drug. Therefore the Agency's top brass pushed for a miracle tool to solve their problems, but after ten years of experimentation, including testing drug and hypnosis prospects, the CIA was unable to find any effective method of control. Its findings were supported by a group of scientists who, in the 1950s, concluded that control of an individual required a responsive subject and that there were severe limitations on influencing a subject when he or she was unwilling. Hypnotizing an unwilling or reluctant subject would be extremely difficult because no relationship of trust and authority could exist between the hypnotist and the unwilling subject.[38]

At first the CIA believed LSD (lysergic acid diethylamide) a mind-altering drug, could solve the problem, but tests showed that the drug left subjects far from controllable. The CIA also couldn't find any evidence that the Soviet and Chinese reeducation programs used any absolute method of mind control. They realized their adversaries had been using the time-honored methods of brutal police interrogation, threats, intimidation, and imprisonment and solitary confinement to force prisoners into confessions, albeit sometimes false statements.[39] The CIA found that people would talk if they were tortured, but no method could be found to effectively gauge whether subjects had told the truth. The Agency abandoned the idea that it was possible to turn human beings into puppets.

CIA scientists were also never able to produce "total amnesia" in a subject. According to an ARTICHOKE and MKULTRA operative, "All experiments beyond a certain point always failed because the subject jerked

himself back [to reality] for some reason or the subject got amnesiac or cata-
tonic," and the Agency's methods occasionally turned the subjects into vegetables who could not do anything, especially the Agency's bidding.[40] A former
MKULTRA official told author John Marks that a foolproof way of triggering
amnesia could not be found: "You had to accept," he said, "that when someone is caught, they're going to tell some things."[41]

The record shows that the CIA made two attempts to produce a
"Manchurian candidate." The first involved a hypnotist hired by the Agency
to hypnotize a suspected Mexican double agent. The hypnotist's job was to
coax the subject to murder a Soviet KGB agent. Eventually, the hypnotist,
code-named "Mindbender," decided the idea was unrealistic and decided
not to continue. The second attempt occurred in 1966 when the CIA hired a
hypnotist to coax a Cuban exile to return to his homeland and assassinate
Fidel Castro. Although the hypnotist tried to coerce three subjects into committing the act, all attempts failed.[42]

Conspiracy advocates frequently cite experiments conducted by CIA
scientist Morse Allen, who they allege was successful in programming an
assassin. Allen hypnotized his secretary, who had a fear and loathing of guns,
to pick up a pistol and shoot another secretary. The gun, of course, was unloaded. After Allen brought the secretary out of the trance, she had no memory
of what she had done.

Those who promoted this experiment as proof of programmed assassins failed to mention that Allen did not give much credibility to it. Allen
believed that he had simply convinced an impressionable young woman volunteer to accept orders from a legitimate authority figure to carry out an
order she likely knew would not end in tragedy.[43] Allen also believed there
were too many variables in hypnosis for it to be a reliable weapon. And all
the participants in such trials knew they were involved in a scientific experiment. An authority figure was always present to remind the subject or
some part of the subject's mind that it was only an experiment.

Psychologist Martin Orne discovered that the same people who were
prepared to commit suggested violent acts under hypnosis were also prepared to commit those same acts while not hypnotized.[44] Dr. Wagstaff arrived at similar conclusions: "Studies have concluded that [such acts] can be
explained primarily in terms of subjects a) wanting to help the hypnotist/
examiner, b) thinking their actions were actually safe, and/or c) making assumptions that someone else would take responsibility for the consequences
of the acts." According to Wagstaff,

> Studies have shown that non-hypnotic subjects are just as likely
> as . . . hypnotic subjects to perform a variety of anti-social or

repugnant acts . . . although some have argued that most subjects are only likely to engage in what appear to be dangerous anti-social acts if they perceive the situation to be safe. . . . Other research indicates that this is not necessarily the case. . . . Calverly and Barber . . . found that almost all of a group of nursing students would sign derogatory, slanderous statements about a superior when emphatically directed to do so, even when they stated that they really believed the statements really would be harmful. Once again it made no difference whether subjects were in hypnotic or non-hypnotic conditions.[45]

Even if it were possible to hypnotize a subject to commit a criminal act against his or her own will, most experts agree the successful hypnosis would have to involve a number of important prerequisites. First, before an unwilling subject became controllable, he or she would have to undergo intense briefing and numerous hypnosis sessions over a long period of time and conducted by an authority figure. Second, the controlling figure would have to establish him- or herself as a valid authority. According to Dr. Herbert Spiegel, who supports the notion that Sirhan was hypnotized at the time of the assassination, "[It could happen if he were] subject to proper programming under control conditions, and subject to some degree of supervision."[46] In Sirhan's case, as discussed in chapter 8, these conditions are unlikely to have been met.

A majority of hypnosis and mind control experts within the scientific community maintain that the possibility of programming an unwitting and unwilling subject like Sirhan is not possible.[47] Hypnosis expert Dr. Etzel Cardena of the Society for Clinical and Experimental Hypnosis told the present author, "Most experts in hypnosis opine that the scenario you describe [i.e., a hypnotically-programmed Sirhan] is implausible."[48] UK hypnosis expert Dr. Wagstaff believes that

Controlled empirical research seems fairly overwhelming to support the view that hypnosis does not have some special coercive power over and above a comparable situation in which people feel motivated or pressured to perform anti-social actions. . . . Perhaps if "experts" in this field directed their energies to the elements of the hypnotic situation that might be relevant to the concept of compulsion or duress rather than automatism, there might be less chance of humiliating or preventing justice for a genuine victim who is using "hypnosis" as a face-saving device, or failing to convict someone who committed a criminal act with no or minimal pressure but is spuriously using hypnosis as a defence.[49]

Leading hypnosis expert James W. Kenney found after many years of forensic experience "that people rarely will do anything that is against their moral beliefs. If they do, it is willingly and a form of experimentation to see if they enjoy it, much like trying to live out a fantasy through someone else's belief system. All hypnosis is self-hypnosis. The hypnotists may offer the road map, but it is the subjects themselves that place themselves into an altered state."[50]

Furthermore, a robotic assassin cannot be guaranteed success; it is an erratic tool. A hypnotist can plant a suggestion in the subject's mind and ask him to forget that suggestion, but there is no foolproof way of preventing another hypnotist from coming along and recovering the memory.

The CIA's ARTICHOKE team concluded that it could not effectively hypnotize a subject even though Allen thought it could be possible. John Gittinger, the MKULTRA case officer on hypnosis, said, "Predictable absolute control is not possible on a particular individual. Any psychologist, psychiatrist or preacher can get control over certain kinds of individuals but that's not a predictable, definite thing."[51]

Following years of research into the subject of possible CIA mind-controlled assassin programs, author John Marks concluded that, "[MKULTRA officials] were not interested in a programmed assassin because they knew in general it would not work and, specifically, that they could not exert total control. The CIA had concluded that there were more reliable ways 'to kill people.'" Marks observed that some MKULTRA officials did, however, concede that a hypnotized patsy could be created, but that the amnesia might not "hold up under police interrogation."[52] Marks could not be positive that the CIA ever found a technique to control people, despite his "definite bias in favor of the idea that the human spirit defeated the manipulators."[53]

Sirhan's "Amnesia" and "Hypnotic State"

Sirhan's Arab roots might have influenced his steely resolve in murdering Robert Kennedy. Many Arabs might have recognized Sirhan's intensity as he pulled the trigger as *Rujuliyah*, a man's awareness of his own masculinity. Rujuliyah likely gave Sirhan his sense of nerve and conviction and took away his fear of death. As the years passed, the idea that Sirhan had been hypnotized to kill Kennedy became a more appealing explanation for the assassin's trancelike state and memory loss than rujuliyah.

During one of their hypnosis sessions Dr. Diamond asked Sirhan if he had been part of a conspiracy. Sirhan answered, "No, no, no."[54] He insisted that he practiced automatic writing as a way to learn mind control and that he learned the method himself by reading books. He said he had hypnotized himself by staring into a mirror shortly before he made his notebook entries.[55] Sirhan's brother Adel testified at the trial that Sirhan would often "talk to himself" and would sit in front of a mirror by his desk, light a candle, and attempt to control the flame with his mind.[56]

Conspiracy advocates did not accept Diamond's thesis that Sirhan hypnotized himself and they began to speculate that there were more sinister reasons for Sirhan's calm, trancelike state and memory loss. Sirhan's defenders pointed to a number of "clues" that indicated conspirators had hypnotized Sirhan:

- After his arrest Sirhan could not remember what he had written in his notebooks; thus his scribblings must have been the product of "automatic writing."
- Sirhan's last memory from the night of the assassination is that he left the Ambassador, walked to his car, found himself too drunk to drive, and returned to the hotel for some coffee at about 11:00 p.m.
- Sirhan was "transfixed" by a teletype machine in the Colonial Room of the Ambassador Hotel shortly before the assassination.
- Arresting officer Arthur Placencia examined Sirhan and concluded the suspect was "definitely under the influence of something."

Conspiracy advocates solicited the opinions of some members of the scientific community to support this evidence. In a June 5, 1992, television documentary by the show *A Current Affair*, psychologist Herbert Spiegel agreed to help Sirhan's present attorney, Lawrence Teeter, in his battle to secure a new trial for Sirhan. In Spiegel's professional opinion, Sirhan might have been under mind control when he committed the murder and he was definitely in the top 5 percent of the most susceptible hypnosis subjects worldwide.

Ex-FBI agent William C. Turner also supported the idea that Sirhan had not hypnotized himself but had been under others' control. Turner wrote in 2003, "Witnesses in the pantry reported to the press that Sirhan exhibited symptoms of being in a trance state (dilated eyes, superhuman strength in resisting being overpowered), but the idea that it was self-induced seemed to be gratuitous. His background yielded no motive for him to want to hypnotize himself to kill the senator."[57]

However, Sirhan's trancelike state, it can be argued, was likely caused by his alcohol intake and his intense concentration (the result of his hypnotic self-improvement exercises) rather than any efforts by conspirators to hypnotize him. Alcohol intake frequently causes amnesia, and it is possible that Sirhan's memory was impaired by the Tom Collins drinks he had had earlier in the evening. Sirhan confessed he had been drunk, although arresting officers disputed this. Hans Peter Bidstrup, an electrician at the Ambassador Hotel, said he believed Sirhan was "half-drunk" around 10:00 p.m. on the night of the shooting. Sirhan said he was not accustomed to alcohol and became intoxicated but did not remember how many drinks he purchased. Sirhan said, "Everybody was—it was like a party—hell, what do people go to parties for? Fun—you know—celebration. So I started drinking."[58] He also stated, "I felt I was quite high in my own self, and if I got more drunk, there was nobody to take care of me."[59] Sirhan said, "I got into the car, but, hell, I couldn't drive. I was too drunk. The idea of driving in the condition that I was in doesn't appeal to me. Then I said, 'Sober up, try to run around the block if you can, get coffee and that's what hit me—go and get some coffee at the Ambassador. And I went down again. I don't remember taking the gun with me."[60]

The credibility of Sirhan's testimony regarding his drunkenness is uncertain because evidence suggests he was, in fact, used to drinking alcohol. His friend Walter Crowe said that Sirhan, in a group of four men who went barhopping on the night of May 2, 1968, shared eight pitchers of beer with friends without claiming memory loss. Sirhan had also visited bars to play pool and consume beer on several occasions in the years before the assassination.

To test his reactions to alcohol defense psychologist Dr. Marcus gave Sirhan a few Tom Collins drinks, which held a total of six ounces of gin. He consumed the drinks in eight minutes and was then given an electroencephalograph (EEG), a test to measure his brain waves. The EEG showed no significant change in Sirhan's brain activity, but doctors observed a drunken behavior in Sirhan, who started shivering violently and became "irrational, agitated and restless." Sirhan swore, cried, and became angry at Dr. Marcus.[61]

Discussing his case with Robert Blair Kaiser, Sirhan said, "This was an assassination in the classical sense of assassinations—where the assassin was—dulled—mentally at the time that he commits the crime. The word assassin itself means hashish—hashashin—persons who are drugged, under the influence of some narcotics, liquor. I wasn't under the influence of marijuana, hashish or heroin or whatever. Just a few mirrors and a couple of shots of Tom Collins was enough to put me in that same state, the same state, mental state, as the ancient assassins were."[62]

During Sirhan's interview with author Dan Moldea in the 1990s, he reiterated that the root of his amnesia might have been his alcohol intake. Sirhan said, "I must have been there but I can't reconstruct it mentally. I mean no disrespect here, but I empathize with Senator Ted Kennedy in the Chappaquiddick incident. He was supposedly under the influence of alcohol and couldn't remember what he had done. When he finally did realize what had happened, someone was dead."[63]

Further, if Sirhan did experience memory lapse, his amnesia was not necessarily the result of hypnosis or drunkenness. In North America and Europe, some criminals convicted of a violent crime—26 percent of men who have been convicted of manslaughter or murder—frequently claim they cannot recall the crime. Some studies indicate that anywhere from 25 to 65 percent of violent criminals say they do not remember committing manslaughter or murder. With regard to actual amnesia as opposed to feigned amnesia, studies have shown that "amnesia is not uncommon in the case of violent crime and in particular homicide where it can occur in 30–40 percent of cases. A related state is 'psychogenic amnesia' which is associated with stress."[64]

Some research shows that intense stress can cause failure to recall anything learned in a given situation. Experts have concluded that the combination of stress hormones in the brain that occurs during intense trauma results in post-incident amnesia in which, immediately after a critical incident, the majority of information will not be remembered. The greater the trauma, the more likely a subject is to experience post-incident amnesia. Keith Ashcroft, head of the Centre for Forensic Psychopathology in Manchester, England, agrees and has concluded that "there are certain psychological defenses which stop people remembering things, and one of those is trauma."[65] FBI profiler Russell Vorpagel also supports the notion that traumatic episodes can lead to amnesia. He believes that forgetting "is a way of subconsciously lying to your conscience."[66]

Alan J. Parkin is skeptical of criminals who use the amnesia defense. He quotes Cantor (1982), who noted, "Amnesia is easily feigned and difficult to disprove in criminal cases, in the 11 year experience of the author . . . no case of psychological (psychogenic) amnesia in the absence of a psychotic episode, brain tumour, or brain syndrome was ever confirmed."[67]

Compelling evidence, presented at his trial, reveals that Sirhan was fully aware of everything around him on the night he killed Robert Kennedy and suggests that he was likely not in a disassociated state. During interviews with police officers following his arrest, Sirhan never once asked why he had been arrested. If he had indeed been hypnotized and then came out of the trance in the early hours of June 5, his most logical first question would have been, "Why have I been arrested?" Sirhan was also fully alert when he was given a police caution that he need not say anything until he sought legal assistance. He refused to give police officers any details about himself, including his name and address.

In fact, Sirhan "played" with his interrogators at the police station. The unremorseful assassin kept his identity secret to "keep it interesting."[68] He told arresting officers, he wanted to wait "until I could see what the hell's going on."[69] Officer Murphy accused Sirhan of "matching wits" with the LAPD and asked him to make his job easier by giving his name. Sirhan replied, laughing, "Again, you might lose interest in the mystery."[70]

Police tapes further confirmed that Sirhan was "alert and evasive" on the night he was arrested, and this observation was confirmed by all police officers present during Sirhan's questioning. The doctor at the county jail who examined Sirhan immediately following his arrest also confirmed his subject's alertness. He said the suspect was "self-satisfied, smug and unremorseful."[71] As prosecutor David Fitts suggested when he cross-examined defense psychiatrist Dr. Eric Marcus, "If he [Sirhan] was suffering from retrograde amnesia [a state induced by emotional shock] he would still be asking questions of the police, like why was he there and what had he done, as if he were suffering from real [organic] amnesia, wouldn't he?" Dr. Marcus agreed, and Fitts continued, "That leaves me with the only working hypothesis—that he was malingering, doesn't it?" Dr. Marcus replied, "Yes, I guess it does."[72]

After listening to the police interrogation tapes, defense psychiatrist Martin Schorr changed his mind about Sirhan's disassociated state in the early hours of June 5. The tapes proved that in the eight hours following the shooting, the assassin was "mentally agile, equipped with a verbal dexterity and able to converse with police officers in a normal way." Schorr concluded that Sirhan sounded "capable."[73]

There is also evidence that Sirhan knew that diminished capacity could be used to excuse acts of murder. Following his arrest, Sirhan asked Officer Frank Foster about the Boston Strangler case, mentioning that Albert DeSalvo had committed the crimes because he had suffered a deprived childhood. Sirhan asked, "but, correct me if I'm mistaken, is it when . . . the man is self-admitting? He admits that he wasn't trying, but they won't believe him? Is this related to it?" Sirhan was effectively stating that DeSalvo had committed his crimes in some kind of disassociated state.[74] Defense investigator Robert Blair Kaiser, who came to know Sirhan better than any of the defense lawyers, believed his client knew that the Boston Strangler committed his crimes in a "disassociated state."[75]

Sirhan had also wanted to discuss the Jack Kirschke case with police officers, thus revealing his knowledge of criminal cases and of how defense lawyers were able to argue for reduced sentences on the basis that the crimes were committed when the perpetrator was emotionally charged. Sirhan's brother Munir revealed that he used to go to trials with Sirhan. Sirhan at first denied this and then admitted he had been learning about the "legal process. . . . [I] was always interested in going down to the courtroom."[76]

At the trial, psychiatrist for the prosecution, Dr. Seymour Pollack, stated that Sirhan demonstrated foresight and planning before the murder, was not in an "altered state" during the shooting, and knew what was going on when he was questioned by the police. Pollack believed that Sirhan lied on two important issues: not remembering what he had written in his notebooks and not remembering the shooting. Pollack said,

> Sirhan's denial of recall of his written notes I interpret as an attempt to avoid some serious condition that would be attributed to his writings, that would be interpreted as evidence of planning, premeditation of killing Kennedy . . . had he been in an altered state of consciousness he would have been perplexed when he awakened . . . he would have raised questions about where he was, what he was there for. . . . And if this amnesia is present, it is retrograde amnesia . . . which developed at least a day or two after he was apprehended. . . . However, if an individual can't deny his act, the next best thing is to say that he didn't remember it, couldn't remember it . . . and if he thinks about this long enough the individual can convince himself that he honestly doesn't remember what took place.[77]

Defense psychiatrist Diamond explained these points away by suggesting that when Sirhan had come out of his trance the first thing he heard was the police warning that anything he said would be used against him. The argument does not, however, explain Sirhan's lack of curiosity about why he had been arrested.

Pollack's theory that Sirhan might have deliberately blocked his memory of the shooting has recently received support from research carried out by scientists at Stanford University. The Stanford study found that if people try hard enough they can forget something they do not want to remember. The study built on Freud's thesis on memory suppression, which suggested that people can be subconsciously influenced by events buried too deeply in their memory to be recalled. The Stanford University scientists found that people in an experiment were able to block certain memories when asked to do so and that scanners could identify which parts of the brain were involved. According to Professor Michael Anderson, "If you consistently expose people to a reminder of a memory that they don't want to think about and they try not to think about it, they don't remember it as well as memories where they were not presented with any reminders at all."[78]

Most evidence, however, proves that Sirhan was feigning amnesia. He said he could not remember writing in his notebooks, "RFK must die," but FBI handwriting analysis concluded that Sirhan had written the entries haphazardly, jumping around from page to page in the notebook, and that he had not written when under the influence of a hypnotic trance.[79] It was also clear to ACLU lawyer Abraham Lincoln Wirin, as discussed in chapter 8, that Sirhan remembered that his notebooks contained incriminating evidence.

And, in fact, after his arrest, Sirhan was disingenuous with the doctors who came to examine him. He was forthright with Diamond when he was under hypnosis, yet he refused to answer important questions when Pollack hypnotized him. Pollack responded to Sirhan's memory blocking, saying, "Whenever we try to get you to talk about these things that are important, you pull away, you fall asleep. We spent a half hour trying to find out where the gun was. How could you carry the gun from your car . . . near Wilshire? How could you carry a gun from there back to the Ambassador Hotel and not know you had it."[80] There is also evidence that Sirhan brushed up on his knowledge of psychology to ready himself for his trial and that he perhaps wanted advice on how to cover up his guilt. He asked a deputy sheriff to order him a book, *Psychology You Can Use*.[81]

Further, in a conversation with Kaiser, Sirhan told the defense investigator that he thought Lee Harvey Oswald and James Earl Ray had acted as cowards by shooting their victims from behind. Kaiser asked Sirhan if his act was less cowardly. Sirhan responded, "Hey, when you shoot a man in the back? There you go! At least Kennedy saw me." Sirhan quickly added, "I think, I don't know."[82]

Conspiracy advocates point to Sirhan's staring at a teletype machine as evidence that he was hypnotized, yet Sirhan frequently became strangely fascinated by things around him. This was part of his makeup and often began to stare when things fascinated him. Sirhan told his police interrogators, "Everything . . . life itself is a challenge. . . . When you watch a barber, sir, I just stand and watch that barber for hours. I . . . from the time I'm watching him I want to be nothing but a barber. You know, if I'm watching a dentist, boy, he fascinates me, and I want to be him. I was talking to [LAPD officer] Frank [Foster]here a while ago. The way he talked, you know . . . I was very fascinated and, you know, I was sort of superimposing myself in his position for . . . temporarily."[83] Readers will also recall that Sirhan's mother said her son experienced trancelike states as a boy growing up in Jerusalem.[84]

Sirhan's defenders believe the assassin's calm and peaceful state at the time he was apprehended proved Sirhan had been in a hypnotic state. However, as FBI profiler John Douglas discovered, Sirhan's calmness was not at all unusual behavior for an assassin. With reference to Mark Chapman, who stalked and then murdered John Lennon in 1980, Douglas wrote, "[Chapman's unusually calm state] squares with the emotions of so many others. . . . Once they decide on their course of action, stress and conflict are lifted."[85] And, of course, Sirhan was under the influence of the calming effect of alcohol. It has long been established that alcohol greatly reduces inhibitions and often produces a glassy-eyed stare effect as well as, in some people, a trancelike look.

Michael McCowan was a private detective who assisted Sirhan's lawyers. He worked for the LAPD for ten years while attending law school. In the period before Sirhan's trial, McCowan spoke to Sirhan about the shooting. In a response to one of McCowan's questions, Sirhan told how his eyes had met Kennedy's in the moment just before he shot him, before Kennedy had fully turned to his left to shake hands with the kitchen staff. McCowan asked Sirhan, "Then why, Sirhan, didn't you shoot him between the eyes?" Without hesitating Sirhan replied, "Because that son-of-a-bitch turned his head at the last second."[86] This statement, not presented at Sirhan's trial, is, in itself, damning evidence that Sirhan lied when he said he did not remember shooting RFK. When Dan Moldea published part of the McCowan interview in his book, *The Killing of Robert F. Kennedy*, in 1995, he was attacked by Lawrence Teeter, who claimed McCowan was lying. Moldea quickly had McCowan "sign a document attesting to this statement."[87]

McCowan's story is supported by an incident reported in Kaiser's book, *RFK Must Die*. During Sirhan's trial, hotel workers Jesus Perez and Martin Patrusky both said Sirhan had approached them to ask if Robert Kennedy was coming through the pantry following his speech. Sirhan had contended he did not remember anything after he collected his gun from his car, but following the hotel workers' testimonies, Sirhan told McCowan, who was seated next to him, that he had not approached either witness. When McCowan reminded Sirhan that he supposedly remembered nothing of this period before the crime, Sirhan "nodded and gulped."[88]

If Sirhan was lying and remembered the assassination, then how was the hypnotic defense constructed in the first place? Sirhan claimed that his lawyers first put forward the idea that he was in a "hypnotic trancelike state" when he shot Kennedy, but some evidence suggests that Sirhan had knowledge of "amnesiac states" before he committed the murder. Sirhan had read Truman Capote's *In Cold Blood*, a book about the murders of a Kansas farmer, his wife, and two teenage children. Perry Smith and Richard Hickock committed the murders in 1959, and Capote's book about the murder, manhunt, trial, and executions of the murderers was published in 1965. Sirhan identified with the short and stocky Perry Smith. He felt great empathy for Smith. Smith, a small-statured man who suffered a deprived childhood, had bouts of shivering and trancelike states and believed in mysticism and fate. According to Capote, Perry Smith "had many methods of passing [time] . . . *among them, mirror gazing . . . every time [he saw] a mirror [he would] go into a trance*." (Emphasis added.)[89]

At the conclusion of his book Capote quoted the opinions of leading psychiatrists Drs. Joseph Satten, Karl Menninger, Irwin Rosen, and Martin Mayman about why people like Smith and Hickock committed such devastating crimes, and what their mental states were like during the commission of the murders. The psychiatrists attempted to assess the criminal responsibility of a number of murderers—"murderers who seem rational, coherent and controlled and yet whose homicidal acts have bizarre, apparently senseless qualities."[90] In their examinations the psychiatrists found a number of similarities between the murderers, including the fact that the men they studied "were puzzled as to why they killed their victims, who were relatively unknown to them, and in each instance the murderer appears to have lapsed into *a dream-like disassociative trance* [emphasis added] from which he awakened to suddenly discover himself assaulting the victim. . . . Two of the men reported severe disassociative trancelike states during which violent and bizarre behavior was seen, while the other two reported less severe and perhaps less well-organized, *amnesiac episodes*." (Emphasis added.)[91]

Conspiracy advocates have never been clear as to when Sirhan was supposedly hypnotized. Some allege that Sirhan was missing from home for a three-month period beginning in January 1968, yet his work record suggests otherwise. They allege a controller, probably the girl in the polka-dot dress, manipulated Sirhan in the Ambassador Hotel, yet they do not explain how, during the weeks preceding the assassination, Sirhan was hypnotized. Their own experts believe Sirhan could have been a hypno-programmed assassin only if he was isolated for a considerable amount of time and subjected to brainwashing techniques. The conspiracy advocates' theories thus become implausible.

10

SIRHAN'S OBSESSIONS

"History has taught us that peace does not lie in characters and covenants alone but in the hearts and minds of people."

—President John F. Kennedy

"You cannot reason a person out of something he did not reason himself into."

— Jonathan Swift

Sirhan and the "Jews"

Conspiracy advocates Philip Melanson and William Klaber in their book *Shadow Play* (1997) wrote, "Nothing in Sirhan's youth appears to lead to the most pivotal moment of his life." Furthermore, the authors argue, "a review of Sirhan's interviews with his doctors and lawyers reveals that he is noteworthy for his lack of hatred for his victim."[1] Sirhan's attorney, Lawrence Teeter, denies that Sirhan was anti-Jewish.[2] However, the evidence in the case, including the testimonies of employers, acquaintances, friends, family, doctors, television and print reporters, and government investigators, disproves these allegations. Not only did Sirhan's hatred for Jews lead him to his fate, but his hatred for Robert Kennedy has been well documented in his own words.

Sirhan's anti-Semitism had its roots in the environment he was raised in, the education he received, and the adults who had an influence on him. During Sirhan's trial his mother related how the intense feelings of the Palestinians remained with the family even though they had been far removed from the conflict when they immigrated to America. She told of how her family had lived in Jerusalem for "thousands of years,"[3] and she spoke of the bitterness and hatred of the Israelis who had "taken their land." Mary Sirhan believed her son killed Robert Kennedy because of his Arab nationalism. She said, "What he did, he did for his country."[4] Sirhan's friend, John Strathman, believed the young Arab was heavily influenced by his mother's views.

Sirhan was doubtlessly influenced by his parents' opinions. Therapists have long known that anything a parent says to a child, especially comments regarding strongly held views about religion and politics, has a way of entering into the child's consciousness and influencing the individual's life-long self-concept. Sirhan's parents taught him that the Jews were evil and stole their family's home. Following the assassination, Bishara Sirhan told reporters that his son's trial would establish the fact that Palestinian Arabs had a legitimate cause: "A nation of our own, not Israeli, not Jordanian but Palestinian. . . . He was a very good boy, a very studious boy. If he did this . . . it was because he was doing something for his country. We know he is a hero."[5] Bishara regretted Kennedy's death, but his hatred and contempt for the politician shone through in a statement he made to reporters in the days following his son's arrest: "I can say that I do not regret his death as Kennedy the American politician who attempted to gain the presidential election by his aggressive propaganda against the Arab people of Palestine. . . . Kennedy was promising the Zionists to supply them with arms and aircraft . . . and thus provoked the sensitive feelings of Sirhan who had suffered so much from the Jews. . . . It is not fair to accuse my son without a full examination of Zionist atrocities against the Arabs—those atrocities which received the support and blessings of Robert Kennedy."[6]

Lebanese-American club owner Lou Shelby, who hired Sirhan's brother Adel as a musician at his club, visited the Sirhans in Pasadena on a number of occasions for musical rehearsals and thus was able to see them in a social setting. According to Shelby, "The Sirhans always struck me as being a weird family. By that I mean something quite strange and unusual. Perhaps the best way to explain it is by saying that though they were Christians, the general quality, the atmosphere, of their family was that of a Muslim family. It was serious and heavy and lacking in the adaptability and quickness which most Arab Christian families here have. And there were their relations with their mother; the sons were fond of her, of course, but she had little influence on them and they didn't take her wishes or feelings into account."[7]

Arab culture was central to the Sirhans way of life. They listened to Arab music, read Arab literature, and thought in the Arab way. The family also had its share of Arab pride—so much that Sirhan became angry when his lawyers argued that he had been mentally ill when he shot Robert Kennedy. In most Arab countries it is better to be a criminal than to admit insanity; Sirhan did not want to suffer the stigma attached to mental illness in Arab culture. Sirhan also adopted the Arab approach to the treatment of women. On May 2, 1968, Sirhan met his friend, Walter Crowe, and they barhopped with two other friends, Ivan Garcia and Joseph Marcovecchio. While they were at the Hi-Life Bar, Sirhan became depressed at the way a stripper demeaned herself in front of the crowd of men. At another bar Sirhan became contemptuous about the way the women dancers cavorted.[8]

Most of Sirhan's biographers haven't considered the effect that teachers, influential adults in the Jerusalem Arab community, and the Palestinian Arabs' general attitude had on Sirhan. The way a nation educates its children about another country's races and religions will often determine the relations between the two countries. Populations are not culturally prone to hatred; they are educated toward it, as studies of Nazi Germany have shown. The anti-Semitism inculcated in German children in the 1930s and '40s remained with them into their old age, and the West German government's postwar attempts to promote anti-fascism had no effect on those who grew up during the Third Reich.[9]

The propaganda used by Palestinians had no less an effect on younger generations from the 1940s to the present day. Educators, family members, and friends taught Sirhan, from an early age, that the Jews were treacherous, an evil enemy, and that it was his duty to rid Palestine of Jews. Sirhan's generation was taught to hate and fear Jews, to believe not only that every self-respecting Arab had the right to fight the Jewish state but also that it was just and desirable to destroy it. As Christopher Hewitt noted, "In so far as the political debate on an issue involves extremist rhetoric, it is presumably more likely to result in violence."[10]

Sirhan's hatred and anger toward the Jews did not originate with any mental illness he may have suffered. In fact his attitude was no different from that of the majority of Palestinians and the rest of the Arab peoples. As Glubb Pasha, an Arab military leader and British officer (and no friend of the Jews), reported in 1945, "They [the Arabs] were painfully conscious of their immaturity, their weakness and their backwardness. They show all the instability and emotionalism of the adolescent [characterized by] their touchiness and . . . readiness to take offence at any sign of condescension by their elders. Slights gave rise to outbursts of temper and violent defiance."[11]

There is little doubt the conflict and the situation Palestinians found themselves in following the 1948 Diaspora had its effect on all Palestinian children. Their dark rage and despair originated from poor leadership within the Palestinian communities and the feeling that they had gone unnoticed by the rest of the world. Theirs were memories of a "lost homeland," the yearning for return passed down from generation to generation and above all outrage, shame, anger, and humiliation. As Palestinian writer Sana Hassan eloquently wrote,

> Living in Beirut as a stateless person for most of my growing up years, many of them in a refugee camp, I did not feel I was living among my Arab brothers. . . . I was a Palestinian. And that meant I was an outsider, an alien, a refugee and a burden. . . . It defeated some of us. It reduced and distorted and alienated others. The defeated, like myself, took off to go away from the intolerable pressures of the Arab world. . . . The reduced, like my parents, waited helplessly in a refugee camp for the world, for a miracle, or for some deity to come to their aid. The distorted, like Sirhan Sirhan, turned into assassins. The alienated, like Leila Khaled, hijacked civilian aircraft.[12]

Before Sirhan immigrated to America at age twelve he was schooled in East Jerusalem, which was annexed by Jordan during the 1948 conflict. After 1948 East Jerusalem and West Bank schools followed the Jordanian curriculum. In the Arab world, including Jordan, educational systems were driven by notions antithetical to the values of tolerance and understanding that are so intently promoted in the West. Hundreds of books published from 1948 in Egypt, Syria, Lebanon, Jordan, and Iraq promoted the liquidation of Israel as not only a political necessity but also a moral imperative. Israel and its people were an evil entity, and it was permissible to destroy them. Arab leaders compiled a curriculum of hatred for their children, and the anti-Israeli and anti-Jewish teachings became a basic element in the study of history in the schools. Arab children were taught that Jews were the ultimate embodiment of evil and should be destroyed. One of Sirhan's contemporaries, A. Dokimos, wrote about his education in Jordan in the early 1960s: "The first song I learned in school . . . [was] titled, 'Arabs our Beloved and Jews Our Dogs.' . . . In an attempt to change the hearts of Palestinians the Israeli television stations would show Holocaust documentaries. . . . I would sit and watch cheering the Germans while I chewed on food. It was impossible for me to change my heart and mind concerning the Jews. . . . Hitler [was] my idol."[13]

Although Sirhan's school was nominally Christian, teachers were mainly drawn from the Arab community, which was predominantly Muslim, with some input from foreign missionary workers. Christian Arabic children used Jordanian textbooks. From 1948 to 1967 Christian schools in East Jerusalem were required to teach the Koran.[14] Following his arrest for the murder of Robert Kennedy, Sirhan told a story about how he had been influenced by one particular teacher in his school, Mr. Suheil, who angrily denounced present-day Arabs and compared them to the Arab warrior Saladin. Suheil tried to indoctrinate his pupils in Arab nationalism and urged them to be like Saladin and fight for the Arab cause.[15]

As the Arab world ignored the United Nations' call to legitimize the State of Israel, Arab Jordanian school textbooks continued to refer to Israel as foreign-occupied Palestine. The texts called for Israel's destruction and made reference to the obligation Palestinians had to defend Islamic land. In the textbooks Jews were portrayed as thieves, occupiers, and enemies of the prophets, as cunning, deceitful, and treacherous, and as wild animals and locusts. The Palestinian narrative linked Jews, Israelis, and Zionism to Western colonialism in the Middle East. The books chronicled the "evil plans against the Muslims. Zionist evil, whose goal was to conquer and destroy the Islamic Holy places, the Dome of the Rock, all of Jerusalem and all that is holy to Islam."[16] They always described Arabs as victims.

The curriculum also exhorted children to violence and described the Jewish state in Nazi-like terms. The textbooks contained emotionally charged scenes of the stoning of Jews and Jewish property—the message being that killing Jews was a worthy and honorable act. In fact the purpose of Arab schooling in Jordan and Egypt was to mobilize the population for future conflict with Israel. Maps in the textbooks did not include Israel and denied its existence. The history and geography books for grades one through six contained maps that portrayed all of Israel as Palestine and called on Palestinian children to liberate all of Palestine by taking up arms against the Jews.

Among the favorite books of Palestinians at the time was *Our Country Palestine* by Murad al-Dabbagh, published in 1947. Dabbagh exhorted his people to take up arms and said that there was "no alternative to destroying Israel."[17] A favorite book in the Arab world was *The Protocols of the Elders of Zion*, an anti-Semitic tract and also a Soviet forgery constructed to fan the flames of hatred toward Jews in Europe. No fewer than seven Arabic translations of *The Protocols* were published between 1949 and 1967. More than any other book of the twentieth century, *The Protocols* provided the ideological justification for the physical destruction of the Jewish people. It has been called "The Father of the Holocaust."[18]

Sirhan's hatred and anger toward the Jews remained with him as he settled in the United States. He believed Jews ran his new country, controlled the American media, and were thus responsible for the slanted view of Arabs presented by the American media.[19] According to Mohan Goel, an acquaintance of Sirhan, "[Sirhan] couldn't understand the Americans, that they let the Jews suck the blood of the nation, and keep putting money in the banks."[20] Sirhan confessed he still felt "towards the Jews as they [the Jews] felt towards Hitler. Hitler persecuted them and now they're persecuting me in the same style."[21]

At John Muir High School, Sirhan became interested in politics and began to express his political views. Once he gave a talk to the Foreign Relations Club. Arriving at the venue Sirhan became disgusted at the audience, which he believed was made up mostly of Jews. When asked if Arabs should accept the status quo and also accept peace, Sirhan became inflamed. He berated his questioner and asked, rhetorically, "Give up our own houses? You want us to give up our own houses?"[22]

As the years went by Sirhan's hatred of the Jews did not dissipate. He once denounced one of his brothers for working for a Jew.[23] He became incensed when he saw the movie *Exodus*. "Every time I hear that [Exodus] song," he later told author Robert Blair Kaiser, "I shut it off. It bugs me. The memories. Those Jews. . . . 'The fucking Arabs' is what they're trying to say every time they play that song."[24] Sirhan refused to see the movie *Lawrence of Arabia* as he believed it to be anti-Arab. He also disliked the movie because it had a Jewish director, Sam Spiegel. His employer, John Weidner, said, "[Sirhan] had a kind of 'hate' I discussed with him. . . . He said 'Mr. Weidner, I would like to be like you and forgive but I cannot.' So when I hear that he had done that [assassinated RFK] I remember that Kennedy had made some statements some days ago. I watched the TV program of the debate and he wanted to help Israel then I was not too surprised that in the emotional concept of his defense of Jordan that he [said] 'That is my enemy.'"[25]

In fact Sirhan became paranoid about Jews in the United States. He confessed that he was not "psychotic . . . except when it comes to the Jews."[26] Once he said, "The Jews are behind the scenes wherever you go. You tell them your name and they freeze. 'SUR-HAN,' [they say]."[27] He felt slighted every time someone mentioned his double-barreled name. He said, "My name! My name! As soon as anyone heard it, everything else stopped."[28]

American friend and fellow radical Walter Crowe said Sirhan was virulently anti-Semitic and professed hatred for the Jews and the state of Israel. Crowe believed Mary Sirhan propagated these views to Sirhan.[29] Crowe, who studied Arabic, attended a meeting of the Organization of Arab Students (OAS) with Sirhan in 1964. In 1965 Sirhan told Crowe of his admiration for President Nasser and expressed the wish that the Arabs would someday rid Palestine of the Jews.[30]

As a part-time gardener Sirhan came to hate the Jews whose gardens he tended. He referred to them as "fucking Jews," "the goddamn Zionists," and the "fucking Zionists." A number of people who knew him, including John Strathman, said Sirhan had been impressed by Hitler's *Mein Kampf* and also by the German leader's solution to the "Jewish problem."[31] John Weidner said, "I soon discovered he had a dislike for the Jewish people as a nation. . . . He said that in America, the Jewish people were on the top and directed things. . . . He said they had taken his home."[32] Following his arrest Sirhan told one of the court-appointed psychiatrists, George Y. Abe, about his political philosophy. Sirhan said he was solidly anti-Zionist and disgusted at the way Jews in America had such a strong influence within the American political system. Sirhan said he believed Robert Kennedy listened to the Jews,[33] and he saw the senator as having sold out to them.[34]

The Arab-Israeli war of 1967 provoked the worst of Sirhan's anti-Semitic rages. Kanan Hamzeh, president of the Organization of Arab Students in Pasadena, said Sirhan had "intense feelings about the Israelis."[35] According to John Strathman, Sirhan was "intense" and "mad" about the Six Days' War. Strathman's wife, Patricia, said Sirhan became "burning mad . . . furious" about the war.[36] On his way to the Ambassador Hotel on the night of June 4, a newspaper advertisement announcing a march on Wilshire Boulevard to commemorate the first anniversary of Israel's victory in the Six Days' War. At his trial Sirhan said, "that brought me back to the six days in June of the previous year. . . . I was completely pissed off at American justice at the time. . . . I had the same emotionalism, the same feelings, the fire started burning inside me . . . at seeing how these Zionists, these Jews, these Israelis . . . were trying to rub in the fact that they had beaten the hell out of the Arabs the year before. . . . When I saw that ad, I was off to go down and see what these sons-of-bitches were up to."[37]

Sirhan and American Society

When the twelve-year-old Sirhan arrived in the United States, he soon discovered he was "different." He was hopeful that what he learned in school—that America was a land of equality—would prove to be true. Eventually, however, he began to believe that America's promises did not apply to him.

In high school he began to develop strong feelings about social and racial discrimination. He identified largely with Mexican Americans, African Americans, and poor Americans and believed political leaders were subverting American ideals. He described himself as a displaced Palestinian Arab living in America. Kanan Hamzeh heard accounts from several of Sirhan's brothers of Sirhan's constant arguments with them as well as with his mother. Hamzeh said all of the brothers were unhappy living in the United States and they were unable to adjust to the social and political atmosphere.

His disillusionment with American society remained with Sirhan as a young adult. John Weidner told NBC News, "When I first heard about it [the RFK assassination] my first reaction was to think about what Kennedy said about Israel a few days ago and that made me believe that it was not impossible that a hot-tempered man like Sirhan, with his fantasies, that he was able to do something like that. I tried to discuss with him about how good it was in America but he didn't want to believe it. He believed that Russia and China were maybe better. . . . He was resentful against authority, against those who possess, and he told me America was a country where there was no freedom. . . . On that subject [Israel] he was [fairly unstable]."[38]

Following his arrest Sirhan's hatred of American society became a central feature in his discussions with his lawyers. He told them that he had read Victor Hugo's *Les Misérables* and was impressed with the book. According to defense investigator and journalist Robert Blair Kaiser, Sirhan especially appreciated the following passage in the book: "Teach the ignorant as much as you can; society is culpable in not providing instruction for all and it must answer for the night which it produces. If the soul is left in darkness, sins will be committed. The guilty one is not he who commits the sin, but he who causes the darkness."[39] Using this passage, Sirhan told Kaiser that American society had left him in darkness, had relegated him to the bottom of the heap, and was responsible for his murderous act.

At his trial Sirhan said, "I always felt that I had no country. I wanted a place of my own where the people would speak my own language, where they would eat my own food, where I could share my own politics and my own—something that I could identify as Arab, a Palestinian Arab, and have my own country, my own city, my own land, my own business and my own everything."[40]

Sirhan would not discuss the Kennedy shooting with police officers following his arrest, but he did reveal his disillusionment with America in conversations with his interrogators. Sirhan asked Officer Frank Foster why he became a police officer. Foster replied he wanted to work in a job that benefited society. Foster told Sirhan, "I don't care if it's the person that— maybe he washes out toilet bowls, I don't know, or the highest person that can gain a position in the world; there's still injustice and maybe misuse of his powers even though its his powers." Sirhan replied, "Let me shake your hand. You're the first man . . . that ever said that and expressed it, you know, in the same way as I felt it."[41] When Foster asked Sirhan what he wanted to get out of life, Sirhan replied, "Nothing. . . . They won't give me it! They won't give me it!"[42]

Sirhan's frustration with and hatred of American society was reflected in his journals when he wrote,

> I advocate the overthrow of the current President of the fucken United States of America. I have no absolute plans yet, but soon will compose some. I am poor—this country's propaganda says that she is the best country in the world—I have not experienced this yet—the U.S.—says that life in Russia is bad. . . . I believe that the US is ready to start declining, not that it hasn't—it began on November 23, 1963, [Sirhan meant November 22, 1963, the day President Kennedy had been assassinated], but it should decline at a faster rate so that the real Utopia will not be too far from being realized during the early 70s in this country.[43]

Sirhan believed his mind had been "wounded," and no one had been there to heal his "scars." "You [the United States] just aggravated them and moved them from chronic to malignant. And it eventually burst," he exclaimed.[44]

Given Sirhan's frame of mind and awareness of his failures in life it is not surprising he empathized with murderer Perry Smith after he read Truman Capote's 1965 book *In Cold Blood*. Both Sirhan and Smith had chips on their shoulders, were short of stature, were embittered with the way their parents brought them up, and suffered unhappy childhoods. Their only sisters had died young. Both were singled out by other children as different. They each, in their own way, acted out the bitterness that had haunted them through their formative adolescent years. Perry Smith reacted through an orgy of violence. Sirhan responded by embracing Arab nationalism, which spoke to his feelings of inferiority and which also gave him pride and self-esteem. After his trial Sirhan told Kaiser that one of the memorable parts of *In Cold Blood* was Perry Smith's confrontation with his parole officer, who let him leave prison before he was ready. Sirhan quoted Smith, "You had me and you let me go!" Then Sirhan turned to Kaiser and said, "You had *me* and you let me go. And look what I did!"[45]

A psychiatrist's profile of Smith, quoted by Capote, revealed,

> Two features in [Smith's] personality makeup stand out as particularly pathological. The first is his 'paranoid' orientation towards the world. He is suspicious and distrustful of others, tends to feel that others discriminate against him, and feels that others are unfair to him and do not understand him. He is overly sensitive to criticisms that others make of him, and cannot tolerate being made fun of. He is quick to sense slight or insult in things others say, and frequently may misinterpret well-meant

communications. He feels he has a great need of friendship and understanding. . . . Akin to this first trait is the second, an ever-present, poorly controlled rage—easily triggered by any feeling of being tricked, slighted, or labeled inferior by others.[46]

According to John Weidner, "You had to be careful not to walk on [Sirhan's] feet. He wanted you to respect him intellectually. He was a man who said, 'I'm going to have my rights.'"[47]

Sirhan was obsessed with his position on the lowest rung of the ladder and grieved that he did not have the skills or opportunity to benefit financially from the American Dream. As criminologist Bryan Vossekuil observed, "A number [of assassins] saw themselves as backed into a corner, in despair and without much hope. They got to that point through, inevitably, a set of sad experiences: life reversals, financial reversals, family situations that were quite unhappy, some instances of child abuse."[48] All of these prerequisites applied to Sirhan.

Sirhan once told his friend Walter Crowe that he wanted to make money, "a lot of of money."[49] And he repeatedly wrote in his notebooks that he wanted to buy a Mustang car, a symbol of American success. John Strathman said, "School wasn't quick enough for him, he wanted success *now*."[50] He told his lawyer, Russell Parsons, "We claim to live in a democracy. Poor, rich, white, all equal before the law, whose votes and opinions count. I never experienced this. Rather the contrary. I experienced the injustice that these people have committed against me."[51]

Sirhan had desperately wanted the life of a typical American citizen—a decent job, family, house, cars. He wasn't satisfied with a simple job and basic material possessions because his ambition demanded more. According to a friend, Patricia Strathman, who met Sirhan when she attended John Muir High School, Sirhan's conversations always turned to horses and money. Sirhan wanted to make, "lots of money . . . fast." He equated success with the acquisition of wealth,[52] but his search for the American Dream became a nightmare, an illusion. Thus, Sirhan believed the American Dream was possible only for someone like Robert Kennedy.[53] He told American Civil Liberties Union (ACLU) lawyer Abraham Lincoln Wirin, "Kennedy was a millionaire. I was poor."[54] Lou Shelby, a family friend, said Sirhan was "definitely" unhappy with the establishment and "frustrated" in his political feelings.[55]

At college Sirhan felt detached from American society and wanted to eventually return to his homeland. However, following the Israeli occupation of East Jerusalem, as well as the Gaza Strip, West Bank, and Golan Heights in the 1967 war, his dream was shattered. He had set his sights on becoming an Arab diplomat but soon came to believe that the odds were stacked against him. He became convinced that only rich people became diplomats and that he had no chance as one of America's poor people. Sirhan said,

> [Diplomat] Ralph Bunche? Yeah, he made it in diplomacy, but he has a manufactured eminence. He spoke at PCC [Pasadena Community College] once. After that I realized that being an Arab is worse than being a Negro. Oh, I worked hard . . . but I stood out in class . . . just my name gave me away. I stood out for that teacher as an example to prove the points he wanted to make to the class about 'acculturation.' Once, during a discussion of adaptation, the problem, the issue of Palestine came up. This was my chance to speak. I really wanted to clobber this fellow, this *blond* [emphasis added] son of a bitch and I did. I put him where he really belonged. I talked for one solid hour. There were two or three colored people in the class. They had to applaud. I was on their side when they got up to tell about their grievances. My argument? Well, I said that if the US was really as benevolent as it claimed to be, why did it send Hitler's Jews to Palestine? Why not to the Mojave desert? Then see how much milk and honey they could produce![56]

Sirhan admired the Black Panthers believing they were just like him—underdogs within American society. He hated Kennedy supporters Rosey Grier and Rafer Johnson and derided their "Uncle Tom" ways. The militants, he said, had not bought RFK's image.[57] Black Panther literature of the time exhorted followers to violence. Cartoons in the Black Panther newspaper depicted Panthers shooting police officers and Black Panther leader Eldridge Cleaver said that "a dead pig is the best pig of all. We encourage people to kill them, because the police constitute an army."[58] Sirhan also was fascinated with the movie *Bonnie and Clyde*, which received much publicity in 1967 for its romantic portrayal of a Depression-era couple who robbed banks that purportedly took the farms and homes away from poor Midwesterners.

In fact, Sirhan initially threw his support behind Robert Kennedy because he thought the senator had proved his commitment to the underdog in society.[59] Of course, Sirhan changed his mind when he learned that Kennedy supported Israel.

Sirhan was also, according to star witness at the trial Alvin Clark, "very prejudiced towards white people."[60] He believed blacks had recently rioted because they had been "pushed too far," and he compared the African Americans to Palestinians. Sirhan once said, "Robert Kennedy was a fascist pig. [Black Panther leader] Eldridge Cleaver said so."[61] In fact, during his trial, Sirhan emulated the Black Panther clenched fist salute. According to his brother Munir, Sirhan also became enamored with the Black Muslims, who were like him culturally. Sirhan attended the Black Muslim Temple in Central Los Angeles until he was told he could not join the organization because he was not black. He did, however, purchase some Black Muslim literature.[62]

William T. Divale, whom the FBI hired to act as an informant on college campuses, said Sirhan, in his May 2, 1968, meeting with mutual friend Walter Crowe, advocated a violent approach to protesting the Vietnam War. Divale said Sirhan would have organized a "guerrilla band, holing up in the mountains somewhere and waging a shooting war against the establishment."[63]

According to Crowe, who unsuccessfully tried to organize Students for a Democratic Society (SDS) events on the PCC campus, Sirhan took a left-wing position on issues such as racism and the Vietnam War but was reactionary when it came to the Arab-Israeli conflict. Because Crowe was a committed communist the LAPD's Special Unit Senator (SUS) questioned the radical student about his connections to Sirhan. The SUS found Crowe to be truthful when he denied he was part of a conspiracy to kill RFK, but Crowe's polygraph test revealed he had lied when he said he did not have foreknowledge of Sirhan's crime. The LAPD Summary Report said, "The results of the [polygraph] test caused investigators to believe that Crowe had some knowledge of Sirhan's intention to kill Kennedy; however, it was considered improbable that Crowe could have influenced Sirhan, based on the conversations with Crowe."[64] It is plausible that Crowe was placed in the same position as Alvin Clark, the garbage collector who heard Sirhan threaten Robert Kennedy. Crowe and Sirhan both held radical political views, and in conversations with Crowe, Sirhan had not held back in expressing those views. While Crowe might have known about Sirhan's intention to strike out in support of his views in some political way, as a communist and hater of the establishment he felt he could not inform the authorities lest he also be accused.

Notwithstanding conspiracy writers' protestations to the contrary, some evidence suggests that Sirhan embraced communist ideology. According to Lisa Pease, "When [private detective Michael McCowan] looked at a collection of books Sirhan owned he jumped to the conclusion that Sirhan was a communist."[65] Sirhan did indeed embrace the communist creed. He became fascinated with revolutionary politics and was intensely interested in Fidel Castro's book *History Will Absolve Me*.[66] His notebooks revealed his radical leftist position. One entry declaimed,

> A list of grievances against US and all its façade of freedom is but an imaginary and an elusive concept granted the American sheep-like bourgeois masses, by their selfish (capitalistically permissible) sinister, and power hungry (whether democratically given to them or not is immaterial) overlords—(who are bribed, paid homage to and toyed with by lobbyists) who are in turn treated the same way—by a lesser power hungry (political and economic) patriotic (understated) individuals (bastards). An individuals [*sic*] freedom of speech is guaranteed as long as he remains aligned, and in accord with what his decadent leaders want him to be. . . . Should you dissent, we will find some means to kill you (economically, socially, politically etc). We will use some of the loop-holes that we have constructed in our legislation. . . . American capitalism will fail . . . give way to the worker's dictatorship. . . . I firmly support the communist cause and its people—whether Russian, Chinese, Albanian, Hungarians or whoever—workers of the world unite. You have nothing to lose but your chains and a world to win. . . . America will soon face a downfall so abysmal, that she will never recover from it. . . . Well, my solution to this type of government that is to do away with its leaders— and declare anarchy, the best form of government—or no govt. The president is your best friend until he gets in power, then he sucks every drop of blood out of you—and if he doesn't like you—you're dead.[67]

Sirhan's bitterness toward the country that gave his family safe haven became greater following the Six Days' War in June 1967. He said that his identification with the Arab cause had an effect on his self-esteem following the Arab defeat. He believed the war was his "denouement," psychologically speaking.[68] In his notebooks he made an entry dated June 2, 1967, in which he railed against the United States. Sirhan wrote,

> A Declaration of War Against American Humanity—When in the course of human events it has become necessary for me to equalize and seek revenge for all the inhuman treatment

committed against me by the American people, the manifesta-
tion of this Declaration will be executed by its supporters as
soon as he is able to command a sum of money ($2,000) and to
acquire some firearms—the specification of which have not
been established yet. The victims of the party in favor of this
declaration will be or are now—the President, vice, etc.—down
the ladder. The time will be chosen by the author at the conve-
nience of the accused. The method of assault is immaterial—
however the type of weapon used should influence it somehow. The author believes that many, in fact multitudes of
people, are in harmony with his thoughts and feelings. The
conflict and violence in the world subsequent to the enforcement of this decree shall not be considered likely by the author of this memoranda, rather he hopes that they be the ini-
tiatory military steps to WWIII—the author expresses his
wishes very bluntly that he wants to be recorded by history as
the man who triggered off the last war.[69]

Sirhan's writings reveal a young and immature man attempting to
emulate a diplomat. Sirhan wrote, in effect, a parody of the Declaration of
Independence, using pretentious and semisophisticated language that reflected his limited education.

Sirhan and "Assassination"

The idea of assassination was in Sirhan's mind for many years prior to the
murder of Robert Kennedy. As a Secret Service report on assassination
concluded, "Potential assassins seek out historical information about assassination, the lives of attackers, and the protectors of their targets. . . . An
attack was a means to achieve an end, such as calling attention to a perceived problem."[70]

As a student at John Muir High School Sirhan underlined passages
in his school textbooks that referred to assassination. In one textbook, *The
Transformation of Modern Europe* by Louis Gottschalk and Donald Lash,
Sirhan underlined the following passage, which makes reference to Gavrilo
Princip's assassination of Archduke Ferdinand, which sparked off World War
I: "It is conceivable that if the chauffeur of the Archduke's car, having taken
the wrong road on the way back from the official reception at the town hall,
had not backed up to correct his error, the assassin would not have been
successful. On the other hand, another assassin might have been, because the
plot to kill the Archduke had been carefully laid under the direction of the

colonel in charge of the intelligence division of the Serbian general staff, and more than one assassin was lying in wait that day."[71]

In *A History of the American People*, Sirhan underlined, "It was his last public utterance. The next day, as he was holding a reception in the Temple of Music, he was shot by a young Polish anarchist named Czolgosz, whose brain had been inflamed by reading the tirades of the yellow press against 'Czar McKinley.' After a week of patient suffering the president died— the third victim of an assassin's bullet since the Civil War." Below the passage Sirhan had written, "And many more will come." Sirhan made no other marks in either book. In a textbook that Sirhan had purchased on January 30, 1964, titled *Readings for College Writers*, he underlined the following sentences: "The enemy is not necessarily a bad man. Indeed, he may be a man of high character and considerable good will."[72]

Like William McKinley's assassin, Sirhan was quiet and shy, with no real close friends apart from his brothers. And, like Leon Czolgosz, he was fascinated with previous assassinations and assassination attempts. Like Czolgosz, he was foreign born and part of an ethnic immigrant community and wanted to strike a blow at a government that "would not listen." Like Czolgosz, Sirhan refused to give his name following his arrest. Czolgosz gave his name as Fred Nieman, which police later realized translated as "Fred Nobody."

Sirhan also displayed further features common to past American presidential assassins, as described by the National Commission on the Causes and Prevention of Violence, which was commissioned by President Johnson following the assassination of Robert Kennedy. According to the commission, assassins of American leaders often were "short and slight of build, foreign born and from a broken family—most probably with a father either absent or unresponsive to the child. He would be a loner, unmarried, with no steady female friends, and have a history of good work terminated from one to three years before the assassination attempt by a seeming listlessness and irascibility. He would identify with a political or religious movement with the assassination triggered by a specific issue which relates to the principles of the cause or movement. Although identifying with the cause, the assassin would not in fact be part of or able to contribute to the movement. Not every presidential assassin has had every one of the foregoing traits but some combination of the above has characterized them all."[73]

Many of America's presidential assassins shared relatively recent foreign roots, possibly contributing to their sense of low esteem and low status in society. Richard Lawrence, who made an attempt on the life of President Andrew Jackson in 1835, was an Englishman who had moved to

America with his parents when he was twelve. John N. Schrank, who made an attempt on the life of former President Theodore Roosevelt in 1912, was a native of Bavaria and moved to the United States when he was thirteen. Giuseppe Zangara, who tried to shoot president-elect Franklin D. Roosevelt in 1933, was born in Italy and immigrated to America when he was twenty-three. Leon F. Czolgosz was born a few months after his parents immigrated to the United States from Poland. Oscar Collazo, who tried to kill President Harry Truman in 1950, was born in Puerto Rico.

David Rothstein analyzed twenty-seven inmates of the Medical Center for Federal Prisoners in Springfield, Missouri, who indicated an intention to attack the president. They each bore stark similarities to Sirhan. Most came from unhappy homes, had ineffectual fathers, and had some connection to the military at an early age. According to Rothstein, the prisoners had in common "youth, unhappy home environments and, typically, an upbringing by a dominant mother while an ineffectual father stood aside."[74] And John Douglas and Robert Ressler, famous for their techniques of profiling serial killers and other murderers, interviewed Sirhan Sirhan and found he displayed many characteristics found in the background profiling of other famous assassins and would-be assassins.

According to Douglas and Ressler, assassin types were generally paranoid and always came from dysfunctional families but in some cases "it was more subtle; the absence of a loving or nurturing atmosphere; inconsistent or non-existent discipline; a kid who, for whatever reason, never adjusted or fit in."[75] Douglas and other experts who worked closely with the Secret Service identified consistent characteristics of assassins. They were generally

- white males who had had troubled childhoods
- loners
- lacking in self-esteem
- "functional paranoiacs"
- diary keepers

According to Douglas, "Another telling characteristic [of assassins] is the way [they] tend to express themselves. A very large number of them will keep diaries or journals recording not just events that happened or the way they're feeling on a particular day as most people would, but also every slight done to them and imagined conspiracies, as well as detailed plans for what to do about them. . . . Since they don't have any close friends or trusted confidants, these social isolates express themselves *to* themselves in these detailed secret communications. . . . In many cases, they actually use this journal writing to program themselves to commit the crime."[76]

Douglas described two types of paranoid personality. "Functional paranoiacs," Douglas explained, were different from "paranoid schizophrenics." Paranoid schizophrenics suffered from a serious psychosis "often described as a shattered personality." They fit fairly normally into society but, according to Douglas and others, display delusional ideas, at least in the sense that they think their crimes will precipitate changes in society, or they are delusional in the sense that there is no correlation between the problem as they've defined it and the action they take to deal with it. This type of criminal does not hear voices or act in response to "God's commands." Douglas maintains that if the basic premise of the assassin's delusions, in this case Sirhan's belief in the Palestinian cause, are accepted as true then he can be called a functional paranoiac.[77]

It may be true that Sirhan's political motive in killing Robert Kennedy was an excuse to satisfy his other needs: fame, notoriety, feeling some kind of worth or success, as Douglas believes. Criminologist Stephen Schafer, in his book *The Political Criminal: The Problem of Morality and Crime*, identified some offenders as "pseudo-convictional," that is, common criminals who use political grievances to mask a motivation centered around their own sense of thrill or adventure, who live beyond and outside the law to share in popular fame and adulation. According to Schafer these offenders' claims of political motive, however strenuously asserted, are mere excuses. Schafer asked, "How then are genuine political offenders to be distinguished from the impostors, those who resort to political motives merely as a cover?"[78] Dan Moldea supports the idea that Sirhan was a "pseudo-convictional assassin," that he acted not out of any strong political motive but rather a desire to achieve infamy. The question that must be asked, therefore, is, Would Sirhan have committed the crime had he not been fueled by Palestinian-Arab nationalism and a hatred for American society? It is true that Sirhan acted out of a need to acquire status and notoriety, but it is also true his act directly related to his political beliefs and, like contemporary Palestinian terrorists, he wanted to become a hero to his people.

Some evidence suggests that Sirhan was fascinated and obsessed not only with assassination in general but also with the JFK assassination in particular. Sirhan followed the JFK conspiracy debate, which was a regular item in news stories during the mid- to late 1960s. In fact he read William Manchester's *Death of a President* and listened to *A Memorial Album: Highlights of Speeches Made by Our Beloved President, JFK*. He once pointed a finger at Robert Blair Kaiser's forehead, made a popping sound, and said, "That's all that rules the world. Lee Harvey Oswald ruled the world for that moment that trigger was pulled."[79]

Sirhan might have been trying to act like Oswald when he was arrested. Following Oswald's arrest the presidential assassin asked to speak to someone from the ACLU. He refused to answer questions that bore directly on the assassination or the murder of Officer Tippit, and he refused to confirm his identity to police officers who found two IDs on his person. Like Oswald, Sirhan refused to give his name, telling the police to figure it out for themselves. Sirhan stripped himself of every piece of identification before the shooting. Like Oswald, Sirhan "toyed" with the police during his interrogations. At his trial Sirhan might have been emulating Oswald when he gave a left-wing clenched fist salute. (It is, of course, possible Sirhan had simply emulated the salute of the Black Panthers, a group he had empathy for.)[80]

Sirhan and Oswald shared additional similarities. Both assassins believed they were underdogs in society. Both had suffered deprived childhoods and grew up in poverty without a meaningful male role model. They spent their formative years adrift from the guidance only fathers can give to young boys. Both assassins looked to a "new world order"—Oswald through his belief in revolutionary socialism, Sirhan through his belief in fanatical Arabism and new age philosophies. Both were angry young men who found it difficult to hold down a job. And both believed, unrealistically, that they were destined for an important role in life. They had narcissistic personalities.

Sirhan and the Occult

Although nominally a Christian, Sirhan abandoned his faith long before June 1968. An associate pastor at the Baptist Church in Pasadena who had several conversations with him described Sirhan as "a very intense atheist." The pastor believed Sirhan had been heavily influenced by a junior high school teacher who provided Sirhan with anti-religious literature.[81]

Sirhan began keeping a diary after he read that political scientist C. Wright Mills used them as starting points for his books. Sirhan was also influenced by his school friend, Walter Crowe, who wrote his political thoughts in notebooks. Sirhan knew that Perry Smith had kept a journal, "The Private Diary of Perry Edward Smith."[82] Dr. Seymour Pollack, the psychiatrist who argued for the prosecution's case in Sirhan's trial, said Sirhan's diaries were not evidence of a psychotic mind but were either doodlings or the rational work of a man setting down his goals to perk up his courage.[83]

Tom Rathke, a stable groom at the Santa Anita Racetrack, inspired Sirhan to pursue the practices of mysticism. Rathke also introduced Sirhan in the practice of self-hypnosis. Rathke believed that Sirhan's unusual personality and "thought waves" calmed the horses. Sirhan had been impressed by Rathke and engaged in long conversations with him about mysticism. Sirhan pursued his interest in the subject by answering an advertisement by the San Jose–based Rosicrucians inviting the public to apply for membership. Sirhan applied and sent $20 for membership.[84]

Patricia Strathman and her husband John both held an interest in mysticism and conversed with Sirhan about the subject. According to John Strathman, "Sirhan used to talk about [Rathke] a lot. . . . I think he was the guy who introduced Sirhan to the occult. He seemed to have Sirhan sort of transfixed. From what Sirhan told me, I got a sinister picture—of Sirhan and Rathke riding around in this old car. Rathke is driving and talking and Sirhan is listening and filling his head with all this junk on the occult."[85]

The Rosicrucians believed that individuals could succeed in any enterprise if they wrote down their objective over and over again while in a trancelike state. Sirhan said his stream of consciousness writings about killing Kennedy before June 5 were inspired by a sermonizing article titled "Put It in Writing" by Arthur J. Fetting that was published in a Rosicrucian magazine dated May 1968.[86] The article exhorted readers to "Try it. Pick a goal. Set a target date. Now, start working to make it come true. . . . Read that goal every morning when you get up and every night before you go to sleep. Read it, believe it, and start doing things you feel you should to make it come true. This simple formula of writing it down and believing works."[87] Sirhan had also read Rosicrucian ideas about hypnotism.[88]

Sirhan went to a meeting of the Rosicrucians the week before the assassination, on Tuesday, May 28, 1968, at Pasadena's Akhnaton Lodge. Twenty-four people attended the meeting, and Willamay Harrison greeted Sirhan when he arrived at the meeting. Sirhan gave his name as "Joe," Munir's nickname. He was asked to put on a membership apron, and Verna C. Miller gave him a nametag. He was alone and hardly spoke to anyone. He left the meeting early but not before he was noticed looking at a display of occult books.[89]

Sirhan had previously attended a meeting of the Theosophical Society in March 1968 at the Adyar Lodge in Pasadena.[90] Theosophy borrows from the philosophy of the Hindu religion without adopting the external forms of Hindu worship and was founded by Madame Blavatsky. Helena P. Blavatsky claimed that cosmic masters asked her to bring about a new age of spiritual enlightenment. In 1888 Blavatsky wrote *The Secret Doctrine*, in which she attempted to set out the principles of God-wisdom, or theosophy, that the God masters of Atlantis had imparted to her. Blavatsky claimed that the God masters were the progenitors of the human race and that while some people retained the Atlantian purity of their ancient ancestors, others, notably the Jews, had not. Propagandists of the Third Reich were the first to latch onto her theories of racial purity. The philosophy's strain of anti-Semitism doubtlessly appealed to Sirhan.

Sirhan's interest in the occult did not begin with his interest in the Rosicrucian Society, however. His mother had dabbled in mysticism, which was basically intuition without human reasoning, and often read people's fortunes in tea leaves. Sirhan was also fascinated with Arab neighbor Linda Massri's fortune telling,[91] and he held the belief that Hitler had hypnotic powers.[92]

Sirhan visited two spinsters, Anna Sylvan and Olive Blackslee, who lived down the block from the Sirhan family, to play Chinese checkers. According to Sylvan and Blackslee, Sirhan did not discuss politics but liked to talk about spiritual ideas, philosophy, and theosophy. They said Sirhan practiced yoga and mentioned "the powers of mind over matter."[93] Sirhan had also read that Perry Smith "foretold events, had premonitions . . . was most respectful of his superstitions. . . . The compulsively superstitious person is also very often a serious believer in fate. . . . Some of his thinking [reflected] a 'magical quality,' a disregard of reality."[94]

According to one of his lawyers, Emile Zola Berman, Sirhan "became concerned with mystical thoughts and searched for supernatural powers of the mind over matter. He started mystical experiments in his own room. For example he would concentrate on a hanging lead sinker to make it swing back and forth by the power of his mind and concentration. He would concentrate on a candle flame and make it dance, first to the right and then to the left."[95] After experimenting Sirhan came to believe he had caused a horse, named Press Agent, to crash against the rails of the racecourse, simply by concentrating his mind.[96] He also believed he could "kill" his former boss, Bert Altfillisch, by using the powers of his mind.

Sirhan believed that his experimentation with the occult spurred him on to murder Robert Kennedy. He said he gained the power to condition his mind for the act by reading *Cyclomancy*, recommended by Tom Rathke, and by developing his powers of "autosuggestion."[97] Munir confirmed that Sirhan would stare into the mirror and make a candle flame flicker and that Sirhan would also make a homemade pendulum swing back and forth after staring at it for some time. Sirhan was also fascinated with "voodoo."[98]

Sirhan began to use his mind control techniques to set his goal of killing Robert Kennedy. He concentrated in front of a mirror and "thought about Senator Kennedy until at last, he saw his own face no longer, but that of Senator Robert Kennedy himself in the mirror."[99] Sirhan wrote in his notebooks, "Senator Kennedy must be sacrificed for the cause of the poor exploited people. . . . The glorious United States of America will eventually be felled by a blow of an assassin's bullet." On May 18 at "9:45 a.m.—68," he wrote, "My determination to eliminate RFK is becoming more the more of an unshakable obsession. . . . RFK must die—RFK must be killed Robert F. Kennedy must be assassinated RFK must be assassinated RFK must be assassinated. . . . RFK must be assassinated before 5 June 68." He told psychiatrist Dr. Bernard Diamond he remembered this entry "very vaguely."[100]

In a 1993 interview with Dan Moldea, Sirhan attempted to explain why he was attracted to the occult. He told Moldea, "It was a kind of meditation, silence and quiet. It's like the New Age movement toward tranquility and peace of mind. . . . I was trying to improve myself. I started to learn about the metaphysical occult after the death of my sister. I was hit hard when she died. . . . A guy I knew when I was down in Corona [Tom Rathke] pushed me along the way to reading more. It was more intellectual and abstract. It was more about Theosophy, which is about the spiritual afterlife. It expanded my knowledge and horizons of life, as well as my own nature and spiritual being."[101]

Sirhan's mind control exercises served a purpose but not the one he described to Moldea. They gave him the ability to channel his hatred and aggression and disappointments in life into positive action, in much the same way the first assassins used the drug hashish to induce concentration, courage, and self-belief in the acts they were about to commit.

11
THE UNAFFILIATED TERRORIST

"They're all trying to dig into my family background. That had no effect on my actions.... Had I killed my wife, had I killed my brother ... [I could] understand their trying to delve into my background. But, you see, this was political."
—SIRHAN SIRHAN, IN AN INTERVIEW WITH ROBERT BLAIR KAISER

"In my mind, my theory has always been ... is what it would be like if I was able to ... shoot Hitler. To the German people I'd be the worst scumbag.... In my own mind, I'd say, 'Hey, I'm a big hero. I did the right thing for the world.' That's the way [Sirhan] struck me. He really believed that he had done the right thing."
—LOS ANGELES POLICE DEPARTMENT SGT. WILLIAM JORDAN, WHO LED SIRHAN SIRHAN'S INTERROGATION ON JUNE 5, 1968

"Sirhan is a political assassin. His murder of Senator Kennedy was an act intended to kill more than a man or woman. It was different. It was an act intended to kill a living and vital part of our democratic and representative government."
—LOS ANGELES DISTRICT ATTORNEY JOHN VAN DE KAMP, 1981

The Origins of Middle Eastern Terrorism

The Middle Eastern terrorism menace has its roots in European totalitarianism, pan-Arabism, and fundamentalist Islam. Its common goal is the annihilation of liberal societies. Nazi theorists in postwar Egypt had a large influence over the Muslim Brotherhood, the ancestors of Al Fatah, and Al Qaeda; Syrian and Iraqi Baathists leaned toward the Soviet Union; and German ultraleftists like the Baader-Meinhof gang allied themselves with Palestinians in the 1970s to murder Jews. Whether the Middle Eastern terrorist groups sought racial purity, class purity, or a reversion to the seventh-century doctrine of Medina, all promised a new world order but produced only hatred, death, and nihilistic destruction.

The most important of the early twentieth-century scholars who gave legitimacy to terrorism was Egyptian philosopher Sayyid Qutb, an anti-materialist Muslim leftist. Qutb initiated a profound pathology within the Arab world centered on the idea that death is "glory." He first popularized the idea that the Christian West was evil because it separated its material life from its spiritual center. Christianity's split personality was seen to threaten the Muslim faith. For Qutb, jihad, which had previously been a defensive strategy to preserve Islam, became a struggle against "infidels" everywhere. The thirty-four tomes of Qutb's commentary on the Koran became the Bible for Arab political movements throughout the Middle East and a mirror image of fascist and communist totalitarian terror.

Qutb believed that Muslims should not only follow their religion but also "strike hard at all those political powers which force people to bow before them and which rule over them, unmindful of the commandments of God and which prevent people from listening to the preaching and accepting the belief if they wish to do so. After annihilating the tyrannical force, whether it be in a political or a racial form, or in the form of class distinctions within the same race, Islam establishes a new social, economic, and political system, in which the concept of freedom of man is applied in practice."[1]

Paul Berman, in his acclaimed book, *Terror and Liberalism* (2003), argues that for the past thirty years or more the West has refused to recognize that terrorism can be fought through aide and negotiation. Since the 1970s Muslim despots and fanatics have exterminated millions of people: in Lebanon, the Sudan, Algeria, Afghanistan, and Iraq. The West, Berman argues, is guilty of failing to recognize that whole societies have succumbed to pathological political tendencies. Fearful of domestic Muslim opinion, the rationalist Western governments blamed themselves for their imperialist past instead of looking outward to Middle Eastern governments that were solely responsible for their own failed societies, and the Islamic world refused to admit that the reason its civilization had lost out to Western modernity lay within itself. The Middle East blamed the West and its imperialism for the calamities that struck Arab people. As a result, any attempt by the West to defend itself against violence was seen as an imperialist attack and any civilian casualties Arabs inflicted were an unfortunate consequence of their defense.

Berman also accuses the liberal West of making terrorism more effective by looking at the problem with a "moral equivalence"—they have their fundamentalism, we have ours—as if non-Muslim faiths in the West represent the same threat to the world as the semi-crazed believers in a death-obsessed culture. Left-wing intellectuals, Berman argues, propagate the argument that terror is acceptable. From Stalin to Mao to Pol Pot, the left has supported, or made excuses for, the oppression and killing of people whose fate was dismissed as the necessary sacrifice for the fantasies of revolutionary socialism. As former Israeli prime minister Ehud Barak observed, "[Muslim fundamentalists] don't suffer from the problem of telling lies that exists in Judeo-Christian culture. Truth is seen as an irrelevant category. There is only that which serves your purpose and that which doesn't. There is no such thing as 'the truth.'"[2]

Defining "Terrorism"

Political scientists are split on the definition of terrorism. Terrorism, by its nature, is difficult to define. As Walter Lacqueur observed, "Even if there were an objective, value-free definition of terrorism, covering all its important aspects and features, it would still be rejected by some for ideological reasons."[3] Even the agencies of the U.S. government cannot agree on a single definition and some countries, like Iran, define the term narrowly according to their own set of beliefs. The 2002 Organization of the Islamic Conference, comprised of fifty-seven Muslim countries, failed to issue a definition of terrorism. The secretary general of the conference called for efforts to fight the unjust attribution of the label "terrorists" to Palestinians and to denounce the "state terrorism" of Israel, practiced through various means of "terrorist acts."[4]

Some definitions of terrorism include:

- Terrorism is the use or threatened use of force designed to bring about political change.[5]
- Terrorism constitutes the illegitimate use of force to achieve a political objective when innocent people are targeted.[6]
- Terrorism is the premeditated, deliberate, systematic murder, mayhem, and threatening of the innocent to create fear and intimidation in order to gain a political or tactical advantage, usually to influence an audience.[7]
- Terrorism is the unlawful use or threat of violence against persons or property to further political or social objectives. It is usually intended to intimidate or coerce a government, individuals, or groups, or to modify their behavior or politics.[8]
- In a criminal sense, terrorism involves the "deliberate evocation of dread," and this dread sets a terrorist act apart from "simple murder or assault."[9]

While there is no universal definition of terrorism, various experts point out that most terrorist acts share common elements, including:

- Acts of terrorism usually are committed by groups who do not possess the political power to change policies they consider intolerable.
- Terrorists choose targets and actions to maximize the psychological effects on society or government.
- Terrorists plan their acts to get as much media exposure as possible.
- Terrorists often justify their acts on ideological or religious grounds.

Bruce Hoffman maintains that an act may be defined as terrorism only if certain features, including "violence committed by non-state entities," are present.[10] He believes that "even though Sirhan Sirhan's assassination of a presidential candidate and United States Senator Robert Kennedy . . . had a political motive . . . it is debateable whether the murder should be defined as a terrorist act since Sirhan belonged to no organized group and acted entirely on his own, out of a deep personal frustration and a profound animus that few others shared."[11] As we have seen, however, Sirhan's act was not committed simply out of a personal frustration not shared by others.

Hoffman's definition is too narrow for the Federal Bureau of Investigation (FBI), which defines a terrorist act as "the unlawful use of force or violence against persons or property to intimidate or coerce a government, the civilian population, or any segment thereof, in furtherance of political or social objectives." The FBI, therefore, believes that terrorists need not be part of any organized or loose group and can act individually without any direction from such groups. Still, it is reluctant to categorize an incident as terrorism unless it is claimed by a group. However, as Christopher Hewitt, wrote, "Most terrorism is organized in the sense that it is carried out by members of terrorist or extremist organizations. . . . [But] even those individuals who are not members of organized groups may have links with wider movements, and respond to what the leaders of extremist movements do and say."[12] Hewitt observed that "Most American terrorism differs from terrorism in other countries in that a significant proportion of terrorist acts have been carried out by unaffiliated individuals rather than by members of terrorist organizations. . . . Such loners will pose the greatest threat to the security of the United States . . . since they are hard to track down. . . . Freelancers are defined as individuals who are not members of a terrorist group, or members of an extremist organization acting under the orders of an official of the organization."[13] Hewitt calls this type of terrorist "unaffiliated."

Paul R. Pillar persuasively argues that political motivation must be a prerequisite of terrorism: "Terrorism is fundamentally different from these other forms of violence, however, in what gives rise to it and in how it must be countered, beyond simple physical security and police techniques. Terrorists' concerns are macrocosms about changing a larger order; other violent criminals are focused on the micro level of pecuniary gain and personal relationships. 'Political' in this regard encompasses not just traditional left-right politics but also what are frequently described as religious motivations or social issues."[14]

From the definitions formulated by many government organizations and some leading political scientists, including Pillar, Sirhan's act of murder can be described as terrorist in nature. Although there is no evidence that he was in league with Palestinian terrorist groups before Robert Kennedy's murder, there is strong evidence to show that Sirhan was influenced by extremist propaganda, that he chose his target on the basis of political motive, and that he believed his actions were legitimate and were ideologically and politically inspired.

Sirhan's Political Motivation

Conspiracy writer Philip Melanson and others have sought to portray Sirhan as having no political motive for killing Kennedy because if Sirhan had no real motive then the idea that he was used as a patsy becomes more compelling. According to Melanson, "To say that Sirhan shot RFK for political reasons asks us to believe something quite improbable—that Sirhan, a man without any history of violent acts, political fanaticism or interest in the impact of RFK's candidacy on the Middle East, suddenly became so obsessed with RFK's support of Israel that he committed murder."[15]

Lisa Pease and James DiEugenio also pour scorn on Sirhan's political motivation: "During his trial, Sirhan burst out that he had killed RFK, 'wilfully, premeditatively, with twenty years of malice aforethought.' This was not very compelling, however, since Sirhan was only 24 years old at the time of the assassination. He would have had to be contemplating the murder of the as yet little-known Kennedy at the age of four!"[16] This outburst, however, was in reality the expression of a political metaphor. Sirhan was referencing the suffering his people had endured since the 1948 war, twenty years previous. He might also have been alluding to his own memories of the violence he witnessed in Jerusalem when he was four years old.

The idea that Sirhan's self-confessed political motivation was spurious did not originate with conspiracy advocates. From the beginning both

Sirhan's lawyers and the U.S. media sought to portray Robert Kennedy's assassination as the act of a deranged individual bent on seeking fame and notoriety. As Christopher Hewitt noted, "The criminal justice system is predisposed to define terrorists as crazy rather than give them a platform to expound their views. . . . In several cases, even against their clients' wishes, defense lawyers have claimed that their clients were mentally unstable. Sirhan Sirhan's attorney strongly opposed any attempt to address his political motives . . . despite the fact that Sirhan repeatedly stated that it was because of Kennedy's support for Israel."[17]

The New York lawyer Emile Zola Berman, a Jew, became one of Sirhan's lawyers and was praised for defending the Palestinian. However, the defense team might have used him simply to negate the political overtones of the crime. Berman advocated that Sirhan's defense be built around the plea of diminished capacity and proof that Sirhan had been mentally ill. Sirhan protested this line of defense. Before the trial he told his lawyers, "Have you ever heard the Arab side of the story? . . . I mean on the TV, the radio, in the mass media? . . . That's what bugs me! There's no Arab voice in America, and goddamn it, I'm gonna show 'em in that courtroom. I'm gonna really give 'em hell about it."[18] During the trial Sirhan repeatedly voiced his political motives, but his lawyers went ahead with their trial strategy after the judge rejected a second-degree murder plea, which would have saved Sirhan from the gas chamber.

Time magazine portrayed the crime, in a way typical of the American press, as the mindless act of a deranged individual, symptomatic of American society in general and a result of weak gun control laws:

> Once again the long journey home, the hushed procession, the lowered flags and harrowed faces of a nation in grief. Once again the simple question: Why? The second Kennedy assassination—almost two months to the day after the murder of Martin Luther King—immediately prompted, at home and abroad, deep doubts about the stability of America. Many saw the unleashing of a dark, latent psychosis in the national character; a stain that had its start with the first settlement of a hostile continent. For the young people, in particular, who had been persuaded by the new politics of Robert Kennedy and Eugene McCarthy to recommit themselves to the American electoral system, the assassination seemed to confirm all their lingering suspicions that society could not be reformed by democratic means.[19]

One year later *Newsweek* editorialized, "but whether Sirhan is ex-ecuted or locked away the trial itself has notably failed to explain, in any profound way, whatever meaning there may be behind the Kennedy assassi-nation. Perhaps, as Albert Camus has pointed out, the only way to under-stand such maniacally absurd events is to see the absurd itself as all the an-swer there is."[20]

Kennedy's assassination can be seen as an absurd act only if there was no obvious rational motive to consider. Yet Sirhan's crime was indeed explicable and rational, both in personal and political terms, as the Arab communities in the United States recognized as soon as the facts of the case were publicized. Henry Awad, the editor and publisher of the *Star News and Pictorial*, the largest Arab newspaper in America, said, "The Arab commu-nity wants this trial. We think it's the only way the US will hear about the Arab cause. . . . Every single Arab in America regrets the killing but the trial will bring us a chance for publicity."[21] The *New York Times* interviewed a celebrated spokesman for the Arab-American community, John Jabara, who believed that Sirhan's trial would bring an "understanding of the Arab cause."[22] *Al Anwar*, an Arab newspaper in Beirut, commented on June 10, 1968, "Regardless of everything, Sirhan's blood-stained bullets have carried Palestine into every American home. The act may be illegal, the price high and the assassination unethical. But American deafness to the cause of the Palestine people is also illegal, unethical and carries a high price."[23]

A Beirut weekly magazine opened a defense fund for Sirhan, and contributions flowed in from every corner of the Arab world. Numerous newspaper reports in the Middle East declared Palestinian joy at the news of the shooting.[24] Even sixteen years after the assassination, M. T. Mehdi, head of the Arab-American Relations Committee, told the U.S. media, "I have said that Sirhan Bishara Sirhan is legally guilty and Robert Kennedy is mor-ally guilty. Sirhan is responsible for the death of one person directly. Robert Kennedy is responsible indirectly for the deaths of thousands of Palestin-ians, Libyans, Syrians. What do you say to that?"[25]

A few media outlets in the United States recognized the nature of Sirhan's act but their voices went unheard. The *Jewish Observer* recognized that Robert Kennedy's assassination would leave a "deep scar on America's relations with the Arab world" and noted how the State Department played down Sirhan's Arab origins in order not to offend Arab states. It also ob-served that members of Congress were avoiding all reference to the Arab-Israeli conflict when discussing the assassination.

Before the start of Sirhan's trial, defense psychiatrists concluded that Sirhan was mentally ill and therefore could not meaningfully understand the gravity of his crime. Dr. Martin Schorr said Sirhan was "paranoid" and trapped in a "rigid, persistent, persuasive system of delusional self-beliefs." Accordingly, concluded Schorr, Sirhan was not able to "maturely and meaningfully reflect upon the gravity of his crime." Dr. Eric Marcus, a psychiatrist appointed by Judge Arthur Alarcon, the arraigning judge, to prepare a report on Sirhan in the weeks following the assassination, said, "In my opinion [Sirhan] was mentally disturbed and became increasingly more disturbed during the spring of [1968]. That is also noted in the psychological tests and I feel that his mental disturbances [were] relevant and directly related to his political views and his feelings about Robert Kennedy; I feel, therefore, that he could not meaningfully and maturely think and deliberate on his actions." However, Marcus conceded that Sirhan was capable of planning and forming "an intent to kill" and could entertain "malice aforethought."[26]

Dr. George Y. Abe, who also interviewed Sirhan, implied that Sirhan's political ideas were irrational. Sirhan, he said, had "paranoid-inclined ideations, particularly in the political sphere, but there is no evidence of outright delusions or hallucinations."[27] Yet the assassin's "motives" were anything but "paranoid" and reflected the thinking of millions of Arabs both in the Middle East and the United States. Dr. Philip S. Hicks, a psychiatrist who interviewed Sirhan in 1986, said that the assassination stemmed from "political fanaticism rather than psychotic violence."[28] As Richard Rhodes argued, "Psychiatry should abandon its failed mental-illness model of criminal violence, replace it with [Lonnie] Athens's evidence-based symbolic-interactionist model and get out of the disreputable business of helping violent criminals avoid taking responsibility for their crimes. After Athens it is possible to argue that some people are violent and mentally ill, but it is no longer defensible to argue that people are violent because they are mentally ill."[29] In Sirhan's case it may be pertinent to add that some criminals are violent, mentally ill, and fully cognizant of their actions.

During Sirhan's trial the prosecution's psychiatrist, Dr. Seymour Pollack, while admitting Sirhan had some form of mental illness, nonetheless stated that the assassin "wanted to kill Senator Kennedy. He appreciated the changes that would take place if he killed Senator Kennedy. He appreciated the change and that is why he wanted to kill him. If Sirhan's deliberations had been accompanied by psychotic or substantially disturbed thinking in the sense that I had meant it—from psychotic delusions—Sirhan would not have had the capacity for meaningful deliberation."[30]

Sirhan's hatred and fanaticism had their origins in the young Palestinian's upbringing, schooling, identification with Palestinian-Arab nationalism, and virulent anti-Semitism. As presented in chapter 10, Sirhan's friends, employers, and acquaintances described the young Arab as intense in his political views. His friends John Strathman and Elsie Boyko said Sirhan had always been intense and emotional whenever he discussed the Arab-Israeli conflict and was critical of American foreign policy regarding Israel. He told his psychiatrist, Dr. Diamond, that he believed he was a fanatical martyr who had acted unselfishly by helping to save the lives of Palestinians and by sacrificing his own life in the process. He told Diamond he was ready to die in the gas chamber.

Sirhan developed the idea of striking out in the year following the Arab defeat in the Six Days' War of 1967, and the idea climaxed during the 1968 primary elections. In the years leading up to the shooting Sirhan's Arab nationalism was fueled by the Arab newspaper *Al Bayan*, published in Brooklyn, which printed anti-Israeli and overtly anti-Semitic rhetoric. Robert Licher, who delivered mail to the Sirhan household from 1963 to 1968, recalled delivering Arab literature addressed to Sirhan. Special Unit Senator (SUS) detectives Sandlin and Dominguez interviewed Licher, who told them that sometimes he delivered packages that were open at the ends, revealing anti-American hate literature. Licher thought the Sirhans came from Egypt because Nasser was depicted on some covers in various victorious poses, "sometimes trampling on the necks of American leaders."[31]

An avid reader of American political periodicals, Sirhan became angry at the way the American press treated the Arabs. He told one of the doctors involved in the case, "I read this magazine article on the 20th anniversary of the state of Israel. . . . I hate the Jews. There was jubilation. I felt they were saying in the article, 'We beat the Arabs.' It burns the shit out of me. There was happiness and jubilation."[32]

Some evidence suggests that Sirhan was not incorrect in his assumptions that the U.S. media had a definite bias against Arab states. In a July 1967 *Time* magazine article titled "The Least Unreasonable Arab," Jordan's King Hussein was described as the only moderate leader in the Middle East. The magazine stated, "Instead of trying to salvage what they can the Arabs are busy blaming just about everybody but themselves for the fact that great globs of territory lie in Israeli hands." In its essay *Time* continued, "Desperately in need of survival training for the 20th century . . . a case of arrested development . . . emotional and political instability . . . suffering from one of history's worst inferiority complexes."[33]

In 1967 the Sirhan family watched television news and read the Los Angeles newspapers for reports about the Six Days' War. The family also received reports about the situation in the Middle East from friends who lived in Jerusalem.[34] A *Los Angeles Times* editorial of June 6, 1967, said that the United States had an obligation to maintain the territorial integrity of Israel, and beginning June 5, 1967, the newspaper devoted many pages to depictions of Arabs as figures of ridicule. Television comedy shows made reference to anti-Arab jokes, and the general atmosphere throughout America was joy at the Israeli victory. Arabs living in the United States found it difficult to understand why the United States sided with Israel, notwithstanding American leaders' oft-stated view of Israel as an island of democracy in a sea of dictatorships. Arab communities in America also failed to understand how the American people supported Israel because it was seen as the underdog, a small nation standing up to the aggression from large Arab states. Furthermore, support for Israel was linked to the Cold War reality that friendships were growing between Arab states, especially Nasser's Egypt, and the Soviet Union.

Sirhan's hatred for Jews was fueled by the speeches and propaganda of Egypt, Syria, and the Palestinian groups that had been waging guerrilla warfare against the state of Israel. Sirhan's hero was Abdul Nasser, and he voiced his love for the Egyptian leader to his friends and relatives. In the years following the Suez Crisis of 1956, Nasser became the greatest Arab leader since Saladin. His following was especially great with Arab youth, and because of new technology and transistor radios, the Egyptian leader's speeches on Arab nationalism had a great impact throughout the Middle East and in Arab communities in America. Nasser believed that the state of Israel had been instituted as a first step in ridding the world of Arab states. "We all know," he said after the 1956 war, "why Israel was established. Not to set up a national home, but to be one of the factors in liquidating Arab nations."[35]

The Egyptian leader also expressed anti-American sentiments in his speeches. According to former Libyan prime minister Abd Al-Hamid Al-Bakkoush, Nasser

> made a war of words against America a reason for revolutions and rebellions against any monarchic regime with any connection whatsoever to America. [Nasser] made fighting America a major element of Arab foreign policy. Many [Arab] governments used the media to implant in our minds hostility towards all things American—to the point where we became suspicious of the patriotism of anyone less than enthusiastic about hating Americans. . . . We indulged in the fantasy . . . that hostility towards America heads our list of priorities. We defined an Arab citizen as either loyal or traitorous according to his outward hostility to the Americans.[36]

Nasser believed in the bogus *The Protocols of the Elders of Zion*. As Amos Elon reveals in his book *A Blood-Dimmed Tide*, the Egyptian leader was influenced by this anti-Semitic Russian forgery, which had been used by Nazi Germany to justify its assault on German Jewry. Nasser believed in the book's thesis and quoted from the paragraph that spoke of "proof beyond all doubt that 300 Zionists, each knowing the others, controlled the fate of the European continent and elected their successors from themselves." The book inspired Nasser to exhort parents to teach their children that the Jews controlled the world's wealth and mass media. Jews had deliberately instigated the French and Russian revolutions and World War I so that they could wipe out the Islamic Caliphate and establish the League of Nations "in order to rule the world by their intermediary."[37] The book went through seven Arabic translations between 1949 and 1967 and was widely disseminated throughout the Arab world.

Nasser's anti-Semitic speeches and press releases likely convinced Sirhan that virulent hatred of Jews was not only based in historical fact but was an obligation for all Arabs to follow. And Nasser's development of strong relationships with the Soviet Union also likely influenced Sirhan in adopting a pro-communist pseudo-ideology. Sirhan wrote in his notebooks, "Long live Communism. Long live Communism, Long Live Communism. Long live Nasser. Nasser. Nasser. Nasser. . . . Nasser is the greatest man who ever lived in this world."

As is the case with many Arabs, Sirhan's Palestinian pride was greatly affected following Arab defeat in the Six Days' War. Sirhan became depressed that the territories gained by Israel during the war would never again belong to the Arabs.[38] At his trial he said,

> when you move a whole country, a whole people bodily from their own homes, from their own land, from their businesses . . . outside their country, and introduce an alien people . . . into Palestine—the Jews and the Zionists—that is completely wrong . . . and it's unjust and the Palestinian Arabs didn't do a thing . . . to justify the way they were treated by the West. . . . It affected me . . . very deeply. I didn't like it. Where is the justice involved? . . . Where is the love . . . for fighting for the underdog? Israel is no underdog in the Middle East. . . . It's those refugees that are the underdogs. And because they have no way of fighting back . . . the Jews . . . the Zionists, just keep beating away at them. That burned the hell out of me.[39]

An unnamed girlfriend of Adel told reporters it was no secret that the Arab community in Los Angeles was upset at the American government's overt support of Israel. In 1967 and 1968 she and others joined in a demonstration with marches on Hollywood Boulevard and the Hollywood Bowl.[40] Adel said his brother became angry with television reports of Arab-Israeli conflicts and would "walk across the room with a sour face very fast and get away."[41] Louis Shelby, owner of the Fez restaurant and friend of the Sirhan family, said that Sirhan was concerned about the United States and the direction it was taking, especially in the area of foreign policy. Sirhan had told Shelby how concerned he was that American foreign policy was not stopping a worldwide Zionist plot and that the United States was responsible for the establishment of Israel.[42]

Sirhan blamed "Western imperialism" for the problems of the Middle East and came to detest American leaders. In a Louis Fischer book about Mohandas Gandhi, Sirhan had underlined a passage and wrote "profound" in the margin. Although the passage was about the colonial situation in India, the situation it described was clearly analogous to that in the Middle East when viewed from the perspective of a Palestinian Arab. Fischer wrote, "The British were masters in somebody else's home. Their very presence was a humiliation. . . . Even if the British had converted India into a land flowing with milk and honey, they would have been disliked. Imperialism, like dictatorship, fears the soul, degrades the spirit and makes individuals small, the better to rule them. Fear and cowardice are its allies."[43] At his trial Sirhan said that he had learned "from history books and reading that the main cause [of the Middle East conflict] was that the West wanted to bring in persecuted Jews from Europe and expel the indigenous Arabs to accommodate the Jews."[44]

Sirhan admitted to "hating President Johnson's guts" and felt the American president was acting duplicitously when he said he upheld the "integrity of all nations in the Middle East." Sirhan said, "That's why I hated him. . . . President Johnson was trying to bring the military groups back from Europe to keep the dollars at home . . . those goddamn Zionists . . . What gives? The riots that were going on then in Newark . . . they were economically inspired and they were taking money out of the country by the truckload . . . and I didn't even have a damn job . . . and here all this money is going out of the country."[45]

Sirhan also developed an intense hatred for other leading American politicians although at his trial he expressed admiration for President Kennedy. He said he had "loved" the president because JFK had worked with Arab leaders to try to bring about a peace settlement in the Middle East. Sirhan believed President Kennedy "was going to put pressure on Israel . . . to help the refugees. . . . He was killed and it never happened."[46]

Aside from JFK, very few American leaders escaped his venomous contempt. In August 1968, when he was awaiting trial, Sirhan told his lawyers that Hubert Humphrey was a "chicken-faced son-of-a-bitch. . . . Humphrey, you better have a million guards around you, because you're gonna get it, you goddamn bastard!"[47] He also railed against Richard Nixon and Ted Kennedy. He told his lawyers, "Nixon! He's worse than Kennedy. To get the Jewish vote, he said he'd help the Israelis. But what good did it do him? Hell, he only got 4 percent of the Jewish vote. Humphrey got most of it, the son-of-a-bitch. Nixon! Hell, I gave him the election! Hell, I gave it to him!"[48] He even believed that, since he had given the election to Nixon, the new president should free him and give him a Jordanian passport and a million dollars.[49] During his pretrial incarceration at the Los Angeles County Jail, he made numerous statements that revealed his contempt for the Kennedy family. During one conversation with his lawyer, Sirhan said, "They've got an article here on Edward Kennedy. . . . Teddy never worked a day in his life."[50] Sirhan became enraged when the United States voiced its support for Israel in the United Nations Assembly and later confessed, "At the time I would have killed [U.S. ambassador to the United Nations, Arthur Goldberg] if I had a gun."[51] He wrote in his diary, "Ambassador Goldberg must die— Goldberg must be eliminated."

Sirhan reserved his burning contempt for Robert Kennedy, who he believed had made statements in support of Israel that went beyond any expressed by the other presidential candidates. He imagined Kennedy had "betrayed" him when he discovered RFK, the candidate who expressed allegiance to the underdog, had now become his bitter enemy. He also targeted Kennedy because of the senator's high potential to become the next president. Sirhan knew RFK's assassination would engender much publicity for the Arab cause.

At his trial Sirhan said that he wanted Robert Kennedy to be president but that love turned to hate when he saw television reports of RFK participating in an Israeli Independence Day celebration. He said,

> At that time, the way I felt about it, if he were in front of me, so help me God, he would have died. I was watching television. That evening I brewed myself some tea—I went into the living room to watch television. As I was flipping the dial, a program on Robert Kennedy came on, a biography that told of

his career as a politician. And I sat down to watch it. It told of his achievements . . . as Attorney General and a close associate of his brother, the President, and how he became Senator from New York. At the last part of the program . . . they were talking about Robert Kennedy always being for the underdog, for the poor, the scum of society. . . . And there he was . . . in a film from 1948 in Israel helping the Jews, as I thought, celebrating . . . the declaration of their new nation. And the emotion with which the narrator spoke . . . that burned me up. Up to that point I liked Robert Kennedy. I hoped he would win the presidency. But he was doing a lot of things behind my back that I didn't know about.[52]

Asked by his lawyer, Grant Cooper, if anyone had put it in his mind that Robert Kennedy was a "bad person," Sirhan replied, "No, no, this is all mine. . . . I couldn't believe it [RFK's support for Israel]. I would rather die . . . rather than live with it. . . . I have the shock of it . . . the humility and all this talk about the Jews being victorious."[53]

Sirhan said he heard a radio broadcast in which "[the] hot news was when the announcer said Robert Kennedy was at some Jewish Club or Zionist Club in Beverly Hills."[54] At the Neveh Shalom Synagogue Kennedy said, "In Israel—unlike so many other places in the world—our commitment is clear and compelling. We are committed to Israel's survival. We are committed to defying any attempt to destroy Israel, whatever the source. And we cannot and must not let that commitment waver." Sharif Sirhan told Egyptian journalist Mahmoud Abel-Hadi that, following the broadcast of the speech on television, "he [Sirhan] left the room putting his hands on his ears and almost weeping."[55]

At his trial Sirhan said the reference to "RFK must be assassinated before 5 June 1968" was in relation to the starting date for the Six Days' War, "the beginning of the Israeli assault, the Israeli aggression against the Arab people." Sirhan was upset that his brothers and mother did not see Robert Kennedy as a malevolent force and they argued about it. According to one of his lawyers at the trial, "[Sirhan] was disturbed that both his mother and his brothers did not see Senator Kennedy as the same destructive and malevolent and dangerous person as Sirhan perceived him to be; and I gather that he and his family . . . had some arguments about this."[56]

Over the years that hatred did not diminish. Sirhan showed little remorse for killing Robert Kennedy and portrayed himself as the victim as the following statements reveal:

"I saw that bastard [RFK] as a mass murderer. He was to the Arabs what
   Hitler was to the Jews." (1968)

"The bastard isn't worth the bullets." (1969)

Following his arrest a police officer asked if Sirhan was ashamed of what he
   did. Sirhan replied, "Hell, No!"

"That bastard is not worth my life." (January 1969)

"Kennedy got what was coming to him." (March 1969)

"In the first place, Robert Kennedy was a fascist pig. Eldridge Cleaver said
   so." (May 1969)

"Every morning I get up . . . I say I wish that son of a gun were alive because
   I wouldn't have to be here now." (May 1969)

"As far as the loss of a human being, loved by his family and all that, loved by
   his children—on that basis my action was indefensible and I acknowledge that. And I am willing to pay the price. But as far as a
   politician, a self-seeker, getting votes and preferring one ethnic group
   against another in this great democracy, for personal interest, I have
   no—what's the word?—I don't feel that he was even fair in that
   respect. . . . Who was Robert Kennedy? Was he a greater creation of
   God? I have been victimized by this country, deprived of my homeland, dispossessed." (August 1979)

In a conversation with his lawyers Sirhan admitted he disliked Kennedy, did
   "not give a damn" about him, and felt he was the one to "stop him."
   (1968)

Sirhan was aware that Palestinian organizations had begun to carry
out terrorist acts in the 1960s. In conversations Sirhan held with his friend,
Walter Crowe, the two politically aware and leftist young men discussed Arab
nationalism. Crowe told Sirhan that the Arab cause was a fight for national
liberation. Echoing sentiments held by many left-wing radicals of the time,
Crowe said the conflict in Palestine was an internal struggle by Palestinians
who were oppressed by the Israelis. Crowe believed Al Fatah's terrorist acts
were justified and that Palestinian terrorists had gained the respect of the
Arab world. Sirhan agreed and spoke of "total commitment" to the cause.[57]
Sirhan was for "violence whenever, as long as it's needed."[58] Crowe said that
Sirhan "could have seen himself as a fighter," and believed that Sirhan saw
himself as a committed revolutionary willing to undertake revolutionary action. Later Crowe came to feel guilt about the part he might have played in
putting ideas of terrorist acts into Sirhan's head and reinforcing Sirhan's
resolve.[59]

In 1959 five Arabs—Yasser Arafat, Khalil al-Wazir, Salah Khalaf, Farouq Qaddoumi, and Khaled al-Hassan, who all met in Kuwait—founded Al Fatah. In June 1967 Al Fatah began promoting its interests in the United States. Fatah (or Al Fatah) is an acronym for Harakat Al-Tahrir Al-Watani Al-Filastini—the Movement for the National Liberation of Palestine. In Arabic, HTF means death; when reversed to FTH it means victory. The organization was heavily influenced by Frantz Fanon's writings about the Algerian War of Independence. Fanon had developed the idea of "sacred violence" as a means to national self-purification, and this idea appealed to Fatah's leaders, who saw themselves as a new generation of Arabs destined to become the "revenge generation."[60] Fatah advocated a revolutionary approach: "An armed Palestinian revolution is the only way to liberate our homeland. In the initial stages at least, the revolution must be conducted by the Palestinian masses, independently of party and state. Although the active support of the Arab world is essential for the success of the operation, the Palestinian people shall retain its discretionary powers and primacy. . . . Only the idea of the armed struggle can bridge ideological differences and accelerate the process of unification."[61] Al Fatah believed there was no room for Israelis in the new Palestine. Its sponsor became the radical faction of the Baath Party in Syria.[62]

From 1965 to 1967 Fatah pursued a policy of terrorist attacks on Israeli settlements. Only a few incursions into Israel were aimed at military targets. The various Palestinian groups, which in addition to Fatah included the Popular Front for the Liberation of Palestine, led by Christian Arab, George Habash, and the Popular Front for the Liberation of Palestine, mounted 113 sabotage and terrorist attacks against Israel during this period. Fatah claimed to have carried out three hundred raids. The attacks were designed to force the Israelis to adopt a hard line toward Arab belligerency, and they eventually led to war in 1967. Following the Arab states' defeat in that conflict, Al Fatah was the first Palestinian group to recover. Its leaders decided that a guerrilla war against Israel was the only viable option, and they launched a major guerrilla offensive. Since 1965 the Palestinians had been building ties to other "liberation" movements, including the communist movement in Cuba. They adopted Leninist philosophy and saw Mao and Che Guevara as heroic "partners." In April 1968 an historic meeting between Arafat and Nasser sealed the ties between the Arab states and the terrorist organization.[63]

In July 1968 Al Fatah joined the Palestine Liberation Organization (PLO), which had been formed in 1964, and the terrorist group became the organization's main component. The PLO created the first terrorist training camps, invented suicide bombings, and became the chief propaganda machine in the West in its attempt to persuade westerners that the terrorist armies were really missionaries for social justice. Relying on Western "imperialist guilt," the PLO sought to tie the conditions of poverty, racism, and oppression of the Palestinians in the Lebanese and Jordanian refugee camps to the Western democracies, which, they argued, were ultimately to blame. The PLO vowed from its inception to have as its main objective the destruction of the Jewish state.[64]

In early 1968 Fatah groups of armed guerrillas were forced to withdraw from Israeli territory and operate from Jordan. In January 1968 Fatah convened with all Palestinian groups at a conference in Cairo to coordinate terrorist activity. The Battle of Karameh on March 21, 1968, was a turning point in the Palestinian struggle against Israel. Approximately 120 Palestinians were killed but the Al Fatah leadership decided they were victorious, and this battle enhanced Al Fatah's stature among young Palestinians. Prior to the battle, Fatah had some two thousand men under arms. By 1970 the terrorist organization had grown to ten thousand fighters.[65]

In March 1968 a group of terrorists used a land mine to destroy a school bus in Israel's Negev Desert. Two adults were killed and twenty-eight children wounded. In April 1968 Israeli police stopped a passenger bus a few miles east of the Sirhan's village, Taibeh. Three young Palestinian terrorists were shot and two of the victims died.[66] The stories were widely circulated within the United States. As a keen student of politics and Middle Eastern affairs Sirhan could not have failed to read about Fatah's exploits. On the West Coast, Arab students received their literature from Arab groups including Al Fatah. Students received copies of Al Fatah statements and communiqués, according to the *Christian Science Monitor*'s Beirut correspondent.[67] The statements exhorted Palestinian Arabs to pursue a more violent agenda to remove the Jews from Palestinian soil. There is no evidence that Sirhan met with any terrorist group representatives, but the Arab community as a group gave its wholehearted support to the Palestinian terror groups and this no doubt influenced and inspired Sirhan.

Sirhan was a student at Pasadena City College from September 1963 until May 18, 1965. During this period two Arab groups were active on campus—the International Club and the Organization of Arab Students in the United States and Canada (OAS)—but they were not recognized by the college. According to writer James H. Sheldon in an article titled "Anti-Israeli Forces on Campus," the OAS was dangerously active in spreading extremist and violent ideas during this period.[68]

Sirhan was involved with the Organization of Arab Students and met the organization's president, Kanan Abdul Latif Hamzeh, through Sharif Sirhan, who was an active member. Sirhan became a de facto member of the organization, which had been set up to assist Arab students in adjusting to academic life away from home but was more politically active than its mission statement professed. According to Hamzeh, Sirhan volunteered to assist in organizing meetings, setting up chairs, and procuring refreshments. Hamzeh also said Sirhan had intense feelings against the Israelis.[69]

It is a myth that terrorists act simply for political reasons. Steve K. Dubrow-Eichel, an expert on cults and the personalities of fanatics, argues that "Fanaticism often begins with a sudden, dramatic shift in world-view, often due to an overwhelmingly disturbing experience that is not readily explainable using 'ordinary' or familiar frameworks. Sometimes this involves betrayals and deep disappointments at the hands of close friends, family, loved ones, or a group/cause with which one strongly identifies. [Osama Bin Laden fits into this mold.] . . . The second step on the road to fanaticism is exposure to a fanatic ideology."[70]

According to Christopher Hewitt, most unaffiliated terrorists suffer from some kind of mental derangement. He asks, "What are the characteristics of these unaffiliated terrorists? . . . Although most terrorists are normal, the rate of psychological disturbance is certainly higher among the loners."[71]

Terrorism expert Jerrold Post, a leading advocate of the idea that most terrorists are mentally ill, has his own psychological hypothesis on terrorism. Although he agrees that terrorists "reason logically," Post argues that a terrorist's reasoning process is characterized by what he terms "terrorist psycho-logic." In his analysis, terrorists do not resort to terrorism as an intentional choice. Rather, he argues that "political terrorists are driven to commit acts of violence as a consequence of psychological forces and that their special psycho-logic is constructed to rationalize acts they are psychologically compelled to commit."[72] Post believes that the most potent form of terrorism exists among those individuals who are bred to hate, from generation to generation. For those terrorists, rehabilitation is nearly impossible because ethnic animosity or hatred is "in their blood" and passes from father to son.

The idea that terrorists are often influenced by events in their own lives is supported by research on Palestinian suicide bombers. The United Kingdom's Channel 4 documentary *Inside the Mind of a Suicide Bomber* revealed how some Palestinian terrorists join terrorist organizations following a personal tragedy. And Dr. Reuven Paz, an Israeli expert on politics in the

Islamic world, highlighted the personal motives of some suicide bombers when he wrote, "In all the recent Palestinian women suicide bombers, the personal motive seemed much stronger than it was among the men. They were driven either by revenge, especially if their family members had been killed by Israeli soldiers, or they had been disappointed in love."[73]

Sunday Times journalist, Christina Lamb, claims to have found evidence that Al Qaeda deliberately sought out would-be terrorists whose lives had been in turmoil. According to Lamb, "Far from searching out the religious fanatics who might be known to the authorities, the terrorists' talent-spotters frequent mosques to seek out those involved in petty crime or those who are in such trouble that they might feel their lives are not worth living. Al Qaeda preys on these weaknesses." She quoted one recruit as stating, "My life had fallen apart anyway and it seemed a way out. There are a lot of young boys in this country (UK) like I was—frustrated with their lives and then inside their heart they feel all these people are killing Muslims in Afghanistan or Iraq, so why not do something to help? . . . I knew they wanted me to do some kind of operation in which I would die but my life was in such a mess that in my mind I was already dead."[74]

Sirhan is no less an example of a terrorist who acted for both personal and political reasons. According to a report prepared under an inter-agency agreement by the Federal Research Division, Library of Congress, authored by Rex A. Hudson, there is no "terrorist mindset" but there are features present in some personalities that are common to many terrorists. The report stated, "Individuals who become terrorists often are unemployed, socially alienated individuals who have dropped out of society. . . . [Some] join out of boredom and a desire to have an action-packed adventure in pursuit of a cause they regard as just."[75]

Psychologist Eric D. Shaw provided a strong case for what he called the "personal pathway model," which includes a socialization process, narcissistic injuries, escalatory events, and those terrorists "who have suffered from early damage to their self-esteem. . . . Family political philosophies may also serve to sensitize those persons to the economic and political tensions inherent throughout modern society. . . . As a group, they appear to have been unsuccessful in obtaining a desired place in society, which has contributed to their frustration."[76]

Sirhan believed his crime was legitimate, and he was intensely proud of his act. He believed he was the Arab equivalent of a "CIA executioner."[77] His former employer, John Weidner said, "I think he did it because he thought he was doing something for his country. . . . [Sirhan] told me that when he was a child, he saw members of his family killed by Jews and he had to flee Jordan when he was a child. He was not a citizen and didn't like the United States."[78] Robert Blair Kaiser, in December 1968, told Sirhan he did not believe the assassin's expressed pro-Palestinian motives. He suggested Sirhan had been "putting him on." Sirhan replied, "I could be sometimes. But it's in me. . . . You know, women, money and horses were my thing, but I still maintain this thing [the assassination] had a political motivation. There was no other . . . involving factor."[79] Sirhan believed he was an important revolutionary; he was in the vanguard of the third world as he expressed it.[80] He thought RFK would be "like his brother," the president, and help the Arabs but, "Hell, he fucked up. That's all he did. . . . He asked for it. He should have been smarter than that. You know, the Arabs had emotions. He knew how they felt about it. But, hell, he didn't have to come out right at the fucking time when the Arab-Israeli war erupted. Oh! I couldn't take it! I couldn't take it!"[81]

Sirhan knew that his crime propagandized a political or ideological point of view; it was "a propaganda of the deed," as the National Commission on the Causes and Prevention of Violence described it. Sirhan attempted to advance his cause through publicity. His crime involved a cause and effect. By killing Kennedy, Sirhan had been advancing the Palestinians' cause, a cause that promoted the return of Arab land from the state of Israel. He said, "They [the Palestinians] want action. They want results. Hey! I produced action for them. I'm a big hero over there."[82]

U.S. policy, especially the installation of U.S. military bases near holy sites in Saudi Arabia, was condemned by many in the Arab world. In 1968, however, most Americans had no conception of the complex nature of Arab-Israeli affairs and the intense hatred pro-Israeli politicians engendered. Most of the media outlets in the Arab world, even while condemning Robert Kennedy's murder, nevertheless gave some level of justification for Sirhan's act. Furthermore, the U.S. media not only downplayed the reality of Arab-Israeli tension but it also was enjoined by the American government, which had attempted to strike a balance while at the same time giving full support to the Israelis. The U.S. government also attempt-ed to downplay the connection between Arab anger and Robert Kennedy's assassination by denying Sirhan had acted in the role of a "terrorist."

12
WHY DID HE KILL?

*"While nothing is easier than to denounce the evildoer, noth-
ing is more difficult than to understand him."*

—FYODOR MIKHAYLOVICH DOSTOYEVSKY

*"Violence is a cleansing force. It frees the native from his in-
feriority complex and from his despair and inaction; it
makes him fearless and restores his self-respect."*

—FRANTZ FANON

The Radical Influence

The investigation into the causes of political violence instituted by President Johnson following the murder of Robert Kennedy inquired into
the timing of the assassination. The commission concluded that assassination events in the United States and around the world correlated highly with
general political turmoil.

In June 1968 violence and protest in the United States had reached
a crescendo. A number of political and social movements justifying violence
as a legitimate tactic in seeking political ends had been voicing their philosophies throughout the period 1963–1968. Sirhan Sirhan had given his approval to some of these groups, specifically the Black Panthers, the Black
Muslims, and fringe groups of the Students for a Democratic Society (SDS).
He later told journalist Robert Blair Kaiser that he identified with the black
militants "very much so" and that "the Negroes bought RFK's image, but
the blacks didn't. The Uncle Toms bought it but not the militants."[1] He paid
visits to the Black Muslim temple in Central Los Angeles and bought a book
about Elijah Muhammad. Sirhan believed he had "struck a blow for the third
world against the West." According to Johnson's commission, violent revolutionary rhetoric, some of which influenced Sirhan, was frequently a pre-
cursor to physical assaults against politically prominent individuals.

Sirhan, no less than assassins in other periods of American history, was caught up in the political turmoil and social disruption. He echoed the sentiments of radical groups in his notebooks, frequently making reference to the violent overthrow of the American government. He told Kaiser, "I will be appreciated not now, but the next time the world goes to war, the next conflict comes up. That's when they're gonna think of Sirhan. Appreciate my own political views."[2] At his trial he frequently raised a clenched fist, the salute of left-wing revolutionaries.

Following the assassination, a number of U.S. radical groups, many supportive of Marxist terror groups around the world, praised Sirhan's act. Effectively, they sanctioned the killing as a legitimate act against a capitalist, unjust, and corrupt society. Sirhan's lack of remorse was a product of the terrorists' way of rationalizing political murder. He told Kaiser, "For the loss of human life, I think I should be dead. But for stopping Robert Kennedy, a fucking politician, who would have been a killer if he had been elected . . . I don't think I should be convicted at all."[3] As David C. Rappaport explained, "All terrorists must deny the relevance of guilt and innocence, but in doing so they create an unbearable tension in their own souls, for they are in effect saying that a person is not a person. It is no accident that left-wing terrorists constantly speak of a 'pig-society,' by convincing themselves that they are confronting animals they hope to stay the remorse which the slaughter of the innocent necessarily generates."[4]

Sirhan and his brothers found it difficult to assimilate into American society. They abhorred U.S. culture, disliked American mores, and most important, hated the support Americans gave to the state of Israel. The family felt they were part of a minority group alienated and misunderstood within the larger community. Stanford University professor Philip G. Zimbardo conducted a series of laboratory experiments dealing with anonymity and aggression. Commenting on the increase of violent acts in the 1960s, Zimbardo said, "What we are observing around us . . . is a sudden change in the restraints which normally control the expression of our drives, impulses and emotions." Zimbardo believed a process of "deindividualization" was gripping society—a process whereby social responsibility was decreasing and citizens were feeling the symptoms of anonymity. Size of cities, he argued, made people feel powerless, and rootlessness and mobility were contributing to the wearing away of the need for group understanding and group help. Zimbardo believed that we no longer felt like we were part of a whole society whereby each citizen felt some kind of responsibility to others in a community.[5]

There is little doubt that, when he fired his shots, Sirhan was in an emotionally charged state and felt anger toward Kennedy. This is evidenced by his cry of "Kennedy, you son of a bitch!" during the shooting. But Sirhan was also attempting to redress the grievances he had built up inside him against the United States, which, in his mind, had treated him badly and relegated him to the bottom of the heap. Radical groups that propagated violent action as a way to change society reinforced Sirhan's beliefs. In effect he was emotionally inoculated by the moral self-justification that the promoters of revolutionary violence had espoused. Sirhan's decision to strike out in a purposeful way, to act as a hero to his people, was his way of heeding the call for radical action. And he chose the last vestiges of his self-esteem, his identity as a Palestinian Arab, to accomplish the feat.

The Personal Motive

Sirhan might have recognized the character traits of Lee Harvey Oswald in his own personality. Oswald had gone on a murderous rampage to be "a somebody," a figure of importance; he had a great need to become a great historical figure. Both assassins were fatherless; both left written accounts of their lives behind; both stalked political figures; both fantasized about success and fame, which, by the very nature of their personalities, were unattainable; both searched for a religious/political meaning to their lives—and both expected to be acclaimed a hero to the downtrodden. Sirhan coveted Oswald's fame.

In 2003 one of the longest academic studies ever conducted on human personality found that many basic character traits are largely fixed by age three. The research, led by Professor Avshalom Caspi of the Insitute of Psychiatry in London, claimed to provide the strongest evidence yet that children's early emerging behavior can foretell their characteristic behavior, thoughts, and feelings as an adult.

Researchers interviewed one thousand children when they were three and then interviewed them again twenty-three years later. They found that characteristics in adults such as ambitiousness, self-confidence, shyness, impulsiveness, and the ability to concentrate were already well established when the subjects were small children. The researchers acknowledged that there were exceptions to this rule and that character often changes under the influences of, for example, upbringing and teaching. However, an important conclusion of the report recognized that the best-adjusted children, 40 percent of the total, were balanced, self-confident, had self-control, and were not easily upset. And by the time they were adults their personalities and characters had not changed.[6]

These results are particularly important when considering the issue of children growing up in war-torn zones. Sirhan's lawyers first proposed the idea that Robert Kennedy's attacker was, in some way, responding to the psychological damage he suffered as a child in Jerusalem during the 1948 Arab-Israeli war and the frequent clashes between Palestinians and Israelis he witnessed as an infant and as a young boy. Their comments received some support from Sirhan's mother, who testified at the trial about her son's experiences growing up in Jerusalem. Following Robert Kennedy's assassination, Bishara Sirhan said, "As a child, Sirhan had seen Arabs in Jerusalem killed by Jewish terrorist gangs and had seen a woman neighbor stabbed by an Israeli soldier. Furthermore, he witnessed the death of one of his childhood friends when an Israeli bomb exploded in the school yard and the little boy died immediately."[7] At Sirhan's trial, clinical psychologist William W. Crain said, with reference to the psychopathology of war, "[Sirhan's] plans to assassinate appear to have had their base in a very deep and long-standing effort on the part of Sirhan to right past wrongs regarding his own life experience. . . . Mr Sirhan's 'premeditation' began, in my judgment, when he was a very small child."[8]

Historically, this theory has some merit. During World War I, psychiatrists cared for many soldiers who had suffered shell shock. Sometimes the word "bomb" would have a profound effect on the injured. Some would react by immediately hiding beneath the hospital bed. These feelings and emotions remained with some of the soldiers for the rest of their lives. Sirhan's experiences no doubt remained with him. He frequently made reference to colleagues and friends to the horrible events he had witnessed and spoke of them in graphic detail. John Weidner's wife remembered, "One day when we were traveling back to the other [Weidner] store and I said, 'You know, Sol, John would have a lot of resentment towards the Germans and the fact his sister died in a concentration camp . . .' and I said if anyone should be resentful he would be and what they did to his sister and I said he's forgiven them, and he said to me, 'Well, do you think the Jews can't be cruel?' And I was a little startled at this, and he said, 'I'm going to tell you something that I never revealed to anyone before, not even my parents.' And then he proceeded to tell me that he had seen an Israeli soldier take a sword and cut the breasts of an Arab woman, which he's never forgotten."[9]

So many people believe that Sirhan was a pawn in the hands of others in part because a number of Sirhan family acquaintances described the assassin as "mild-mannered" and "nonviolent." Sirhan's acquaintances believed someone matching that description could hardly have fit the profile of a violent assassin. Many who actually knew Sirhan, however, would dispute this characterization. But even if the description were accurate, scientific research into criminal behavior has revealed that predicting what personality type is most likely to commit murder is never easy. Research by Lee,

Zimbardo, and Berthoff, psychologists who tested and interviewed nineteen murderers in California prisons, concluded that ten of the murderers "never committed any criminal offense prior to the current homicide—their murders were totally unexpected given their mild-manner and gentle disposition.... [the] majority was shy. These 'shy sudden murderers' killed just as violently as did the habitual criminals, and their victims died just as surely, but it would have been impossible to predict this outcome from any prior knowledge of their personalities that were so different from the more obvious habitual criminals." Terrorism expert Martha Crenshaw has written, "The outstanding common characteristic of terrorists is their normality."[10]

As he grew older, Sirhan became seriously disturbed until he at one point experienced a diminished sense of self. His life became increasingly without purpose; he felt locked in a cell of isolation, despair, and anger—anger toward others who saw him as less than a full citizen of his adopted country, toward a social system that did not recognize his talents, and toward a nation that gave support to his enemy. His profound sense of disillusionment translated into a general cynicism about where his life was headed. If he could not elevate himself to a professional position with all the riches and status that follows, he would look to his politics to find a way of succeeding. It was far easier for him to reach his goal by killing Kennedy than by constantly pursuing position and wealth that always seemed to escape him. With the assassination Sirhan exercised power in a way that had been denied him since birth.

In many ways Sirhan's act was a resentment murder. He spoke of his hatred for RFK's wealth and status and for the love the politician engendered throughout the nation. His deep-seated hatred of the senator was also rooted in his belief that America was hostile to people of dark skin and foreign origin. He told Robert Blair Kaiser, "If every man had the right to work, equality and justice, none of this would have happened."[11]

Sirhan stalked Robert Kennedy in the weeks before the assassination. He purchased a pistol and practiced rapid-fire shooting. He was a bitter and angry young man who felt the United States had treated him with disdain because of his Arab heritage. He told an acquaintance he wanted to kill Robert Kennedy. On the day of the shooting he drank enough alcohol to steel himself to commit the murder. And he weighed the consequences of arrest, having acquired some knowledge of how the U.S. criminal justice system worked. He was also aware of his legal rights and of how other criminals had escaped the full weight of the law by claiming they were in a dissociative state and thus were not really responsible for their crimes. He knew that Los Angeles prosecutor, Jack Kirschke, had gotten away with a light sentence for a premeditated double homicide and thought perhaps he could too. Psychiatrist for the prosecution, Seymour Pollack, believed that Sirhan expected to get "a couple of years in prison [for the murder]. It is the same kind of thinking that a black nationalist has who doesn't think he should get too much time for killing somebody in a racially justified situation. He thought it was good to kill Senator Kennedy. He believed he was right . . . and that is not necessarily a delusion. . . . He thought he would be looked up to and would be considered a hero. . . . He believed he was doing what was not only right but should be done, a good thing."[12]

There is little doubt that Sirhan had been experiencing psychological exhaustion and that his positive self-image had been slowly disintegrating. A reexamination of Sirhan's Rorschach was recently carried out using psychostructural and psychodynamic analyses and also using reliable and valid methodology that was unavailable at the time of examination. The researchers concluded, "In contrast to the defense experts at trial who diagnosed paranoid schizophrenia, the data suggest a depressed and suicidal individual organized at a borderline level of personality. Character pathology is hysterical, paranoid, and dependent. When the Rorschach findings are compared to the development history of Sirhan and the behavior around the time of the assassination, the data are somewhat consistent with the theme of psychic trauma, are very consistent with the theme of recurrent loss and pathological mourning, and validate a characterological distrust and hatred of, yet hysterical dependence on, the object world."[13]

Self-image is vital to everyone. Many young men and women are often shy, awkward, and insecure because their mirror does not reflect a positive image. Other people's opinions create a self-image. These opinions reflect back to form a definite mental picture of who we are. This is why young people require positive comments from role models, parents, and employers: the comments help to form their self-images, to create distinct personas. Activity is also important because doing creates a sense of purpose and gives meaning to our lives; this in turn helps create a positive self-image. Sirhan's lack of meaningful employment was a crucial factor in his decision to commit the crime. Research into unemployment reveals that one's self-image is destroyed when he or she loses a job. Unemployment leads to depression, and often depression leads to violence or antisocial acts. Furthermore, without a creative outlet and a sense of purpose the mind has no direction and wanders into the realm of fantasy, as Sirhan's case shows.

Sirhan had no capacity for inner direction. The vicious streak in him, which became apparent to some observers in the year before the murder, was the result of exhaustion and frustration at the creative level. His life was heading nowhere, and he was becoming arrogant and indignant at the perceived slights he received from "White America." He failed to secure a real education or success as a jockey and the American Dream was slipping away. Sirhan became fascinated with the occult and turned to New Age philosophies in the hope they would provide an answer to his perilous state of hopelessness. They did nothing but fill him with the nonsensical idea that he could will himself to succeed. Frustrated, he turned to the one thing that would ensure his success in life—his Arab identity. And Sirhan's criminal act not only developed his self-image but also made him feel like he achieved success by inflicting punishment on a society that deserved it.

Sirhan's decision to strike out could have been avoided if his capacity for self-actualization had been greater. His dislike of his new country was an act of self-defense. Having nearly attained the success attached to immigrant sons who acquire a college education, Sirhan was brought down to earth by his inability to meet the demanding level of his studies. Unskilled in any career or profession, he dreamed of Mustang cars, money, and glory. He was not insane in the layman's sense of the word; he was simply angry, frustrated, and bitter about his second-class citizenship. Like Lee Harvey Oswald, he craved recognition and believed his intellectual skills should have made him a "somebody." Sirhan, fixated at the self-esteem level, showed a preoccupation with the idea of intellectual or creative eminence and became the semi-educated type of individual who used big words to impress. His political insights were simplistic, the product of shallow reasoning and unobjective truth. They were the protestations of a fanatic possessing fixed views about complex issues. In this state of failure and emotional fatigue, he resorted to the ugly level of his psyche—anti-social resentment. And he killed because he hated himself, hated what he had become—an anonymous entity without a country, an identity, and a calling.

His crime may also have had a sexual dimension to it. A 1969 study of assassinations stated that "the emergence of charismatic figures, at various points in the history of a constitutional democracy such as the United States, tends to generate assassination attempts by marginal, anomic men estranged from strata of society. . . . Individuals who are driven to attempt such assassinations have strong, unfulfilled sex drives; are afflicted with abnormally intense envy and feel alienated from society and from themselves."[14] According to Dr. Edwin A. Weinstein, who worked at the Walter Reed Hospital's Division of Neuropsychiatry, Sirhan's language and his repeated use of a particular word indicated a strong sexual component in Sirhan's hatreds. He wrote in his notebooks, "the fucken USA." RFK was a "fucken politician." He said Kennedy had "fucked up" by advocating sending "fucken jet bombers" to Israel so the "fucken Jews" could "fuck the Arabs."[15]

Sirhan was shy around women, according to his brothers, and he was rejected many times by female students with whom he tried to form a relationship. According to an acquaintance, Robert Comfort, a former student at Pasadena City College (PCC), Sirhan asked a few girls out for dates but none accepted. He said girls typically said of him, "He is a nice guy, but I'd feel funny if I went out with him." Gwen Gumm was a student at PCC and was a contestant for Carnival Queen in 1964 when she first met Sirhan. She was sitting in a booth collecting donations for the carnival. Votes for the contest were counted as a cent each. Sirhan gave her a $10 bill. Sirhan asked her for dates after that, but she always declined.[16]

Sirhan became obsessed with Peggy Osterkamp, who worked at the Del Rio Ranch, and he admired her from a distance, but he was unwilling or, more likely, unable to form a relationship with her. In fact, he may have stalked her. He went to Corona often in the months preceding the assassination, giving the excuse that it was a beautiful area to visit. Osterkamp was introduced to Sirhan at the ranch where he also worked. Once, she was having lunch in a restaurant with friends, and Sirhan saw her, strolled by her table, and picked up the check. He did this without saying a word, paid the bill, and left the shop. He fantasized about marrying her, writing in his notebooks, "Peggy Sirhan." Fellow workers knew that someone of Sirhan's physical stature and background simply had no hope in attracting her. They were poles apart. Kaiser once suggested that if Sirhan had developed a loving relationship with a woman in the spring of 1968 RFK might not have been murdered. Sirhan did not reject Kaiser's analysis.

Sirhan harbored thoughts of murder before he killed RFK. He even considered killing his former employer, ranch boss Bert C. Altfillisch. As Sirhan's indignation at his life in America grew, it became more obvious he had to do something—to make someone pay for the position he had been placed in. Considering his state of mind, Sirhan's actions begin to seem logical. The majority of murders, RFK's assassination included, are crimes of passion. At the time the murder is committed, the perpetrator cannot think of anything that is more important than the murder itself, but afterward he or she looks back on the act as a moment of insanity. Sirhan might have been suffering from catathymia, a condition that involves a steady buildup of anger and frustration leading to a violent explosion.

Sirhan felt a bond with Americans who had been relegated to the bottom of the heap. He told Kaiser that Arabs were treated like second-class citizens in the United States. "Just because we're Arabs in this country," he said, "we have no power, no prestige, no influence, no money—nothing, really. We can be treated like dogs, like ants. Had it not been for me . . . Munir would be out there in one of those [Palestinian refugee] camps. He would have been deported [for having a criminal conviction]. . . . The whole world knows 'Sirhan' now. If they had deported his younger brother from America that would show an injustice on the part of America. . . . But even without me, what's all the difference? Munir was just a good-for-nothing Aye-rab."[17]

Since his birth Sirhan had experienced the four stages of "violentization," which criminologist Lonnie Athens believes are the crucial elements that create aggressive individuals. Athens interviewed hundreds of violent criminals before he reached the conclusion that the social development of criminals was warped; they experienced a "violent socialization," or "violentization," in which they are brutalized into learning that they will not be protected by the system responsible for them and that they must brutalize others or be brutalized themselves.[18] With relevance to Sirhan's background, the four stages are:

1. Brutalization: Sirhan's formative childhood years were spent in Jerusalem at a time of open conflict between Arabs and Jews. Sirhan frequently observed horrific scenes of violence. At the same time he underwent beatings by his father, who was culturally conditioned to administer extreme violence in the upbringing of his son. According to a childhood friend, Ziad Hashimeh, Sirhan's father was "too emotional." Hashimeh observed that Sirhan's father beat his son "quite a few times . . . on the bottom, the back, everywhere . . . with a stick . . . anything he could lay his hands on."[19] His father also ill-treated his wife and eventually abandoned her to return to his native land. In the United States Sirhan was "coached" by radical Palestinian literature into recognizing that violence was an effective way of changing his people's condition. Walter Crowe also coached Sirhan, telling him that the use of violence in a revolutionary situation was justified. Another element of coaching in Sirhan's world was the glorification of violence, especially that directed toward the Jews, in Arab newspapers, and periodicals. Sirhan was also "brutalized" by a long period of unemployment.

2. Belligerency: After being brutalized himself, Sirhan was determined not to have anyone treat him as inferior and aggressively challenged anyone who slighted him or insinuated he was a "second-class citizen." Although he avoided getting into fights with strangers, he often clashed with his brothers and physical fights erupted from time

to time. Sirhan, upset he had been dumped as a jockey, also toyed with the idea of killing one of his horse-trainer bosses.

3.   Violent performance: The novice commits himself to use serious violence. Sirhan vowed, through his diary entries, to use violence to propagate Arab nationalism.

4.   Virulency: The violent actor is now committed to using violence in a serious way and resolves to act.[20] Sirhan convinced himself through self-hypnosis that he was a powerful person capable of carrying out his mission to kill Robert Kennedy. He discovered the advantages of being famous even if fame was in the form of notoriety.

In 1998 the U.S. Secret Service, in consultation with mental health experts, published the findings of an ongoing study that looked at eighty-three people who had displayed threatening behavior or committed violent acts against public figures at some point since 1949. About half those studied were found to have behaved in a delusional or psychotic manner at some point in their lives. All of the eighty-three believed that the government was their enemy. Other motivations, with relevance to Sirhan's situation, included:

- **A desire for fame and notoriety.** The morning after his arrest he asked one of the guards to bring him some newspapers. He was disappointed when he could not find any stories about himself. The papers had gone to press before news of the assassination was released.

- **An attempt to avenge a perceived wrong.** Sirhan saw himself as an individual who had been wronged by American society. As an individual within a larger group, Palestinian Arabs, he believed that the world had ignored his people's plight and that America, the Jews, and Western colonialism were responsible for the Palestinian condition.

- **A desire to develop a special relationship with the target.** At first Sirhan expressed "love" for Kennedy. Acting as though he had a personal relationship with the senator, Sirhan became angry when RFK started "doing things behind his back" (i.e., giving support to Israel).

- **A desire to bring about political change.** Sirhan knew that he would be seen as a "hero" to his people and that his act would lead to world recognition of Palestinian grievances.

- **To cast attention on a personal or public problem.** Sirhan believed his act would show that "Arabs had guts" and would in some way take away the stain of humiliation the Arabs suffered following their defeat by the Israelis in the Six Days' War.

- **To bring an end to personal pain by risking death.** Sirhan's life was going nowhere. He was depressed and angry. At his trial he repeatedly told the court and his lawyers that he was willing to die for the Palestinian cause.

- **To save the country or the world.** Sirhan's notebooks show he believed that violent revolution was the answer to the world's problems.[21]

Sirhan had a long-standing morbid fascination with assassinations. In fact he had been thinking about assassination since childhood. Sirhan underlined a passage on the assassination of Archduke Ferdinand in one high school textbook. In another he underlined a paragraph that made reference to the slaying of President McKinley with a marginal note, "and many more will come." Sirhan made no other marks in either book.

As John Douglas and Robert Ressler discovered, many assassins kept diaries and many murderers fantasized about their crimes years before the events. Just as the sexual predator's crimes begin in fantasy, so did Sirhan's. The fantasy was reinforced each time he sat down to write in his journal and also each time he read a news story about Kennedy or saw his image on television. Sirhan's diaries were a dress rehearsal for the assassination. And the fantasies became increasingly realistic as he began to stalk Robert Kennedy.

Sirhan was a young man who wanted a higher degree of reward than society was willing to offer. Frustrated, he tried to grab the reward without earning it. Sirhan's reward was not tangible but rather came with the instant enrichment of celebrity. Following his arrest Sirhan became excited at the amount of mail he received from young women. He poured over the letters he received that called him a hero. When one of the prosecuting lawyers termed his crime a political assassination, he became excited. He reveled in his celebrity—"[I believe I have] gained something. They can gas me. But I am famous. I achieved in a day what it took Kennedy all his life to do."[22]

Whether or not Sirhan was suffering some form of mental illness when he committed the murder is debatable. Figuring out the inner workings of a criminal is never a precise business. What can be said about Sirhan is that he was fully aware and rational following his arrest despite conspiracy advocates' descriptions of him as being in a state of altered consciousness. His trancelike state can better be described as "drunklike"; he had also steeled himself through self-hypnosis and the knowledge that his actions would make him a hero to his people. As Kaiser wrote, "How did he come to be so focused? As late as May 5, 1969, Sirhan was still groping for an answer; he told me then in his cell that he may have been like the original assassins, the Hashshashin, members of a secret Mohammedan cult who drugged themselves before they committed their appointed murders, 'It must have been something like that with me,' he said."[23]

The jury came to recognize that Sirhan fully understood his act's implications and the difference between right and wrong. As Dr. Frederick Wertham observed, with reference to recent psychiatric defense arguments, "Zacarias Moussaoui, the only 9/11 terrorist who was captured, was considered insane by his lawyers. The possibility that Moussaoui is a political terrorist seems to escape mental health experts. The possibility that 'normal people' might engage in acts of violence is, to them, beyond the realm of reasonable assumption."[24]

If Sirhan was indeed suffering from some kind of mental illness, it does not necessarily follow that he was without reason or suffered from a split personality. Instead, the mental condition Sirhan experienced might best be described as "detached," as if surrounded by cotton wool or standing outside the reality of the chaos and violence that he engendered. Many murderers experience this condition. It is also true that Sirhan failed to resist aggressive impulses and allowed himself to engage in destructive acts. People who commit these acts are no different from anyone else, but they are no longer able to control their urges. They disassociate themselves from their own actions, often experiencing an hysterical blindness. They are blind to the darkness within themselves. And, as Lonnie Athens has concluded, the violent criminal is "violentized" by his upbringing and coaching by influential "actors."

Dan Moldea might have been correct when he said that Sirhan committed the act of murder simply to show he could do it, that he was not a "gutless Arab," that it was an attempt to assert that he was capable of action. What can be said is that RFK's violent murder was connected to Sirhan's need to be something more than he was; Sirhan chose to play the role of his people's "avenger."

Would Sirhan have killed Robert Kennedy, or indeed, committed some other form of extreme violence had there been peace between Arabs and Jews? It is possible. Sirhan fit the profile of an American assassin bent on striking out at a country he felt had betrayed him. He was a disillusioned man who wanted to attain "fame" in the classical tradition of American assassins. However, Sirhan's political motives gave him pride, self-esteem, and also a deep-rooted anger. These sentiments spurred him to act.

The Political Catalyst

From the beginning, the American media and American leaders approached the sensitive issue of Sirhan's professed motive with caution. Newspapers and television news broadcasts looked inward, instead, to explain why the crime was yet another example of sick American society. The media was awash in stories about gun control laws, the connection between poverty and crime, and the violent roots of U.S. history. The issue of violence in America played a crucial role in many of the RFK shooting reports. One reporter noted that the United States would, with its rash of assassinations in the 1960s, appear to outsiders to be "some sort of violent society."[25] Dr. King's successor as the president of the Southern Christian Leadership Conference aimed his criticism more pointedly in the direction of President Lyndon Johnson and the conflict in Vietnam by saying that Kennedy had worked against "the violence, the hatred, and the war mentality" that had been poisoning America. Senator Eugene McCarthy, Kennedy's opponent in the Democratic primary elections, echoed this sentiment in his condemnation of violence at home and abroad. Some twelve hours after the shooting, Johnson responded to criticism in a special address in which he denounced violence "in the hearts of men everywhere" and suggested the establishment of a commission to investigate the causes of violence in American society. Johnson said the murders of Martin Luther King Jr., and the Kennedy brothers gave "ample warning that in a climate of extremism, of disrespect for law, of contempt for the rights of others, violence may bring down the very best of us."[26]

There were also voices of reason. Alistair Cooke recognized that the political motive for the crime had been shunted aside. A few days after Robert Kennedy was murdered, Cooke said in one of his famous BBC radio broadcasts, "Letters from America," "I still cannot rise to the general lamentations about a sick society. I, for one, do not feel like an accessory to a crime and I reject almost as a frivolous obscenity the sophistry of collective guilt the idea that I, or the American people, killed John Fitzgerald Kennedy and Martin Luther King and Robert Francis Kennedy. I don't believe, either, that you conceived Hitler and that in some deep, unfathomable sense all Europe was responsible for the extermination of six million Jews. With Edmund Burke, I do not know how you can indict a whole nation. To me this routinely fashionable theme is a great folly."[27]

As most Americans were unaware of the Palestinian issue, very few journalists examined Sirhan's background as a Palestinian Arab in an attempt to explain the tragedy. Instead, commentators wrote off Sirhan as yet another misfit with a gun who stalked and then murdered a leading public official with no apparent motive except his own demons.

In time, Sirhan's defenders found it difficult to accept that the murder had a political motive at its roots. In fact, it was necessary to disprove a political motive if the controlled assassin thesis was to have any credibility. According to Klaber and Melanson, "If the accused assassin was making a heroic gesture on behalf of his people, why would he not remember the crime or say he did not remember the crime, while at the same time not denying or challenging his guilt? Sirhan's lack of memory simply does not fit with the act as a political event."[28] Sirhan's lawyer Lawrence Teeter said his client had no motive in killing Kennedy and that the "Phantom jets to Israel" argument was false. However, as we have seen, Sirhan's hatred for Robert Kennedy was not predicated simply on Kennedy's advocacy of sending jets to Israel. Teeter has deliberately ignored the wealth of evidence that proves Sirhan's animus toward Kennedy began some time before the jets to Israel statement.

Sirhan's self-confessed motive was entirely consistent throughout the weeks, months, and years following his act. Immediately following the shooting he cried out that he did it for his country. His insistence that his crime was political was followed up with repeated protestations that no other motive existed except a love for his people. "June 5th stood out for me . . . more than my own birth date!" he said. "I felt Robert Kennedy was coinciding his own appeal for votes with the anniversary of the [Six Days'] war."[29] From numerous statements he made to his lawyers and family it is clear he believed he had been adventurous, daring, and brave.

Sirhan's personality reflected the Arab identity as described by leading Arab intellectual Al-Afif Al-Akhdar, who wrote, "In the head of almost everyone of us [Arabs] is something of Dr. Jekyll and something of Mr Hyde: a mind simultaneously demented and wretched. An [historic] narcissistic wound is a frustration that makes its victims despise himself, a blow that makes [the victim] see himself as nothing. . . . It is symbolic castration that causes a crushing sense of shame and inferiority, and in our case, a constant [sense] of this. . . . The Arabs experienced their defeats by European imperialism and Israel on both the conscious level and the collective subconscious level . . . as a national humiliation whose shame can be purged only by 'blood, vengeance and fire' as the Arab national motto [states]."[30]

In the hours and days following the shooting Sirhan must have realized the shame he had brought upon his mother. How could he accept guilt as a political assassin and at the same time escape culpability? The answer was to feign amnesia, an idea he first learned about by reading Truman

Capote's *In Cold Blood*, while at the same time maintaining that he "must have shot Kennedy." It was impossible for him to claim otherwise considering his murderous act was carried out in full view of dozens of individuals. His claim to have suffered amnesia held out some hope that his conviction might some day be overturned but also guaranteed him praise from fellow Arabs and Palestinians.

The crime, as the notebooks and prosecution witnesses testified, was premeditated. As prosecutor David Fitts told the jury, "This defendant did not act in a rash or impulsive manner . . . when he fired a bullet into the brain of the senator. . . . Put it all together, the notebooks, the outspoken hatred for Kennedy, the clipping in his pocket, his visits to the pistol range, his rapid-fire shooting there, Sirhan's uncharacteristic interest in attending a public assembly, his inquiry in the pantry [whether Kennedy would pass that way], his condition at the time of the shooting, the cute way he avoided identifying himself to the police, leaving his identification in the glove box of his vehicle."[31] The jurors had no doubt Sirhan was guilty. First of all, they believed Sirhan had showed specific intent to kill, that is, he had a clear purpose. Second, they believed his act was indeed premeditated. Third, the jurors believed Sirhan committed the murder "with malice."

The Palestinian-Arab cause is the sine que non of the assassination, and this thesis was supported by Arab intellectual, the late Edward Said. As a poor working class immigrant, Sirhan identified with his downtrodden people living as refugees in Jordan, Egypt, Syria, and Lebanon. The period 1967–68, the year following the Six Days' War, became a crucial time in Sirhan's life because it was the time when Israel, having successfully defended itself against Arab aggression, became dominant in the region. Having failed to eject the Jews from Israel/Palestine, Arabs throughout the world felt powerless and weak, and Arab pride was severely damaged. Their condition exaggerated Sirhan's feelings of inadequacy even though he lived thousands of miles away from the conflict. Many exiled Palestinians sought retribution and began to formulate plans to kill innocent civilians and hijack planes. Sirhan answered these problems by killing a major American politician who advocated support for Israel.

Sirhan could have targeted any of the leading presidential candidates that year to publicize, through a violent act, the cause of the Palestinians. Hubert Humphrey, Eugene McCarthy, Richard Nixon, and Nelson Rockefeller supported military aid to Israel and believed in the continuing American-Israeli alliance. So why did Sirhan choose RFK?

Initially, Sirhan would likely have been satisfied with any opportunity to kill a leading American politician. He had also been obsessed with assassinating an American president and wrote in his notebooks, "Sirhan ... Sirhan Sirhan. Must begin work on ... solving the problems and difficulties of assassinating the 36th President of the glorious United States ... the so called president of the United States must be advised of their punishments for their treasonable crimes against the state more over we believe that the glorious United States of America will eventually be felled by a blow of an assassin's bullet—bullets bullets."

Unfortunately for Sirhan, President Johnson had tight Secret Service security around him and rarely campaigned around the United States, especially during the period after he announced his decision not to seek reelection. Sirhan told Robert Blair Kaiser he had been upset with Humphrey the week before the Democratic Convention in Chicago because "even after the assassination [of RFK] Humphrey said he would send bombers to Israel—just to spite me! He said that just to spite me! Humphrey, you better have a million guards around you, because you're gonna get it, you goddamn bastard."[32]

In the years between 1963 and 1968, American political culture was dominated by the idea of a "Kennedy Dynasty" and myths surrounding JFK's assassination. Year after year books, movies, television documentaries, and political news stories gave cult status to JFK's assassin, Lee Harvey Oswald. Sirhan, too, desired fame. Killing any of the other candidates would certainly have given him status throughout the Arab world, but his true target had an even greater symbolism attached to him. Sirhan would become the "Second Kennedy Assassin." He knew that killing RFK could give him greater world exposure than the other candidates could provide. It was no accident that Sirhan set his sights on the candidate who was the brother of the martyred president. It was no accident that Sirhan chose the candidate who was most likely to become the next president.

One of Sirhan's doctors said the assassin was "not a raving maniac. He's got a keen sense of justice, but it is from his private world." However, this "sense of justice" was not from Sirhan's "private world." Defense psychiatrist Dr. Martin Schorr, along with the majority of the American people, did not yet understand the logic of terrorist acts. Not only was Sirhan's act logical, although malicious, but it was embraced, condoned, and applauded throughout the Arab world. As Martha Crenshaw wrote, "Terrorism has an extremely useful agenda-setting function. If the reasons behind violence are skillfully articulated, terrorism can put the issue of political change on the public agenda. By attracting attention it makes the claims of resistance a salient issue in the public mind. . . . The message to the world [is] 'to take us seriously.'"[33] As Sirhan said, "[My act] was a warning to the US. You'd better listen. Be more cautious. Be more fair. Remember Kennedy. Remember Kennedy."[34]

To the Western mind, terrorists are deranged and evil. However, their acts are not the product of insanity; rather they possess a logic all their own. Terrorists have rational, if sometimes bizarre, motives. It is also true that many terrorists (like Al Qaeda's Ramzi Yousef and Zacarias Moussaoui) display symptoms of a psychopathic nature—they are cold-blooded and carry out their acts of terror without remorse. But their acts are not the products of delusional or irrational minds, and Sirhan's wasn't either. He did indeed crave attention and success. He was depressed that society had relegated him to the bottom of the heap. He felt an allegiance and empathy with assassins of the past. And he dreamed of infamy. But without Sirhan's Arabness and without the bitterness and hatred toward Jews that had their roots in the conflict in the Middle East, it is unlikely he would have assassinated Robert Kennedy. All the hatred that spewed forth from Sirhan's gun can ultimately be traced back to one source—Palestinian nationalism. And this may have been the first act in an international political drama that culminated with 9/11.

AFTERWORD

"The Senator's lips moved. A friend leaned over to listen. 'Jack, Jack,' he murmured, and then lapsed into unconsciousness from which he never recovered."

—RICHARD GOODWIN, *REMEMBERING AMERICA*

"Toasts: To the State Board of Parole, for its action last week in denying parole to Sirhan Sirhan, the assassin of Robert F. Kennedy. In addition to killing the New York senator, Sirhan's bullets pierced the dreams of a generation of Americans. We don't know what would have happened if RFK had been elected in 1968; but it's likely that the Vietnam War wouldn't have dragged on for another seven years, and we certainly wouldn't have had to endure Watergate. Sirhan has been denied parole 13 times; may he be denied for another 13, and more."

—*TIMES STANDARD*, EUREKA, CALIFORNIA, MARCH 20, 2006

The Funeral

On Thursday, June 6, 1968, family and friends accompanied Robert F. Kennedy's body home. A cortege including a blue hearse and nine limousines with police motorcycles left Good Samaritan Hospital at 12:40 p.m., for the twenty-mile freeway trip to the airport. RFK's wife Ethel and JFK's widow Jackie rode in the front limousine. Many onlookers threw flowers in front of the hearse. On arrival at the airport the African mahogany casket, chosen by Edward M. Kennedy, was placed at the rear of an Air Force 707 jet that had been sent by President Lyndon Johnson. A red carpet leading to the jet was lined with roses and carnations. At first Jackie Kennedy thought she was traveling on the same plane that carried her and her husband to Washington following the Dallas assassination, but it was pointed out to her that the plane was different. The airliner took off from Los Angeles International Airport at 1:28 p.m., as Secret Service agents were stationed in strategic positions around the area. The plane had originally been scheduled to leave at 10:00 a.m., but the flight was delayed by the lengthy autopsy, which had been especially thorough so as to avoid any controversy such as the one that to this day surrounds the slaying of President Kennedy in Dallas.

The plane held a group of seventy-one friends and staff. Their names read like a Who's Who in the fields of government, the arts, show business, and sports, and they included mountaineer Jim Whittaker; architect Fernando Para; civil rights leader Charles Evers, brother of the assassinated Medgar Evers; singer Andy Williams; author George Plimpton; and Coretta Scott King, the widow of Martin Luther King Jr.

During the flight Ethel Kennedy chatted with other passengers and later fell asleep beside RFK's coffin. When the silver and blue presidential jet landed at New York's La Guardia airport at 8:58 p.m., more than a thousand grieving New Yorkers were waiting in muggy eighty-three-degree heat. As the jet rolled to a halt, Ted Kennedy was the first to appear in the front door of the plane with fifteen-year-old Joe Kennedy and fourteen-year-old Robert F. Kennedy Jr. The three helped move the coffin onto a lift, which lowered it.

The coffin was transferred to a gray Cadillac hearse as Archbishop Terence J. Cooke intoned a brief prayer. New York police imposed tight security as the cortege moved out of the airport and headed for Manhattan. Tens of thousands lined the nine-mile route as the cortege made its way to the Triborough Bridge, through the corner of Spanish Harlem on its way to East River Drive and then on to St. Patrick's Cathedral. When the convoy arrived the casket was carried up the steps through the bronze doors to the altar. After a brief service, the Kennedys went by motorcade to the Waldorf-Astoria Hotel, passing a number of storefronts, draped in black crepe, that displayed RFK's photo.

Thousands of New Yorkers and tourists remained standing all night behind police barricades around St. Patrick's, waiting for the cathedral to open the following morning for public homage to Robert Kennedy. As the doors opened at 5:30 a.m. a vast stream of people moved forward in the line to view the closed coffin. Many waited in ninety-degree heat to file past the bier at the rate of one hundred people per minute. Police estimated that 151,000 people filed past the bier in twenty-four hours.

The casket rested on a bier draped in purple in the crossing of the cathedral, and mourners reached out to touch the casket in an old Irish ritual of preventing the Devil from troubling the deceased's soul. Six candles in tall bronze holders flanked the coffin, and an American flag covered it. Throughout the day, an honor guard of six men, consisting interchangeably of members of the armed forces, relatives, friends, and the senator's staff, stood vigil. As the day wore on the intense heat began to take its toll, and the Red Cross treated sixty-five people for heat exhaustion.

The funeral mass, presided over by seventy-two-year-old Cardinal Cushing, took place on Saturday, June 8, 1968, and was attended by six cardinals, six archbishops, eighteen bishops, and more than two hundred priests. During the mass Senator Ted Kennedy delivered a eulogy in a strong but sometimes quivering voice. "My brother need not be idealized or enlarged in death," he intoned, "beyond what he was in life. He should be remembered as a good and decent man, who saw wrong and tried to right it, saw suffering and tried to heal it, saw war and tried to stop it. . . . As he said many times, in many parts of this nation, to those he touched and who sought to touch him, 'Some men see things as they are and say why. I dream things that never were and say why not.'"

President Johnson attended the mass and so did the major presidential candidates, including Vice President Hubert Humphrey, Senator Eugene McCarthy, Governor Nelson Rockefeller, and former Vice President Richard Nixon. After the mass RFK's body was taken by motorcade to New York's Pennsylvania Station and placed aboard a twenty-one-car funeral train for the journey to Washington, D.C. During the 226-mile trip the railway tracks were lined by hundreds of thousands of Americans waiting to pay homage to the assassinated senator. Kennedy's funeral train left New York City at 1:00 p.m. and arrived in Washington eight hours later. When the southbound train emerged from the Hudson River tunnels and reached Newark mourners mobbed the station platform to pay their respects. Americans of every race, class, and creed gathered five-deep along the tracks to register their grief, disbelief, and anger.[1]

"Something about that kind of loss breaks down barriers," photographer Paul Fusco observed.[2] As testament to the kind of social cohesion that Robert Kennedy offered his country, many of Fusco's pictures showed blacks and whites standing side by side, in awe of the passing train.

When the train arrived at Washington's Union Station, it was greeted by a 106-member armed services honor guard, President Johnson, and Vice President Humphrey. Following the playing of the Navy hymn at 9:35 p.m., the caravan of black limousines made its way to Arlington National Cemetery. Thousands of people lined the route as the hearse carried RFK's body past the Senate Office Buildings and the Justice Department to the Lincoln Memorial, where the U.S. Army hearse stopped while a choir sang "The Battle Hymn of the Republic," before crossing Memorial Bridge to the cemetery. The hearse arrived at the base of the JFK gravesite at 10:24 p.m. Pallbearers carried the coffin a distance of one hundred yards to the burial site. Archbishop Philip M. Hannan of New Orleans, a family friend, gave the final brief liturgy. Astronaut John Glenn handed the flag to Ted Kennedy, who passed it to RFK's son, Joe, who in turn handed the flag to his mother.

Robert Kennedy was laid to rest, by the light of flickering candles and a spring moon, within sight of the eternal flame over his brother Jack's grave. For the following four decades he was remembered not so much for what he accomplished but, like his brother, for what he promised. Robert Kennedy had conservative personal values—patriotism, law and order, family, work, religious faith—but he also gave a voice to the powerless minorities in American society, articulating their concerns in an authentic and sincere manner. He was a bridge in American society between the haves and the have-nots. His legacy endures to this day, and it has influenced nearly every major Democratic presidential candidate, including Bill Clinton and John Kerry, for the past thirty-five years. As Arianna Huffington wrote, "John Kerry has said that he would one day like to write a book entitled simply *1968.* In fact, it was impossible to watch [PBS's] *RFK* and not be struck by the many historical parallels between 1968 and today, by how much the legacy of Bobby Kennedy animates John Kerry's run for the White House—and how Kerry is in a unique position to complete Kennedy's unfinished mission of ending a misguided war, returning real compassion to our domestic agenda, and bringing us together as a nation."[3]

The nation became permanently set on a precarious course with RFK's death. A single savage murder changed the direction of the country and might have sent thousands to their deaths. When Sirhan murdered Robert Kennedy, he also set in motion events that eventually led to the killing of four young people at Kent State University in 1970 and the deaths of approximately twenty thousand Americans who, after 1968, gave their lives in Vietnam's jungles. If not for Kennedy's assassination, Cambodia might have remained neutral and stable and a million innocents might not have perished in the Pol Pot holocaust. Watergate would have remained simply a luxurious hotel and apartment block, and years of racial animosity might have been avoided.

Corcoran State Prison

Sirhan Sirhan's death sentence was commuted to life imprisonment in 1972 after the California State Supreme Court declared the death penalty unconstitutional. Sirhan was also at that time given the right to seek parole. Following incarceration at San Quentin Prison's death row, Sirhan was eventually moved to Soledad Prison in 1975.

In 1992 Sirhan was moved to Corcoran State Prison in King's County near Fresno, California, 150 miles north of Los Angeles. Corcoran State stands starkly isolated in the middle of the state's agricultural heartland in the San Joaquin Valley. It is a high-tech maximum security prison, surrounded by lethal electric fences, and it is ranked highest in the United States for inmate killings, with routine reports of torture and cover-up by prison guards. It had been common practice, up to the turn of the century, for Corcoran State guards to pair off rival inmates like roosters in cockfights, complete with spectators. In March 1999 Sirhan fell victim to the prison's regime when some of its convicts gave him a badge-of-honor beating up. He had been held, along with other notorious prisoners like Charles Manson, in the protective housing unit of the prison, where, a prime target for violence, he was closely monitored. When a door to the exercise yard was left open, three assailants burst in. Sirhan suffered minor cuts and bruises before guards intervened.

Sirhan's anger did not abate following his murder conviction. In 1971 he wrote a threatening letter to his lawyer, Grant Cooper, and also threatened the life of defense investigator Robert Blair Kaiser. Sirhan admitted both threats to a parole board. In 1975 he threatened Soledad correctional officer Vern Smith for failing to provide him with immediate medical attention when he suffered a toothache. In 1981 Los Angeles district attorney John Van de Kamp gave evidence to Sirhan's parole board that indicated Sirhan had not changed. According to Van de Kamp, an inmate of Soledad prison had spoken to Sirhan about the 1980 presidential campaign and the possibility of Ted Kennedy's candidacy. In that conversation, Sirhan said, "I know he would [be assassinated]. . . . If I get out of here in 1984 and he's still president I'll take care of him myself."[4]

Since the time of his trial, the assassin has continually repeated his assertion that he does not remember shooting Kennedy. In the past ten years he has accepted the claims made by conspiracy advocates that he had been hypnotized before the murder and used by conspirators as a Manchurian Candidate–type assassin. This despite Sirhan's own words that contradict those who said he had been programmed to murder RFK and then forget about it. From a letter Sirhan wrote to his lawyer, Grant Cooper, regarding Robert Blair Kaiser: "Hey Punk. Tell your friend Robert Kaiser to keep mouthing off about me like he has been doing on radio and television. If he gets his brains splattered he will have asked for it like Bobby Kennedy did. Kennedy didn't scare me; don't think that you or Kaiser will: neither of you is beyond my reach. [A]nd if you don't believe me—just tell your ex-monk [Kaiser had studied for the priesthood] to show up on the news media again—I dare him. R.B.K. must shut his trap, or die."[5]

Sirhan's lawyer, Lawrence Teeter, who died in 2005, appeared regularly in the media claiming his client was not responsible for the crime. The purpose of the conspiracy, Teeter alleged, was to prevent Kennedy, an opponent of the Vietnam War, from winning the presidency. The military-industrial complex wanted to continue the war, and therefore the winner of the

1968 presidential election could not be an anti-war candidate. Teeter said Sirhan's head injury made the young Palestinian "one of the most deeply hypnotizable people in the world. It will be part of our case at a new trial that the CIA discovered this when Sirhan was in hospital. We will show that from that point on, he went into the CIA assassination program. Part of that program was to ensure that Sirhan would have no recall of how he had been programmed and by whom."[6]

Teeter also denied that Sirhan was anti-Jewish or that the assassin was aware of Kennedy's support for Israel, despite the overwhelming evidence that proves the contrary. Teeter and his colleague Lynn Mangan, a Sirhan family friend, provided no credible evidence to show that Sirhan was framed despite the voluminous material they have collected, including mutilated gun tags and police memos, that highlights errors in the collection and retention of the physical evidence.

In January 2003 Teeter lost a Supreme Court appeal of Sirhan's conviction. The judges refused to consider claims that Sirhan's original defense lawyer secretly worked for the government to win his conviction. Although this ruling did not prevent Sirhan's defenders from continuing their battle to secure the assassin a new trial, a consensus among experts emerged. Most reputable historians, journalists, and media commentators now reject the idea that the Kennedy assassination involved anything more than an individual attacker with a political grievance. In 2003 eighty-one-year-old former prosecuting lawyer Lynn Compton summed up the general attitude about the case when he said, "The case itself was a slam dunk. Roosevelt Grier was standing across the table from Kennedy when Sirhan put the gun up to Kennedy's head. Grier jumps across the table and grabs him, gun in hand. Yet we spent the majority of our time running down the possibility of any other people involved. That somebody had put him up to it. There were so many reasons that wouldn't be true because it was just too dumb and such a stupid way it was performed. Nobody who was trying to hire a hit man to get Kennedy would have hired him [Sirhan]."[7]

Author Dan Moldea, who interviewed Sirhan in prison in the early 1990s and who initially thought the Palestinian had been wrongly convicted, said during their talks he began to understand Sirhan's strategy in claiming not to have had any memory of the shooting: "I finally began to understand. . . . As long as people like me continued to put forth supposed new evidence, he still had a chance to experience freedom. And, more than any other person in recent years, I had been keeping this case alive with all of my supposed new revelations about alleged extra bullets and the possibility that at least two guns had been fired at the crime scene. . . . As I sat there I became furious with myself for nearly being hoodwinked by Sirhan and the circumstances of this entire case. I didn't even attempt to hide my feelings."[8]

The RFK assassination story took a new turn, when in 2001, the *Washington Post*'s Petula Dvorak reported that Sirhan might have had foreknowledge of the September 11 terror attacks. Dvorak said that Corcoran prison guards told officials that, a week before the attack on the World Trade Center and the Pentagon, Sirhan had shaved his head and, for the first time, asked for a television set. A prison spokesman, Lt. Johnny Castro, told Dvorak, "These are unusual requests for him; he is usually pretty much isolated and reclusive." Dvorak reported that Sirhan frequently mails letters to outsiders and that the FBI was investigating whether Sirhan's letters were monitored because they were written in Arabic. Lawrence Teeter denied his client had had foreknowledge of the attacks.[9]

As the new millennium arrived, RFK assassination conspiracy theories continued to surface. Following the attacks of 9/11, it was reported that an FBI surveillance tape had recorded the voice of a leading Al Qaeda terrorist telling a colleague that Sirhan had been given three years of terrorist training in the Middle East—a preposterous statement considering the fact that Sirhan's whereabouts in the years preceding the assassination are fully accounted for.[10]

The facts of this case indicate that Sirhan was indeed motivated by political considerations but that he was an unaffiliated terrorist rather than someone who had plotted with a terrorist group to kill Kennedy.

In 2003 the U.S. Supreme Court refused to consider freeing Sirhan. Sirhan's challenge was based on a claim that his defense lawyer was engaged in a secret arrangement with the government to gain his conviction. He also argued that a judge tainted the appeals process. Later in the year Sirhan was denied parole for the twelfth time. Officials sited his deteriorating mental condition and said that he would pose a danger to society. The board reviewed Corcoran Prison officials' assessments of Sirhan, which described his anger and inability to cope. According to a spokesman for California's Board of Prison Terms, Bill Sessa, "He would be an unreasonable risk to society if he were released. His mental skills, his ability to cope in prison seem to be eroding. He seems far more angry and agitated than he has been in years past. To the board it was just another sign that he would pose an unacceptable risk if he were released to society."[11]

When Sirhan was denied parole for the thirteenth time in 2006, Tip Kindel of the California Department of Corrections and Rehabilitation said, "Essentially, the board found he continues to be a danger to public safety and is not suitable to parole." Kindel said that psychiatric exam results presented to the board indicated that Sirhan "hates Americans and, if released, wants to be involved in Middle East politics." Sirhan opted not to attend the parole board hearing and did not send anyone to represent him. Kindel said, "Essentially, the board found he continues to be a danger to public safety and is not suitable to parole. He was given two opportunities by the panel to show up, and declined." The board concluded that Sirhan killed Kennedy in a "cold, calculated and callous manner" with disregard for the senator and those with him.[12]

Despite the overwhelming evidence that Sirhan knowingly murdered Robert Kennedy and that he acted alone, the American public continues to question the conclusions of the government reports and the findings of "lone assassin" investigative reporters. However, recent advances in science might settle once and for all whether or not Sirhan has been lying for the past four decades. Brain fingerprinting has already been ruled admissible evidence in U.S. courts. A brain fingerprinting test, unlike the old-fashioned polygraph test, is conducted using an electroencephalograph (EEG), a hairnet of electrodes that can pick up faint electrical flickering in the brain. Subjects are first fitted with the electrodes, and then they are made to listen to sounds or shown a series of pictures or words, associated with the crime. If the person's brain contains a memory of any of this evidence, the EEG will pick up a characteristic electrical brain wave, which should peak about three hundred milliseconds after the brain receives the stimulus.[13] It is not yet clear if this method can be used on someone with Sirhan's deteriorating mental state. However, if leading medical experts agree that the method is suitable, Sirhan should be given the chance to give substance to his assertions that he has no memory of having killed Kennedy.

This case began with a straightforward answer to "Who Killed Robert Kennedy?" Although questions were asked about the evidence prior to Sirhan's trial, the assassin's guilt seemed to be clearly established. Some independent researchers rightly pursued the story behind the mistakes made by official investigations, and they contributed to a greater understanding of the murder. Others, however, started a process of paranoia and suspicion that led to the public perception that Robert Kennedy was murdered by sinister forces within the U.S. government. The conspiracy theorists' research was characterized by an unwillingness to accept reasonable answers to questions about seemingly suspicious acts. They did nothing but muddy the waters for future objective investigations. Perhaps now, at the beginning of a new century, we can finally establish the truths about RFK's murder and Sirhan Sirhan's guilt—and use those truths to understand the sources of hatred that provoked the assassin's demons.

APPENDIX A

REPORT ON RFK'S WOUNDS
BY BALLISTICS EXPERT LARRY STURDIVAN

Larry Sturdivan is an acclaimed and recognized expert on wound ballistics. He has a bachelor of science in physics from Oklahoma State University and a master of science in statistics from the University of Delaware. He worked at the U.S. Army's Ballistics Research Laboratory, Aberdeen Proving Ground, Maryland, from 1964 to 1972, and then at the Edgewood Research, Development, and Engineering Center, Aberdeen Proving Ground, from 1972 through 1995. In 1964 he observed ballistics tests conducted at the Biophysics Laboratory of Edgewood Arsenal in support of the Warren Commission's investigation into President John F. Kennedy's assassination. He has held positions from bench-level research to management, and he was the associate technical director for technology at Edgewood. He wrote the majority of the casualty criteria for bullets, fragments, etc., used by the United States and the North Atlantic Treaty Organization (NATO) and has had contracts to update them. In 1978, as a senior researcher, he was made the U.S. Army's contact in helping the House Select Committee on Assassinations (HSCA) as it reinvestigated the JFK assassination. He is currently a consultant in mathematical and statistical modeling for LMS Scientific Applications. He has written a book entitled The JFK Myths: A Scientific Investigation of the Kennedy Assassination, *which was published in 2005.*

Author's note: Larry Sturdivan wrote the following report dated May 16, 2006, for the author in response to an RFK conspiracy writer's article on a JFK conspiracy website. In the article, Critic H claimed that the RFK autopsy report proved that the senator's gun shot wounds were too large to have been caused by Sirhan's .22-caliber pistol, so a second gunman had to have been involved in the shooting.

Expanding bullets are usually designed to open up in soft tissue, but not to fragment. The extent of expansion is somewhat variable in soft tissue and unpredictable in bone. The back pressure from the solid bone may, under some circumstances, restrict expansion. Under other circumstances, the strength and density of the bone may cause the bullet to fracture into two or more pieces. The expanded bullet tends to travel in a nearly straight line while the bullet fragments will travel in different, and unpredictable, directions. In rare cases, the trajectory of a fragment will curve so dramatically that it will exit back out of the surface penetrated initially. In most cases, the paths will diverge in a "cone" of variable size.

The penetration of a bullet into a person does not cause an injury like that which would result from a cork borer. It does not remove (or destroy, or any other word of your choice) an amount of tissue the size of the bullet's diameter or expanded diameter. It pushes the tissue rapidly aside, stretching and disrupting the soft tissue or fracturing the bone. The diameter of the damaged area surrounding the bullet's path depends on the shape, size, orientation, and velocity of the bullet and the elasticity and strength of the tissue. For instance, the entry wound in the skin is often smaller than the diameter of the bullet because the skin is strong and elastic and the bullet is in a low-drag orientation as it penetrates skin and some of the pressure that would otherwise move the skin aside may be relieved by surface effects (think of the skin bulging outward). Muscle and other tissue lying beyond the "surface effect depth" will usually be damaged to a diameter larger than the diameter of the projectile—sometimes much larger for a high-velocity, high-drag yawing bullet or fragment. Bone has much greater strength than soft tissue, but no elasticity, so the entry hole in the front table (hard surface layer) must be as large or larger than the size of the bullet as it penetrates, including expanded diameter (from penetrating skin) or change in orientation (no longer point first). In addition, the bone will be "cratered" on the exit side, as the projectile perforates. The cratering again depends on the size, shape, and velocity of the projectile and anatomical and physical properties of the bone. Sometimes the crater can be less than twice the diameter of the penetrating projectile and sometimes large chunks can be "scabbed" off the exit side of the bone. Thus, the size of the crater is inherently unpredictable.

So let us go through the sequence of events in the [RFK] head injury in question. First, the bullet probably started to expand as it penetrated the scalp, leaving a hole in the surface slightly smaller than the diameter of the unexpanded bullet (it did not instantaneously expand on impact). As it penetrated the skull, it probably continued to expand and may have started to fracture. It left a crater that widened from the entry hole toward the inner table of the skull. The crater likely was irregular and as large or larger than twice the diameter of the expanded bullet. If the bullet was still relatively intact, it probably was irregularly deformed by penetrating the skull, so that it would have curved off in the path dictated by its shape and orientation, creating an unpredictable amount of "lift" that would curve the path. If it were broken, pieces would have traveled in an unpredictable manner. Though unlikely, one could have curved sharply to return to strike the skull at some point near the entry hole. It would probably have stopped on the inner table of the skull. More likely, the pieces would have penetrated in random directions through the brain until they stopped.

The brain is very inelastic and weak, so the area of injury about the trajectory (or trajectories) would be larger than the projectile that caused them. Because it is contained in a rigid container, the skull, the outward motion of the tissue from the bullet's trajectory can cause motion at locations remote from the bullet or trajectory sufficient to cause damage in the fragile brain tissue. In blunt injury, this remote damage is termed "contra-coup" injury. The largest amount of damage, however, would have been at the location where the bullet/fragment(s) passed through the skull, where the velocity was highest. In the fragile brain tissue, this area of damage would have been much larger than the "diameter" of the deformed bullet (the point I was trying to make in my initial comment). If the target were a gelatin block, this would be the end of the damage cycle. As soon as this initial damage was inflicted, the dynamic, still-living brain continued the physical and physiological processes that could have contributed to further damage. The damaged tissue immediately began to swell, as blood leaked through ruptured capillaries, like the puffiness that surrounds a bruise. This swelling could have pushed the damaged, already-swollen tissue into the crater and entry hole of the bone, causing further damage (called "herniation" in Noguchi's autopsy). If so, the size of the crater (in the inner table, next to the brain) is already much larger than the deformed bullet. Or, if the hole were already occluded by a bone chip and/or other debris, no herniation damage would have been produced.

The physician at the scene (of the RFK shooting), noting no bleeding, tried to clear the obstruction to keep the back pressure from the arteries that supply the brain from slowing and eventually stopping the flow altogether. The inserted finger could have pushed a bone chip or metallic fragment into intact tissue, causing further damage. This was unlikely, but possible. At surgery, the entry hole in the scalp and skull were enlarged enough

to attempt repair. Even with due care, this could have caused further damage. Once opened wider, even momentary pressure could have caused further herniation damage in the enlarged hole (if the blood pressure were still
high enough). Or not.

During all of the above, medical personnel were trying to keep blood
flow going so that back pressure would not deprive the undamaged brain of
oxygen. The flow was undoubtedly flushing debris from the wound, including detached brain tissue, bone fragments, and possibly bullet fragments.
Even those bone and bullet fragments that were not carried out were probably moved from their original position by the massive amount of blood flowing from the disrupted transverse sinus and arteries all along the wound
track. Bullet fragments and even whole bullets have sometimes been pushed
into veins and ended up in remote parts of the body. Local movement of at
least some fragments is almost certain.

At autopsy, Noguchi only saw the aftermath of all of the above. He
could not peer into the past to determine if any given bit of damage was caused
by one of the above and not by another. Initial damage alone is sufficient to
have produced a swollen area of the size he described, without requiring any
herniation damage. On the other hand, there is nothing to preclude the additional herniation damage he reported, but it could have resulted from herniation into the crater and entry hole in the skull. The caliber of the undeformed
bullet cannot be determined by the evidence contained in the autopsy report.
Even the entry hole in the skull was likely produced by an expanded bullet
that bore little or no indication of the original diameter of the undeformed
bullet. The damage described, indeed, could have been caused by any number
of different bullets, but I saw nothing in [Critic H's] essay that would constitute proof that it was not a bullet from Sirhan's gun that caused the injury. In
fact, I saw nothing that indicates that the damage was even *more likely* to
have been caused by a different bullet.

[Some critics] continue to speak of a .22-caliber bullet as though it
were never expanded. I cannot know . . . what the expanded diameter of the
bullet was when it exited the inner table of the skull to enter the brain, but it
was larger than .22 inches. The crater in the inner table was larger than the
diameter of the expanded bullet, as cratered entry holes always are. Again
we have no way of determining the size of the base of the crater. As the crater
is made by cracking off pieces of the inner table of skull, it is irregular. The
dura does not remain intact at the site of the entry wound. It, too, is torn by
an expanded bullet and the bone chips. Damage 1 centimeter in radius from
the track of the bullet, a reasonable amount of damage in the fragile brain

from the penetration of an expanded bullet, would indeed be a 2-centimeter diameter. Again, that damage would be all along the track, largest at the highest velocity (the entry) and diminishing to about the size of the bullet or fragment of a broken bullet where it stopped. The brain would swell around the wound track whether confined or not. The bullet did not enter the brain tissue by magic; the brain, at the entry point, was injured and would swell, just as it would all along the track. We cannot know how much damage was done by penetrating bone fragments, but any such damage would also contribute to surface swelling. In short, I still see no physical evidence that would prove a conspiracy in the Robert Kennedy killing.

APPENDIX B

ANALYSIS OF "THE PRUSZYNSKI TAPE" BY ACOUSTICS EXPERT PHILIP HARRISON

Philip Harrison is a full-time consultant and director for J. P. French Associates, the United Kingdom's longest established independent forensic speech and acoustics laboratory. The company prepares reports for the defense and prosecution in criminal cases on speaker identification, transcription, authentication and enhancement of recordings, acoustic investigation, and other related areas, including the analysis of recorded gun shots, and is regularly involved in some of the most important and high profile cases in the United Kingdom and around the world. Philip has worked on over eight hundred such cases. He has been involved in undertaking analysis in cases such as the United Kingdom's "Who Wants to Be a Millionaire" fraud, the United Nations' prosecution of war criminals in the former Yugoslavia, the conviction of the Yorkshire Ripper Hoaxer John Humble, the shooting of Police Constable Ian Broadhurst on Boxing Day 2003, and the Bloody Sunday Inquiry. He holds a first-class honors degree (bachelor of engineering) in acoustic engineering from the Institute of Sound and Vibration Research, University of Southampton, and a master of arts with distinction in phonetics and phonology from the Department of Language and Linguistic Science at the University of York. He is an elected member of the Institute of Acoustics (MIOA) and the International Association of Forensic Phonetics and Acoustics. He is also involved in research in forensic speech analysis, the subject of his growing body of publications.

Author's note: In 2006 the present author obtained a previously unreported tape recording of the gunshots in the pantry from the California State Archives. The recording was made by Stus Pruszynski, a journalist. Pruszynski informed the Los Angeles Police Department (LAPD) that he was in the pantry at the time of the assassination. He claimed his cassette recorder was running all through the shooting. It is the only recording of the gunshots in existence that was taken in the pantry, and it is a record of all the shots fired from beginning to end.

I have listened to and analyzed the CD copy of the Pruszynski recording within specialized audio analysis software. In doing so I have discussed my findings and conclusions with a colleague, Professor Peter French, who is in agreement with my interpretations. My comments and conclusions are as follows:

There are seven impulse sounds with very similar characteristics both in terms of how they sound and their appearance within spectrograms (displays showing sound energy across frequency over time). If these sounds were considered in isolation outside of the context of the recording it would not be possible to conclude with any certainty that they are the sounds of a .22-caliber revolver being fired. However, taking into account the events of the early hours of June 5, 1968, and considering the entirety of the recording and the characteristics of the seven sounds, it is fair to conclude that these are the sounds of Sirhan's gun being fired.

It is generally accepted that Sirhan's gun held eight bullets and that all eight of them were fired. This leaves the sound of an eighth shot unaccounted for. Assuming that the shot was fired and since the sound cannot be readily identified it must be masked to some extent by other sounds. There are three candidate locations for this shot; the first is between the shots marked 6 and 7, and is simultaneous with some unclear speech. If this were the location then the regular spacing of the shots would hold across all eight. There is a vertical bar visible within the spectrogram that is indicative of an impulse sound but the characteristic higher frequency features of the other seven shots cannot be seen and there is no auditory similarity. The second is 0.19 seconds after shot 7. Again, there is a vertical bar in the spectrogram but the higher frequency content is different and the auditory quality is not consistent with the shots. Also, it would require the trigger to be pulled in a very short space of time following shot 7. The third and final candidate is simultaneous with the scream that follows the shots. The potential location is not clear as there are the vestiges of several vertical bars and higher frequency areas that could be considered consistent with those of the other seven shots. However, the level of the scream is too high to allow any definitive conclusions to be reached.

There are several other impulse sounds surrounding the shots and many others across the thirty-five minutes of recording. Determining the

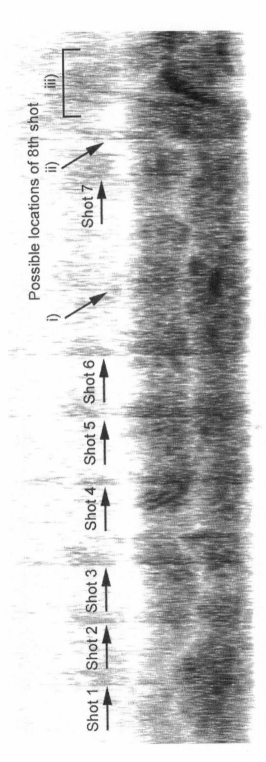

Philip Harrison's spectrogram of the Pruszynski Tape. *Philip Harrison*

actual source of these sounds is not viable as the quality of the recording is not adequate and there are no reference sounds with which to compare them. It is, however, possible to state that there is no evidence to support the claim that there are shots from a .38-caliber gun in the recording. There is no trace of a sound that has the characteristics of such an acoustic event.

The sounds preceding the shots do not bear any resemblance to a .38 shot or the other seven .22 shots. It is not possible to determine their source but this is not necessary as the important question is whether another gun was fired, not what is the source of all sounds in the recording.

Another point that has been raised is the sound that occurs 0.14 seconds after the third shot. This is again an impulse sound as there is a vertical bar within the spectrogram, but the remaining structure and auditory quality is different from that of the seven shots. The impulse is simultaneous with speech apparently from a woman saying the words "come here." The impulse is roughly contemporaneous with the /k/ of "come" but the level of energy here is greater than one might associate with the audible release of this plosive consonant. Whilst one cannot arrive at a definitive interpretation of what this sound is, one can state categorically what it is not, namely, the sound of a .38 revolver being fired in the room. The acoustic signature bears no resemblance whatsoever to that. Suggestions have been made that it could be either an echo from the previous shot or the bullet from the previous shot striking a solid object within the ceiling. If it were an echo, one would expect to find echoes of the other shots within the recording and one does not. Also, given the timing between the impulses and assuming a speed of sound of 340 meters per second, the sound-reflecting surface creating the echo would have to be over twenty-three meters away. The impulse could be the sound of the bullet striking something within the ceiling, but the amplitude and timing of the impulse relative to the gunshot cause me to doubt this interpretation.

How The Discovery Channel Duped The American Public About The RFK Assassination Acoustics Debate by Mel Ayton

The article below was published on History News Network following the broadcast of a Discovery Channel Times documentary in June 2007 which purported to prove that more than 8 shots had been fired in the pantry of the Ambassador Hotel on the night Robert Kennedy was assassinated.

In June 2007 the Discovery Times Channel broadcast a documentary, '*Conspiracy Test – The RFK Assassination*', which relied on unscientific practices to sensationalize their story of how a second gunman acted with Sirhan Sirhan to murder Senator Robert F. Kennedy. (http://www.you tube.com/watch?v = TaF6pW45d0o) The documentary challenged the 'Pruszynski Tape' acoustics research carried out by two teams of experts - Philip Harrison and Professor Peter French of J P French Associates in the UK and Steve Barber, Dr Chad Zimmerman and Michael O'Dell in the US - for my book 'The Forgotten Terrorist'.

J P French Associates is the United Kingdom's longest established independent forensic speech and acoustics laboratory. The company prepares reports for the defense and prosecution in criminal cases on speaker identification, transcription, authentication and enhancement of recordings, acoustic investigation, and other related areas, including the analysis of recorded gun shots, and is regularly involved in some of the most important and high profile cases in the United Kingdom and around the world.

Philip Harrison has worked on over one thousand such cases. Harrison analyzed the 'Pruszynski Tape' using three different methods, both independently and simultaneously. These involved (1) listening analytically to the recording via high quality headphones, (2) examining visual representations of the recording's waveform (oscillographic displays), and (3) analyzing spectrograms (plots of sound energy across frequency over time), all using specialized computer software. Harrison's findings were agreed by Professor Peter French, a colleague and lecturer in forensic speech and audio analysis at the University of York. They found no more than 8 shots were present on the recording.

Both the UK and US teams had independently examined the tape then Barber and Harrison consulted with each other.

Further research carried out by these two teams after the airing of the Discovery Times Channel documentary casts serious doubt on the findings of their acoustics experts. The Discovery Times' acoustics research was led by Philip Van Praag, electrical engineer and author of 'Evolution of the Audio Recorder'. Wes Dooley, forensic analyst and manufacturer of ribbon microphones, was brought in to independently consider the recording. Van Praag claimed that he had identified 'approximately 13 shot sounds' on the Pruszynski Tape, whilst Dooley and his team located 10. Van Praag also insisted 'certainly more than 8 shots were fired'. As Dan Moldea observed after watching the documentary, "Van Praag has concluded - and stated on national television - that thirteen shots were fired at the crime scene...... Even the kookiest kook hasn't suggested that."

The history of how the new acoustics evidence became known to the world began, not with the Discovery Channel documentary as the producers alleged in their press release, but with Steve Barber. The Prusynzki Tape had been widely publicized in Steve Barber's HNN article. (http:// hnn.us/articles/36915.html)

In early 2006 I obtained from the California State Archives an audio cassette copy of the previously unreported 'Pruszynski Tape'. It is a tape recording containing of the sound of the gunshots in the Ambassador Hotel pantry on the night Robert Kennedy was assassinated. The recording was made by Stanislaw Pruszynski, a journalist. Pruszynski informed the Los Angeles Police Department (LAPD) that he was in the pantry at the time of the assassination. He claimed his cassette recorder was running all through the shooting. It is the only recording in existence that was taken in the pantry, and it is a record of all the shots fired from beginning to end.

In May of 2006 I asked Genevieve Troka of the California State Archives if they had facilities to make a high quality digital copy of the material which was on the cassette tape they had previously sent me. Their response was to inform me that the previous year 'an audio expert', Philip Van Praag, visited the California State Archives and made a digital copy of the 'Stanislaw Pruszynski Audio Tape'. I contacted Van Praag and asked him to send a copy of his digitized version of the tape to Steve Barber who in turn forwarded the recording to Philip Harrison. Harrison and Barber had agreed to examine the tape and digitized copy for me and provide a report of their findings. After examining the digitized version of the tape Steve Barber characterized it as "…identical to the cassette in every way, except that it is much clearer."

In April 2007 I was asked to participate in a Discover Times Channel documentary about the RFK assassination. I was informed by one of the producers that the documentary would be balanced and fair. During pre-production correspondence the producer informed me that her company, 'Creative Differences', had hired an independent acoustics firm to analyze the tape but they refused to name the company.

The Creative Differences producer would also not release any of their experts' findings because the company had negotiated a 'secrecy' agreement and their results were not allowed to be publicized until the Discovery Times program was broadcast. The producer was well aware that I had asked two teams of experts to examine the tape and their results were included in Steve Barber's HNN article and in the galleys of my book 'The Forgotten Terrorist' which the Creative Differences producers obtained from my publishers. Their acoustics team was thus at an advantage in that they had access to J P French Associates' acoustics report and also the results of the Barber, Zimmerman and O'Dell research.

During production of the Discovery Times documentary, the 'Creative Differences' documentary team asked that one of the experts I enlisted to examine the Pruszynski Tape, be present for interview. I asked Philip Harrison to attend. During this period they also told us their acoustics experts had identified 'more than 8 shots on the Pruszynski Tape'. My response was to ask Creative Differences for a copy of their acoustics report for consideration before filming. However, their analysts, consisting of Van Praag, Wes Dooley and his assistant, had not even produced a written report but had simply been filmed on camera examining the recording.

Despite having grave reservations concerning the lack of any written report and also of not having the opportunity to respond to their experts' findings, Philip Harrison and I agreed to be interviewed as we were assured the outcome would be 'fair and balanced'. Thus, during filming, Philip was not able to respond to the Discovery Channel's acoustics findings even though they had *his* report in full.

The Discovery Channel documentary, as suspected, managed to provoke a dramatic media and internet response, in the main because they had sensationalized everything about the RFK case. Furthermore, the documentary makers skewed everything in favour of conspiracy as I suspected after first reading the press release which, as I previously mentioned, had wrongly attributed the tape's revelation to the world to themselves when in fact Steve Barber was the first to publicize it worldwide in an article for History News Network.

'Discovery Times' was also remiss in not telling its viewers the whole story about the acoustics research carried out for me. I had told their producers there had been *two teams* of experts (Harrison/French and Barber/Zimmerman/O'Dell) looking at the Pruszynski Tape with a view to publishing the findings in my book 'The Forgotten Terrorist'. I named all the contributors to the research. This fact appears to have been lost on the producers.

Contrary to the inferences made by the Discovery Times' documentary, we have, in reality, *three* experts in the United States - Philip van Praag, Wes Dooley and his assistant, Paul Pragus and *one* expert in Denmark, Eddie Brixen, who examined the tape and who concluded there were 10 or 13 shots fired - but we have *five* experts (* Author's note – see below) in the US and UK who found no more than the acoustic signatures of 8 shots fired. Philip Harrison provided a written report of his findings. Harrison's work was agreed by forensic speech and acoustics expert Professor Peter French of J P French Associates and York University. Steve Barber was interviewed for my book and his comments about his team's research is included within the narrative of my book. The Discovery Times Channel 'teams' have produced no written report nor have they published their findings in any book or journal. It should be quite obvious to *every* person in the scientific community that Van Praag's and Wes Dooley's findings should never have been characterized by Discovery Times' producers as 'scientific fact' without publication of their research for peer review. As Harrison observed, "The only way in which to fully assess and respond to what they are saying is for them to prepare a comprehensive written report and provide us with copies of all the materials on which they've relied. This is the way that science is done."

Had the documentary producers insisted on having their acoustics team's results examined by J P French Associates and Steve Barber's team they would have discovered the many flaws in the acoustics evidence presented by their experts.

Following the airing of the documentary Harrison and Barber decided to look at the acoustics evidence again and found a number of problems with the presented analyses:

'The program claimed that the 'fourth expert', Philip Harrison, wasn't using the best quality recordings and that he didn't take into account the position of the Polish journalist doing the recording. The Discovery Times narrator added, "Harrison was working from a single copy of Van Praag's recording from the California State Archives. Not from Van Praag's masters. Harrison was also not aware of the details surrounding the events of that night at the Ambassador. Most importantly, he did not know the location of Pruszynski's microphone and how it was moving when the shots were fired." He also later claims that "with these important differences it's no surprise that Wes Dooley and Paul Pragus as well as their colleague in Denmark found more shots". These statements are misleading. It is clearly stated in the documentary that Eddie Brixen had only been provided with a single copy of the recording and there is no indication that he was given information about Pruszynski's movements. So the relevance of this information, which was claimed to be "critical to an accurate analysis of the recording", seems somewhat less significant as Brixen also appeared to locate more than 8 shots.

'Philip Harrison had been working initially from the CSA cassette tape and then Van Praag's digitized version. Van Praag had this to say about the copy of the digitized version sent to Steve Barber who in turn forwarded it to Philip Harrison: "The copy I made for you. . . . I did not apply any filtering to the recording you obtained from me. The transcription I made utilized the FINEST studio professional console analog equipment for playback (quite necessary), along with multiple digital and analog machines on the record side." As Steve Barber noted, "Van Praag said that he sent us the digital copy from his archives, which came from the same CSA source that we got our cassette copy from and confirmed to me that he didn't do 'any type of filtering'". Digitized copies lose nothing in the transaction. As Michael O'Dell observed, "The bit about Ayton's expert (in the documentary) was spin by the narrator. . . . none of this analysis would be changed by having the master copy." Furthermore, Harrison has taken issue with the degree of importance attached to Van Praag's multiple copies of the Pruszynski Tape. Harrison stated, "Since he only played back the recording once the numerous versions will have limited value for the analysis."

*Harrison and Barber were obviously interested in the new, albeit limited, information available from the documentary and were intrigued as to the details of Van Praag's work that had resulted in such different findings. Therefore, Harrison and Barber contacted Van Praag but he was not willing to discuss his findings in detail. Harrison then contacted Wes Dooley. According to Harrison, "Dooley revealed some interesting information including the fact they had to destroy all their files after the filming and that Dooley didn't seem to consider his findings to be as conclusive as the documentary might have made out".

*Van Praag did admit to Steve Barber that Creative Differences had produced their own audio level graph with 13 numbers 'popping up' and Van Praag had no idea who constructed it. Van Praag said it 'in no way' necessarily represented what his findings revealed and that the documentary makers had stooped to a low level in presenting his findings. So if Creative Differences misunderstood Van Praag's research (even though he did say 13 shots had been identified) it is not a great leap of the imagination to assume their interpretation of Van Praag's work shown in the documentary was erroneous. Another of Van Praag's comments to Steve Barber following the broadcast of the Discovery Times documentary ("Until I finish sorting it [my analysis] out …..a day, a week, a month…") is also revelatory. Van Praag thus presented his findings to Discovery viewers when, by his own admission, he had not completed his research.

*Discovery's acoustics 'experts' arrived at their number of gunshots fired, not by an examination of the Pruszynski Tape alone, but by also considering the location of Pruszynski and his microphone at the time of the shots. The location information appeared to be derived by synching a thump sound on news broadcast footage with the same sound on the Pruszynski Tape. According to the documentary Pruszynski was said to have walked behind the podium when RFK and his retinue left the Embassy stage and down the steps to the right of the stage (viewed from the front) and is last seen approaching the stage door that leads back in the direction of the pantry. Van Praag's description was that Pruszynski is seen "walking down the stairs and at this point we hear a thump just as he's beginning to enter the kitchen pantry area and we know from Pruszynski's recording that that is the point where the shots are fired".

Steve Barber and Philip Harrison were able to locate the thump, which was played several times on the documentary, on a section of news footage obtained from the California State Archives. However, this material is in color and is not the black and white footage in which Pruszynski can be seen in the documentary. It therefore must be assumed that Van Praag had synchronised the images of the color footage with those of the black and white footage and the thump sound to obtain Pruszynski's location at the time of the shots. Barber and Harrison then attempted to locate the thump sound on the Pruszynski recording. Despite there being a few candidate impulse sounds none were similar enough to the news footage thump for them to be able to accurately determine which sound Van Praag considered to be the thump.

In view of their serious doubts over Van Praag's synchronisation Barber and Harrison contacted him again to try to obtain confirmation that the 'thump' that was played during the documentary was the same one he had used. However, he was not prepared to enter into correspondence on the subject. Van Praag's description of the timing of events indicate that the thump occurs very shortly before the shots. This raises further issues in relation to the images seen on the color TV footage. There are over 8 seconds of material after the thump before there is a break in the recording. During those 8 seconds there are no indications of panic within the ballroom crowd and no shot sounds can be heard. There is a further short recording with a duration of 6 seconds and again there are no obvious signs of panic in the crowd. It isn't until the next recording, some 14 seconds after the thump (not including time elapsed whilst the camera was not recording) that signs of panic start to become apparent. If Van Praag's timings are correct then why did it take so long for the crowd to react?

Van Praag's 13 shot scenario is based on a compilation of various sounds on the tapes which on first examination appear to be gunshots. Steve Barber is convinced Van Praag was confusing 'thump' sounds with gunshots i.e. the two sounds identified as 'thumps' in his HNN article; the string of 8 shots; plus the sound between shots 3 and 4; and this brings the total to 11. Furthermore, as one of the thumps rises in pitch it is extremely unlikely it was the sound of a gunshot. Close inspection of one of the plots produced by Eddie Brixen, which is shown in the documentary, appears to show that he is only convinced of 8 shots. Other features are marked including two that are labelled 'probably a shot'. This shows that there isn't even a consensus between those who believe that the recording contains more than 8 shots. One of Wes Dooley's closing remarks is that the recording 'merits closer examination'.

˙In addition to the issue concerning the number of total shots fired, the show also said at least two of the shots on the tape were fired too closely to have come from the same gun. They even go to a firing range where a firearms expert conducts experiments using the same type of gun as Sirhan. These show that it would not be possible to fire two shots from that gun in the time required by the recording. This is presented as corroborating evidence for a second gunman when the crucial point is completely ignored - what is the actual evidence for the second sound being a shot?

Having highlighted serious concerns about the reliability and usefulness of both the location information and Van Praag's extra copies of the recording, it is clear that the bottom line is that the differences between the findings of the analysts is simply a matter of interpretation. All of the analysts involved would agree that there are more than 8 impulse sounds in the Pruszynski recording in the area of the shots. (Impulse sounds are characterised by a sharp onset and rapid decay. They are caused by a wide range of events, for example a gun being fired, a balloon bursting, a firecracker being let off or one object hitting another.) There are, in fact, many other impulse sounds throughout the entire recording and to simply attribute other impulse sounds in the region of the shots to a second gunman without being able to provide a reasoned scientific argument is reckless.

The documentary provides no information about why Van Praag considers the location of Pruszynski to be so important or how it accounts for the differences between the analysts' findings. The same is true for Van Praag's different recordings. More importantly no explanation is given for why the documentary's experts discount all other possible sources for the impulse sounds and instead conclude that they are gunshots.

H. L. Mencken once ridiculed "the virulence of the national appetite for bogus revelation." These truths seem to be more prevalent now in the internet age and in the public's appetite for television sensationalism. The danger in well-presented documentaries of this kind and their dissemination throughout the internet is that they provide the only historical information source for the majority of Americans, especially the youth of America. As RFK assassination expert, Dan Moldea, stated, " ...... I thought that this program was very exciting and well done, just as I thought that Oliver Stone's *JFK* was very exciting and well done. The problem is that both presentations defy belief. In other words, good dramas, terrible history."

There is also an additional danger – although Van Praag's and Wes Dooley's findings will be rejected by the scientific community on the basis they have not provided a written report for consideration by their peers, they have unwittingly (or consciously) provided scientifically unsupported results to conspiracists who have their own agenda in promoting an unproven conspiracy to murder Robert F. Kennedy.

* AUTHOR'S NOTE: Barber and Harrison's findings are, to some extent, supported by another acoustics expert, Robert Berkovitz. In 2006 Berkovitz had been asked by CNN journalist Brad Johnson to look at the Pruszynski Tape "…. preliminary to an analysis of all extant recordings made during the Robert Kennedy assassination and known and available to Johnson. Johnson sought to hire us to analyze this material as part of a cable TV project, but nothing came of it." Berkovitz emailed me and stated "My final words to Johnson, shortly before he informed me of his withdrawal from the project, were that unless some way could be found to prove that the thumps or bangs in question were gunfire, any conclusions about their significance would rest on sand. One question I would have wanted to answer was whether the relative amplitudes of the shot-like impulses in the numerous recordings could be used to locate their sources" Berkovitz sent a spectrogram he had made in 2006 "……of a 4-second segment of the Pruszynski recording. Audible impulsive events have been numbered, and we found eight of these. The red-tinted rectangular portion at the left side of the spectrogram corresponds to a vocalization, "Ow!" that follows the first event. The more prominent event at the right side of the spectrogram, following impulse No. 8, is a scream."

APPENDIX C

EXCERPTS FROM SIRHAN SIRHAN'S NOTEBOOKS

we know what we are doing in
viet Nam — were keeping the
economy going through our war spending.
We will keep bussy here working
on pecagunish matters to impress you —
all what we really want to do is
fuck you os up — get fat and then
quit
Well, my solution to this type of
government that is to do away
with its leaders — and declare
anarchy the best form of gout — or no
gout.
~~I contend that what is my solution
than to shoot for president~~
the President debt is your best friend until
he gets in power then to i ~~your
most exploing fucker~~ suck every
os drop of flood out of you — ~~fat~~ and
if he dosent like you — you're dead —

intentional - us - extentional.
connotation vs. denotation.
implicit. Equality before and <u>after the law</u>

I advocate the overthrow of the
current president of the fucken United
States of america, I have no absolute
plans yet - but soon will compose some
I am poor — This country's propoganda
says that she is the best country in
the world — I have not experienced this
yet - the U. S - Says that life in
Rusia is bad — Why — ~~the~~ Supposedly
No <u>average american</u> has ever
lived in a slave society so how
can he tell if it is good or bad —
isn't his goat putting words in his
mouth.

Anyway — I believe that the U. S is
ready ~~to start~~ start declng, not that
it hasn't - it began in Nov 23, 63 —,
but it should decline at a ~~fast~~
faster rate, so that the real <u>utopia</u>
will not ~~the~~ be to far from being
realized during the early 70's in this
country.

I firmly support the communist
cause and its people — wether Rusian, chinese

7 & per hour

seven cents per hour

razor

Clothes
vitamins-
Blanket
tools car - gallon container extra tire, tubes
Books- . pens-
I'm have to stay   where does one

to keep up with all of them or all of those
you're goddamned right

you will not be requested to do anything that
may require any great or ungreat

Stipulation against the arab people -
is told is is paid to say
is is paid to say say

while any one is is not required to
perform in any way that is thus is
possible -

لاتذری بی.........
آنہا.... لاتذری ....

...دودلا آتذری...

...وو چای...
Sudan (Sultan?)

Kennedy must fall Kennedy must fall
please pay to the order of Sirhan Sirhan

the amount of Sirhan Sirhan and do not
forget to become any more of a
he prder   Senator R. Kennedy
Second group of American Sailors-
must   must be disposed of.
We believe that Robert F. Kennedy must
be sacrificed for the cause of the
poor exploited people

we believe that we can effect
such action and produce such results —
the hand that is writing doing this
writing is going to do the slaying of
the above mentioned victim
One wonders what it feels like to do any
assassination that might do some
illegal work —   please pay to

I believe that I can effect the
death of Bert C. Allfillisd

Kennedy must die / Kennedy must fall

Kennedy must fall Kennedy must fall
Kennedy must fall Kennedy must
fall Kennedy must fall

NOTES

Inroduction

1. Robert A. Houghton, *Special Unit Senator: The Investigation of the Assassination of Senator Robert F. Kennedy* (New York: Random House, 1970), 93.
2. Dan E. Moldea, "Investigating the Murder of Robert Kennedy (IV): When Wisdom Comes Too Late," *Moldea.com*, June 22, 2000, http://www.moldea.com/RFK4.html.
3. Steven Waldman, "Closing the Case on RFK," *Newsweek*, June 12, 1995, 42.
4. Gordon Thomas, "Was Robert Kennedy's Assassin Brainwashed?" *Americanfreedomnews.com*, September 4, 2002, http://www.american freedomnews.com (accessed January 1, 2003).
5. Dan E. Moldea, *The Killing of Robert F. Kennedy: An Investigation of Motive, Means, and Opportunity* (New York: Norton, 1995), 122.
6. Ibid., 322, 323.
7. Paul Nellen, "An Interview with Prof. Philip Melanson," *The RFK Assassination—Interviews*, 1994, http://homepages.tcp.co.uk/~dlewis/me-lanson.htm.
8. William Klaber and Philip H. Melanson, *Shadow Play: The Murder of Robert F. Kennedy, the Trial of Sirhan Sirhan and the Failure of American Justice* (New York: St. Martin's Press, 1997), 65.
9. John H. Davis, *The Kennedys: Dynasty and Disaster* (London: Sidgwick and Jackson, 1985), 555.
10. Michael D. Evans, "Remember Who Killed Robert Kennedy?" www.therefinersfire.org/sirhan-killed-kennedy.htm (accessed April 20, 2004).
11. William Sullivan, *The Bureau: My Thirty Years in Hoover's FBI*, with Bill Brown (New York: Norton, 1979), 56–57.
12. Joseph A. Palermo, *In His Own Right: The Political Odyssey of Senator Robert F. Kennedy* (New York: Columbia University Press, 2001), 248.

13. Evan Thomas, *Robert Kennedy: His Life* (New York: Simon & Schuster, 2000), 391.

14. Nellie Bly, *The Kennedy Men: Three Generations of Sex, Scandal and Secrets* (New York: Kensington Books, 1996), 158.

Chapter 1: The Ambassador Hotel

1. George Volgenov, "Roll Up the Red Carpet: Hotel of the Stars to Close Its Guest Register," *Detroit Free Press*, October 28, 1988, 1–2.

2. Ian Brodie, "Every Day He Knew His Life Could Be in Danger," *Daily Telegraph*, June 6, 1968, 8.

3. Houghton, *Special Unit Senator*, 233.

4. Hays Gorey, "Memories of a Historic Ride," *Time*, May 9, 1988, 20.

5. Brodie, "Every Day He Knew his Life Could Be in Danger."

6. The Los Angeles Police Department Records of the Robert F. Kennedy Assassination Investigation, 1969 Final Report (10-volume edition used by LAPD to indicate expurgated portions of the 1969 report), 4, California State Archives, Sacramento, CA. (Hereafter referred to as LAPD Summary Report.)

7. Ibid., 3.

8. Gorey, "Memories of a Historic Ride," 20.

9. LAPD Summary Report, 120.

10. Larry Sneed, "NBC News Report," June 6, 1968, Larry Sneed Audio Tape Archives.

11. Godfrey H. Jansen, *Why Robert Kennedy Was Killed: The Story of Two Victims* (New York, Third Press, 1970), 199.

12. Robert Blair Kaiser, *RFK Must Die: A History of the Robert Kennedy Assassination and Its Aftermath*. (New York: E. P. Dutton, 1970), 12.

13. Houghton, *Special Unit Senator*, 108.

14. LAPD Summary Report, 2.

15. Daryl F. Gates, *Chief: My Life in the LAPD* (New York: Bantam Books, 1993), 148.

16. Ibid., 150.

17. LAPD Summary Report, 37.

18. Ibid., 5.

19. Ibid., 5.

20. Ibid., 6.

21. John Pilger, *Heroes* (London: Vintage, 2001), 128.

22. Houghton, *Special Unit Senator*, 282

23. Griel Marcus, "Chronicle of a Death Foretold," *The Guardian* (UK), July 13, 2002, 12.

24. Houghton, *Special Unit Senator*, 286

25. Steve Bell, "June 5, 1968: The Day Robert Kennedy Was Shot," *Jim Bafaro Show*, ABC Radio News transcript, June 1998, www.abcnews.com.

26. David L. Wolper, *Producer: A Memoir* (New York: Simon & Schuster, 2003), 76.

27. Houghton, *Special Unit Senator*, 288.

28. Virginia Guy, taped interview, in "Appendix E: Lists of the Investigation Records Audio Tapes," Los Angeles Police Department Records of the Robert F. Kennedy Assassination Investigation, CSAK82, I-21, California State Archives, Sacramento, CA.

29. Mark Miester, "Eyewitness to History," *Tulanian*, Spring 1998, http://www2.tulane.edu/article_news_details.cfm?ArticleID = 2923.

30. "Bobby's Last, Longest Day," *Newsweek*, June 17, 1968, 30.

Chapter 2: RFK and Israel

1. James Reston, "The Qualities of Robert Kennedy," *New York Times*, June 7, 1968, www.nytimes.com.

2. Alan Dershowitz, *The Case for Israel* (Hoboken, NJ: John Wiley, 2003), 54.

3. Ibid., 58.

4. Ibid., 159.

5. Ibid., 68.

6. Debroah Hart Strober and Gerald S. Strober, *The Kennedy Presidency: An Oral History of the Era* (Washington, DC: Brassey's, Inc., 2003), 226.

7. Dershowitz, *Case for Israel*, 81.

8. Ibid., 69.

9. David Harsanyi, "The Media's Occupation Myth," *FrontPagemagazine.com*, March 29, 2002, http://www.jr.co.il/articles/politics/media.txt.

10. Laurence Leamer, *The Kennedy Men: 1901–1963: The Laws of the Father* (New York: William Morrow, 2001), 286.

11. Dershowitz, *Case for Israel*, 5.

12. Ibid., 28.

13. Ibid., 87.

14. Myron Love, "Arab Journalist Puts Lie to Palestinian Claims," *The Canadian Jewish News*, February 21, 2002, http://www.cjnews.com/pastissues/02/feb21-02/front3.asp.

15. Abraham David, "Issues on the Mythical Palestine," www.masada.org, June 13, 2003.

16. Dershowitz, *Case for Israel*, 92.

17. Ibid., 7.

18. Ibid.

19. Ibid.

20. David, "Issues on the Mythical Palestine."

21. Efraim Karsh, *Arafat's War: The Man and His Battle for Israeli Conquest.* (New York: Grove Press, 2003), 125.

22. Kathleen Christison, "The History of Anti-Palestinian Bias, from Wilson to Bush," *CounterPunch*, July 15, 2002, http://www.counter punch.org/kchristison0715.html.

23. Warren Bass, *Support Any Friend: Kennedy's Middle East and the Making of the US-Israel Alliance* (New York: Oxford University Press, 2003). See in particular the introduction.

24. Robert Silverberg, *If I Forget Thee O Jerusalem: American Jews and the State of Israel* (New York: William Morrow, 1970), 550.

25. Arthur M. Schlesinger, *A Thousand Days: John F. Kennedy in the White House.* (London: Andre Deutsch, 1965), 494.

26. Strober and Strober, *Kennedy Presidency*, 226.

27. Ibid., 229.

28. Ibid., 229.

29. Ibid., 232.

30. Arthur M. Schlesinger, *Robert Kennedy and His Times* (New York: Ballantine Books, 1979), 80.

31. Ibid.

32. Jansen, *Why Robert Kennedy Was Killed*, 163.

33. Schlesinger, *Robert Kennedy and His Times*, 75.

34. Ibid., 82.

35. Ibid., "Appendix."

36. Ibid.

37. Ibid.

38. Margaret Laing, *The Next Kennedy* (London: MacDonald, 1968), 236.

39. Jansen, *Why Robert Kennedy Was Killed*, 179.

40. *New York Times*, September 18, 1964, quoted in Jansen, *Why Robert Kennedy Was Killed*, 178.

41. Schlesinger, *Robert Kennedy and His Times*, 69.

42. Jansen, *Why Robert Kennedy Was Killed*, 178.

43. Ibid., 179.

44. Ibid., 187.

45. Ibid.

46. Ibid.

47. Thomas, *Robert Kennedy*, 386.

48. Jansen, *Why Robert Kennedy Was Killed*, 189.

49. "The Non-Debate," *Time*, June 7, 1968, 40.
50. Davis, *Kennedys*, 544.

Chapter 3: Sirhan and Palestine

1. Jansen, *Why Robert Kennedy Was Killed*, 39.
2. Ibid., 40.
3. Ibid., 41.
4. Ibid., 52–53.
5. Kaiser, *RFK Must Die*, 306.
6. James W. Clarke, *American Assassins: The Darker Side of Politics* (Princeton, NJ: Princeton University Press, 1982), 79.
7. Kaiser, *RFK Must Die*, 418.
8. Ibid., 166.
9. Ibid., 277.
10. Jansen, *Why Robert Kennedy Was Killed*, 60.
11. Ibid., 78.
12. Ibid., 79.
13. Ibid., 79.
14. Ibid., 82.
15. Kaiser, *RFK Must Die*, 403.
16. Jansen, *Why Robert Kennedy Was Killed*, 82.
17. Ibid., 83.
18. Ibid., 83.
19. Kaiser, *RFK Must Die*, 196.
20. Ibid.
21. Jansen, *Why Robert Kennedy Was Killed*, 95.
22. Kaiser, *RFK Must Die*, 166.
23. Houghton, *Special Unit Senator*, 162.
24. Jansen, *Why Robert Kennedy Was Killed*, 93.
25. Houghton, *Special Unit Senator*, 162.
26. Kaiser, *RFK Must Die*, 404.
27. Houghton, *Special Unit Senator*, 163.
28. Ibid., 164.
29. Jansen, *Why Robert Kennedy Was Killed*, 105.
30. Ibid., 114.
31. Ibid., 121.
32. Kaiser, *RFK Must Die*, 439.
33. Ibid., 198.
34. Jansen, *Why Robert Kennedy Was Killed*, 121–123.
35. Ibid., 123.

36. Kaiser, *RFK Must Die*, 203.

37. Houghton, *Special Unit Senator*, 164.

38. Moldea, *Killing of Robert F. Kennedy*, 294.

39. Kaiser, *RFK Must Die*, 112.

40. Ibid., 198.

41. Jansen, *Why Robert Kennedy Was Killed*, 105.

42. "Acquaintances Characterize Robert Kennedy's Suspected Assassin," description of film footage, Independent Television News, June 6, 1968, www.itnnews.co.uk.

43. Jansen, *Why Robert Kennedy Was Killed*, 105.

44. Kaiser, *RFK Must Die*, 103.

45. Jansen, *Why Robert Kennedy Was Killed*, 116.

46. Kaiser, *RFK Must Die*, 279.

47. Ibid., 279.

48. Jansen, *Why Robert Kennedy Was Killed*, 140.

49. LAPD Summary Report, 379.

50. Jansen, *Why Robert Kennedy Was Killed*, 116.

51. LAPD Summary Report, 49.

52. Ibid., 350.

53. Ibid., 112.

54. Kaiser, *RFK Must Die*, 198.

55. Ibid., 252.

56. Ibid., 158.

57. Ibid., 483.

58. Jansen, *Why Robert Kennedy Was Killed*, 115.

59. LAPD Summary Report, 49.

60. Jansen, *Why Robert Kennedy Was Killed*, 116.

61. Kaiser, *RFK Must Die*, 422.

62. Ibid., 256.

63. LAPD Summary Report, 65.

64. "Sirhan Brother Convicted of Threatening Mrs. Meir," *New York Times*, June 14, 1973, 35.

65. Ibid., 48.

66. Ibid., 350.

67. Jansen, *Why Robert Kennedy Was Killed*, 118.

68. Ibid., 138.

69. Clarke, *American Assassins*, 86.

70. LAPD Summary Report, 51.

71. Ibid., 56.

72. Jansen, *Why Robert Kennedy Was Killed*, 73.

73. Ibid., 126.

74. Kaiser, *RFK Must Die*, 202.

75. Moldea, *Killing of Robert F. Kennedy*, 294.

76. Larry Sneed, "Interview with Jack Perkins,"NBC News Radio, May 22, 1969, Larry Sneed Audio Tape Archives.

77. Kaiser, *RFK Must Die*, 206.

78. Ibid., 207.

79. LAPD Summary Report, 385.

80. Houghton, *Special Unit Senator*, 181.

81. Francine Klagsbrun and David C. Whitney, eds., *Assassination: Robert F. Kennedy, 1925–1968* (New York: Cowles, 1968), 109.

82. Houghton, *Special Unit Senator*, 41.

83. Kaiser, *RFK Must Die*, 207.

84. Ibid., 282.

85. Ibid., 208.

86. Houghton, *Special Unit Senator*, 188.

87. Jansen, *Why Robert Kennedy Was Killed*, 129.

88. Houghton, *Special Unit Senator*, 191.

89. Jansen, *Why Robert Kennedy Was Killed*, 129.

90. Kaiser, *RFK Must Die*, 213.

91. Ibid., 209.

92. Houghton, *Special Unit Senator*, 191.

93. Klagsbrun and Whitney, *Assassination*, 110.

94. Kaiser, *RFK Must Die*, 212.

95. Jansen, *Why Robert Kennedy Was Killed*, 133.

96. Time-Life Books, eds. *Assassination* (Alexandria, VA: Time-Life Books, 1994), 69.

97. Klaber and Melanson, *Shadow Play*, 204.

98. Kaiser, *RFK Must Die*, 211.

99. Ibid., 274.

100. Ibid., 418.

101. Houghton, *Special Unit Senator*, 193.

102. Ibid., 194.

103. Kaiser, *RFK Must Die*, 214.

104. LAPD Summary Report, 384.

105. Houghton, *Special Unit Senator*, 195.

106. Jansen, *Why Robert Kennedy Was Killed*, 132.

107. "Acquaintances Characterize Robert Kennedy's Suspected Assassin."

108. Houghton, *Special Unit Senator*, 196.

109. Jansen, *Why Robert Kennedy Was Killed*, 135.

110. Ibid., 134.

111. Ibid., 137.

112. Larry Bortstein, "Guard Has a Leg Up on Opening Day," *OC Register*, December 24, 2006, http://www.ocregister.com/ocregister/sports/other/article_1397207.php.

113. Jansen, *Why Robert Kennedy Was Killed*, 139.

114. Moldea, *Killing of Robert F. Kennedy*, 296.

115. Jansen, *Why Robert Kennedy Was Killed*, 134.

116. Kaiser, *RFK Must Die*, 216.

Chapter 4: The Shooting

1. Danny G. Bobbitt, taped interview, May 6, 1968, in "Appendix E," CSAK19, I-110.

2. Houghton, *Special Unit Senator*, 246.

3. Moldea, *Killing of Robert F. Kennedy*, 134.

4. Kaiser, *RFK Must Die*, 293.

5. Houghton, *Special Unit Senator*, 262.

6. "Sirhan Takes the Stand," *Newsweek*, March 17, 1969, 17.

7. "Robert F. Kennedy Assassination—(Summary)," *Report Consisting of the Los Angeles County Board of Supervisors Independent Investigation by Special Counsel Thomas F. Kranz*, FBI Records, http://foia.fbi.gov/foiaindex/rfkasumm.htm. (Hereafter referred to as Kranz Report.)

8. Houghton, *Special Unit Senator*, 264.

9. Kaiser, *RFK Must Die*, 249.

10. Ibid., 332, 328.

11. LAPD Summary Report, 9.

12. Ibid.

13. Kaiser, *RFK Must Die*, 71.

14. Houghton, *Special Unit Senator*, 267.

15. Jansen, *Why Robert Kennedy Was Killed*, 200.

16. Klaber and Melanson, *Shadow Play*, 205.

17. Ibid., 366.

18. Moldea, *Killing of Robert F. Kennedy*, 300.

19. Jansen, *Why Robert Kennedy Was Killed*, 201.

20. Houghton, *Special Unit Senator*, 275–276.

21. LAPD Summary Report, 301.

22. Ibid.

23. Ibid.

24. Kaiser, *RFK Must Die*, 187.

25. LAPD Summary Report, 38.

26. Houghton, *Special Unit Senator*, 276.

27. Ibid., 279.

28. LAPD Summary Report, 39.

29. Ibid., 38.

30. Ibid., 144.

31. Ibid., 9.

32. Klagsbrun and Whitney, *Assassination*, 168.

33. LAPD Summary Report, 144.

34. Ibid., 9.

35. Kaiser, *RFK Must Die*, 75.

36. Ibid., 26.

37. Ibid.

38. Houghton, *Special Unit Senator*, 21.

39. Ibid., 256.

40. Klagsbrun and Whitney, *Assassination*, 24.

41. Ibid.

42. Kaiser, *RFK Must Die*, 26.

43. Kranz Report, Section 1, 26.

44. Ibid.

45. LAPD Summary Report, 150.

46. Ibid., 25.

47. Ibid., 24.

48. Ibid., 27.

49. Jules Witcover, *85 Days: The Last Campaign of Robert Kennedy* (New York: Ace, 1969), 50.

50. C. David Heymann, *RFK: A Candid Biography* (London: William Heinemann, 1998), 499.

51. LAPD Summary Report, 25.

52. Witcover, *85 Days*, 267.

53. Kranz Report, Section 1, 7.

54. "Eye of the Hurricane," *Newsweek*, March 3, 1969, 20.

55. Heymann, *RFK*, 499.

56. Kaiser, *RFK Must Die*, 186.

57. Carl George, "Interview with Dr. Marcus McBroom," NBC Radio News, June 5, 1968, Larry Sneed Audio Tape Archives.

58. Jansen, *Why Robert Kennedy Was Killed*, 224.

59. Klagsbrun and Whitney, *Assassination*, 30.

60. Steve Lopez, "Ex-Busboy Will Never Forget Bobby Kennedy," *Los Angeles Times*, June 1, 2003.

61. John Seigenthaler, *A Search for Justice* (Nashville: Aurora Publishers, 1971), 228.

62. "Eye of the Hurricane," 21.
63. Houghton, *Special Unit Senator*, 99.
64. Joe Gerringer, "Robert Kennedy Assassination: Revisions and Rewrites," *Court TV Crime Library*, 2005, http://www.crimelibrary.com/terrorists_spies/assassins/kennedy/5.html.
65. LAPD Summary Report, 12.
66. Klagsbrun and Whitney, *Assassination*, 30.
67. Kranz Report, Section 1, 6.
68. Ibid., 7.
69. Seigenthaler, *Search for Justice*, 236.
70. *People v. Sirhan*, 7 Cal.3d 710, Crim. No. 14026, June 16, 1972, http://caselaw.lp.findlaw.com/ca/cal3d/7.html, 497.
71. Moldea, *Killing of Robert F. Kennedy*, 78.
72. LAPD Summary Report, 42.
73. Ibid., 42.
74. Ibid., 10.
75. Gerringer, "Robert F. Kennedy Assassination."
76. *People v. Sirhan*, 739.

Chapter 5: The Trial

1. "Verdict on Sirhan," *Newsweek*, April 28, 1969, 22.
2. "Trials: Round One," *Newsweek*, February 3, 1969, 23.
3. Seigenthaler, *Search for Justice*, 205.
4. Ibid.
5. Ibid.
6. "Trials: Round One," 23.
7. "Trials: Smiling Through," *Newsweek*, January 27, 1969, 17.
8. "Sirhan: Tragedy of the Absurd," *Newsweek*, March 24, 1969, 22.
9. Klaber and Melanson, *Shadow Play*, 271.
10. Seigenthaler, *Search for Justice*, 228.
11. "Test Case," *Newsweek*, April 7, 1969, 66.
12. The McNaughton Rule was named after the man who tried to assassinate the British prime minister, Sir Robert Peel, but who instead murdered the prime minister's secretary, Edward Drummond, in a case of mistaken identity. Daniel McNaughton, the courts learned, was an intelligent, law-abiding citizen who was sometimes given to violent rages. His outbursts often resulted in broken furniture, and he ranted about how devils in human form were out to get him. He was unable to sleep, became physically ill, and made frequent visits to the local police station to request protection. He began to blame his troubles on the Tories,

purchased a pair of pistols, and sought Sir Robert Peel out as a target. Following Drummond's assassination and McNaughton's subsequent arrest, the defendant was tried and then acquitted on the grounds of insanity. He was sent to a mental institution, where he remained for the rest of his life until his death in 1865. Bernhardt J. Hurwood, *Society and the Assassin: A Background Book on Political Murder* (London: Parents Magazine Press, 1970), 82.

13. Seigenthaler, *Search for Justice*, 208.
14. Hurwood, *Society and the Assassin*, 82.
15. "Verdict on Sirhan," *Newsweek*, April 28, 1969, 24.
16. Seigenthaler, *Search for Justice*, 300.
17. Ibid., 227.
18. Kaiser, *RFK Must Die*, 439.
19. Seigenthaler, *Search for Justice*, 269.
20. Kaiser, *RFK Must Die*, 446.
21. "The Assassins: Who Did It—and Why?" *Newsweek*, March 24, 1969, 23.
22. Ibid.
23. "Sirhan's Trance," *Newsweek*, April 7, 1969, 31.
24. Ibid.
25. Ibid.
26. Ibid.
27. Ibid.
28. Ralph Blumenfeld, "New Questions: The Death of RFK," *New York Post*, May 23, 1975.
29. LAPD Summary Report, 909.
30. Ibid., 103.
31. Seigenthaler, *Search for Justice*, 239.
32. Kranz Report, Section 1, 9.
33. Kaiser, *RFK Must Die*, 467.
34. Ibid., 468.
35. Seigenthaler, *Search for Justice*, 308.
36. "The Other Sirhan," *Newsweek*, April 14, 1969, 22.
37. Kaiser, *RFK Must Die*, 469.
38. Ibid., 473.
39. *People v. Sirhan.*
40. Ibid.
41. Clarke, *American Assassins*, 100.
42. "Assassins," 23.
43. Kaiser, *RFK Must Die*, 242.
44. Ibid., 388.

45. Ibid., 345.
46. Klaber and Melanson, *Shadow Play*, 76.
47. Kaiser, *RFK Must Die*, 218.
48. Klaber and Melanson, *Shadow Play*, 285.
49. Kaiser, *RFK Must Die*, 218.
50. Alan Dershowitz, "Put Arafat on Trial," *Ha'aretz Daily*, September 13, 2002, www.frontpagemagazine.com.
51. *Life* editorial, May 1969, 5.
52. Seigenthaler, *Search for Justice*, 369.
53. Frederic Wertham, *Turning Criminals into Mental Patients and Mental Patients into Criminals*, 2002, http://www.cinemaniastigma.com (accessed April 21, 2003).
54. "Test Case," 66.
55. "The Jury v. Sirhan," *Newsweek*, May 5, 1969, 20.
56. "Verdict on Sirhan," 23.
57. "The Jury v. Sirhan," 20.
58. "The Letter and the Law," *Newsweek*, June 2, 1969, 26.
59. Ibid.

Chapter 6: Controversies: The Physical Evidence

1. Houghton, *Special Unit Senator*, 70.
2. Ibid., 69.
3. Seigenthaler, *Search for Justice*, 225.
4. LAPD Summary Report, 496.
5. Kaiser, *RFK Must Die*, 426.
6. Houghton, *Special Unit Senator*, 69, 183.
7. Kaiser, *RFK Must Die*, 215.
8. Lisa Pease and James DiEugenio, eds., *The Assassinations:* Probe Magazine *on JFK, MLK, RFK and Malcolm X* (Los Angeles: Feral House, 2003), 556.
9. Ibid., 540.
10. Moldea, *Killing of Robert F. Kennedy*, 186.
11. John Hunt, "Oops, Dan Moldea Accidently Uncovers the Conspiracy to Kill RFK," *JFK Lancer*, 2005, http://www.jfklancer.com/hunt/moldeas.htm.
12. Moldea, *Killing of Robert F. Kennedy*, 310.
13. John Hunt, "Robert Kennedy's Headwounds: The Case For Conspiracy," *JFK Lancer*, 2006, http://www.jfklancer.com/hunt/rfk_pt1.htm.
14. Larry Sturdivan, letters to the author, February 27, 2006, and/or May 16, 2006.

15. Sturdivan letter, February 27, 2006.

16. Dan E. Moldea, letter to the author, May 7, 2006.

17. Larry Sturdivan, letter to the author, November 28, 2006.

18. Seigenthaler, *Search for Justice*, 229; and Kranz Report, Section 2, 13.

19. Moldea, *Killing of Robert F. Kennedy*, 210.

20. Ibid., 212.

21. Kranz Report, Section 2, 13.

22. Moldea, "Investigating the Murder of Robert Kennedy."

23. Moldea, *Killing of Robert F. Kennedy*, 313.

24. Ibid., 311.

25. Houghton, *Special Unit Senator*, 46.

26. Heymann, *RFK*, 498.

27. Moldea, *Killing of Robert F. Kennedy*, 312.

28. Thomas Noguchi, interview by Douglas Stein, November 1986, http://www.geocities.com/marilynmonroesplace/noguchi.html.

29. Carl George, "Interview with Dr. Marcus McBroom," NBC News Radio, June 5, 1968, Larry Sneed Audio Tape Archives.

30. Moldea, *Killing of Robert F. Kennedy*, 225.

31. Thomas T. Noguchi, *Coroner to the Stars* (London: Corgi Books, 1983), 102.

32. Moldea, *Killing of Robert F. Kennedy*, 233.

33. Ibid.

34. Ibid., 239.

35. Houghton, *Special Unit Senator*, 97.

36. Moldea, *Killing of Robert F. Kennedy*, 232.

37. Ibid.

38. Ibid., 253.

39. Ibid., 315.

40. Ibid., 253.

41. Ibid., 259.

42. Ibid., 277.

43. Ibid., 318.

44. Ibid., 315.

45. Gates, *Chief*, 151.

46. "Officer Ordered Items Destroyed," *Santa Monica Evening Outlook*, August 21, 1975; and "Our Times," *Los Angeles Times*, undated, www.latimes.com.

47. Klaber and Melanson, *Shadow Play*, 310.

48. Moldea, *Killing of Robert F. Kennedy*, 172.

49. Ibid., 173.

50. Ibid., 164.
51. Ibid., 162.
52. Kranz Report, Section 2, 25.
53. Ibid., 27.
54. Moldea, *Killing of Robert F. Kennedy*, 321.
55. Ibid., 141.
56. Gates, *Chief*, 152.
57. Kranz Report, Section 2, 35.
58. Ibid., 63.
59. Moldea, *Killing of Robert F. Kennedy*, 47.
60. Carl Rivera, "Man Wins Battle with City over Kennedy Assassination Photos," *Los Angeles Times*, August 23, 1996.
61. Klaber and Melanson, *Shadow Play*, 360.
62. Ibid.
63. Moldea, *Killing of Robert F. Kennedy*, 91.
64. Ibid.
65. See http://mcadams.posc.mu.edu/odell/,http://mcadams.posc.mu.edu/barber.htm.
66. Steve Barber, letter to the author, May 1, 2006.
67. Ibid.; and Steve Barber, letter to the author, May 7, 2006.
68. Michael O'Dell, letters to the author, May 7, 2006, May 9, 2006.
69. The Pruszynski tape, June 4–5, 1968, is mentioned in "Appendix E," CSAK123, I-4837.
70. Steve Barber, letters to the author, May 1, 2006, May 10, 2006, June 26, 2006, June 28, 2006.
71. O'Dell letter, May 9, 2006.
72. Chad Zimmerman, letters to the author, April 30, 2006, May 5, 2006, June 19, 2006.
73. Steve Barber, letters to the author, May 12, 2006, May 14, 2006, June 23, 2006.
74. Philip Harrison, letters to the author, June 15, 2006, June 21, 2006.

Chapter 7: Controversies: The Witnesses

1. Houghton, *Special Unit Senator*, 243.
2. Ibid., 301.
3. Gates, *Chief*, 151.
4. John Kelin, "The RFK Panel," 2002, http://www.parapolitics.info/copa/copa2002gallery/ (accessed April 21, 2003).
5. Moldea, *Killing of Robert F. Kennedy*, 150.
6. Kranz Report, Section 2, 7.

7. Ibid., 8.
8. Moldea, *Killing of Robert F. Kennedy*, 205.
9. Philip H. Melanson, *The Robert F. Kennedy Assassination: New Revelations on the Conspiracy and Cover-up* (New York: Shapolsky, 1991), 80.
10. Moldea, *Killing of Robert F. Kennedy*, 201.
11. Ibid., 202.
12. Ibid., 216.
13. Ibid., 289.
14. Ibid., 298.
15. Kaiser, *RFK Must Die*, 305.
16. Judith Groves, taped interview, June 28, 1968, in "Appendix E," CSAK29, I-375.
17. Klaber and Melanson, *Shadow Play*, 147.
18. Gloria Farr, taped interview, June 21, 1968, in "Appendix E," CSAK82, I-392.
19. Melanson, *Robert F. Kennedy Assassination*, 227.
20. Ibid., 230; and Booker T. Griffin, taped interview, July 7, 1968, in "Appendix E," CSAK11, I-76.
21. Melanson, *Robert F. Kennedy Assassination*, 225. Other witnesses reported seeing a woman in a polka-dot dress of varying descriptions on the night RFK was killed. Judith Groves, John Ludlow, Eve Hansen, Nina Ballantyne, and Jeannette Prudhomme reported seeing the woman with a Sirhan look-alike or "acting in suspicious circumstances."
22. Seigenthaler, *Search for Justice*, 233.
23. Houghton, *Special Unit Senator*, 125.
24. LAPD Summary Report, 411.
25. Kaiser, *RFK Must Die*, 125.
26. LAPD Summary Report, 412.
27. Kaiser, *RFK Must Die*, 125.
28. Kranz Report, Section 2, 47.
29. Houghton, *Special Unit Senator*, 119.
30. Ibid., 121.
31. LAPD Summary Report, 415.
32. Klaber and Melanson, *Shadow Play*, 166.
33. Houghton, *Special Unit Senator*, 178.
34. Moldea, *Killing of Robert F. Kennedy*, 101.
35. Houghton, *Special Unit Senator*, 103.
36. Moldea, *Killing of Robert F. Kennedy*, 114.
37. Houghton, *Special Unit Senator*, 126.
38. Ibid.

39. Houghton, *Special Unit Senator*, 123.

40. Ibid., 121.

41. Ibid., 142.

42. Robert Blair Kaiser, "The case is still open. I'm not rejecting the Manchurian Candidate aspect of it," http://www.rfkmustdie.com (accessed April 25, 2003).

43. Dennis Weaver, taped interview, June 21, 1968, in "Appendix E," CSAK84, I-623.

44. Kaiser, *RFK Must Die*, 35.

45. Cathy Fulmer, taped interview, June 7, 1968, in "Appendix E," CSAK91, I-4589.

46. Kaiser, *RFK Must Die*, 121.

47. Moldea, *Killing of Robert F. Kennedy*, 208.

48. LAPD files, CSA-K84, I-3959, June 21, 1968.

49. Kelin, "The RFK Panel."

50. LAPD Summary Report, 531.

51. Moldea, *Killing of Robert F. Kennedy*, 110.

52. Kaiser, *RFK Must Die*, 156.

53. Moldea, *Killing of Robert F. Kennedy*, 111.

54. LAPD Summary Report, 530–532.

55. Klaber and Melanson, *Shadow Play*, 131.

56. Kranz Report, Section 2, 3. Evan Freed reported seeing a second gunman but later retracted his story. Conspiracy writers accused him of having been influenced in his retraction by his job as a Los Angeles city deputy attorney. Marcus McBroom, nearly twenty years after the assassination, said that he saw a woman running out of the pantry shouting "We shot him!" and that she was followed by a man with a gun hidden under a newspaper. McBroom said an ABC cameraman and a man named "Sam Strain" witnessed the incident. However, no reports by these individuals confirming McBroom's statement have been forthcoming.

57. Ibid.

58. Moldea, *Killing of Robert F. Kennedy*, 147.

59. Jane Kirtley, "Defamation Judgement Puts Onus on Media," *American Journalism Review*, January/February 1999, www.ajr.org.

60. Pease and DiEugenio, *Assassinations*, 592.

61. Moldea, *Killing of Robert F. Kennedy*, 294.

62. LAPD Summary Report, 61. Following false leads is a grave problem for investigating agencies. Nearly every famous crime in modern American history has generated false sightings of fugitives and co-conspirators and false confessions of guilt. Following Hitler's death, for example, people

all over the United States started to claim that they had seen the German dictator. One thousand FBI agents were following up on these reported sightings at any one time. They generated over twelve hundred separate documents and reports on "Hitler's Escape." (Federal Bureau of Investigation, *Hitler's FBI File*, National Archives and Records Administration, Washington, DC.)

Chapter 8: Distorted Truths

1. William F. Buckley, "Murder Heaven: The Law Is a Quagmire," *National Review*, November 18, 2003.
2. Kaiser, *RFK Must Die*, 118.
3. LAPD Summary Report, 78.
4. Houghton, *Special Unit Senator*, 96.
5. Elaine Wilson, "KLKI's Broadcasters Stretch Retirement Age," *www.SkagitBIZ.com*, February 11, 2004, http://www.klki.com/whatshappening.cfm.
6. Gates, *Chief*, 153.
7. Michael Baden and Marion Roach, *Dead Reckoning: The New Science of Catching Killers* (London: Arrow, 2002), 9.
8. Eric Hamburg, *JFK, Nixon, Oliver Stone and Me* (New York: Public Affairs, 2002), 273.
9. Manuel Chavez, e-mails to the author, December 1–3, 2006.
10. Manuel Chavez, e-mail to the author, December 9, 2006.
11. Grayston Lynch, e-mail to the author, December 2, 2006.
12. Don Bohning, e-mail to the author, December 1, 2006.
13. Ibid.
14. Karen Lynch, e-mail to the author, December 5, 2006.
15. Dan E. Moldea, e-mail to the author, December 3, 2006. "In November 2007 O'Sullivan identified the purported agents as Bulovar Watch salesmen Michael D. Roman ('Campbell') and Frank Owens ('Joannides'). The salesmen's families confirmed the identifications."
16. Lamar Waldron and Thom Hartmann, Ultimate Sacrifice: John and Robert Kennedy, the Plan for a Coup in Cuba, and the Murder of JFK (London: Constable, 2005), 781.
17. John H. Davis, *Mafia Kingfish: Carlos Marcello and the Assassination of John F. Kennedy* (New York: McGraw-Hill, 1989), 351.
18. David E. Scheim, *The Mafia Killed President Kennedy* (London: Virgin, 1988), 349.
19. Lisa Pease, "Sirhan and the RFK Assassination: Part 1, The Grand Illusion," *Probe Magazine*, March/April 1998.
20. Klaber and Melanson, *Shadow Play*, 179.

21. Melanson, *The Robert F. Kennedy Assassination*.

22. LAPD Summary Report, 488.

23. "The Kennedy Love Triangles," *www.etyahoo.com*, June 2, 2004, http://www.etyahoo.com/.

24. Mel Ayton, *Questions of Controversy: The Kennedy Brothers* (Sunderland, UK: University of Sunderland Press/BEP, 2001), 214.

25. Peter Evans, *Nemesis: Aristotle Onassis, Jackie O, and the Love Triangle That Brought Down the Kennedys* (New York: Regan Books, 2004), 231.

26. Moldea, *Killing of Robert F. Kennedy*, 108.

27. Stuart M. Speiser, *The Deadly Sins of Aristotle Onassis* (Ozark, AL: ACW Press, 2005), 352.

28. Ibid., 354.

29. *The Assassination of Robert Kennedy*, produced by Chris Plumley, Exposed Films Production for Channel 4 in association with the Arts and Entertainment Network, UK, 1992.

30. Michael Haggarty, taped interview, June 19, 1968, in "Appendix E," CSAK83, I-227.

31. Greg Lynch, "Interview with Adel Sirhan," *Over the Shoulder: The RFK Assassination*, NPR Radio, 2000, www.npr.com.

32. Jansen, *Why Robert Kennedy Was Killed*, 195.

33. Ibid.

34. Peter Knight, *Conspiracy Nation: The Politics of Paranoia in Post War America* (New York: New York University Press, 2002), 58.

35. Klaber and Melanson, *Shadow Play*, xiii.

36. Seigenthaler, *Search for Justice*, 261.

37. Kaiser, *RFK Must Die*, 94.

38. Ibid., 484.

39. Ibid., 469.

40. William Turner, *Rearview Mirror: Looking Back at the FBI, the CIA and Other Tales* (Granite Bay, CA: Penmarin Books, 2001), 256.

41. Seigenthaler, *Search for Justice*, 276.

42. Andrew Cook, "Lone Assassins," *History Today* (UK), November 2003, http://www.historytoday.comdt_issue.asp?gid = 19652&aid = &tgid = &amid = &g19652 = x&g30026 = x&g20991 = x&g21010 = x&g19965 = x&g19963 = x.

43. "A Possible Explanation for Conspiracy Theories," *The Economist*, July 9, 2004, 34.

Chapter 9: *The Manchurian Candidate* Assassin

1. Moldea, *Killing of Robert F. Kennedy*, 135.

2. "Sirhan's Trance."

3. Ibid.
4. Kaiser, *RFK Must Die*, 304.
5. Moldea, *Killing of Robert F. Kennedy*, 298.
6. Klaber and Melanson, *Shadow Play*, 86.
7. Bernard Diamond, "Dr. Diamond Speech to the Northern California Hypnosis Society," July 23, 1981, in J. Quen, *The Psychiatrist in the Courtroom: Selected Papers of Bernard L. Diamond, M.D.* (Mahwah, NJ: Analytic Press, 1995), 144.
8. Moldea, *Killing of Robert F. Kennedy*, 155.
9. Lisa Pease, "Sirhan and the RFK Assassination: Part II, Rubik's Cube," *Probe Magazine*, March/April 1998.
10. Philip Melanson, *Who Killed Robert Kennedy?* (New York: Odonian Press, 1993), 75.
11. David Cogswell, "New Trial for Sirhan?" *Media Review*, November 24, 2002, www.davidcogswell.com/Political/NewTrialSirhan.html.
12. Nellen, "An Interview with Prof. Philip Melanson."
13. Melanson, *Robert F. Kennedy Assassination*, 204.
14. Greg Roberts, "RFK Assassination Conspiracy Theory Hypnotist Found Dead in Las Vegas," *Hollywood Reporter*, March 21, 1977.
15. Thomas, "Was Robert Kennedy's Assassin Brainwashed?" 2.
16. Isabel Vincent, "Kennedy's Killer Demands Re-Trial," *National Post*, June 11, 2003.
17. Melanson, *Who Killed Robert Kennedy?* 69.
18. Ibid.
19. Pease and DiEugenio, *Assassinations*, 534.
20. M. H. Erikson, *The Nature of Hypnosis and Suggestion* (New York: Irvington, 1980), 8.
21. W. C. Coe and K. Ryken, "Hypnosis and Risks to Human Subjects," *American Psychologist* 10:6 (August 1979), 23.
22. Robert Allen Baker, *They Call It Hypnosis* (Buffalo, NY: Prometheus Books, 1990), 23–27.
23. Robin Waterfield, *Hidden Depths: The Story of Hypnosis* (London: Macmillan, 2002), xxiv.
24. Ibid., 313.
25. Ibid., 314.
26. Dr. Graham Wagstaff, letter to the author with attachment, "Hypnosis and Forensic Psychology," March 15, 2003.
27. Waterfield, *Hidden Depths*, 237.
28. Ibid., 269.
29. Ibid.

30. Ibid., 31–41.

31. Ibid., 229.

32. Ibid.

33. Robert Todd Carroll, "Hypnosis, " *The Skeptic's Dictionary*, November 27, 2006, http://skepdic.com/hypnosis.html.

34. Waterfield, *Hidden Depths*, 381.

35. John Marks, *The Search for the Manchurian Candidate: The CIA and Mind Control* (New York: Norton, 1979), 30.

36. Senate Intelligence Committee, Foreign and Military Intelligence, Select Committee to Study Governmental Operations with Respect to Intelligence Activities, Foreign and Military Intelligence, *Final Report*, 94th Cong., 2d sess., 1976, Rep. 94-755, 8.

37. Marks, *Search for the Manchurian Candidate*, 38.

38. Waterfield, *Hidden Depths*, 388.

39. Marks, *Search for the Manchurian Candidate*, 110.

40. Ibid., 154.

41. Ibid., 200.

42. Waterfield, *Hidden Depths*, 385.

43. Marks, *Search for the Manchurian Candidate*, 196.

44. Waterfield, *Hidden Depths*, 229.

45. Wagstaff letter.

46. *Assassination of Robert Kennedy*.

47. Waterfield, *Hidden Depths*, 229.

48. Dr. Etzel Cardena, letter to the author, January 21, 2004.

49. Wagstaff letter.

50. James W. Kenney, letter to the author, September 25, 2003.

51. Marks, *Search for the Manchurian Candidate*, 198.

52. Ibid., 204.

53. Ibid., 223.

54. Kaiser, *RFK Must Die*, 365.

55. Ibid., 366.

56. Seigenthaler, *Search for Justice*, 254.

57. Turner, *Rearview Mirror*, 243.

58. Kaiser, *RFK Must Die*, 250.

59. Seigenthaler, *Search for Justice*, 263.

60. Kaiser, *RFK Must Die*, 251.

61. Ibid., 230.

62. Ibid., 517.

63. Dan E. Moldea, "Confronting Sirhan," *Moldea.com*, 2000, http://www.moldea.com/Seven-8.html.

64. Daniel L. Schacter, *Searching for Memory: The Brain, the Mind, the Past* (New York: Basic Books, 1997), 227.

65. Clint Witchalls, "Murder in Mind," *Guardian Weekly*, April 15, 2004, 20.

66. Russell Vorpagel, Profiles in Murder: An FBI Legend Dissects Killers and Their Crimes (New York: Dell, 1998), 142.

67. Alan J. Parkin, *Memory and Amnesia* (New York: Psychology Press, 1997), 175.

68. Houghton, *Special Unit Senator*, 51.

69. Kaiser, *RFK Must Die*, 293.

70. Houghton, *Special Unit Senator*, 51.

71. Kaiser, *RFK Must Die*, 86.

72. Seigenthaler, *Search for Justice*, 285.

73. Ibid., 279.

74. Kaiser, *RFK Must Die*, 70.

75. Ibid., 70.

76. Ibid., 342.

77. Seigenthaler, *Search for Justice*, 297.

78. "Freud Was Right: Mind Can Block Memories if They Are Too Painful," *The Independent* (UK), January 9, 2004.

79. "Sirhan's Trance," 31.

80. Melanson, *Robert F. Kennedy Assassination*, 163.

81. Kaiser, *RFK Must Die*, 201.

82. Ibid., 518.

83. Houghton, *Special Unit Senator*, 52.

84. Kaiser, *RFK Must Die*, 204.

85. John Douglas and Mark Olshaker, *The Anatomy of Motive* (London: Pocket Books, 1999), 240.

86. Moldea, *Killing of Robert F. Kennedy*, 326.

87. Dan E. Moldea, "Re: DiEugenio's 'The Curious Case of Dan Moldea,'" *Moldea.com*, undated, http://www.moldea.com/2000june3.html.

88. Kaiser, *RFK Must Die*, 388.

89. Truman Capote, *In Cold Blood* (London: Penguin Books, 1967), 13.

90. Ibid., 290.

91. Ibid., 292 n.; M. Cima, H. Merckelbach, H. Nijman, E. Knauer, and S. Hollnack, "I Can't Remember, Your Honor: Offenders Who Claim Amnesia," *German Journal of Psychiatry*, February 25, 2001, http://www.gjpsy.uni-goettingen_de/gjp-article-cima.pdf.

Chapter 10: Sirhan's Obsessions

1. Klaber and Melanson, *Shadow Play*, 370, 328.

2. Kenneth Ofgang, "California Supreme Court Again Denies Freedom to Sirhan," *Metropolitan News Enterprise*, March 20, 2003.

3. Klaber and Melanson, *Shadow Play*, 200.

4. Kaiser, *RFK Must Die*, 422.

5. Ibid., 301.

6. Mohammed Taki Mehdi, *Kennedy and Sirhan: Why?* (New York: New World Press, 1968), 88.

7. Jansen, *Why Robert Kennedy Was Killed*, 138.

8. Kaiser, *RFK Must Die*, 227.

9. Avi Davis, "Textbook Incitement," *Aish.com*, December 23, 2003, http://www.aish.com/jewishissues/middleeast/Textbook_Incitement.asp.

10. Christopher Hewitt, *Understanding Terrorism in America: From the Klan to Al Qaeda* (New York: Routledge, 2002), 25.

11. Alan Caruba, "The Dogs of War and the Winds of Change in the Middle East," *The Progressive Conservative* 5:235 (September 22, 2003): 4.

12. Sana Hassan, "Israel and the Palestinians," *New York Review of Books* 21:18 (November 14, 1974).

13. A. Dokimos, "The Testimony of a Palestinian Muslim Turned Christian in Israel," www.dokimos.org/shepherdsvoice (accessed June 20, 2003).

14. Andrea Levin, "Jenning's Jerusalem Jihad," *CAMERA*, December 31,1996, http://www.camera.org/index.asp?x_context=3&x_outlet=1&x_article=32.

15. Jansen, *Why Robert Kennedy Was Killed*, 80.

16. National Christian Leadership Conference for Israel, "Palestinian Textbooks: Selections," www.nclci.org/issues/palestinian-textb (accessed July 25, 2004).

17. Ibid.

18. Joseph E. Katz, "Modern Arab Propaganda Has Incorporated Nazi Propaganda," *EretzYisroel.org*, 2001, http://www.eretzyisroel.org/~samuel/nazi.html#2.

19. Kaiser, *RFK Must Die*, 357.

20. Houghton, *Special Unit Senator*, 231.

21. Kaiser, *RFK Must Die*, 363.

22. Ibid., 199.

23. Ibid., 187.

24. Ibid., 188.

25. John Dancy, "Interview with John Weidner," NBC News Radio, June 5, 1968, Larry Sneed Audio Tape Archives.

26. Kaiser, *RFK Must Die*, 277.

27. Ibid., 200.

28. Klaber and Melanson, *Shadow Play*, 57.

29. Houghton, *Special Unit Senator*, 165.

30. Ibid., 166.

31. Ibid., 231.

32. Seigenthaler, *Search for Justice*, 268.

33. Kaiser, *RFK Must Die*, 166.

34. Seigenthaler, *Search for Justice*, 296.

35. LAPD Summary Report, 488.

36. Houghton, *Special Unit Senator*, 232.

37. "Sirhan Takes the Stand," 17.

38. Dancy, "Interview With John Weidner."

39. Kaiser, *RFK Must Die*, 200.

40. "Trials: Death without Dread," *Time*, March 14, 1969, 26.

41. Kaiser, *RFK Must Die*, 80.

42. "The Assassins," 23; and "Sirhan: Tragedy of the Absurd," 23.

43. "Sirhan's Notebooks," in LAPD Summary Report.

44. Kaiser, *RFK Must Die*, 516.

45. Ibid., 514

46. Capote, *In Cold Blood*, 289.

47. Klagsbrun and Whitney, *Assassination*, 40.

48. "Mind of the Assassin," *60 Minutes II*, August 15, 2000, http://www.cbsnews.com/stories/2000/03/14/60II/main171812.shtml?CMP = ILC-SearchStories.

49. Kaiser, *RFK Must Die*, 227.

50. Houghton, *Special Unit Senator*, 231.

51. Kaiser, *RFK Must Die*, 219.

52. Houghton, *Special Unit Senator*, 231.

53. Kaiser, *RFK Must Die*, 516.

54. Ibid., 108.

55. LAPD Summary Report, 400.

56. Kaiser, *RFK Must Die*, 199.

57. Ibid., 513.

58. Hewitt, *Understanding Terrorism in America*, 63.

59. Kaiser, *RFK Must Die*, 166.

60. Klaber and Melanson, *Shadow Play*, 180.

61. Kaiser, *RFK Must Die*, 514.

62. Ibid., 214.

63. Melanson, *Robert F. Kennedy Assassination*, 294.

64. LAPD Summary Report, 71.

65. Pease and DiEugenio, *Assassinations*, 629.

66. Kaiser, *RFK Must Die*, 168.

67. "Sirhan's Notebooks."

68. Kaiser, *RFK Must Die*, 209.

69. "Sirhan's Notebooks."

70. Robert A. Fein and Bryan Vossekuil, *Protective Intelligence and Threat Assessment Investigations* (Washington, DC: National Institute of Justice, 1998), 16, http://www.secretservice.gov/ntac/ntac_pi_guide_state.pdf.

71. Kaiser, *RFK Must Die*, 171.

72. Ibid., 169.

73. James F. Kirkham, Sheldon G. Levy, and William J. Crotty, *Assassination and Political Violence: A Staff Report to the Commission on the Causes and Prevention of Violence* (New York: Bantam/Matrix Books, 1970), 83.

74. David A. Rothstein, "Presidential Assassination Syndrome" *Archives of General Psychiatry* 11 (September 1964): 245–54.

75. Douglas and Olshaker, *Anatomy of Motive*, 31.

76. Ibid., 220.

77. Ibid., 219.

78. Stephen Schafer, *The Political Criminal: The Problem of Morality and Crime* (New York: Free Press, 1974), 156.

79. Kaiser, *RFK Must Die*, 271.

80. Mel Ayton, *The JFK Assassination: Dispelling the Myths* (West Sussex, UK: Woodfield, 2002), 297.

81. LAPD Summary Report, 58.

82. Capote, *In Cold Blood*, 142.

83. "The Other Sirhan."

84. Kaiser, *RFK Must Die*, 286, 292, 343.

85. Ibid, 292.

86. Ibid., 425.

87. Ibid.

88. Ibid., 295.

89. Ibid., 273.

90. Houghton, *Special Unit Senator*, 248.

91. Jansen, *Why Robert Kennedy Was Killed*, 113.

92. Houghton, *Special Unit Senator*, 231.

93. Ibid., 248.

94. Capote, *In Cold Blood*, 40, 289, 286.

95. Seigenthaler, *Search for Justice*, 227.

96. Kaiser, *RFK Must Die*, 307.

97. Ibid., 276.

98. Ibid., 375.

99. Seigenthaler, *Search for Justice*, 227.

100. Kaiser, *RFK Must Die*, 294.

101. Moldea, *Killing of Robert F. Kennedy*, 297.

Chapter 11: The Unaffiliated Terrorist

1. Robert Spencer, *Onward Muslim Soldiers: How Jihad Still Threatens America and the West* (Washington, DC: Regnery Publishing, 2003), 227.

2. Anne Coulter, *Treason: Liberal Treachery from the Cold War to the War on Terrorism* (New York: Crown Forum, 2003), 291.

3. Walter Lacqueur, *The Age of Terrorism* (New York: Little, Brown, 1987), 149.

4. Kevin M. Cherry, "Defining Terrorism Down," *National Review Online*, April 4, 2002, www.nationalreview.com.

5. Brian Michael Jenkins, et al., *Countering the New Terrorism* (Washington, DC: Rand, 1999), 3.

6. Lacqueur, *Age of Terrorism*, 10.

7. James M. Poland, *Practical, Tactical and Legal Perspectives of Terrorism and Hostage Taking*, with Michael J. McCrystle (new York: E. Mellon Press, 1999), 12.

8. George H. W. Bush, *Public Report of the Vice President's Task Force on Combating Terrorism* (Washington, DC: Government Printing Office, February 1986), http://www.population-security.org/bush_and_terror.pdf.

9. Jessica Stern, *The Ultimate Terrorists* (Cambridge: Harvard University Press, 1999), 11. This definition underlay the court ruling that the 2002 Washington snipers could be charged under Virginia's anti-terrorism law.

10. Bruce Hoffman, *Inside Terrorism* (London: Weidenfeld and Nicholson, 1998), 25.

11. Ibid., 42.

12. Hewitt, *Understanding Terrorism in America*, 57.

13. Ibid., 79.

14. Paul R. Pillar, *Terrorism and US Foreign Policy* (Washington, DC: Brookings Institution Press, 2001), 13.

15. Melanson, *Who Killed Robert Kennedy?* 68.

16. Pease and DiEugenio, *Assassinations*, 532.

17. Hewitt, *Understanding Terrorism in America*, 74.

18. Kaiser, *RFK Must Die*, 262.

19. "For Perspective and Determination," *Time*, June 14, 1968, 9.

20. "The Assassins," 24.
21. Lacey Fosburgh, "Sirhan Trial—It Stirs Deep and Conflicting Emotions," *New York Times,* January 19, 1969.
22. Douglas E. Kneeland, "Sirhan Trial Seen Plodding Along in World of Own," *New York Times,* February 2, 1969.
23. Jansen, *Why Robert Kennedy Was Killed,* 221.
24. Klagsbrun and Whitney, *Assassination,* 70.
25. Melanson, *Assassination of Robert F. Kennedy,* 143.
26. Klaber and Melanson, *Shadow Play,* 231.
27. Kaiser, *RFK Must Die,* 166.
28. Melanson, *Assassination of Robert F. Kennedy,* 144.
29. Richard Rhodes, *Why They Kill: The Discoveries of a Maverick Criminologist* (New York: Vintage Books, 1999), 321.
30. Kaiser, *RFK Must Die,* 472.
31. Houghton, *Special Unit Senator,* 222.
32. Kaiser, *RFK Must Die,* 181.
33. "The Least Unreasonable Arab," *Time,* July 14 1967, http://www.time.com/time/magazine/article/0,9171,899627,00.html.
34. Jansen, *Why Robert Kennedy Was Killed,* 150.
35. Katz, "Modern Arab Propaganda Has Incorporated Nazi Propaganda."
36. Abd Al-Hamid Al-Bakkoush, "The US and the Complexities of the Arab Mind," Middle East Media Research Institute, February 22, 2002, www.memri.de.
37. Amos Elon, *A Blood-Dimmed Tide* (New York: Columbia University Press, 1998), 93.
38. Kaiser, *RFK Must Die,* 111.
39. Seigenthaler, *Search for Justice,* 258.
40. Kaiser, *RFK Must Die,* 97.
41. Ibid., 254.
42. LAPD Summary Report, 400.
43. Kaiser, *RFK Must Die,* 168.
44. Seigenthaler, *Search for Justice,* 253.
45. Ibid., 257.
46. Ibid., 258.
47. Kaiser, *RFK Must Die,* 217.
48. Ibid., 240.
49. Ibid.
50. Ibid., 205.
51. Seigenthaler, *Search for Justice,* 258.

52. Ibid., 255.

53. Kaiser, *RFK Must Die*, 253.

54. Ibid., 256.

55. Witcover, *85 Days*, 218.

56. Jansen, *Why Robert Kennedy Was Killed*, 195.

57. Clarke, *American Assassins*, 92.

58. Kaiser, *RFK Must Die*, 516.

59. Ibid., 165.

60. Karsh, *Arafat's War*, 36.

61. Dr. Ely Karmon, "Fatah and the Popular Front for the Liberation of Palestine," Institute for Counter-Terrorism, 2001, http://www.ict conference.org/aarticles/c1847.php.

62. Karsh, *Arafat's War*, 37.

63. Ibid., 38–46.

64. Ibid.

65. Ibid., 27.

66. Jansen, *Why Robert Kennedy Was Killed*, 188.

67. Ibid., 151.

68. LAPD Summary Report, 488.

69. Ibid.

70. Steve K. Dubrow-Eichel, "The Mind of the Fanatic," The Rick A. Ross Institute for the Study of Destructive Cults, Controversial Groups and Movements, September 23, 2001, http://www.rickross.com/reference/ brainwashing/brainwashing16.html.

71. Hewitt, *Understanding Terrorism in America*, 80.

72. Walter Reich, ed., *Origins of Terrorism* (Washington, DC: Woodrow Wilson Center Press, 1998), 25–40.

73. Hala Jaber, "The Avengers," *Sunday Times* (UK), December 7, 2003.

74. Christina Lamb, "Gambling Habit Led Briton into Deadly Clutches of Al Qaeda," *Sunday Times* (UK), May 9, 2004.

75. Rex A. Hudson, "The Sociology and Psychology of Terrorism: Who Becomes a Terrorist and Why?" *(report prepared under an Interagency Agreement* by the Federal Research Division, Library of Congress, *September 1999), http://www.fas.org/irp/threat/frd.html.*

76. Ibid.

77. Kaiser, *RFK Must Die*, 385.

78. Klagsbrun and Whitney, *Assassination*, 40.

79. Kaiser, *RFK Must Die*, 183.

80. Ibid., 283.

81. Ibid., 270.
82. Ibid., 515.

Chapter 12: Why Did He Kill?

1. Kaiser, *RFK Must Die*, 513.
2. Ibid., 283.
3. Ibid., 265.
4. Hudson, "Sociology and Psychology of Terrorism," 40.
5. W. J. Arnold and D. Levine, *1969 Nebraska Symposium on Motivation* (Lincoln: University of Nebraska Press, 1970), 237–307.
6. Roger Dobson, "We're Stuck with Our Personality at Age of Three," *Sunday Times* (UK), April 7, 2004.
7. Mehdi, *Kennedy and Sirhan*, 88.
8. Kaiser, *RFK Must Die*, 449.
9. John Dancy, "Interview with Mrs. John Weidner," NBC News Radio, June 5, 1968, Larry Sneed Audio Tape Archives.
10. Reich, *Origins of Terrorism*, 26.
11. Kaiser, *RFK Must Die*, 513.
12. Seigenthaler, *Search for Justice*, 297.
13. J. R. Malloy, "Revisiting the Rorschach of Sirhan Sirhan," *Journal of Personality Assessment* 58:3 (June 1992): 548–570.
14. Sidney J. Slomich and Robert E. Kantor, "Our Assassins: From Booth to Ray: Study Finds They Were Outcasts, Misfits," *Chicago Daily News*, March 13, 1969.
15. Kaiser, *RFK Must Die*, 291.
16. LAPD Summary Report, 383.
17. Kaiser, *RFK Must Die*, 364.
18. Rhodes, *Why They Kill*, 109–140.
19. Seigenthaler, *Search for Justice*, 252.
20. Rhodes, *Why They Kill*, 109–140.
21. "Lone Attackers Are Greatest Threat," *USA Today*, July 27, 1998.
22. "Trials: Round One," 23.
23. Kaiser, *RFK Must Die*, 535.
24. Wertham, "A Sign of Cain: An Exploration of Human Violence," in *Turning Criminals into Mental Patients*.
25. "Bobby's Last, Longest Day," *Newsweek*, June 17, 1968, 25.
26. Ibid.
27. Alistair Cooke, "The Death of Robert Kennedy," BBC Archives, June 9, 1968.
28. Klaber and Melanson, *Shadow Play*, 182.

29. Kaiser, *RFK Must Die*, 219.
30. Al-Afif Al-Akhdar, "Arab Identity Crisis and Education in the Arab World," *Free Republic*, June 2003, http://www.freerepublic.com/focus/f-news/986824/posts.
31. Seigenthaler, *Search for Justice*, 307.
32. Kaiser, *RFK Must Die*, 217.
33. Reich, *Origins of Terrorism*, 18.
34. Kaiser, *RFK Must Die*, 219.

Afterword

1. Milton Benjamin, Ed Rogers, and Mike Feinsilber, "Funeral Train," in *Assassination*, eds. Klagsbrun and Whitney, 197–202.
2. Jessica Dawson, "RFK's Funeral Train: Images Along: Ties That Bound," *Washington Post,* May 30, 2002.
3. Arianna Huffington, "John Kerry and Bobby Kennedy's Unfinished Mission," *The Huffington Post*, May 19, 2004, www.ariannaonline.com/columns.
4. "Another Kennedy Death Threat," *Newsweek*, August 24, 1981, 29.
5. "'Hey Punk' Letter from Sirhan Sirhan to His Attorney, Grant Cooper," *Moldea.com*, undated, http://www.moldea.com/Sirhan-HeyPunk.html.
6. Cogswell, "New Trial for Sirhan?"
7. Adele Ferguson, "Olympia Watch," *Anacortes American*, December 17, 2003, http://www.goanacortes.com/articles/2003/12/17/columnists/ferguson.txt.
8. Moldea, *Killing of Robert F. Kennedy*, 303.
9. Jim Robinson, "Did Sirhan Know?" *Free Republic*, October 12, 2001, http://www.freerepublic.com/focus/f-news/546255/posts.
10. *Wall Street Journal*, November 26, 2001.
11. "Kennedy's Assassin Denied Parole," *CNN.com*, March 7, 2003, http://www.cnn.com/2003/LAW/03/06/crime.sirhan.reut/.
12. Juliana Barbassa, "Robert Kennedy's Convicted Killer Denied Parole for 13th Time," Associated Press, March 16, 2006, http://pqasb.pqarchiver.com/ap 1009255311.html?did = 1009255311&FMT = ABS&FMTS = FT&date = Mar + 16 % 2C + 2006&author = JULIANA + BARBASSA&pub = Associated + Press&desc = Robert + Kennedy % 27s + convicted + killer + denied + parole + for + 13th + time.
13. Julie Wheldon, "The Truth, the Whole Truth, as Shown by the Brain Scan," *Daily Mail* (UK), January 31, 2006. In a 2005 U.S. study, eleven volunteers were asked questions after taking part in a mock shooting. While under "brain scanners," five were told to tell the truth and six to

lie. In those who lied, fourteen areas of the brain lit up. This compared with seven in those who told the truth. The frontal lobe was also particularly active in the liars. The method proved to be far more accurate than the polygraph, which looks for clues such as increased perspiration, a racing heartbeat, quicker breathing, and sometimes even leg movements or facial expressions. The method uses MRI scanners, which hospitals use to detect tumors.

BIBLIOGRAPHY

U.S. Government Reports, State Records, and Files

"Appendix C: List of Motion Picture Films." Los Angeles Police Department Records of the Robert F. Kennedy Assassination Investigation. California State Archives, Sacramento, CA.

"Appendix E: Lists of the Investigation Records Audio Tapes."

Los Angeles Police Department Records of the Robert F. Kennedy Assassination Investigation. California State Archives, Sacramento, CA.

Bush, George H. W. *Public Report of the Vice President's Task Force on Combating Terrorism.* Washington, DC: Government Printing Office, February 1986. http://www.population-security.org/bush_and_terror.pdf.

Federal Bureau of Investigation. *Hitler's FBI File.* National Archives and Records Administration, Washington, DC.

Fein, Robert A., and Bryan Vossekuil. *Protective Intelligence and Threat Assessment Investigations.* Washington, DC: National Institute of Justice, 1998. http://www.secretservice.gov/ntac/ntac_pi_guide_state.pdf.

Hudson, Rex A. "The Sociology and Psychology of Terrorism: Who Becomes a Terrorist and Why?" R*eport prepared under an Interagency Agreement* by the Federal Research Division, Library of Congress, September 1999. http://www.fas.org/irp/threat/frd.html.

Kirkham, James F., Sheldon Levy, William J. Crotty. *Assassination and Political Violence: A Report to the National Commission on the Causes and Prevention of Violence.* Washington, DC: Government Printing Office, 1969.

Kranz, Thomas F. "Robert F. Kennedy Assassination—(Summary)." Report Consisting of the Los Angeles County Board of Supervisors Independent Investigation. FBI Records. http://foia.fbi.gov/foiaindex/rfkasumm.htm.

1969 Final Report. 10 vols. Los Angeles Police Department Records of the Robert F. Kennedy Assassination Investigation. California State Archives, Sacramento, CA.

People v. Sirhan. 7 Cal.3d 710, Crim. No. 14026, June 16, 1972. http://caselaw.lp.findlaw.com/ca/cal3d/7.html

Senate Intelligence Committee, Foreign and Military Intelligence, Select Committee to Study Governmental Operations with Respect to Intelligence Activities, Foreign and Military Intelligence. *Final Report.* 94th Cong., 2d sess., 1976, Rep. 94-755.

Research on the Acoustics Evidence in the RFK Case Was Carried Out By:

Steve Barber: A drummer/percussionist whose work was seminal in proving that the Dictabelt recorded by the Dallas Police Department that allegedly contains sounds of the shots in the JFK assassination was actually recorded elsewhere. He worked directly with a panel of the Committee on Ballistic Acoustics (CBA), which included two Nobel prize-winning physicists, Norman F. Ramsey, chairman of the committee, and the late Luis Alvarez. The Justice Department hired the CBA to reexamine earlier findings of the House Select Committee on Assassinations acoustics experts, who had concluded that the Dictabelt contained the gunshots that killed President Kennedy.

Philip Harrison: See Appendix B.

Michael O'Dell: A technical analyst who worked with the Ramsey Panel on its rebuttal of research that attempted to invalidate the panel's criticisms of the House Select Committee on Assassinations JFK assassination acoustics findings. See http://mcadams.posc.mu.edu/odell.

Chad R. Zimmerman: A chiropractor from Sioux City, Iowa, with a strong interest in the JFK case. He presently also serves as one of the three moderators on the newsgroup alt.assassination.jfk. He is interested in firearms aspects of the shooting and was part of the Discovery Channel special program that investigated the "magic bullet." In September 2004 he visited the National Archives and viewed the original autopsy photos and X-rays with Larry Sturdivan. He has a website at www.zimmermanjfk.com.

Research about RFK's Wounds Was Carried Out By:

Larry M. Sturdivan: See Appendix A.

Books and Articles

"Acquaintances Characterize Robert Kennedy's Suspected Assassin." Description of film footage. Independent Television News, June 6, 1968. www.itnnews.co.uk.

Al-Akhdar, Al-Afif. "Arab Identity Crisis and Education in the Arab World." *Free Republic*, June 2003, http://www.freerepublic.com/focus/ f-news/986824/posts.

Al-Bakkoush, Abd Al-Hamid. "The US and the Complexities of the Arab Mind." Middle East Media Research Institute, February 22, 2002, www.memri.de.

"Another Kennedy Death Threat." *Newsweek*, August 24, 1981.

Arnold, W. J., and D. Levine. *1969 Nebraska Symposium on Motivation.* Lincoln: University of Nebraska Press, 1970.

"The Assassins: Who Did It—And Why?" *Newsweek*, March 24, 1969.

Ayton, Mel. *The JFK Assassination: Dispelling the Myths.* West Sussex, UK: Woodfield Publishing, 2002.

———. *Questions of Controversy: The Kennedy Brothers.* Sunderland, UK: University of Sunderland Press/BEP, 2001.

Baddely, A. D. *Human Memory: Theory and Practice.* Boston: Allyn and Bacon, 1997.

Baden, Michael. *Unnatural Death: Confessions of a Forensic Pathologist.* London: Sphere Books, 1989.

Baden, Michael, and Marion Roach. *Dead Reckoning: The New Science of Catching Killers.* London: Arrow, 2002.

Baker, Robert Allen. *They Call It Hypnosis.* Buffalo, NY: Prometheus Books, 1990.

Ballard, Travis. "Children in America: Fatherless and in Need of Immediate Intervention." National Congress for Fathers and Children, Novermber 27, 1995. www.ncfc.net.

Barbassa, Juliana. "Sirhan Denied Parole for 13th Time." *Associated Press*, March 16, 2006. http://pqasb.pqarchiver.com/ap/1009255311. html?did = 1009255311&FMT = ABS&FMTS = FT&date = Mar + 16 % 2C + 2006&author = JULIANA + BARBASSA&pub = Associated + Press&desc = Robert + Kennedy % 27s + convicted + killer + denied + parole + for + 13th + time.

Bass, Warren. *Support Any Friend: Kennedy's Middle East and the Making of the US-Israel Alliance.* New York: Oxford University Press, 2003.

Bell, Steve. "June 5, 1968: The Day Robert Kennedy Was Shot." *Jim Bafaro Show*, ABC Radio News transcript, 1998. www.abcnews.com.

Berman, Paul. *Terror and Liberalism.* New York: Norton, 2003.

Blumenfeld, Ralph. "New Questions: The Death of RFK." *New York Post*, May 23, 1975.

Blumenthal, Sid, and Harvey Yazijian, eds. *Government by Gunplay: Assassination Conspiracy Theories from Dallas to Today.* New York: New American Library, 1976.

Bly, Nellie. *The Kennedy Men: Three Generations of Sex, Scandal and Secrets.* New York: Kensington Books, 1996.

"Bobby's Last, Longest Day." *Newsweek,* June 17, 1968, 30.

Brodie, Ian. "Every Day He Knew His Life Could Be in Danger." *Daily Telegraph* (UK), June 6, 1968.

Brown, Nathan J. "Democracy, History, and the Contest over the Palestinian Curriculum." George Washington University report prepared for the Adam Institute, Washington, DC, November 2001.

Buckley, William F. "Murder Heaven: The Law Is a Quagmire." *National Review,* November 18, 2003.

Capote, Truman. *In Cold Blood.* London: Penguin Books, 1967.

Carroll, Robert Todd. "Hypnosis." *The Skeptic's Dictionary,* November 27, 2006. http://skepdic.com/hypnosis.html.

Caruba, Alan. "The Dogs of War and the Winds of Change in the Middle East." *The Progressive Conservative* 5:235 (September 22, 2003).

Cherry, Kevin M. "Defining Terrorism Down." *National Review Online,* April 4, 2002. www.nationalreview.com.

Christison, Kathleen. "The History of Anti-Palestinian Bias, from Wilson to Bush." *CounterPunch,* July 15, 2002. http://www.counterpunch.org/kchristison0715.html.

Cima, M., H. Merckelbach, H. Nijman, E. Knauer, and S. Hollnack, "I Can't Remember Your Honor: Offenders Who Claim Amnesia." *German Journal of Psychiatry,* February 25, 2001. http://www.gjpsy.uni-goettingen.de/gjp-article-cima.pdf.

Clarke, James W. *American Assassins: The Darker Side of Politics.* Princeton, NJ: Princeton University Press, 1982.

Coe, W. C., and K. Ryken. "Hypnosis and Risks to Human Subjects." *American Psychologist* 10:6 (August 1979).

Cogswell, David. "New Trial for Sirhan?" *Media Review,* November 24, 2002, http://www.davidcogswell.com/Political/NewTrialSirhan.html.

Cook, Andrew. "Lone Assassins." *History Today* (UK), November 2003. http://www.historytoday.com/dt_issue.asp?gid = 19652&aid = &tgid = &amid = &g19652 = x&g30026 = x&g20991 = x&g21010 = x&g 19965 = x&g19963 = x.

Cooke, Alistair. "The Death of Robert Kennedy." BBC Archives, June 9, 1968.

———. *Talk about America: 1951–1968.* London: Penguin Books, 1981.

Coulter, Anne. *Treason: Liberal Treachery from the Cold War to the War on Terrorism.* New York: Crown Forum, 2003.

Crotty, William J., ed. *Assassinations and the Political Order.* New York: Harper and Row, 1971.

David, Abraham. "Issues on the Mythical Palestine." *www.masada.com*, June 13, 2003.

Davis, Avi. "Textbook Incitement." *Aish.com*, December 23, 2003. http://www.aish.com/jewishissues/middleeast/Textbook_Incitement.asp.

Davis, John H. *The Kennedys: Dynasty and Disaster*. London: Sidgwick and Jackson, 1985.

————. *Mafia Kingfish: Carlos Marcello and the Assassination of John F. Kennedy*. New York: McGraw-Hill, 1989.

Dawson, Jessica. "RFK's Funeral Train: Images Along: Ties That Bound." *Washington Post,* May 30, 2002.

Dershowitz, Alan. *The Case for Israel*. Hoboken, NJ: John Wiley, 2003.

————."Put Arafat on Trial." *Ha'aretz Daily*, September 13, 2002. In *Frontpage Magazine*, October 1, 2002. http://www.frontpage mag.com/Articles/ReadArticle.asp?ID = 3073.

Dobson, Roger. "We're Stuck with Our Personality at Age of Three." *Sunday Times* (UK), April 7, 2004.

Dokimos, A. "The Testimony of a Palestinian Muslim Turned Christian in Israel." 2002. www.dokimos.org/shepherdsvoice. Accessed June 20, 2003.

Douglas, John, and Mark Olshaker. *The Anatomy of Motive*. London: Pocket Books, 1999.

————. *The Cases That Haunt Us*. London: Pocket Books, 2000.

————. *Mindhunter: Inside the FBI Elite Serial Crime Unit*. London: Arrow Books, 1997.

Dubrow-Eichel, Steve K. "The Mind of the Fanatic." The Rick A. Ross Institute for the Study of Destructive Cults, Controversial Groups and Movements, September 23, 2001. http://www.rickross.com/reference/brainwashing/brainwashing16.html.

Eland, Ivan. "Does US Intervention Overseas Breed Terrorism? The Historical Record." *Cato Foreign Policy Briefing No. 50*, December 17, 1998. http://www.cato.org/pubs/fpbriefs/fpb-050es.html.

Elliott, Paul. *Assassin! The Bloody History of Political Murder*. London: Cassell Illustrated, 1999.

Elon, Amos. *A Blood-Dimmed Tide*. New York: Columbia University Press, 1998.

Erikson, M. H. *The Nature of Hypnosis and Suggestion*. New York: Irvington, 1980.

Evans, Michael D. "Remember Who Killed Robert Kennedy?" 2003. www.therefinersfire.org/sirhan-killed-kennedy.htm. Accessed April 20, 2004.

Evans, Peter. *Ari: The Life, Times and Women of Aristotle Onassis*. London: Penguin Books, 1987.

———. *Nemesis: Aristotle Onassis, Jackie O, and the Love Triangle That Brought Down the Kennedys*. New York: Regan Books, 2004.

"Eye of the Hurricane." *Newsweek*, March 3, 1969, 20.

Ezzell, Carol. "Scientific American Gets Hypnotized." *Scientific American.com*, July 2001. http://www.sciamdigital.com/index.cfm?fa = Products.ViewIssuePreview&ARTICLEID_CHAR = EF2A5B86-3CCC-4271-B4D0-244D8F753F4.

Farr, B. "Sirhan Threatened to Kill Ted Kennedy Told." *Los Angeles Times*, August 13, 1981.

Fein, Robert A., and Bryan Vossekuil. "Assassination in the United States: An Operational Study of Recent Assassins, Attackers, and Near-Lethal Approachers." *Journal of Forensic Sciences* 44:2 (March 1999).

Ferguson, Adele. "Olympia Watch." *Anacortes American*, December 17, 2003. http://www.goanacortes.com/articles/2003/12/17/columnists/ferguson.txt.

Fosburgh, Lacey. "Sirhan Trial—It Stirs Deep and Conflicting Emotions." *New York Times*, January 19, 1969.

Frank, Gerold. *The Boston Strangler*. London: Pan Books, 1967.

Freed, Donald. *The Killing of RFK*. London: Sphere Books, 1976.

"Freud Was Right: Mind Can Block Memories if They Are Too Painful." *The Independent* (UK), January 9, 2004.

Gates, Daryl F. *Chief: My Life in the LAPD*. New York: Bantam Books, 1993.

Gerringer, Joe. "Robert Kennedy Assassination: Revisions and Re-writes." *Court TV Crime Library*, 2005. http://www.crimelibrary.com/terrorists_spies/assassins/kennedy/5.html.

Goldberg, Robert Alan. *Enemies Within: The Culture of Conspiracy in Modern America*. New Haven: Yale University Press, 2001.

Goodwin, Richard N. *Remembering America: A Voice from the Sixties*. New York: Little, Brown, 1988.

Gorey, Hays. "Memories of a Historic Ride." *Time*, May 9, 1988, 20.

———. *Robert Kennedy: The Last Campaign*. New York: Harcourt Brace, 1993.

Gorney, Cynthia. "Sirhan." *Washington Post*, August 21, 1979.

Halberstam, David. *The Unfinished Odyssey of Robert Kennedy*. London: Barrie and Jenkins, 1968.

Hamburg, Eric. *JFK, Nixon, Oliver Stone and Me*. New York: Public Affairs, 2002.

Hansen, Suzy. "Why Terrorism Works: An Interview with Alan Dershowitz." *Salon.com*, September 12, 2002. http://dir.salon.com/story/books/int/2002/09/12/dershowitz/index.html.

Hare, Robert D. *Without Conscience: The Disturbing World of the Psychopaths Among Us*. New York: Guilford Press, 1993.

Harsanyi, David. "The Media's 'Occupation' Myth." *FrontPagemagazine.com*, March 29, 2002. http://www.jr.co.il/articles/politics/media.txt.

Hassan, Sana. "Israel and the Palestinians." *New York Review of Books* 21:18 (November 14, 1974).

Hazelwood, Roy, and Stephen G. Michaud. *Dark Dreams: A Legendary FBI Profiler Examines Homicide and the Criminal Mind*. New York: St. Martin's Paperbacks, 2001.

Hewitt, Christopher. *Understanding Terrorism in America: From the Klan to Al Qaeda*. London: Routledge, 2003.

Heymann, C. David. *RFK: A Candid Biography*. London: William Heinemann, 1998.

Hoffman, Bruce. *Inside Terrorism*. London: Weidenfeld and Nicholson, 1998.

Holland, Andrew. *The RFK Assassination*. Towers Productions Inc. for the History Channel, 2005.

Houghton, Robert A. *Special Unit Senator: The Investigation of the Assassination of Senator Robert F. Kennedy*. New York: Random House, 1970.

Huffington, Arianna. "John Kerry and Bobby Kennedy's Unfinished Mission." *The Huffington Post*, May 19, 2004. www.ariannaonline.com/columns.

Hunt, John. "Oops, Dan Moldea Accidentally Uncovers the Conspiracy to Kill RFK." *JFK Lancer*, 2005. http://www.jfklancer.com/hunt/moldeas.htm.

———. "Robert Kennedy's Headwounds: The Case for Conspiracy." *JFK Lancer*, 2006. http://www.jfklancer.com/hunt/rfk_pt1.htm.

Hurwood, Bernhardt J. *Society and the Assassin: A Background Book on Political Murder*. London: Parents Magazine Press, 1970.

Hyams, Edward. *Killing No Murder: A Study of Assassination as a Political Means*. London: GB Nelson, 1969.

"Interview with Dr. Herbert Spiegel." *A Current Affair*, television documentary, June 5, 1992.

Jaber, Hala. "The Avengers." *Sunday Times* (UK), December 7, 2003.

Jansen, Godfrey H. *Why Robert Kennedy Was Killed: The Story of Two Victims*. New York: Third Press, 1970.

Jenkins, Brian Michael, et al. *Countering the New Terrorism*. Washington, DC: Rand Publications, 1999.

"The Jury v. Sirhan." *Newsweek*, May 5, 1969, 20.

Kaiser, Charles. *1968 in America: Music, Politics, Chaos, Counterculture, and the Shaping of a Generation*. London: Weidenfeld and Nicolson, 1988.

Kaiser, Robert Blair. *RFK Must Die: A History of the Robert Kennedy Assassination and Its Aftermath.* New York: E. P. Dutton, 1970.

———. "The case is still open. I'm not rejecting the Manchurian Candidate aspect of it," http://www.rfkmustdie.com. Accessed April 25, 2003.

Karmon, Dr. Ely. "Fatah and the Popular Front for the Liberation of Palestine." Institute for Counter-Terrorism, 2001. http://www.ict conference.org/aarticles/c1847.php.

Karsh, Efraim. *Arafat's War: The Man and His Battle for Israeli Conquest.* New York: Grove Press, 2003.

Katz, Joseph E. "Modern Arab Propaganda Has Incorporated Nazi Propaganda." *EretzYisroel.org,* 2001. http://www.eretzyisroel.org/~samuel/nazi.html#2.

Kelin, John. "The RFK Panel." 2002. http://www.parapolitics.info/copa/copa2002gallery. Accessed April 21, 2003.

Kennedy, Robert F. *The Enemy Within.* New York: Popular Library, 1960.

"The Kennedy Love Triangles," *www.etyahoo.com,* June 2, 2004, http://www.etyahoo.com/.

"Kennedy's Assassin Denied Parole," *CNN.com,* March 7, 2003, http://www.cnn.com/2003/LAW/03/06/crime.sirhan.reut/.

Kirkham, James F., Sheldon G. Levy, and William J. Crotty. *Assassination and Political Violence: A Staff Report to the Commission on the Causes and Prevention of Violence.* New York: Bantam/Matrix Books, 1970.

Kirtley, Jane. "Defamation Judgement Puts Onus on Media." *American Journalism Review,* January 1999. www.ajr.com.

Kittrie, Nicholas N. *Rebels With a Cause: The Minds and Morality of Political Offenders.* Boulder, CO: Westview Press, 2000.

Klaber, William, and Philip H. Melanson. *Shadow Play: The Murder of Robert F. Kennedy, the Trial of Sirhan Sirhan and the Failure of American Justice.* New York: St. Martin's Press, 1997.

Klagsbrun, Francine, and Whitney, David C., eds. *Assasination: Robert F. Kennedy, 1925–1968.* New York: Cowles, 1968.

Kneeland, Douglas E. "Sirhan Trial Seen Plodding Along in World of Own." *New York Times,* February 2, 1969.

Knight, Peter. *Conspiracy Culture: From Kennedy to the X Files.* London: Routledge, 2000.

———. *Conspiracy Nation: The Politics of Paranoia in Post War America.* New York: New York University Press, 2002.

Lacqueur, Walter. *The Age of Terrorism.* New York: Little, Brown, 1987.

Laing, Margaret. *The Next Kennedy.* London: MacDonald, 1968.

Lamb, Christina. "Gambling Habit Led Briton into Deadly Clutches of Al Qaeda." *Sunday Times* (UK), May 9, 2004.

Lance, Peter. *1000 Years for Revenge: International Terrorism and the FBI.* New York: Regan Books, 2003.

"The Last Hero." *Time*, May 9, 1988, 18–21.

"The Law: Selling a Client's Story." *Time*, January 19, 1970, 48.

Leamer, Laurence. *The Kennedy Men, 1901–1963.* New York: William Morrow, 2001.

"The Least Unreasonable Arab." *Time*, July 14, 1967. http://www.time.com/time/magazine/article/0,9171,899627,00.html.

Lerner, Jonathan. "I Was a Terrorist." *Washington Post*, February 24, 2002.

"The Letter and the Law." *Newsweek*, June 2, 1969, 21.

Levin, Andrea. "Jenning's Jerusalem Jihad." *CAMERA*, December 31, 1996, http://www.camera.org/index.asp?x_context=3&x_outlet=1&x_article=32.

"A Life on the Way to Death." *Time*, June 14, 1968, 10–16.

"Lone Attackers Are Greatest Threat." *USA Today*, July 27, 1998.

Lopez, Steve. "Ex-busboy Will Never Forget Bobby Kennedy." *Los Angeles Times*, June 1, 2003.

Love, Myron. "Arab Journalist Puts Lie to Palestinian Claims." *The Canadian Jewish News*, February 21, 2002. http://www.cjnews.com/pastissues/02/feb21-02/front3.asp.

Lynch, Greg. *Over the Shoulder: The RFK Assassination.* NPR Radio, 2000, www.npr.org.

Malloy, J. R. "Revisiting the Rorschach of Sirhan Sirhan." *Journal of Personality Assessment* 58:3 (June 1992): 548–70.

Marcus, Greil. "Chronicle of Death Foretold." *The Guardian* (UK), July 13, 2002.

Marks, John. *The Search for the Manchurian Candidate: The CIA and Mind Control.* New York: Norton, 1979.

McKinley, James. *Assassination in America.* New York: Harper and Row, 1977.

Mehdi, Mohammed Taki. *Kennedy and Sirhan: Why?* New York: New World Press, 1968.

Melanson, Philip H. *The Robert F. Kennedy Assassination: New Revelations on the Conspiracy and Cover-up.* New York: Shapolsky, 1991.

———. *Who Killed Robert Kennedy?* New York: Odonian Press, 1993.

Miester, Mark. "Eyewitness to History." *Tulanian*, Spring 1998. http://www2.tulane.edu/article_news_details.cfm?ArticleID=2923.

"Mind of the Assassin." *60 Minutes*, August 15, 2000. http://www.cbsnews.com/stories/2000/03/14/60II/main171812.shtml?CMP=ILC-SearchStories.

Moldea, Dan E. "Confronting Sirhan." *Moldea.com*, 2002. http://www.moldea.com/Seven-8.html.

———. "The History Channel on the RFK Murder." *Moldea.com*, January 17, 2000. http://www.moldea.com/HisChan-RFK.html.

———. "Investigating the Murder of Robert Kennedy (IV): When Wisdom Comes Too Late." *Moldea.com*, June 22, 2000. http://www.moldea.com/RFK4.html.

———. *The Killing of Robert F. Kennedy*. New York: Norton, 1995.

———. "Re: DiEugenio's 'The Curious Case of Dan Moldea.'" *Moldea.com*, undated. http://www.moldea.com/2000june3.html.

Morrow, Robert D. *"The Senator Must Die."* Roundtable Publishing, Inc. 1988. Santa Monica, CA.

National Christian Leadership Conference for Israel. "Palestinian Textbooks: Selections." http://www.nclci.org/issues/palestinian-textb. Accessed July 25, 2004.

Nellen, Paul. "An Interview with Professor Philip Melanson." *The RFK Assassination—Interviews*, 1994. http://homepages.tcp.co.uk/ ~ dlewis/melanson.htm.

Noe, Denise. "Sirhan Sirhan: Assassin of Modern US History." *Crime Magazine*, May 27, 2004. http://www.crimemagazine.com/04/bobbykennedy,0527.htm.

Noguchi, Thomas T. *Coroner to the Stars*. London: Corgi, 1983.

"The Non-Debate." *Time*, June 7, 1968, 12.

"Officer Ordered Items Destroyed." *Santa Monica Evening Outlook*, August 21, 1975.

Ofgang, Kenneth. "California Supreme Court Again Denies Freedom to Sirhan." *Metropolitan News Enterprise*, March 20, 2003.

"The Other Sirhan." *Newsweek*, April 14, 1969, 22.

"Our Times," *Los Angeles Times*, undated, www.latimes.com.

Palermo, Joseph A. *In His Own Right: The Political Odyssey of Senator Robert F. Kennedy*. New York: Columbia University Press, 2001.

Parkin, Alan J. *Memory and Amnesia*. New York: Psychology Press, 1997.

Parrish, Michael. *For the People: Inside the Los Angeles County District Attorney's Office 1850–2000*. Los Angeles: Angel City Press, 2001.

Pease, Lisa. "Sirhan and the RFK Assassination: Part I, The Grand Illusion." *Probe Magazine*, March/April 1998. http://www.webcom.com/ ~ lpease/collections/assassinations/rfk.htm.

———. "Sirhan and the RFK Assassination: Part II, Rubik's Cube." *Probe Magazine*, March/April 1998. http://www.webcom.com/ ~ lpease/collections/assassinations/rfk.htm.

Pease, Lisa, and James DiEugenio, eds. *The Assassinations:* Probe Magazine on *JFK, MLK, RFK and Malcolm X*. Los Angeles: Feral House, 2003.

Peters, Jean. *From Time Immemorial*. Emeryville, CA: JKAP Publications, 2001.

———. "The Origins of the Arab-Jewish Conflict over Palestine." *EretzYisroel.org*, 1984. http://www.eretzyisroel.org/~peters/.

Pilger, John. *Heroes*. London: Vintage, 2001.

Pillar, Paul R. *Terrorism and US Foreign Policy*. Washington, DC: Brookings Institution Press, 2001.

Pipes, Daniel. *Conspiracy: How the Paranoid Style Flourishes and Where It Comes From*. New York: Free Press, 1997.

Poland, James M. *Practical, Tactical and Legal Perspectives of Terrorism and Hostage Taking*. With Michael J. McCrystle. New York: E. Mellon Press, 1999.

"A Possible Explanation for Conspiracy Theories." *Economist*, July 9, 2004. www.theeconomist.com.

Quen, J. *The Psychiatrist in the Courtroom: Selected Papers of Bernard L. Diamond, M.D.* Mahwah, NJ: Analytic Press, 1995.

Reich, Walter, ed. *Origins of Terrorism*. Washington, DC: Woodrow Wilson Center Press, 1998.

Ressler, Robert K., and Tom Shachtman. *Whoever Fights Monsters*. London: Pocket Books, 1993.

Reston, James. "The Qualities of Robert Kennedy." *New York Times*, June 7, 1968.

"RFK's Last Campaign." *Newsweek*, June 8, 1998, 32–51.

Rhodes, Richard. *Why They Kill: The Discoveries of a Maverick Criminologist*. New York: Vintage Books, 1999.

Rivera, Carl. "Man Wins Battle with City over Kennedy Assassination Photos." *Los Angeles Times*, August 23, 1996.

Roberts, Greg. "RFK Assassination Conspiracy Theory Hypnotist Found Dead in Las Vegas." *Hollywood Reporter*, March 21, 1977.

Robinson, Jim. "Did Sirhan Know?" *Free Republic.com*, October 12, 2001. http://www.frontpagemag.com/Articles/ReadArticle.asp?ID=3073.

Rogers, Warren. *When I Think of Bobby: A Personal Memoir of the Kennedy Years*. New York: HarperPerrenial, 1993.

Rothstein, David A. "Presidential Assassination Syndrome." *Archives of General Psychiatry* 11 (September 1964): 245–254.

Schacter, Daniel L. *Searching for Memory: The Brain, the Mind, the Past*. Philadelphia: Basic Books, 1997.

Schafer, Stephen. *The Political Criminal: The Problem of Morality and Crime*. New York: Free Press, 1974.

Scheim, David E. *Contract on America: The Mafia Murders of John and Robert Kennedy.* New York: Shapolsky, 1988.

———. *The Mafia Killed President Kennedy.* London: Virgin, 1988.

Schlesinger, Arthur M. *Robert Kennedy and His Times.* New York: Ballantine Books, 1979.

———. *A Thousand Days: John F. Kennedy in the White House.* London: Andre Deutsch, 1965.

Scott, Peter Dale, Paul L. Hoch, and Russell Stetler, eds. *The Assassinations: Dallas and Beyond: A Guide to Cover-ups and Investigations.* New York: Random House, 1978.

Seigenthaler, John. *A Search for Justice.* Nashville, TN: Aurora Publishers, 1971.

Shihab, Aziz. *Sirhan.* Sacramento, CA: Naylor, 1969.

Silverberg, Robert. *If I Forget Thee O Jerusalem: American Jews and the State of Israel.* New York: William Morrow, 1970.

"Sirhan: Tragedy of the Absurd." *Newsweek*, March 24, 1969, 22.

"Sirhan Takes the Stand." *Newsweek*, March 17, 1969, 17.

"Sirhan's Trance." *Newsweek*, April 7, 1969, 31.

Slomich, Sidney J., and Robert E. Kantor. "Our Assassins: From Booth to Ray: Study Finds They Were Outcasts, Misfits." *Chicago Daily News*, March 13, 1969.

Smith, Matthew. *Vendetta: The Kennedys.* Edinburgh: Mainstream Publishing, 1993.

Speiser, Stuart M. *The Deadly Sins of Aristotle Onassis.* Ozark, AL: ACW Press, 2005.

Spencer, Robert. *Onward Muslim Soldiers: How Jihad Still Threatens America and the West.* Washington, DC: Regnery Publishing, 2003.

Stern, Jessica. *The Ultimate Terrorists.* Cambridge: Harvard University Press, 1999.

Strober, Deborah Hart, and Gerald S. Strober. *The Kennedy Presidency: An Oral History of the Era.* Washington, DC: Brassey's, Inc, 2003.

Sullivan, William. *The Bureau: My Thirty Years in Hoover's FBI.* With Bill Brown. New York: Norton, 1979.

"Test Case." *Newsweek*, April 7, 1969, 66.

"There Just Hasn't Been a Nicer Boy." *Newsweek*, June 17, 1968, 16.

Thomas, Evan. *Robert Kennedy: His Life.* New York: Simon & Schuster, 2000.

Thomas, Gordon. "Was Robert Kennedy's Assassin Brainwashed?" *Americanfreedomnews.com*, September 4, 2002. http://www.americanfreedomnews.com. Accessed January 1, 2003.

Time-Life Books, eds. *Assassination.* Alexandria, VA: Time-Life Books, 1994.

"Trials: Death without Dread." *Time*, March 14, 1969, 23.

"Trials: Round One." *Newsweek*, February 3, 1969, 23.

"Trials: Smiling Through." *Newsweek*, January 27, 1969, 17.

"Trials: Studies in Killing." *Newsweek*, March 31, 1969, 29.

"Trials: The Sirhan Verdict." *Time*, May 5, 1969, 21.

"Trials: The Wanderer." *Newsweek*, January 13, 1969, 36.

Turner, William. *Rearview Mirror: Looking Back at the FBI, the CIA and Other Tails.* Granite Bay, CA: Penmarin Books, 2001.

Turner, William W., and John G. Christian. *The Assassination of Robert F. Kennedy: A Searching Look at the Conspiracy and Cover-up 1968–1978."* New York: Thunders Mouth Press, 1993.

"Verdict on Sirhan." *Newsweek*, April 28, 1969, 22.

Vincent, Isabel. "Kennedy's Killer Demands Re-Trial." *National Post*, June 11, 2003.

Volgenov, George. "Roll Up the Red Carpet: Hotel of Stars to Close Its Guest Register." *Detroit Free Press*, October 28, 1988.

Vorpagel, Russell. *Profiles in Murder: An FBI Legend Dissects Killers and Their Crimes.* New York: Dell, 1998.

Waldman, Steven. "Closing the Case on RFK." *Newsweek*, June 12, 1995, 42.

Waldron, Lamar, and Hartmann, Thom. *Ultimate Sacrifice: John and Robert Kennedy, the Plan for a Coup in Cuba, and the Murder of JFK.* London: Constable, 2005.

Waterfield, Robin. *Hidden Depths: The Story of Hypnosis.* London: Macmillan, 2002.

Wertham, Frederic. "A Sign for Cain: An Exploration of Human Violence." In *Turning Criminals into Mental Patients and Mental Patients into Criminals*, 2002, http://www.cinemaniastigma.com. Accessed April 21, 2003.

Wheldon, Julie. "The Truth, the Whole Truth, as Shown by the Brain Scan." *Daily Mail* (UK), January 31, 2006.

Wilson, Elaine. "KLKI's Broadcasters Stretch Retirement Age." *www.SkagitBIZ.com*, February 11, 2004. http://www.klki.com/whatshappening.cfm.

Witchalls, Clint. "Murder in Mind." *Guardian Weekly*, April 15, 2004.

Witcover, Jules. *85 Days: The Last Campaign of Robert Kennedy.* New York: Ace Publishing, 1969.

———. *The Year the Dream Died: Revisiting 1968 in America.* New York: Warner Books, 1997.

Wolper, David L. *Producer: A Memoir.* New York: Simon & Schuster, 2003.

Zimbardo, Philip G. "The Human Choice: Individuation, Reason and Order

Versus Deindividuation, Impulse and Chaos." In *1969 Symposium on Motivation*. Edited by W. J. Arnold and D. Levine. Lincoln: University of Nebraska Press, 1970.

Audio and Video Recordings

The Assassination of Robert Kennedy. Produced by Chris Plumley. Exposed Films Production for Channel 4 in association with the Arts and Entertainment Network, UK, 1992.

Sneed, Larry A. Live ABC Radio, CBS Radio and NBC Radio News Broadcasts in Larry Sneed Audio Tape Archives. Supplied by kind permission of JFK assassination author and Kennedy researcher.

Personal Correspondence

Cardena, Dr. Etzel. Letter to the author, January 21, 2004.

Kenney, James W. Letter to the author, September 25, 2003.

Wagstaff, Graham. Letter to the author, March 15, 2003.

INDEX

ABOUT THE AUTHOR

MEL AYTON lives in Durham, England, with his wife Sheila and has two grown children, Laura and Tim. He has a BA honors degree in politics and history and an MA from Durham University, where he specialized in historiography and the teaching of history in American schools. In 1988 he was selected as a Fulbright teacher and taught in schools in Michigan.

Mel Ayton's book *The JFK Assassination: Dispelling the Myths* was an examination of the claims made by JFK conspiracy theorists. He decided to write the book following a 1988 conversation with U.S. senator Arlen Specter in which Specter expressed his dismay at the way the JFK conspiracy theorists had misused the evidence in the case. In 2001 the University of Sunderland Press published Mr. Ayton's book *Questions of Controversy: The Kennedy Brothers*, which examined the controversial issues surrounding the lives of John, Robert, and Edward Kennedy.

In 2003 Mr. Ayton acted as the historical adviser for the BBC's television documentary *The Kennedy Dynasty*, which was broadcast in the United Kingdom in November 2003. He has also written widely praised articles for Ireland's leading history magazine, *History Ireland*; David Horwitz's *Frontpage Magazine*; *History News Network*; and *Crime Magazine*. In 2006 he was interviewed about *The Forgotten Terrorist* for the NBC documentary *Conspiracy: Mind Control*.